PRAISE FOR T
ULTIMATE GUIDE

"[One of the] best new running books."
Runner's World

"THE ULTIMATE GUIDE TO MARATHONS *lifts the sport of marathoning another notch by providing key information better enabling marathoners to make informed decisions which may determine the success or failure of their race. I wish I'd had this guide years ago."*
Bill Rodgers, Four-time Boston Marathon Winner

"It's a winner! Whether you are planning to run a marathon or just want to live vicariously through reading about one (or 180) - **THE ULTIMATE GUIDE TO MARATHONS** *is for you. Once you start reading [it] you will find it difficult to put down."*
The Miami Runners Club "Big Kick" Newsletter

"An excellent marathoner's resource book....This is the first real comprehensive marathon course book and a must for anyone planning to travel to a new marathon."
Foot Prints, Houston Area Road Runners Association

"[THE ULTIMATE GUIDE TO MARATHONS] is a must for marathon enthusiasts and great reading for any runner or walker."
Footprints, New Orleans Track Club

"I am MUCH IMPRESSED."
The Buffalo Enquirer, Buffalo Chips Running Club

"You will find **[THE ULTIMATE GUIDE TO MARATHONS]** *to be a perfect aid in determining the best marathon for you. You'll feel this book was written especially for you. The authors have done an excellent job ... vividly describing over 180 U.S. and Canadian marathons. I recommend it."*
Columbus Roadrunners

*"You can tell that the authors of this handy volume are runners. It's loaded with statistics organized and reorganized six ways from Sunday. **THE ULTIMATE GUIDE TO MARATHONS** looks to be a great addition to a runner's resource library."*
Hartford Track Club

*"***[THE ULTIMATE GUIDE TO MARATHONS]*** is just what you have been waiting for. Everything that you might want to know as a runner has been covered. This is an indispensable guide; something that should be on the bedside table of anyone planning to run a marathon."*
Paul Hargrave's Book Reviews, FTC

"There is, to my knowledge, no substitute to **[THE ULTIMATE GUIDE TO MARATHONS]**. *Congratulations to the authors for a job well done."*
L T B , Amazon.com

THE ULTIMATE GUIDE TO
INTERNATIONAL
MARATHONS

BY DENNIS CRAYTHORN AND RICH HANNA

MP

MARATHON PUBLISHERS, INC.
SACRAMENTO, CALIFORNIA

The elevation profiles contained in this book are for illustrative purposes only. They are not intended as exact reproductions of the elevation changes along each course.

Library of Congress Catalog Card Number: 98-091304
ISBN 0-9655187-1-X
Distributed to the book trade by Independent Publishers Group (800.888.4741).

Individuals and specialty stores may order directly from the publisher. In the United States call toll-free (888.586.9099), fax (916.492.8964) or e-mail (Marapub@aol.com) your order with your Visa or MasterCard number and expiration date. Outside the United States, please call (+1.916.492.8966), fax (+1.916.492.8964), or e-mail (Marapub@aol.com). Orders may also be sent to Marathon Publishers, Inc., P.O. Box 19027, Sacramento, California, 95819, USA.

FRONT COVER PHOTO: London Marathon, Tim Matthews (Allsport)
BACK COVER PHOTO: Honolulu Marathon, Ken Lee

Printed in Canada

PREFACE

As we toured the country for our first book, **THE ULTIMATE GUIDE TO MARATHONS**, many runners asked us about marathons outside the United States and Canada. We said that we'd like to know about them, too, but that **THE ULTIMATE GUIDE TO MARATHONS** was difficult enough to research and write. Soon it became clear, however, that we didn't have a choice in the matter. **THE ULTIMATE GUIDE TO MARATHONS** was selling extraordinarily well (so well in fact that it just went into its second printing) and runners clearly were becoming more mobile and global. Not just Americans and Canadians, but runners around the world were heading to foreign countries to run marathons. These runners needed a single resource containing the best marathons in the world – an international marathon all-star book.

So in March, 1997, we plunged into the deep end. And boy was that water cold! We thought **THE ULTIMATE GUIDE TO MARATHONS** was a challenge. Add in thousands more miles, scores of different languages, and much higher costs, and suddenly the pool grew. As runners, though, we have a certain amount of perseverance and intrepidity. After some initial research, we quickly realized that two parts of the world – North America and Europe – remain the center of the running universe in terms of having a large number of high quality races. Of course, there are other strong marathoning countries, like South Africa, Australia, New Zealand, and Japan, but no other region can match North America and Europe in marathon density. So Dennis renewed his passport and put that graduate degree in international affairs to good use by spending three months in Europe going from marathon to marathon. In all he visited over 25 races or courses, and met with the race directors of many other marathons.

Of course, one challenge with writing a book like this is that it must be done quickly, otherwise the information grows stale. This ruled out extensive trips to all reaches of the globe. Although we visited over 18 countries, we could not hit them all. For those marathons we were unable to see first-hand, we relied on several sources of information: race organizers, local runners, other runners who had recently done the race, and the internet. Together, these sources, we believe, gave us a solid sense of the races we were unable to attend.

Now that this book exists, we wish to issue a word of caution. We did not write this book so that runners could make it their personal quest to attend all 104 races in one year (or even one lifetime). If that's what they want to do, then nobody can stop them. However, we urge you not to lose sight of the benefits of running abroad – gaining new cultural insights, making friends with runners from around the world, learning bits of the language – by forging headlong into a marathon collection, whereby each race merely becomes another notch on your running shoes. There is much more to running (and life) than that. Soak in the richness and uniqueness of the place. Visit museums. Roam the countryside. Mingle with locals in the pub. Try *escargot*. We implore you not to judge yourself or your fellow runners on the basis of numbers, like personal records or number of marathons. In the end, who really cares about that? What's important is that your running leads you to new places, physically, intellectually, emotionally. And when you are in these new places, that you take full advantage of them and enjoy them completely.

This book contains 104 great races in all parts of the world. Pick a few and let them melt in your mouth, saturating your taste buds with flavor. You can always dream about the rest.

Dennis Craythorn
Rich Hanna
February, 1998

ACKNOWLEDGMENTS

· To all of the thousands of runners who bought THE ULTIMATE GUIDE TO MARATHONS, we thank you. Your support has made this book possible. Thanks also to the hundreds of other runners we have met at marathons around the country and the world. Your warm comments have been truly gratifying.

Again we must thank our parents, Sheldon and Dorothy Craythorn, and Bob Hanna and Muriel Hanna, for their exceptional support and patience. Suzanne Rogers and Brian Plant remain our staunchest allies in the business world, as well as our very dear friends.

Several individuals reviewed portions of the manuscript, giving us very valuable comments and insights. We would particularly like to thank Suzy Martinez and Sandra Hatcher.

Many people in Europe helped Dennis during his lengthy travels there while researching this book. He especially thanks the utterly charming Ann Marie Burns, who saved him on the Eurostar to London and tipped him off to two great races – the Chambord Marathon and the Loire Valley Marathon. Vivacious and talented Julia Jones, a fellow Californian now living near Pisa, bicycled the Florence Marathon course with him, babysat him in Turin, and generally kept him up to date on the always volatile Italian marathon scene. Thanks Julia for all of your help! Indro Neri, who publishes *Podismo* magazine in Florence and manages the Run The Planet web site, not only gave him a bed to sleep in, but great insights into a number of Italian marathons and race organizations. And to that hustler in Rome, Dennis says, "I'll be back!" Dennis would also like to thank the Association of International Marathons (AIMS), especially Gordon Rogers and Hugh Jones, for allowing him to attend their World Congress in Enschede, Holland. Gordon was particularly gracious in providing an important contact or inroad at several critical times. We hope to see you in Maui, Gordon!

To supplement our own research, we enlisted the assistance of several local runners or people with unique knowledge on marathons in a particular part of the world. Bill Belew, Hiroaki Saito, and Jan Lester gave us critical information on Japanese races. We could not have completed the book without you! For South America, Eduardo Proisman, Margarita Altimirano, and Edson Sanchez helped Rich hurdle the cultural wall. We would like to thank the author and publisher of Tom Cottrell's *Runners' Guide to Road Races in South Africa* (Southern Directories, 1997) for allowing us to use portions of their course description of the Two Oceans Marathon.

We are extremely pleased and fortunate to count the wacky Dave Stringer of *The Runner's Schedule* among our good friends and trusted advisors. *The Runner's Schedule* has been very generous in their support of us, thanks to Dave and its publisher, Kees Tuinzing.

Ardis Bow was the lucky graphics artist who had to decipher some terrible elevation profiles and make them both readable and useful.

Bucking the trend of lazy race directors are: Nicola Stella and his assistant Sylvia, Anders Olsson, Tara Lowe, Christiana Rosso, Bob Craver, Wally Kastner, Scott Schneider, Les Smith, Annemarie Sainsbury, Carey Pinkowski, Mike Nishi, Michael Schild, Wolfram Gotz, Dennis Kenny, Jonathan DeHart, Paul Samaras, Colin Atkinson, and Gordon Rogers.

Traveling is a necessary and expensive part of writing a book like this. Doug Hanna came through with hotel assistance and his great sense of humor, making the book a bit less expensive, but infinitely richer.

We must again thank our distributor, Independent Publishers Group, and its president, Curt Matthews, for believing in us and our company; and our printer, Transcontinental, especially Arnold Krause and Renee Hamel. Phillips Design came up with some great new ads and designed the front cover of this book. Thanks Lee Phillips and Jill Chan. Finally, thanks to all of the photographers and individuals who sent us the great shots used in the book.

TABLE OF CONTENTS

TABLE OF CONTENTS

INTRODUCTION

HOW TO USE THIS BOOK

This book was written for runners around the world who want to travel to a marathon, whether it be for a vacation or to try for a PR. It is divided into five main sections – North America, Europe, Africa/Middle East, Asia/Pacific, and Latin America/Caribbean. Within each section, races are listed chronologically. In all, the 104 best races in the world are discussed, including two half marathons, three ultramarathons, and one climbing race. The Appendix contains a number of fun and useful rankings, and course profiles, arranged in alphabetical order, for nearly half of our races.

HOW TO READ THE RATINGS

Beneath the title of each entry there is a series of ratings. The overall rating indicates our cumulative assessment of the race as a destination marathon, i.e., a marathon that a runner may want to travel to and perhaps build a vacation around. The top-ranked marathon, the Stockholm Marathon, was assigned a score of 100, and every other race's score is a percentage of Stockholm's. The factors that make up the overall score are: course beauty, destination value of the location, race organization, and level of crowd support. The next five ratings (course beauty, course difficulty, appropriateness for first timers, race organization, and crowd support) are based on a 10-point scale and are modified by pluses and minuses, just like school grades. Therefore, a score of 9- exceeds an 8+. The following legend applies to our scores for course beauty, appropriateness for first timers, and race organization:

10	EXCEPTIONAL
9	VERY GOOD
8	GOOD
7	FAIR
<6	POOR

For course difficulty, the following legend applies:

9-10	EXTREMELY DIFFICULT
7-8	VERY DIFFICULT
5-6	MODERATELY DIFFICULT, ROLLING WITH SOME GOOD GRADES
4	AVERAGE DIFFICULTY, MOSTLY ROLLING
3	SLIGHTLY ROLLING
2	MOSTLY FLAT
1	PERFECTLY FLAT, FEW TURNS

For crowd support, the following legend applies:

9-10	EXCEPTIONAL
7-8	VERY GOOD
5-6	MODERATE
3-4	LIGHT
1-2	VERY LITTLE
0	JUST YOU AND THE WIND

The **COURSE BEAUTY** rating scores just that. We tend to mark down courses that pass strip malls, urban blight, and industrial parks. We also tend to cast disfavor on monotonous scenery and never-ending brownness. So much for our biases. The **COURSE DIFFICULTY** rating considers the elevation changes along the route (i.e., hills), number of turns, running surface, altitude, and average weather conditions. The higher the score, the more difficult the course. A course difficulty rating of 3 indicates a relatively fast course, while an 8 denotes a very challenging route. You may use this rating as our equivalent of the relative quickness of the course. Races with the notation (**SEE APPENDIX**) have an elevation profile in the Appendix. The **RACE ORGANIZATION** score consists of an overall evaluation of the race structure. It considers a wide range of factors, including professionalism of race personnel, amount and quality of race amenities (aid stations, pre/post-race activities, transportation, awards), volunteers, and general quality of the race. The **APPROPRIATENESS FOR FIRST TIMERS** is our attempt to help novice marathoners choose the right race for them. To us, the perfect first-timer marathon has a scenic course, excellent race organization, lots of aid stations, few hills, and huge crowds. We consider all of these factors in compiling this score. Finally, **CROWD SUPPORT** indicates the approximate number of spectators along the route. It also considers course-side entertainment.

WHAT'S IN AN ENTRY?

Following the ratings is a boxed section called **RACE DATA** containing useful information about the race. First it gives the overall ranking of the race, its quality ranking, and its quickness ranking. Next it tells you where to write or call to obtain an application; the general date of the race (which should always be considered tentative); race start time; time course closes; number of runners in the most recent year; the general course layout (such as loop, point to point, out and back); whether the course is certified and by whom (times run on certified courses may be used for entry into the Boston Marathon); course records for open and masters runners where available (many races do not maintain masters records); whether the race offers anything special to elite runners (e.g., free entry, expenses, transportation, lodging, prize money); entry fees (all amounts are in the local currency unless otherwise noted); age groups; whether walkers are welcome; any requirements to enter the race; average temperatures on race day (ranges indicate start time and noon); the number of aid stations on the course; and the location of split times.

The first narrative section consists of race **HIGHLIGHTS**. Here we try to capture the essence of the race; what makes this marathon special or not so special. Some races have interesting or noteworthy **RACE HISTORIES**. These histories follow the highlights section. The **COURSE DESCRIPTION** contains a detailed account of the course from a runner's perspective. It tells you what you see along the way and the location of major hills and terrain changes. **CROWD/RUNNER SUPPORT** discusses the level of crowd support along the course and the locations of the greatest concentration of spectators. It also details the aid stations, medical assistance, and entertainment during the race. **RACE LOGISTICS** explains how to get to the race start and back. **ACTIVITIES** enumerates the pre- and post-race activities offered by the event, including where to get your race packet, the pasta dinner, expo, victory party, awards ceremony, and any other activities. **AWARDS** lets you know about T-shirts, medals, age-group awards, prize money, and other relevant goodies. Races that have programs for elite runners contain an **ELITE RUNNERS INFORMATION** section. It explains the race's criteria for elite status, what the race may offer you, and breaks down the prize money structure, including course record bonuses. A few races give **SPECIAL INFORMATION FOR FIRST TIMERS**. We also list some **ACCOMMODATIONS** convenient to the race site, including the host hotel, hotels offering discounts to marathon entrants, and in some cases other lodging options. All prices are in the local currency unless otherwise noted, i.e., amounts under Canadian races are given in Canadian dollars. **RELATED RACES/EVENTS** lists other races that run in conjunction with the marathon, such as a marathon relay, half marathon, 10K, 5K, and kids races. Finally, the **AREA ACTIVITIES** section gives you a general idea of the sights and things-to-do in the area. Not an exhaustive list, this section is intended only to help you decide whether to attend that particular marathon. You may still need to buy a relevant travel guide for that area should you want to linger before or after the race.

A NOTE ON TELEPHONE NUMBERS

All telephone numbers are listed from the perspective of people dialing from the United States or Canada. To dial overseas from the United States, you must first dial 011, followed by the country code, city code, and then the telephone number. The number preceded by a plus (+) sign indicates the country code necessary to call to that country. The number following the slash (/) denotes the city code (which is equivalent to our area code). If you are dialing long-distance within that country (say from Melbourne to Sydney), you may need to add a 0 or 9 to the city code. The numbers after the dash (-) are the telephone number of the party you are calling. Be aware that city codes often change. If you have trouble dialing any international number, contact the international operator for assistance.

APPENDIX:
RANKINGS AND COURSE PROFILES

Most of the rankings in this section are self evident, except perhaps for our **WORLD'S TOP 30 FASTEST MARATHONS** ranking and the **MARATHON QUALITY** ranking. The fastest marathons ranking indicates what we believe to be the fastest races (of those in the book) in the world. Similar rankings in other publications have used such things as course records, percentage of PRs, and the like. We believe such criteria are misleading at best. Instead, we try to consider the factors that affect a runner's performance at a given race. It is our firm belief that many variables determine whether a race is fast or slow. Our ranking considers three broad factors in descending order of importance: course difficulty, race organization, and crowd support. The most important ingredient is the course. Is it flat, rolling, or hilly? Where are the biggest hills, early or late? Are there many turns that could disrupt a runner's rhythm? What is the running surface? The second ingredient to producing a fast race is organization. The more support a runner has before, during and after a race the better his prospects for a fast time. Fewer hassles mean less energy spent worrying about details and logistics, and more energy reserved for running. The third ingredient is crowd support. Any runner can tell you that the extra lift provided by spectators can make the difference between pushing through the hurt and giving in to the struggle. The energy at Boston, New York, and Hamburg contribute to faster times than would otherwise be run on those courses. We believe that the ranking of the fastest races based on our formula is the most accurate yet produced. There is always room for fine-tuning, however, and we welcome your comments. The **RACE QUALITY** ranking considers the race organization and the level of crowd support. These are the "big-deal" events that are known throughout the world.

AN IMPORTANT NOTE TO FELLOW RUNNERS (A.K.A. DISCLAIMER)

Races change constantly. We have made every conceivable effort to ensure the information in this book is as up-to-date and accurate as possible. However, there will be changes after this book is printed. So, please, before making any plans or final decisions, contact the races themselves to get the latest information, *especially race dates*. Every year, many races change their dates for a variety of reasons. Once the book is printed, there is little or nothing we can do about it. It is therefore incumbent upon you to check with the race before you make any reservations, buy any tickets, or request any time off from work. We cannot be responsible for any inconvenience, loss, or other unhappiness you encounter. If you do have any suggestions, updates, or differing opinions, please let us know. Be as specific and constructive as you can; generic comments are of little use. For example, telling us we missed a huge hill toward the end of the race does us no good. But informing us that we missed a steep, half-mile hill at the 20-mile mark is very useful. Your comments will play a large role in improving the next edition of THE ULTIMATE GUIDE TO INTERNATIONAL MARATHONS.

Direct all correspondence to:

THE ULTIMATE GUIDE TO INTERNATIONAL MARATHONS

c/o Marathon Publishers, Inc.

P.O. Box 19027

Sacramento, CA 95819

USA

NORTH AMERICA

WALT DISNEY WORLD MARATHON

OVERALL: 85.7

COURSE BEAUTY: 9-

COURSE DIFFICULTY: 3-

APPROPRIATENESS FOR FIRST TIMERS: 9

RACE ORGANIZATION: 9

CROWDS: 4

R A C E   D A T A

Overall Ranking: 62
Quality Ranking: 51
Quickness Ranking: 30
Contact: Walt Disney World Marathon
P.O. Box 10,000
Lake Buena Vista, FL 32830-1000
USA
Tel. (407) 939-7810

Date: Generally first or second Sunday in January
Start Time: 6:00 a.m.
Time Course Closes: 1:00 p.m.
Number of Finishers: 6,426 in 1998
Course: Loop
Certification: USATF
Race Records: Male: (open) 2:11:50; (masters) 2:20:26
Female: (open) 2:31:54; (masters) 2:49:44
Elite Athlete Programs: No
Cost: $50
Age groups/Divisions: 18-24, 25-29, 30-34, 35-39, 40-44, 45-49, 50-54,
55-59, 60-64, 65+ (F), 65-69, 70+ (M)
Walkers: No
Requirements: 18 years old
Temperature: 35°- 65° (2°C - 18°C)
Aid/Splits: 16 / digital clocks every mile

HIGHLIGHTS Do you remember running through Walt Disney World as a child, rushing from the Pirates of the Caribbean to It's a Small World? Or maybe you never got a chance to visit the home of Mickey Mouse, Goofy, Tinkerbell, and all their friends. Well, here's your opportunity to run as fast as you like through the Magic Kingdom without pesky parents telling you to slow down. The Walt Disney World Marathon is blooming into a compelling, runner-friendly event with Disney's one-of-a-kind flair. Heeding runners' suggestions to improve the event, race organizers have worked out early kinks with the course and transportation. Now runners complete a fun, entertaining, and flat course, weaving through three theme parks in the 30,000 acre Disney World property. As you would expect, Disney puts on quite a spectacle, including light shows, a torrent of fireworks, lasers, music, and even snow flurries! The race offers a number of packages from $169 to $573, including entry fee, two-nights accommodations, carbo-load party, and transportation. Walt Disney World is a particularly great race for families. Leon Roby Blue of Searcy, Arkansas says, "*It is a good* *way to include the whole family in the marathon experience. Something for everyone."*

COURSE DESCRIPTION The Disney Marathon begins near Epcot and winds through the Magic Kingdom, Disney-MGM Studios, Epcot, and Disney's snow-themed water park, Blizzard Beach. The race also passes through several Disney resorts. Extremely flat, with a total elevation change of only 30 feet, the course runs mostly on asphalt, although the surface changes at several points. Many runners report that while flat, the course is not especially fast due to the large number of turns and tight spots.

Mickey Mouse fires the starting gun just outside Epcot with a new entertainment theme each year. Making it across the start line may take a while, not only because of the large number of runners, but more importantly because of a popular Disney tradition for runners to high-five Mickey and his friends. Running along Epcot Drive for just under 2 miles, you enter Epcot into Future World with lighted musical fountains. While passing eleven nations by dawn, you are greeted by frolicking lasers over World Showcase Lagoon. Runners exit Epcot at about 2.8 miles and return to Epcot Drive for the next 3 miles before merging onto World Drive headed toward the Magic Kingdom. At about 7.6 miles, runners veer left onto Floridian Way, passing the Polynesian Resort (just before the 9-mile mark) and the Grand Floridian Beach Resort. You enter the Magic Kingdom at mile 10 and stream through Caribbean Plaza, Frontierland, Liberty Square, and right through Cinderella Castle to Fantasyland. Then you jump to Tomorrowland, down Main Street, and by mile 11, it's all over as you exit the Magic Kingdom and head toward Blizzard Beach (just after mile 18) encountering snow flurries in Florida. Your next destination is Disney-MGM Studios where a gaggle of Disney stars greet you (mile 20.7). By mile 25, you're back at Epcot where you circle the Lagoon and finish in the parking lot with the Epcot sphere behind you.

CROWD/RUNNER SUPPORT Once known as one of the loneliest marathons because of thin crowds, the Walt Disney World Marathon has made significant strides in remedying this concern. Monorail takes spectators to several sites along the course, but most of the onlookers stay in Epcot and the other theme parks. In part to make up for smaller crowds, Disney packs in the entertainment along the course from Disney characters, to light presentations, to music. Steve Bainbridge of Fairbanks, Alaska calls the race, *"A sensory overload! Nonstop entertainment."*

RACE LOGISTICS Runners take the monorail system or shuttle buses from their Disney Resort hotels to the start. The same transportation can return runners back to their hotels following the race. If you stay outside the Disney complex, you must provide your own ride.

ACTIVITIES On Friday and Saturday visit the Health and Fitness Expo located at Disney's Wide World of Sports Complex. On Saturday evening, devour mounds of pasta at the carbo-loading dinner at the Contemporary Resort. Following the race you can reload at the generous food tables. The day after the marathon, complete results and finishers certificates are available at the Wide World of Sports Complex.

AWARDS Every entrant receives a long-sleeve T-shirt and an official race program. Marathoners who finish under seven hours are awarded heavy Mickey Mouse Medallions and finishers' certificates. The top five finishers in each division earn additional awards.

ACCOMMODATIONS Stay in one of the 16 distinctly Disney resorts since it will add significantly to your convenience on race day. Offering a number of race packages at all of its resorts, Disney includes two-nights lodging, one race entry fee and carbo-load dinner, free transportation around Walt Disney World, and early theme park admission. Packages start at $169 for campsites at the Fort Wilderness Resort, and continue to: $240 at the All-Star Resorts, $293 for the Port Orleans and Dixie Landings Resorts, $382 at the headquarters Contemporary Resort (Tower) or $429 for the garden view, and $429 for the Wilderness Lodge and Polynesian Resort. For top of the line accommodations, try the Grand Floridian Beach Resort at $573. For more information on resort packages call (407-939-7810) and reference Walt Disney World Marathon registration.

RELATED EVENTS / RACES   A half marathon now runs alongside the full marathon for the first 13.1 miles. The half marathon had almost 3,000 finishers in 1998. FamilyFun magazine presents the FamilyFun Run on Saturday morning beginning at 7:30 a.m. at Epcot. Open to the public, the 5K runs through Epcot and ends at the marathon finish line. Participants receive T-shirts. There are also shorter events for youngsters to earn their Mickey Mouse medals.

AREA ATTRACTIONS   The big attraction in the area is the Walt Disney World complex itself, with its three theme parks, nighttime entertainment complex, three water parks, a zoological park, golf, tennis, and even an Indy Car track. The 200-acre, state-of-the-art Wide World of Sports Complex includes something for any sport fan, such as the Atlanta Braves' new spring training facility, an 11-court tennis center, beach volleyball courts, a track and field stadium, basketball courts, and the Official All-Star Cafe, a sports-themed family restaurant owned by several sports celebrities. In all, the facility will accommodate some 32 sports.

HOUSTON MARATHON

OVERALL: 85.8

COURSE BEAUTY: 6+

COURSE DIFFICULTY: 2+

APPROPRIATENESS FOR FIRST TIMERS: 9

RACE ORGANIZATION: 10

CROWDS: 9-

RACE DATA

Overall Ranking:	61
Quality Ranking:	5
Quickness Ranking:	11
Contact:	Methodist Health Care Houston Marathon
	720 North Post Oak Road, Ste. 335
	Houston, TX 77024
	USA
	Tel. (713) 957-3453
	Fax (713) 957-3406
	http://www.houstonmarathon.com
Date:	Generally third Sunday in January
	(January 17, 1999)
Start Time:	8:00 a.m.
Time Course Closes:	1:30 p.m.
Number of Participants:	6,200 in 1997
Course:	Loop
Certification:	USATF
Course Records:	Male: (open) 2:10:04
	Female: (open) 2:27:51
Elite Athlete Programs:	Yes
Cost:	$40/50
Age groups/Divisions:	≤19, 20-24, 25-29, 30-34, 35-39, 40-44, 45-49, 50-54, 55-59, 60-64, 65+ (F), 65-69, 70-74, 75+ (M)
Walkers:	No
Requirements:	None
Temperature:	45° - 50° (7°C - 10°C)
Aid/Splits:	24 / every mile from mile 2

HIGHLIGHTS Do you like hoopla, the noisy, uplifting, and often crazy entertainment along so many marathons routes today? Pioneering the hoopla phenomenon, the Houston Marathon does it better than most. With nearly every mile packed with some form of entertainment, the course loops through the city and its suburbs. A good place to try for a PR, the race offers excellent organization, superb runner support, usually ideal weather conditions, and substantial crowds.

RACE HISTORY A five-mile loop course marked by a parked station wagon debuted as the Houston Marathon in December 1972. Seventy-three runners endured that race and were treated to beef stew afterwards. Taking up sponsorship of the race in 1980, Tenneco Energy helped it blossom. In fact, in 1992, Houston was the site of the women's Olympic Marathon Trials. Houston also has been chosen as the site of the U.S. Corporate Athletics Association Marathon Championship. Tenneco ended its support of the race in 1996, ending one of the longest standing marathon partnerships. The race has shown little impact, however, and in 1998 Houston hosted the U.S. Women's Marathon Championships. Over the years, Houston has witnessed some remarkable races, including perhaps the closest marathon finish in U.S. history: in 1984, a photo revealed that Charlie Spedding literally won by his foot.

COURSE DESCRIPTION The Houston Marathon's loop course starts and finishes downtown at the George R. Brown Convention Center. Passing through many of Houston's ethnically diverse neighborhoods, the race is completely closed to vehicular traffic. Houston sports a dual start, with men departing from LaBranch Street and women beginning on Crawford Street. After the cannon-blast start, runners head for the Elysian Viaduct. At mile 1, which is on the viaduct, the course reaches one of its highest points at 85 feet. One of Houston's oldest neighborhoods, a Hispanic barrio in the near north side, awaits runners on the down side of the viaduct and provides a fiesta atmosphere as runners pass mariachi bands and dancers. As the men and women merge at 2.5 miles, they head back into downtown, crossing the Main Street Bridge in front of the University of Houston's Downtown campus. After passing the 5-mile mark in the midst of downtown sky-scrapers, runners continue south down Main Street toward its booming Asian office and retail centers. Mile 7 takes runners through a middle class neighborhood where residents bring the kids out to view the race. Mile 8 brings the Herman Park Rose Garden and the Mecom Fountain. Between 8 and 9, enjoy the oak trees arching over Main Street as you run toward the beautiful Rice University Campus. Around 10.5 miles, runners enter trendy, fashionable West University Place, featuring some of Houston's finer homes. Soak in the encouragement here to fortify yourself for the Westpark Hump at the halfway point, a 35-foot climb over a quarter mile, and the following commercial sections of the course. Houston's well-known Galleria shopping area provides good crowd support and takes runners past the Transco Tower, the tallest building in the country that is outside a downtown area, and its sculptured "Water Wall." It's a tough time for runners as they again turn away from downtown at mile 15. Between 15 and 20 miles you pass through the residential and commercial areas Riverway, Tangelwood, and Church. At mile 18 you head toward downtown, passing George Bush's church. Look for the former president as he's usually watching the runners as they continue downtown toward the finish. Miles 20 to 21.5 lead you through Memorial Park, the training ground for Houston's runners. Leaving the park, runners sense the finish, but must conquer the hills of Allen Parkway, actually two street underpasses that at 23.5 can be difficult for many marathoners. After making it through the Allen Parkway bumps, runners make one last pass through downtown. The last mile decorated with confetti streamers is a welcome sight, with the

Convention Center finish within view.

CROWD/RUNNER SUPPORT The Houston Marathon provides unparalleled hoopla lining most of the marathon route. The entertainment consists of everything from belly dancers, bands, ballet, gymnastics, and bagpipers, to cheerleaders. Complementing the hoopla are approximately 250,000 spectators at various sections of the course. Add on to that water stations and split times every mile, and you have outstanding runner support. Together with the other 6,500 runners, you shouldn't be too lonely out there. The Houston Marathon also supports the Run for a Reason program, where marathoners help raise money for any number of area charities.

RACE LOGISTICS The GRB Convention Center offers excellent indoor facilities for runners before and after the race.

ACTIVITIES Houston hosts a large, two-day Health and Fitness Expo at the GRB Convention Center on Friday and Saturday. There you can attend numerous seminars on running and fitness topics, pick up your race packet, or register late. There is no race-day registration or packet pick-up. After the marathon, relax at the post-race party in the Convention Center.

AWARDS Each entrant receives a marathon T-shirt. Runners who finish under five and one-half hours also are awarded finisher T-shirts, glass mugs, and certificates. Trophies are given to age-group winners, while top athletes compete for about $150,000 in prize money. The first local male and female finishers receive a trip to a top international marathon.

ELITE RUNNERS INFORMATION World-class runners could be offered lodging, travel, and expenses. Elite runners compete for the approximately $150,000 prize money. Open winners receive $20,000, with $15,000 for second, $8,000 for third, $6,000 for fourth, $4,000 for fifth, $2,000 for sixth, $1,500 for seventh, $1,000 for eighth, $500 for ninth, and $250 for tenth. The top three American runners also receive $5,000, $2,000, and $1,000 respectively. Masters prize money goes five deep, with $1,500 for first and $200 for fifth.

ACCOMMODATIONS The DoubleTree Hotel at Allen Center, 400 Dallas Street (800-231-6310), serves as the headquarters hotel for the Houston Marathon. The DoubleTree offers runners special room rates. Also convenient are the Hyatt Regency, 1200 Louisiana (800-233-1234); the Four Seasons Hotel, 1300 Lamar Street (800-332-3442); and The Lancaster, 701 Texas Avenue (800-368-5966). A little further out, try the Allen Park Inn, 2121 Allen Parkway (800-231-6310); Harvey Hotel, 2712 Southwest Freeway (713-523-8448); and Ramada Hotel-Galleria, 7787 Katy Freeway (713-681-5000).

RELATED EVENTS/RACES Houston also hosts the Southwestern Bell Spirit of Texas Charity 5K, starting just after the marathon at the GRB Convention Center. The 5K draws more than 1,500 runners and tours the downtown area. There is no race-day registration.

AREA ATTRACTIONS While in Houston, you may want to catch a Houston Rockets basketball game at The Summit, 10 Greenway Plaza. Also tour Space Center Houston for hands-on exhibits and a behind-the-scenes peek at the Johnson Space Center. Bone up on Texas' battle for independence at the San Jacinto Battleground State Historical Park. Houston boasts numerous museums, including the Houston Museum of Natural Science, and its Cockrell Butterfly Center, the Museum of Fine Arts, the Contemporary Arts Museum, and the Menil Collection.

NAPA VALLEY MARATHON

OVERALL: 87.7

COURSE BEAUTY: 9+

COURSE DIFFICULTY: 3- (SEE APPENDIX)

APPROPRIATENESS FOR FIRST TIMERS: 9-

RACE ORGANIZATION: 9

CROWDS: 2

RACE DATA

Overall Ranking:	48
Quality Ranking:	70
Quickness Ranking:	35
Contact:	Sutter Home Napa Valley Marathon
	P.O. Box 4307
	Napa, CA 94558-0430
	USA
	Tel. (707) 255-2609
Date:	Generally first Sunday in March
Start Time:	7:00 a.m.
Time Course Closes:	12:30 p.m.
Number of Finishers:	1,354 in 1997
Course:	Point to point
Certification:	USATF
Course Records:	Male: (open) 2:16:20; (masters) 2:26:04
	Female: (open) 2:39:42; (masters) 2:54:46
Elite Athlete Programs:	Yes
Cost:	$45/50/60
Age groups/Divisions:	≤19, 20-24, 25-29, 30-34, 35-39, 40-44, 45-49,
	50-54, 55-59, 60-69, 70+
Walkers:	No
Requirements:	None
Temperature:	40° - 70° (4°C - 21°C)
Aid/Splits:	12 / miles 1, 5, 10, halfway & 20

H I G H L I G H T S Low key, rural, the Napa Valley Marathon ("NVM") runs along the famed Silverado Trail through vineyards swept with pruned grape vines, emerald grasses, and golden mustard. Stir this incredible setting into Napa's world-class attractions, add a competent, runner-friendly race organization, and you've corked one of the top destination marathons in North America. A particularly fine choice for runners who appreciate serenity but don't like to be out there alone, NVM also seems to be blessed with near-perfect weather, raining only once in 19 years.

R A C E   H I S T O R Y Designed as an intimate, rural marathon, the Napa Valley Marathon began in 1979 by the Silverado Striders, a Napa-based running club. The fact that the distance between Calistoga, at the northern end of the valley, and Napa, at the southern end, happened to be 26 miles seemed too coincidental to overlook.

A number of local companies with national reputations have acted as the race's primary sponsors. For the first dozen years, the Calistoga Mineral Water Company sponsored the race — NVM's start line is just 50 yards from the Calistoga plant. Sutter Home Winery took up sponsorship in 1993, and has installed a permanent trophy (a 7-liter bottle of Zinfandel) in its tasting room along Highway 29 south of Helena. Each year the male and female winners' names and times are etched into the bottle.

Throughout its first 10 years, the marathon remained a local secret, with 800 to 1,000 participants. However, in 1987 the race won notoriety when Dick Beardsley, the then second-fastest marathoner in America, used the course to make his comeback after a near career-ending leg injury. Intending to qualify for the 1988 U.S. Olympic Marathon Trials, he cruised to a course record of 2:16:20. The 1996 race was the first-ever RRCA California State Marathon Championship, the 1997 race was the RRCA Western Regional Marathon Championship, and the 1998 version is the RRCA National Marathon Championship.

COURSE DESCRIPTION NVM's paved, gently rolling, point-to-point course, framed by wooded hills and picturesque vineyards, follows the Silverado Trail, a two-lane country road, for approximately 23 miles before turning into Napa's side streets on its way to the Vintage High School finish. The first 13 miles and the final 3 are completely closed to traffic, while cones protect the runners on the shoulder the middle ten miles. At times the road's camber makes finding a comfortable place to run difficult, particularly from 13 to 23.

The race starts just outside downtown Calistoga. About mile 1.25, runners hit a good, winding upgrade to 1.6, followed by a nice downhill to the 2-mile mark. The course then flattens briefly, going gently up from 2.2 to 2.75. This second hill is again followed by a good downhill. The final significant hill, the largest and steepest of the race, lies at 5.25 miles. As the course descends following the rise, a particularly nice panorama of forested hills greets the runners. From there to the 21-mile mark, the course gently rolls, with some longer, gradual inclines and declines, but no major surprises. Runners pass some excellent wineries during this stretch, including Villa Mt. Eden at 12.7, Mumm at 13.5, Z-D Wines at 13.9, hilltop Silverado Vineyards just after 19, the low, stone buildings of Stag's Leap Wine Cellars at 21.5, followed closely by the ivy-covered Clos du Val. From 21 miles the course flattens. Runners reach the 23-mile mark on a small bridge on Oak Knoll Avenue, just after the turnoff from the Silverado Trail, and pass Monticello Cellars at 24 miles. After the right turn on El Centro, the route becomes residential until the Vintage High School finish.

CROWD/RUNNER SUPPORT As you might expect, small numbers of spectators come out to cheer the runners, mostly family and friends who congregate at several major intersections on the Silverado Trail. NVM supports the runners well with 12 aid stations offering water, electrolyte replacement drink, sponges, medical supplies, and portable toilets. On the last half of the course, fruit is also available. The race will also put out your own special drinks at the aid stations you designate. The relatively short aid stations mean you will probably have to slow down to find and retrieve your bottle, but having your special brew may more than make up for the delay. The mile markers, located at ground level, may be a bit hard to spot if you're in a group.

RACE LOGISTICS The race provides free bus transportation to the start. Monitors will direct you to the parking area at Vintage High School, with buses leaving between 5:15 a.m. and 5:30 a.m. sharp. With limited parking in Calistoga, it's best to use the bus. In addition, runners who park in Calistoga will have to find their own way back to the start, unless their handlers can meet them at the finish.

ACTIVITIES On Saturday, pick up your race packet at the Sports and Fitness Expo, held in the Napa Valley Marriott. The smallish expo also features guest speakers and panels, and NVM veterans discuss course strategy. Buy a raffle ticket for a chance to win some great Napa Valley prizes on Saturday with the proceeds benefitting local charities. Later that evening, hit the pasta feed (about $15 in Napa, $12 in Calistoga). After the race, enjoy some delicious hot soup, bread, fruit, and drink. All registered runners are eligible for random draw prizes, including wine. The drawing is held just prior to the awards ceremony.

AWARDS Every entrant receives a T-shirt, and finishers earn a medal and a pat on the back for a job well done. Plaques are awarded three deep in most age divisions. The top three overall winners receive prizes, including tasty Sutter Home wine. The top local finisher is also recognized.

ELITE RUNNERS INFORMATION Lack of prize money means most big-name runners stay away from NVM, but fast runners may be offered complimentary entry and possibly free lodging. Top prizes include a 6-liter etched bottle of Sutter Home Zinfandel and a set of luggage.

ACCOMMODATIONS The Napa Valley Marriott Hotel, 3425 Solano Avenue, Napa (707-253-7433), serves as the official race hotel, offering discounted rates to runners. Other possibilities in Napa include: Inn at Napa Valley, 1075 California Blvd. (707-253-9540); Best Western Inn, 100 Soscol Avenue (707-257-1930); John Muir Inn, 1998 Trower Avenue (707-257-7220); or Chablis Lodge, 3360 Solano Avenue (707-257-1944).

RELATED EVENTS/RACES NVM also sponsors the Three R's 5K Run, beginning and ending at the marathon finish line, and staged by the Vintage High School English Department. Run proceeds help upgrade the school's computer lab.

AREA ATTRACTIONS The Napa Valley Mustard Festival, with food, drink, and tasting of hundreds of mustards, coincides with NVM. Of course you must tour some of Napa's or nearby Sonoma's fabled wineries. Talk to locals to get tips on finding some lesser-known gems, or wander at will to make your own discoveries. After the marathon, pamper yourself with a spa and mud bath treatment in Calistoga. If the marathon didn't provide enough excitement, try a hot air balloon ride. Those who prefer more conventional locomotion can ride the Wine Train. Napa and Sonoma boast great restaurants and quaint shops. And if by some freak of nature you get bored, San Francisco lies nearby.

CATALINA ISLAND MARATHON

OVERALL: 83.7

COURSE BEAUTY: 10-

COURSE DIFFICULTY: 7+ (SEE APPENDIX)

APPROPRIATENESS FOR FIRST TIMERS: 4

RACE ORGANIZATION: 9-

CROWDS: 1+

RACE DATA

Overall Ranking:	70
Quality Ranking:	79
Quickness Ranking:	95
Contact:	Catalina Island Marathon
	Pacific Sports
	1500 S. Sunkist Street, Suite E
	Anaheim, CA 92806 USA
	Tel. (714) 978-1528
	Fax (714) 978-1505
Date:	Generally second or third Saturday in March
	(March 14, 1998)
Start Time:	7:00 a.m. (6:30 a.m. for walkers)
Time Course Closes:	NA
Number of Participants:	600
Course:	Point to point
Certification:	None
Course Records:	Male: (open) 2:39:58
	Female: (open) 3:15:20
Elite Athlete Programs:	No
Cost:	$75
Age groups/Divisions:	15-18, 19-24, 25-29, 30-34, 35-39, 40-44, 45-49,
	50-54, 55-59, 60-64, 65-69, 70-74, 75+, Buffalo
	Division (open and masters): men over 200 lbs., and
	women over 150 lbs., Island Residents
Walkers:	Yes
Requirements:	15 years old
Temperature:	50˚ - 65˚ (10˚C - 18˚C)
Aid/Splits:	12 / none

HIGHLIGHTS Celebrating its 21st anniversary in 1998, the Catalina Island Marathon promises one of the most challenging and scenic runs of your life. A peaceful paradise 22 miles off the Los Angeles coast, Catalina Island features rugged mountain wilderness (complete with several hundred bison) encircled by 54 miles of pristine shoreline. Its breathtaking vistas soften the edges of a challenging, mostly dirt course that includes 3,700 feet of total climbing from the start in Two Harbors to the finish in Avalon. One of the top trail marathon destinations, Catalina's temperate weather and unspoiled beauty make for a perfect race-weekend getaway.

COURSE DESCRIPTION Catalina's point-to-point course starts at sea level in Two Harbors on the west side of the island and ends at sea level in Avalon on the island's east side. In between, spectacular scenery and 3,700 feet of total climbing await you. Most runners finish about 20-25 minutes slower than their best road marathon time. From Two Harbors, the course starts flat but abruptly climbs 825 feet to the west summit around the 2.5-mile mark. Dropping and rolling until you veer left onto Empire Landing Road, the course reaches an elevation of 920 feet at Big Springs Reservoir 4 miles into the race. Although pretty rough, the road flows mostly downhill from there to the junction of Big Springs Road. After a right turn on Big Springs, you continue downhill to Little Harbor Road, hitting sea level at Little Harbor (8.5 miles). You then begin two climbs with a peak of 350 feet at 10.8 miles. At this point you turn left onto Old Eagles Nest Trail — a now permanent detour made necessary by horrendous storms in 1995. Beginning downhill to an elevation of 260 feet, the trail has a series of three climbs with a peak of 700 feet. From that point it drops down toward Eagles Nest Lodge where you turn left onto Middle Ranch Road at 500 feet. From Eagles Nest, you begin a long steady and gradual uphill through Middle Ranch — often the hottest section of the course. Middle Ranch stretches for about 5 miles rising from 500 feet to 1,000 feet. Here, the infamous "Pumphouse Hill" awaits with a 360-foot rise in less than a mile; you finally reach the top at about 19 miles. Continuing to climb up a picturesque ridge featuring spectacular views of Avalon and the harbor below, you finally veer right past the Wrigley Reservoir back onto a dirt road and again head uphill along Divide Road. This section of the course is a series of rolling hills with a peak at 1,560 feet. At 23 miles, you begin to drop (almost literally) into Avalon, going from 1,500 feet to 270 feet in 2 miles. You enter the final stretch at 25 miles, heading downhill on paved Avalon Canyon Road, on your way to the finish near Front Street.

C R O W D / R U N N E R   S U P P O R T   With no rental cars allowed on the island, spectators stay in the start and finish areas. Encouragement is limited to aid station volunteers and Catalina's considerable wildlife population – most notably over 300 bison (descendants of 14 buffalo brought to the island in 1924 for a silent movie called "The Vanishing American").

R A C E   L O G I S T I C S   Because the race is limited to 600 runners, your first consideration involves sending your registration early as the race generally fills by March 1. Next, participants must be on the island Friday night. Catalina-bound ferries leave regularly from the Los Angeles-area ports of Long Beach, San Pedro and Newport Beach, costing between $25 and $40 for the 60-70 minute ride. For reservations, call Catalina Cruises, Long Beach (800-228-2546), Catalina Passenger Service, Newport Beach (714-673-5245), or Catalina Express, Long Beach and San Pedro (310-519-1212). If you stay in Avalon Friday night, you need to reserve a seat on the Avalon-to-Two Harbors Marathon Boat leaving at 5:00 a.m. race morning (request a reservation on your entry form). The race provides a truck to transport your personal gear back to Avalon. Additionally, if your family or friends would like to be with you in Two Harbors on Friday night, the race provides a bus leaving from the start at 7:30 a.m., arriving in Avalon by 9:00 a.m. in plenty of time to catch the finish. Catalina welcomes marathon walkers and allows them and slower runners to start at 6:30 a.m. The race provides portable toilets at five locations on the course.

A C T I V I T I E S   Packet pick-up occurs Friday night in Avalon at the Landing Bar and Grill from 4:00 p.m. to 9:00 p.m. and in Two Harbors from 4:00 p.m. to 9:00 p.m. After finishing the race, enjoy food and beverages while you await the awards ceremony starting at 2:00 p.m.

A W A R D S   Each marathon finisher receives a long-sleeve T-shirt, medal, pin, and special memorabilia. The top three overall and Buffalo division winners receive plaques and merchandise awards. The top three finishers in each age group also receive awards, as do the first male and female Catalina residents and the second and third men and women in the Buffalo division.

A C C O M M O D A T I O N S   The marathon runs before the prime tourist season so accommodations are generally not hard to find. Marathon participants stay in either Avalon or Two Harbors. Avalon offers the Hermit Gulch Campground located just off Avalon Canyon Road one mile from Avalon (310-510-8368). Avalon hotels include: Pavilion Lodge, 513 Crescent Avenue (310-510-7788); Seaport Village Inn (800-2-Catalina); Hotel Atwater (310-510-2000); Catalina Canyon Hotel, 888 Country Club Drive (310-510-0325); Hotel Vista Del Mar, 417 Crescent Avenue (310-510-1452); and Hotel St. Lauren, Metropolis and Beacon (310-510-2299). If you'd rather awake in tiny Two Harbors on race morning, camp at the Little Fisherman Cove Campground, or on marathon weekend only, at the unimproved Buffalo Park behind the restaurant. The Banning Lodge (310-510-0303), a turn of the century hunting lodge, is available for those who care to stay indoors.

R E L A T E D   E V E N T S / R A C E S   Catalina offers non-marathoners the opportunity to race on beautiful shorter courses in Avalon. At 8:00 a.m., a challenging 10K treats runners to stunning views of Avalon and its bay. A flat 5K gets going at 8:10 a.m. and takes runners along the water's edge and through the town of Avalon. Leaving no runner out, Catalina holds a half-mile Kid's Run for those under age 7, and a 1-mile run for those ages 7-12, starting at 9:00 a.m.

A R E A   A T T R A C T I O N S   Catalina offers visitors more than just her beauty. Some of the best scuba diving anywhere exists at Avalon's Underwater Park off Casino Point. If you'd rather see marine life from a further distance, hop on a glass bottom boat tour of a nearby cove. Touring the elegant estates of the Wrigley family and Zane Grey, the western novelist, are other options.

MAUI MARATHON

OVERALL: 90

COURSE BEAUTY: 10-

COURSE DIFFICULTY: 4-

APPROPRIATENESS FOR FIRST TIMERS: 7+

RACE ORGANIZATION: 9

CROWDS: 2

RACE DATA

Overall Ranking:	32
Quality Ranking:	70
Quickness Ranking:	67
Contact:	Bob Craver
	Valley Isle Road Runners Association
	P.O. Box 330099
	Kahului, Maui HI 96733
	USA
	Tel. (808) 871-6441
	E-mail: bark@maui.net
	http://www.mauimarathon.com
Date:	Generally second or third Sunday in March (March 15, 1998)
Start Time:	5:30 a.m.
Time Course Closes:	1:30 p.m.
Number of Participants:	1,289 in 1997; Limited to 1,700 in 1998
Course:	Point to point
Certification:	AIMS / USATF
Course Records:	Male: (open) 2:24:31
	Female: (open) 2:49:30
Elite Athlete Programs:	Yes
Cost:	US $50/60/75; Non-US $60/75/100
Age groups/Divisions:	18-24, 25-29, 30-34, 35-39, 40-44, 45-49, 50-54, 55-59, 60-64, 65-69, 70+
Walkers:	Yes
Requirements:	18 years old
Temperature:	68˚ - 82˚ (20˚C - 28˚C)
Aid/Split:	17 / Yes

HIGHLIGHTS If your idea of a great marathon includes incredible scenery, excellent organization, small-race charm, and an unsurpassed vacation destination, then the Maui Marathon may be just your race! A well-kept secret for 27 years, the Maui Marathon word is starting to get out. The race grew from 574 runners in 1995 to 1,289 in 1997. For 1998, there is a 1,700 runner limit. Why the tremendous growth? In addition to the above, we know of no other race where you can watch humpback whales frolic offshore while you run, making the marathon's slogan, Run With The Whales, well suited. The race also hosts perhaps the best carbo-load party in the world, held at sunset on Kaanapali Beach with views of palm trees, the Pacific Ocean, and neighboring Lanai. The event boasts live Hawaiian music, hula dancers, entertainers, microbrewed beer, and a generous banquet spread. A great alternative to the Honolulu Marathon, Maui offers a lower-key event. Like Honolulu, there is a large Japanese contingent, just under half of the field. One of the main sponsors of the race is Ryutaro Kamioka, the "Johnny Carson of Japan." He plugs the Maui Marathon regularly on his television show and radio programs in Osaka, which contributes to the large Japanese showing.

RACE HISTORY The Maui Marathon has a surprisingly rich and long history. The oldest continuously held race in Hawaii, the event is one of the oldest in the United States, with 1998 marking the 28th running. Ironically, the Maui Marathon began on Oahu in the early 1940s and was known as the Hawaiian AAU Marathon. At that time, Hawaii's top runner was Norman Tamanaha. In 1971, Mr. Tamanaha convinced the newly formed Valley Isle Road Runners to bring the race to Maui, and the Norman Tamanaha Marathon was run in Maui that same year. In 1974, the race officially became the Maui Marathon which consistently attracted about 600 runners in the late 1970s and early 1980s. Between 1985 and 1993, participation levels dropped following the national trend in marathon running. Beginning in 1995, the race obtained Japanese sponsorship from Ryutaro Kamioka and Runner's Inc., the premiere running publication of Japan. As part of the sponsorship agreement, 25% of contributed funds are donated to a local charity. Seeing hearty growth since 1994, race organizers annually place a maximum number on entries allowed.

COURSE DESCRIPTION The point-to-point course starts in Kahului at Kaahumanu Center (near the airport) and finishes in Kaanapali Resort at Whalers Village. The first 2 miles run in the dark on residential streets. The race then proceeds onto the shoulders of Highways 380 and 30 for the next 6 miles, covering the flat Central Valley sugar cane fields to Maalea fishing village. As you make the turn onto Honoapiilani Highway 30 after the 6-mile mark, there's a good chance you'll be pushed by a nice tailwind as you approach the rolling hills between miles 9 and 12.5. Sunrise over 10,023-foot dormant volcano Haleakala on your left and the rugged West Maui mountains on the right set the stage for inspired running. The next 4 miles hug the Pali (ocean cliffs) where humpback whales can be often seen playing in the waters below. The most difficult part of the course, this section includes moderate rolling hills between miles 9 and 12.5. Lacking large inclines, the hills come early enough so you should still be relatively fresh. If you are not concerned with time, whale searching can take your mind off the hills and the long road ahead. At mile 12.5, a welcomed, albeit short, break from the sun greets you in the form of a 100-meter tunnel. The tunnel signals the end of the hills and the beginning of a .25-mile downhill stretch prefacing the second half of the race. From this point to the finish, the course is flat and stays within 50 feet of sandy beaches and the Pacific Ocean, offering spectacular views of neighboring islands. At about mile 22, the course turns down Front Street into downtown Lahaina, a historic whaling town with many outstanding restaurants and shops. The final two miles are back onto the shoulder of Highway 30 and into Kaanapali Resort to the finish in Whalers Village. Well-marked, the course consists of asphalt in excellent condition as well as a not-too-steep camber of the shoulder. The one disadvantage with the course is that it cannot be closed to vehicle traffic (except for Front Street) since the highways are the only route to the airport and other destinations. The occasional passing tour bus can cause quite a gust in your face, but most traffic travels fairly slowly.

CROWD/RUNNER SUPPORT Excellent for supporters to follow the race, the course highways are open to traffic and provide sufficient space on the side of the road to pull over and root for your favorite runner. Providing plenty of support, the aid station volunteers do a great job dispensing fluids and aid. Manned by various community groups, the aid stations compete for the "best aid station award" as chosen by the runners. Crowds along the course are sparse except for the start, Front Street in Lahaina, and the finish area. Announcers read the names of finishers as they come down home stretch. If you're lucky, your name will also be read in Japanese!

RACE LOGISTICS Race organizers provide bus service from the Kaanapali Resort area to the start, with departures beginning around 3:30 a.m. (ouch!). Buses are limited and

service can take a little time, so race officials urge runners to provide their own transportation if possible. Since most visitors to Maui rent a car anyway, this is not a big deal. Also, if your friends and family want to watch your progress, a car is the only way to go. If you do take the bus, the race will transport any clothes you may wish to have waiting for you at the finish. Though there is a good deal of parking at both the start and finish areas, arrive early. Additionally, shuttle buses are provided to return runners to Kaahumanu Center after the race.

ACTIVITIES The Maui Marathon holds a Sports and Fitness Expo where you also can pick up your race packet, get a course briefing, and have your body kneaded. With an incredible view, party atmosphere, and great food, Maui's carbo-load party may be the best in the world. Held at the Maui Marriott, oceanfront at the Makai Garden, the party includes live music, Hawaiian entertainment, and an all-you-can-eat buffet with a wide variety of food. Refreshingly, there is not the usual parade of celebrity runners to bore you. Instead, the festive atmosphere abounds partly because it is held two nights before the race so runners feel free to partake in the all-you-can-drink beer. Tickets are $25 in advance and $30 at the door. Note that the party is limited to 900 guests and is practically guaranteed to sell out early. On the morning before the race, there is a short (2.6 miles) charity fun run around Kaanapali Resort. Completely noncompetitive, the run could serve as a nice day-before warm-up if you like to get up early. Otherwise, sleep in. All marathon finishers are treated to a post-race massage and refreshments.

AWARDS Every finisher receives a nice Maui Marathon T-shirt, medallion, and finisher's certificate (available for pick up on Monday at the Maui Marriott). There are age-group awards three deep in all categories. A finishers party with awards ceremony is held late afternoon at the Maui Marriott. The party includes free beer, soda, and snacks while they last!

ELITE RUNNERS INFORMATION Runners with PRs under the current course records will be considered for assistance with accommodations and inter-island airfare on an individual basis. In addition, the race offers a small amount of prize money (about $6,500) for the top finishers. Contact the assistant race director for more information.

ACCOMMODATIONS By far the most convenient area to stay is in Kaanapali Resort which boasts six beachfront hotels and four resort condominiums. The race headquarters hotel is the Maui Marriott (800-761-1333 or 808-667-1200). A discount for Maui Marathon participants makes it a good deal, but book early. Other Kaanapali possibilities are the Hyatt Regency (808-661-1234); and Westin Maui (808-667-2525). For less luxurious digs, try the Aston Maui Park (808-669-6622) located further down the highway and off the beach, or Lahaina. For other arrangements, call the marathon's official travel agency, Get Up and Go Travel (888-874-2535).

RELATED EVENTS/RACES A 5K race is held to coincide with the marathon. This is a good way for family and friends to participate in race-day activities as the course finishes at about mile 23 of the marathon, allowing 5K runners to cheer on the marathoners as they run through Lahaina. In addition, a week-long celebration recognizing the humpback whale leads up to the marathon and 5K with many family-oriented activities. Marathoners can also get special sight-seeing tours, including cruises, whale-watching expeditions, helicopter tours, and snorkeling trips through the Do Maui Club (808-877-5303).

AREA ATTRACTIONS There is no shortage of activities on Maui, including lying on the beach, snorkeling, golfing, whale watching, shopping, hiking, and trips to neighboring islands. You will not get bored here, and if you do, see a psychiatrist.

A KAMIOKA CHARITY

Sunday, March 15, 1998
Sunday, March 21, 1999

1999 date subject to change

"One of the ten most scenic marathons in America"
- Runners' World, February 1996

We welcome you to experience the Maui Marathon, considered by many to be the most beautiful and challenging international running event in the world.

Because the field is limited, we recommend that you register in advance. For information call Valley Isle Road Runners at **(808) 871-6441** or visit our website @ www.mauimarathon.com

VISIT MAUI...

Conde´ Nast readers' voted Maui as *"#1Island in the World"* 1994, '95, '96 and '97.

WIN A MARATHON TRIP!

Enter the *Ultimate Guide's* 1999 Maui Marathon Sweepstakes - see information in this edition!

The Maui Marriott Resort on Kaanapali Beach is our Official Headquarters Hotel. The Maui Marriott will be the location of all race week events.

LOS ANGELES MARATHON

OVERALL: 91

COURSE BEAUTY: 6+

COURSE DIFFICULTY: 4+ (SEE APPENDIX)

APPROPRIATENESS FOR FIRST TIMERS: 9+

RACE ORGANIZATION: 9+

CROWDS: 10

RACE DATA

Overall Ranking: 27
Quality Ranking: 12
Quickness Ranking: 73
Contact: Los Angeles Marathon Office
11110 W. Ohio Avenue, Suite 100
Los Angeles, CA 90025
USA
Tel. (310) 444-5544
Fax (310) 473-8105
E-mail: raceinfo@lamarathon.com
http:\\www.lamarathon.com

Date: March (March 29, 1998; March 14, 1999)
Start Time: 8:45 a.m.
Time Course Closes: 2:30 p.m.
Number of Finishers: 15,847 in 1997
Course: Loop
Certification: USATF
Course Records: Male: (open) 2:10:19
Female: (open) 2:26:23
Elite Athlete Programs: Yes
Cost: $40/55
Age groups/Divisions: ≤17, 18-24, 25-29, 30-34, 35-39, 40-44, 45-49, 50-54,
55-59, 60-64, 65-69, 70-74, 75-79, 80+
Walkers: Yes
Requirements: None
Temperature: 59° (15°C)
Aid/Splits: 25 / digital clocks every mile

HIGHLIGHTS The Los Angeles Marathon continues California's trend to lead the nation in innovation. LA was the first U.S. marathon to use the Real Time ChampionChip, a personal digital timing device. If you like carnivals, and the entertainment capital of the world attracts you, you'll love the LA Marathon. The third-largest marathon in the United States, LA enjoys tremendous community support. Among the other highlights are excellent aid stations, a completely closed course, and entertainment every mile. We hope you're not hungry though because this course may pass more fast food joints than any other marathon in the world!

RACE HISTORY The LA Marathon grew out of the 1984 Olympic Games held in Los Angeles. Fresh from the success of the Games, the City wanted to institutionalize the marathon. In 1986, the inaugural LA Marathon became the largest first-time marathon in the world with

10,787 runners. Ten years later, participation had doubled. The race has added the financial muscle of American Honda Motor Company, which should only enhance the event's high quality.

Perhaps the most memorable race in its 12-year history occurred in 1994. Paul Pilkington of Roy, Utah, won the race under controversial and unusual circumstances. As the race rabbit, Paul was paid to lead the race through the halfway point to ensure a fast winning time. Race rabbit protocol suggests the rabbit should drop out after meeting the terms of the pace-setting agreement. However, on this particular day, Pilkington, feeling fresh, continued to lead the way out of the sight of trailing competitors. Luca Barzaghi of Italy crossed the finish line in 2:12:53 with his arms in the air celebrating what he thought was a major marathon victory only to learn that Pilkington had not dropped out but was the winner of the race, a new car, and a sizeable check.

COURSE DESCRIPTION Race organizers reversed the direction of the course in 1996 presumably to make it faster. Even with the new direction, the course challenges all runners. While PRs are possible here, the course is not especially fast. The LA Marathon offers an urban route, and like many urban courses, it is not particularly scenic, traveling through the major cultural centers of Los Angeles. The race starts on Figueroa in downtown LA. A nice, newly paved, wide street, Figueroa can accommodate the large number of runners. The course continues down Figueroa for about 3.1 miles, passing the LA Convention Center and the University of Southern California (USC) turning right on Martin Luther King Blvd. The course skirts the LA Sports Arena and Memorial Coliseum before going right on Vermont. The route then heads down Exposition, going through lower-income residential neighborhoods for a couple miles. Runners encounter the first hill, a freeway overpass, near mile 7, then proceed gradually uphill for the next mile. Miles 8 and 9 gently roll with hills. Runners turn right on Olympic Blvd. (9.1 miles) on their way through Koreatown (9-11), where they encounter a series of short (50 yards) uphills and downhills, followed by two slightly longer upgrades to Wilshire Blvd. After the turn onto Wilshire (11.4 miles), a 200-yard descent precedes a quick uphill, followed by a long, gradual decline. This section is mostly commercial. Near mile 13, the course moves into wealthy residential neighborhoods, which includes a couple of short but good uphills. After mile 14.5, runners traverse N. Highland Avenue which features a palm-tree-lined median and Spanish-style homes. The course becomes more commercial a mile later as it reaches Melrose. As runners turn left on Vine Street, they face a long, gradual uphill until the left on W. Sunset Blvd. around mile 17. The course strolls down Hollywood Blvd. for nearly three miles, past tacky shops on rolling terrain into Sunset Blvd. Sunset contains a couple of long, tough hills at a tough time in the race — after 21 miles. Between miles 22 and 24, the course runs along Santa Monica Blvd. and Virgil Avenue before returning to Wilshire. Here runners stream into downtown, passing McArthur Park near mile 25. A left turn on Flower leads to the finish near the Public Library.

As one would expect from a race of this caliber, the course is completely closed to traffic and is well monitored. Streets are in very good condition for the majority of the race. Quite visible, large mile markers stretch across the street. But beware — the banners don't necessarily mark the precise mile points. Look for the digital clocks.

CROWD/RUNNER SUPPORT The LA community strongly supports the marathon, with more than one million spectators cheering your every step. Over 115 live bands and performers provide entertainment along the course, with eleven designated entertainment centers meant to be representative of LA's diversity — including rock, rap, and Latin music. Lining both sides of the marathon route, 3,700 community volunteers effectively staff the 25 aid stations. The community also gets involved by training local residents for the marathon through the Los Angeles Roadrunners Training Program and Students Run LA. Created in 1987 by teacher Harry Shabazian, Students Run LA is designed to train nearly 1,700 "at-risk" Angeleno students who wish to run the LA Marathon.

RACE LOGISTICS The start/finish area lies near the downtown hotels, so transportation is not a concern. Shuttle vans roam between miles 7 and 24 to return runners to the

finish area should they not be able to complete the race. In addition, the LA Metro Rail system offers free rides on the Green, Red, and Blue Lines the day of the race, delivering runners and spectators to within 100 yards of the start/finish lines.

ACTIVITIES The LA Marathon features a huge, three-day Quality of Life Expo with over 400 exhibitors, seminars, demonstrations, and games. Runners pick up their race packets here. Held at the LA Convention Center, 100,000 people annually attend the expo. The race hosts a carbo-load dinner (about $10) the night before the marathon. The dinner, which draws 4,000 runners, family, and friends, features music and live entertainment and sells out each year. After runners pass through the finish chute, they are provided with water, electrolyte replacement drink, and lots of food. The race hosts the Family Reunion Festival, a day-long party offering arts and crafts booths, entertainment, massage, medical tent, food, and restaurant kiosks; the festival serves as the meeting place for runners, their family, and friends.

AWARDS Every entrant receives a marathon T-shirt, poster, and stuffed goodie bag, all of which are obtained at the Quality of Life Expo. In addition, finishers earn an original medallion.

Age-group winners earn plaques and other prizes.

FIRST TIMERS INFORMATION The LA Marathon is perfect for first-timers — the course is not difficult (although not easy either), aid stations exist every mile, performers entertain almost every step of the way, excellent crowds line the route, and thousands of fellow runners ensure you will never be lonely regardless of your pace. LA weather in March is variable, at times rather chilly, and other times warm and humid. Plan accordingly.

ELITE RUNNERS INFORMATION LA actively recruits between 50 to 100 elite runners and has been particularly successful in recruiting top Mexican athletes. The race offers excellent prize money, incentives for breaking course records, accommodations, transportation, expenses, and new Honda automobiles for overall winners. The amount of cash and prizes varies yearly. In 1997, the open cash prize pool totaled $66,000, with $15,000 (plus a Honda Accord EX V-6 Sedan) for first, $10,000 for second, $5,000 for third, $2,000 for fourth, and $1,000 for fifth. Contact race officials for the current prize structure.

ACCOMMODATIONS The Biltmore Hotel serves as the official race headquarters (213-624-1011). Perhaps even more convenient is the Omni Los Angeles Hotel (800-THE-OMNI). Adjacent to the race starting line, the Omni usually offers reduced rates for marathon entrants, about $110. For cheaper accommodations, try the Hotel Figueroa (800-421-9092), situated about one mile from the start/finish areas and within blocks of the LA Convention Center. Rates are about $50 to $60 per night. Many other hotels are convenient to the start/finish lines. Contact the marathon office for a complete listing of hotels.

RELATED EVENTS/RACES Within the marathon, corporate, law enforcement, and fire department teams compete against each other for top honors. Marathon organizers also host two other events, The Los Angeles Marathon 5K and the Los Angeles Marathon Bike Tour. The 5K is held immediately following the marathon start and has its own pre-race and post-race activities and entertainment at the Convention Center. Celebrities, politicians and other VIPs often join in the 5K. LA is unique (some say for a reason) in offering a Marathon Bike Tour, a 21-mile ride that draws over 15,000 cyclists. Held before the marathon at 6:00 a.m., the tour features T-shirts, finisher medals, and a finish line festival.

AREA ATTRACTIONS A diverse city, LA offers a plethora of activities, including museums, Hollywood, Disneyland, and Venice Beach.

BOSTON MARATHON

OVERALL: 97.9

COURSE BEAUTY: 8

COURSE DIFFICULTY: 4- (SEE APPENDIX)

APPROPRIATENESS FOR FIRST TIMERS: NA

RACE ORGANIZATION: 10

CROWDS: 10+

RACE DATA

Overall Ranking:	10
Quality Ranking:	1
Quickness Ranking:	53
Contact:	Guy Morse
	Boston Athletic Assn.
	131 Clarendon
	Boston, MA 02116
	USA
	Tel. (617) 236-1652
	Fax (617) 236-4505
Date:	Third Monday in April
Start Time:	Noon
Time Course Closes:	6:00 p.m.
Number of Finishers:	10,471 in 1997
Course:	USATF
Certification:	Point to point
Course Records:	Male: (open) 2:07:15
	Female: (open) 2:21:45
Elite Athlete Programs:	Yes
Cost:	$75
Age groups/Divisions:	18-34, 35-39, 40-44, 45-49, 50-54, 55-59, 60-64, 65-69, 70+
Walkers:	No
Requirements:	Qualifying time (see table)
Temperature:	50˚ - 55˚ (10˚C - 13˚C)
Aid/Splits:	12 / every mile

HIGHLIGHTS   The Mother of all Marathons, running's best friend, running's Mecca. Call it what you like, the 102-year-old Boston Marathon stands as the benchmark by which all other marathons are measured. Virtually all certified marathons in North America attest to Boston's preeminence in the sport by noting on their entry blank, "This is a Boston Qualifier." In addition to its age, part of the Boston mystique stems from the rigid qualification standards used to limit its field. If you're talented enough to qualify, expect to have an incredible running experience. One and a half million spectators frame the most famous course in the world: Hopkinton, Wellesley College, Heartbreak Hill, the Citgo sign, and Copley Square are all familiar landmarks of this landmark race.

RACE HISTORY   Unchallenged as the world's oldest and most prestigious annual marathon, the Boston Marathon started on April 19, 1897 after Boston Athletic Association member and U.S. Olympic Team manager John Graham, so impressed with the spirit of the Olympic marathon, decided to stage one in the Boston area. Fifteen men participated in that first race, the second marathon ever held in the United States (New York held a marathon the previous year). Held on Patriot's Day, commemorating Paul Revere's famous ride marking the American Revolution, Boston remains a race of tradition and distinction for its participants, volunteers, and spectators. Starting with John J. McDermott's inaugural win, Boston lore includes Clarence DeMar's record seven victories, John Kelley's two victories and 58 finishes, Roberta Gibb and Kathy Switzers' barrier breaking efforts for women runners, Bill Rodger's record performances, and current stars Cosmas Ndeti and Uta Pippig. While the world's elite marathoners dream of winning Boston, qualifying to run remains an aspiration of most other marathoners worldwide. After instituting qualifying times in the early 1970s, Boston has spurred many marathoners to times they never imagined possible. Whether an elite athlete, qualifier, spectator or volunteer, Boston represents the pinnacle of marathoning.

COURSE DESCRIPTION Starting on Main Street in the rural hamlet of Hopkinton, Boston's point-to-point course features a 450-foot elevation loss as it winds through seven towns before finishing near Copley Square in Boston's Back Bay. Following Route 135, the race heads downhill through Ashland past the impressive Ashland clock tower and the stirring waters of the Sudbury River between miles 4 and 5. Here, runners enter Framingham, passing the historic Framingham Train Depot at the 10K mark. Continuing mostly downhill, the route skirts tranquil Lake Cochituate at 9 miles and the Natick Town Green at 10.5 miles. The male runners always seem to quicken their step as they near the halfway point to the screaming sirens of Wellesley College. Once there, however, many don't seem to be in any hurry. Now on Route 16, runners climb 50 feet between miles 15 and 16 before crossing the Charles River into Newton Lower Falls. After turning right at the fire station onto Commonwealth Avenue, the route traverses the Newton Hills (the infamous Heartbreak Hill) rising 175 feet between miles 17 and 22, paying homage to the John Kelley Statue at 19.5 miles. The course then descends 200 feet over the last 4 miles to the finish. Bearing right at the Chestnut Hill Reservoir, the route makes its way onto Beacon Street continuing mostly downhill past the landmark Citgo sign at the 25-mile mark in Kenmore Square. Here, the course rejoins Commonwealth Avenue turning right onto Hereford Street, then left onto Boylston Street to the finish line.

CROWD/RUNNER SUPPORT The largest single-day sporting event in New England, the Boston Marathon's crowd support is unparalleled, attracting more than 1.5 million spectators. Held on a holiday, the race draws onlookers over 10 deep at several points. Generations of families come out to cheer the runners, with kids holding out orange slices or water, dreaming of the day when they will take part in the spectacle. Several thousand volunteers help coordinate the start, finish and course logistics. If you miss one of the aid stations located every 2 miles, don't worry; unofficial neighborhood aid stations saturate the entire course. Additionally, American Red Cross aid stations occur every mile to assist anyone requiring medical attention. If it's media not medical attention you want, you have a very good chance of being captured in print or television by the approximately 1,100 media personnel representing more than 300 media outlets from around the world who cover the Boston Marathon each year.

RACE LOGISTICS Part of Boston's attraction comes from its unique qualification standards. The following qualifying times must be run between October 1 of the previous year and March 1 of the year you would like to run Boston:

AGE GROUP	18-34	35-39	40-44	45-49	50-54	55-59	60-64	65-69	70+
MEN	3:10	3:15	3:20	3:25	3:30	3:35	3:40	3:45	3:50
WOMEN	3:40	3:45	3:50	3:55	4:00	4:05	4:10	4:15	4:20

In 1997, the race instituted a 15,000 runner limit. If the limit is reached prior to March 1, you are out of luck. Foreign athletes must be registered with their country's federation. On race morning, shuttle bus transportation to the start is provided to runners from South Street and State Park.

ACTIVITIES   Race packets may be picked up at the race headquarters hotel during the extraordinary, 2-day Sports and Fitness Expo all day on Saturday and Sunday. You may do more gawking than eating at the celebrity-laden Boston Marathon Pasta Party on Sunday night. After the race, enjoy the awards ceremony and the Post-Race Dance Party, including dinner, live music and entertainment.

AWARDS   Each entrant receives a long-sleeve T-shirt and an official full-color Race Program. Runners finishing under 6 hours receive pewter medallions and certificates of completion. An official Results Booklet which chronicles the race and lists all official finishers is mailed after the event. Elite athletes compete for a portion of the $600,000 prize purse — largest in the sport. Division winners also receive special awards.

ELITE RUNNERS INFORMATION   The B.A.A. recruits elite runners from every part of the globe, specifically men with sub-2:15 credentials and women under 2:35, though elite status may not always be this straightforward. The race covers travel, lodging and food expenses for elites. Prize money for open men and women extends 15 places with the winner receiving $100,000 and 15th place netting $1,500. Masters men and women compete for prize money extending 5 places with $12,000 earmarked for the winner and $1,000 for 5th place. In addition, bonuses are awarded for course records and world best performances.

ACCOMMODATIONS   Hotels abound in the Boston Metropolitan area. In addition to the race headquarters hotel, the Copley Plaza Hotel (617-267-5300), your lodging options include: Four Seasons Hotel, 200 Boylston Street (617-338-4400); Ritz Carlton Hotel, 15 Arlington Street (617-536-5700); Sheraton Boston, 39 Dalton Street (617-236-2000); Westin, 10 Huntington Avenue (617-262-9600); and Marriott Copley, 110 Huntington Avenue (617-236-5800).

AREA ATTRACTIONS   Not only the site of marathoning's most historic race, Boston rates as one of the country's best walking cities. You can visit some of the city's historic landmarks along the two-and-a-half mile red-painted line of the Freedom Trail through downtown Boston. Explore the Boston Massacre site, Paul Revere's House, and Bunker Hill Monument. Before catching a Boston Red Sox game at Fenway Park, the oldest major league ballpark, spend some time milling about the book stores and cafes of Harvard Square in nearby Cambridge. Shop on trendy Newbury Street near the marathon finish.

BIG SUR INTERNATIONAL MARATHON

OVERALL: 98.8

COURSE BEAUTY: 10+

COURSE DIFFICULTY: 6+ (SEE APPENDIX)

APPROPRIATENESS FOR FIRST TIMERS: 7-

RACE ORGANIZATION: 10

CROWDS: 5-

RACE DATA

Overall Ranking: 5

Quality Ranking: 21

Quickness Ranking: 91

Contact: Big Sur International Marathon
P.O. Box 222620
Carmel, CA 93922-26200 USA
Tel. (408) 625-6226; Fax (408) 625-2119
E-mail: info@bsim.org
http://www.bsim.org/

Date: Generally last Sunday in April (April 26, 1998; April 25, 1999; April 30, 2000)

Start Time: 7:00 a.m.

Time Course Closes: 12:30 p.m.

Number of Finishers: 2,511 in 1997

Course: Point to point

Certification: USATF

Course Records: Male: (open) 2:16:39
Female: (open) 2:41:34

Elite Athlete Programs: Yes

Cost: $60/70/75

Age groups/Divisions: 16-19, 20-24, 25-29, 30-34, 35-39, 40-44, 45-49, 50-54, 55-59, 60-64, 65-69, 70-74, 75-79, 80+, Active Military, Monterey County, Clydesdales (males over 195 lbs., females over 150 lbs.), Mozarctic, Professional

Walkers: Yes

Requirements: 16 years old

Temperature: 50° - 60° (10°C - 16°C)

Aid/Split: 12 / every mile, including pace & projected finish time

HIGHLIGHTS Big Sur has it all — a breathtaking course, first-rate race organization, exceptional entertainment, and an unbeatable location for a getaway vacation. Big Sur's only problem? Every race thereafter seems anticlimactic. An experience to savor, Big Sur should be sipped. The difficult course and the spectacular scenery make PRs unimportant. And make no mistake, Big Sur is a very challenging race. Instead, take it all in: the Robert Louis Stevenson Orchestra, Jonathan Lee on the piano, the Bixby Bridge, the jagged coastline, and especially running down famous Pacific Coast Scenic Highway 1. Many runners describe Big Sur in spiritual or mystical terms. After you run it, you may be speaking in tongues as well — if you can speak at all.

RACE HISTORY We do our best thinking on a run. Evidently, despite being a runner, Bill Burleigh does his best thinking in a car. While driving on Highway 1 from Carmel to his home in Big Sur, Bill noticed a road sign: "26 miles to Big Sur." Bill put twenty-six and point two (.2) together and founded one of the world's great marathons.

Debuting in 1986, Big Sur has become extremely popular lately. The race now quickly fills to its 3,000 runner capacity. Despite (possibly because of) the majesty of the surroundings, Big Sur organizers encourage humor and whimsy. One popular BSIM tradition, the naming contest started in 1988, asks runners to name everything from the 520-foot hill at mile 10 (Hurricane Point), the last hill at mile 25.5 (D minor Hill at D major Time), the 700-pound heifer mascot who gave birth near the course in 1989 (Tchaicowsky), a skeleton dressed in running clothes at mile 25.5 (DeComposer), and the slow-footed race founder (Bachward Burleigh). You may notice the classical music thread here, and for good reason; race organizers give extra points to classical connections.

COURSE DESCRIPTION The Big Sur International Marathon runs along U.S. Highway 1 from Big Sur to Carmel, passing spectacular redwoods, incomparable coastline, and seaside ranches. Runners have the whole road to themselves. Although downhill (the race starts at 300 feet and ends at 25 feet), the course contains plenty of uphills, providing a serious challenge for all levels of runners.

BSIM starts on fairly narrow Highway 1 just south of Pfeiffer State Park at the State Park Maintenance Area. Redwoods dominate the early going, which lies away from the ocean. While BSIM loses 300 feet during the first 5 miles, it contains some strong undulations. The race goes mostly on a nice downgrade from the start until mile 1, where it climbs slightly to about 1.3 miles at the Fernwood Motel. Undulating downward, the course continues to wander under redwoods, in the shadow of the surrounding hills, to the Big Sur Village at mile 2.5. Soon out of the redwoods' embrace, runners face a good bump at 3.7 and another small hill at mile 4.5. After the downside of the hill, the race passes Andrew Molera State Park at the 5-mile mark. Quickly up another hill, runners view the Pacific Ocean for the first time at 5.4 miles. Flattening around 5.5 miles, the grassy Big Sur headlands appear, with textured hills and seaside ranches full of cows. The course rises from miles 6.4 to 6.7, 7.3 to 7.5, and 7.8 to 8.1. A mound of rock rises to the left, and by mile 8.8 runners descend the curvy highway to Point Sur at the 9-mile mark. Here you can make out the climb up Hurricane Point ahead of you. While you still have your breath, enjoy the incredible views of the Big Sur headlands and the crashing blue surf. Still gently down, the course ducks in a cove at 9.8 miles, crossing the Little Sur River Bridge; now the steady, 2-mile climb up 520 feet to Hurricane Point begins. Winds often intensify the challenge of the ascent. Once you top Hurricane Point, the route falls quickly downhill with more great views of the headlands, hills, and rugged, Big Sur rocks pounded by the ocean. At the halfway point, runners cross the famous Bixby Creek Bridge, preceding another winding downhill with incredible scenery. After another incline, the race heads back down past Palo Colorado Canyon. At mile 15.3, the road climbs about 80 feet to Rocky Point at 15.6 miles. Coming down Rocky Point, runners have a nice downgrade to the Garrapata Bridge at mile 16.8. Strongly rolling, with stretches of downgrade, the course forges the Granite Canyon Bridge at 18.2, where it continues to roll past Soberanes Point (mile 19). More stunning views appear after rounding the point. Still up and down, the course reaches the Carmel Highlands at mile 21.8 and a 90-foot hill to Yankee Point at 22 miles. The route here turns ever so slightly more residential as it pulls gently away from the water. You now enter the race's final stages, with another rise from mile 22.3 to 22.5. With a nice downgrade, you run over the Wildcat Creek Bridge at 22.9. With several discernible hills and rolls, you reach Point Lobos around 24 miles and can make out the town ahead. At 24.8 you head down to the Carmel River State Beach, where the course flattens before heading up "D minor Hill at D major Time" at mile 25.3. This tough little 80-foot hill, which should sap your legs of any remaining strength, leaves you more than ready for the finish line. You finish on a well-deserved downgrade into the Crossroads Shopping Center in Carmel. Congratulations. You are now a proud member of the Hurricane Point Survivors Association.

CROWD/RUNNER SUPPORT The Big Sur course naturally limits spectators' access to the race. As a result, the vast majority of crowds lie at two points on the course: the 10-mile point and the finish. However, musical inspiration awaits each runner along various parts of the route: the 26-piece Robert Louis Stevenson Orchestra performs at Hurricane Point; Jonathan Lee plays a concert piano at Bixby Bridge; the Wild Coast Brass Quintet entertains at Rocky Point (mile 15); and Youth Music Monterey inspires at mile 17. At Point Lobos, brace yourself for the 60-member choral group, I Cantori. Bagpipes, radio stations, and a few other surprises support you on the majestic course. Aid stations stock water, electrolyte replacement drink, sponges, and fruit. Medical aid and toilet facilities are also available.

RACE LOGISTICS Race organizers provide shuttle bus service from Monterey to the start, and from the finish area to the start. Since the morning bus ride to the start travels the course in reverse, runners receive an excellent opportunity to check out the route. There is also transportation for your clothing and personal items to the finish.

ACTIVITIES The two-day Expo is held at race headquarters, the Monterey Conference Center. The good-sized expo contains all the usual goodies. On Saturday afternoon, race organizers offer a clinic on "How to Run the Big Sur Course." The clinic is presented by runners of all levels who have completed past races. On Saturday night, attend the group carbo meal for a pasta buffet, locally-grown artichokes, and live jazz (about $14). Reserve early since it sells out well ahead of time. After the race, relax to a classical music concert while receiving a well-deserved complimentary massage. You can shower up then celebrate at the post-race party with beer, fresh fruit juice, and a variety of foods and snacks. Awards ceremony follows.

AWARDS   The entry fee for BSIM is one of the highest around and worth every penny. Each entrant receives a dri-release microblend, long-sleeve T-shirt, official results book, and race-day program. Finishers earn hand-crafted ceramic medals created by a local sculptor. Finishers also become members of the Hurricane Point Survivors Association, which entitles them to discounts on future BSIM entry fees. Unique awards, including merchandise prizes, go to the top five in each age division. Other random awards are doled out on race day. There is also approximately $20,000 in prize money.

ELITE RUNNERS INFORMATION   The top three finishers get reimbursed for transportation and lodging, and the top five receive prize money ($2,500 for first, $1,000 for second, $500 for third, $250 for fourth, and $175 for fifth). Overall winners also receive round-trip airline tickets. If you do well, you can return as an invited elite runner and receive complimentary accommodations. Male runners who have run a recent 2:30, and females with a recent 2:40 could qualify as an elite athlete at BSIM. Non-invited elites receive free entry. A $2,000 bounty goes to the runner who sets a new course record.

ACCOMMODATIONS   If you like to sleep in, try to stay in Big Sur with its 242 rooms and cabins and 431 campsites. For cabins call (800-424-4787). For more luxurious surroundings, try the award-winning Ventana Inn, starting at $195 (408-667-2331); or the Post Ranch Inn Resort, with rates beginning at $285 and a two-night minimum (from California 800-527-2200; others 408-667-2200). Monterey boasts a wider range of lodging but requires transportation to the bus-loading area. Call Monterey Travel (408-649-4292), and let them find you Monterey accommodations in your price range.

RELATED EVENTS/RACES   For those of you who don't want to run the marathon, but would like to experience Big Sur, BSIM also offers 7, 10, and 21-mile walks that start in the middle of the marathon route, a marathon relay for 5-member teams, and a 5K that starts and ends at the marathon finish area. Most of the 5K race runs along the Pacific Ocean, and it serves as the USATF Pacific Association 5K Championship.

AREA ATTRACTIONS   Big Sur has all the ingredients for a wonderful vacation. First and foremost is the coastline. You can also visit the Monterey Bay Aquarium, Cannery Row, Laguna Seca race track, shop in Carmel, golf at Pebble Beach or Spyglass, or just linger along 17-mile drive.

Big Sur
International Marathon

The Walk   the KION 5K   the Power Walk   the Relay

ALWAYS RUN
THE LAST SUNDAY IN APRIL

"The best marathon in North America"
—The Ultimate Guide to Marathons

Photo: David J. Gubernick   Design: Laurie Albrecht

For more information and an entry form, send a self-addressed, stamped, business-size envelope with an international reply coupon to: **BSIM, P.O. Box 222620, Carmel, CA 93922-2620.** United Airlines is offering discounts on all published fares. Call 1-800-521-4041, or Monterey Travel at (408) 649-4292, and identify yourself as a Big Sur Marathon Runner. **THE BIG SUR MARATHON SOLD OUT LAST YEAR!** *Explore the Big Sur Marathon on the Internet.* http://www.bsim.org

AVENUE OF THE GIANTS MARATHON

OVERALL: 83.5

COURSE BEAUTY: 10

COURSE DIFFICULTY: 2+ (SEE APPENDIX)

APPROPRIATENESS FOR FIRST TIMERS: 8+

RACE ORGANIZATION: 8+

CROWDS: 1-

RACE DATA

Overall Ranking: 73

Quality Ranking: 92

Quickness Ranking: 23

Contact: Avenue of the Giants
281 Hidden Valley Road
Bayside, CA 95524
USA
Tel. (707) 443-1226

Date: Generally first Sunday in May (May 3, 1998)

Start Time: 9:00 a.m.

Time Course Closes: 2:00 p.m.

Number of Participants: 466 in 1996

Course: Two out and backs

Certification: USATF

Course Records: Male: (open) 2:17:43
Female: (open) 2:45:40

Elite Athlete Programs: No

Cost: $40/45/50

Age groups/Divisions: ≤19, 20-29, 30-34, 35-39, 40-44, 45-49, 50-54, 55-59, 60-64, 65-69, 70-74, 75-79, 80+

Walkers: No

Requirements: None

Temperature: 45° - 70° (7°C - 21°C)

Aid/Splits: 9 / miles 1, 5, 15 & 20

HIGHLIGHTS Few marathons match the natural beauty contained in northwestern California's Avenue of the Giants Marathon. Staged in Humboldt Redwoods State Park, Avenue's gently undulating route weaves along the South Eel River Valley through a canopy of prehistoric Giant Redwoods that in some places barely allows enough sunlight to nourish the luscious ferns and wild iris growing below. In its heyday 20 years ago, Avenue reigned as one of California's most popular marathons, filling its 2,000 runner limit in days. While participation has waned recently due to other excellent races coming along, the race remains a quality event through one of earth's most remarkable environments.

COURSE DESCRIPTION Avenue of the Giants runs on the same L-shaped course as autumn's Humboldt Redwoods Marathon, except Avenue completes the Bull Creek leg first and the Avenue of the Giants leg second, while Humboldt does the reverse. See Humboldt Redwoods Marathon (page 103) for more detail.

CROWD/RUNNER SUPPORT If your performance hinges on the support of boisterous spectators, the almost eerie quiet of Avenue may not be for you. Your greatest support, in addition to the aid station volunteers every 2.5 to 3 miles, comes from the "ambassadors from another time," as John Steinbeck referred to the mammoth redwoods. These goodwill ambassadors provide a protective canopy for most of the route, effectively insulating you from wind and direct sunlight.

RACE LOGISTICS Unless camping nearby, you'll probably need to drive to the start since lodging is scarce in the immediate vicinity. If you are traveling north on Hwy. 101, take the Founder's Tree exit, while southbound travelers should take the second Redcrest exit. The race's staging area lies on the north side of the Dyerville Bridge and overlooks the convergence of the south and main forks of the Eel River. Parking is located on the Eel River flats adjacent to the staging area. You can avoid the congestion by arriving early.

ACTIVITIES Containing none of the pomp and circumstance that you find at many other marathons, Avenue's principal attraction is its spectacular course. The American Legion Hall in Fortuna serves as the race registration site on Saturday from 2:00 p.m. to 5:00 p.m. Avenue allows race-day registration from 7:30 a.m. to 9:00 a.m. Since few restaurants exist around the area, three separate pasta feeds are available Saturday night from 4:00 p.m. to 7:00 p.m. Choose between the American Legion Halls in either Fortuna or Weott and South Fork High School in Miranda. After the race, enjoy refreshments while waiting for the awards ceremony at 1:00 p.m.

AWARDS All participants receive race T-shirts, and finishers receive medals. Overall and age-group winners receive plaques. A results booklet is mailed to each participant a few months following the event.

ACCOMMODATIONS Avenue does not have an official race hotel, but several hotels exist in nearby small towns. In Weott (about 2 miles away), try the Sequoia Motel, 151 Weott Heights Road (707-946-2276). Possibilities in Myers Flat (8 miles away) include: Log Chapel Inn, Avenue of the Giants (707-943-3315); and Myers Flat Country Inn, Avenue of the Giants (707-943-3259). Redcrest (4 miles away) houses the Redcrest Motor Inn on the Avenue of the Giants (707-943-4208); and Garberville (25 miles away) offers the Benbow Inn, 445 Lake Benbow Drive (707-923-2124); and Motel Garberville, 948 Redwood Drive (707-923-2422). Campgrounds dot the area; campsite assignments are made at Burlington Campground near Humboldt Redwoods State Park Headquarters, 1.5 miles south of Weott on the Avenue of the Giants. For other accommodations, see the entry for Humboldt Redwoods Marathon.

RELATED EVENTS/RACES You don't have to be a marathoner to enjoy a gorgeous run through the redwoods. Avenue offers a related 10K which starts at 9:10 a.m. heading south on an out-and-back course along the redwood-lined Avenue of the Giants.

AREA ATTRACTIONS Although your kids will go nuts over some of the touristy attractions like the Drive-thru Tree near Leggett, the best way to appreciate the majestic redwoods involves escaping to the less crowded trails. Rockefeller Forest (which you pass in the first half of the marathon) contains a grove with the largest redwoods in the world. If you have some time, obtain a hiking guide and explore the dramatic sea cliffs and rugged wilderness along the nearby Lost Coast, so named because no coastal highway exists along its 31 miles. (For other options, see Humboldt Redwoods Marathon.)

CLEVELAND MARATHON

OVERALL: 83.4

COURSE BEAUTY: 8-

COURSE DIFFICULTY: 2+

APPROPRIATENESS FOR FIRST TIMERS: 9-

RACE ORGANIZATION: 9+

CROWDS: 5+

RACE DATA

Overall Ranking:	75
Quality Ranking:	31
Quickness Ranking:	15
Contact:	CVS-Cleveland Marathon
	P.O. Box 550
	Twinsburg, OH 44087
	USA
	Tel. (216) 487-1402
Date:	First Sunday in May (May 3, 1998)
Start Time:	8:00 a.m.
Time Course Closes:	1:30 p.m.
Number of Participants:	1,360 in 1997
Course:	Out and back
Certification:	USATF
Course Records:	Male: (open) 2:11:59; (masters) 2:19:21
	Female: (open) 2:32:14; (masters) 2:49:23
Elite Athlete Programs:	Yes
Cost:	$25/30
Age groups/Divisions:	≤14, 15-19, 20-24, 25-29, 30-34, 35-39, 40-44,
	45-49, 50-54, 55-59, 60-64, 65-69, 70+
Walkers:	No
Requirements:	None
Temperature:	50˚ - 73˚ (10˚C - 23˚C)
Aid/Splits:	15 / every mile

HIGHLIGHTS   When the Cuyahoga River caught fire in the 1970s, Cleveland residents realized something had to be done to clean up their city. An all-out revitalization effort ensued that has transformed Cleveland from the butt of all jokes to a pleasant place to live and a vibrant tourist destination. The Cleveland Marathon takes runners past many of the city's new showpieces such as Jacobs Field and The Flats, all the while surrounding runners with expert race organization. Cleveland offers 15 aid stations, pre- and post-race massages, and one of the richest prize purses in North America. It also offers a flat course, which means Cleveland should appeal to those runners seeking good times.

COURSE DESCRIPTION   The Cleveland Marathon's out-and-back course begins at the Cleveland State University campus at E. 18th and Euclid Avenue, first making a loop to the northeast, returning downtown, and then heading west paralleling the shore of Lake Erie. About six blocks into the race, on Euclid Avenue, runners pass Playhouse Square, the second largest theater district in the United States. After rounding the corner toward Superior Avenue, runners pass Public Square (mile .75), site of the modern BP America Building, Soldiers & Sailors Monument, and the U.S. Courthouse. Just beyond lie the Cleveland Public Library and the Federal Reserve Bank. Runners turn left on E. 45th and then left on St. Claire Avenue (mile 3) to begin the trek back to the heart of downtown. At mile 4.75 near the Galleria, crane your neck to the north up E. 9th Street to catch a glimpse of The Rock 'n' Roll Hall of Fame and the Great Lakes Science Museum. You hit the other side of Public Square near mile 5, going left on Ontario with the distinctive spires of the Terminal Tower (mile 5.25) and the Landmark Tower (mile 5.4) coming into view. At mile 5.5, the course goes by Jacobs Field, home of the Cleveland Indians, and the Cavaliers' Gund Arena. Runners cross the Hope Memorial Bridge, an early 1900s span overlooking the Cuyahoga River and the industrial flats, at mile 6 and enter the West Side Market (mile 6.9), a beautiful farmers market with Old World charm. By mile 8 on Detroit Avenue, the course turns residential with some views of Lake Erie. Lakewood, an eclectic middle-class neighborhood, lies near mile 10, and gracious Rocky River near 14. Runners turn around at mile 15.5, retracing their steps on Lake and Detroit Avenues (miles 15.5 to 24). As you return downtown via the Veterans Memorial Bridge, look down at The Flats entertainment area (mile 24.25) bordering the Cuyahoga River. Once over the bridge's hump, you have practically a straight shot for the final 1.2 miles through the city to the finish at Cleveland State University.

CROWD/RUNNER SUPPORT The largest crowds gather downtown and in the westside neighborhoods of Lakewood and Rocky River. One happy consequence of Cleveland's former status as a constant punch line is that its residents go out of their way to project a positive image of their city to guests. Many residents hold marathon parties, where friends and neighbors congregate to spur on the runners and celebrate their own good judgment for not entering the race. While many a church delegation has forced a marathon to change its starting time to accommodate its flock, one Cleveland church actually changed its hours so that members could participate as volunteers! Including the church delegation, Cleveland's plentiful volunteers man the 15 aid stations well stocked with water, electrolyte replacement drink, sponges, petroleum jelly, and bandages.

RACE LOGISTICS Several downtown hotels are within walking distance of the start. Runners staying at other hotels will have to drive; parking is available near the start and in CSU lots. The race maintains a secured area for your sweats in the gymnasium at the CSU Physical Education Building, 2451 Euclid Avenue.

ACTIVITIES Stop by the CSU Physical Education Building for race packet pick-up, late registration, and the runners expo. Hours are Friday, noon to 8:00 p.m., Saturday 10:00 a.m. to 6:00 p.m., and race day at 6:30 a.m. to 8:00 a.m. Work out your pre-race jitters with a free massage. To supply your carbo-load needs, the race coordinates Restaurants for Runners, where a number of area restaurants offer special deals to marathon participants. After the race, shower in the CSU gym, and then replenish those glycogen stores with the post-race food and beverages.

AWARDS Every marathon entrant bags a T-shirt and results booklet. If you make it through the 26.2 miles under the cut-off, you also receive a custom medallion, personalized certificate, and results postcard (within two days). The top three finishers in each age group receive awards, and the fastest overall and masters runners compete for approximately $115,000 in prize money.

ELITE RUNNERS INFORMATION Cleveland does recruit elite runners, men under 2:13 (sometimes under 2:15) and women under 2:40. Depending on your resume, you could be offered travel, lodging, expenses, and entry. Regardless, you will have a shot at the $115,000 prize purse. The top seven overall rake in $15,000, $10,000, $7,500, $5,000, $3,000, $2,000, and $1,000, respectively (plus $10,000 for a course record). The first Ohioan receives $1,000. The first three masters runners earn $1,000, $750, and $500, respectively, and the top Ohioan masters runner receives $250. Note that you may not win two awards; simply take the highest amount.

A C C O M M O D A T I O N S   Remember to book your hotel early to get the special rates because many out-of-towners come for the large CVS Cleveland 10K race. The Marriott Society Center, about .75 miles from the race start, 127 Public Square (800-228-9290), serves as the official host hotel. Other downtown hotels with special deals for Cleveland runners include: Comfort Inn Downtown, 1800 Euclid Avenue, 1 block from the start (800-221-2222); Holiday Inn Lakeside City Center, 1111 Lakeside Avenue, 1 mile from the start (216-241-5100); Omni International Hotel, 2065 E. 96th Street, 3 miles from the start (800-THE OMNI); Radisson Plaza Suite Hotel Cleveland, 1701 E. 12th Street, .4 miles from the start (800-333-3333); Ritz-Carlton Hotel Cleveland, 1515 W. Third Street, .75 miles from the start (800-241-3333); Sheraton Cleveland City Centre Hotel, 777 St. Clair Avenue, 2 miles from the start (800-321-1090); and Wyndham Cleveland Hotel at Playhouse Square, 1260 Euclid Avenue, 2 blocks from the start (800-WYNDHAM).

R E L A T E D   E V E N T S / R A C E S   Gobs of runners enter the fast CVS Cleveland 10K. Run mostly in downtown Cleveland, the 10K attracts top runners from around the world, and about 5,700 others. In the 1996 race, Joseph Kimani of Kenya set a road 10K World Record (27:20), which fell soon thereafter.

A R E A   A T T R A C T I O N S   Music fans should take note of the Rock 'n' Roll Hall of Fame, 1 T Plaza. The respected Cleveland Museum of Art, 11150 East Blvd., also may catch your interest. If not, watch the Indians play in awesome Jacobs Field, or catch the Cavaliers at Gund Arena. For nighttime entertainment, head to The Flats, the restored warehouse district on the banks of the Cuyahoga River now bursting with nightclubs, bars, restaurants, and shops.

PITTSBURGH MARATHON

OVERALL: 88

COURSE BEAUTY: 8-

COURSE DIFFICULTY: 3 (SEE APPENDIX)

APPROPRIATENESS FOR FIRST TIMERS: 9

RACE ORGANIZATION: 10-

CROWDS: 8

RACE DATA

Overall Ranking:	45
Quality Ranking:	13
Quickness Ranking:	32
Contact:	Larry Grollman
	City of Pittsburgh Marathon, Inc.
	200 Lothrop Street
	Pittsburgh, PA 15213-2582
	USA
	Tel. (412) 647-7866
	Fax (412) 647-7320
	http://www.upmc.edu/pghmarathon
Date:	Generally first Sunday in May
	(May 3, 1998; May 2, 1999)
Start Time:	8:30 a.m.
Time Course Closes:	2:30 p.m.
Number of Participants:	2,230 in 1997
Course:	Near loop
Certification:	USATF
Course Records:	Male: (open) 2:12:02; (masters) 2:20:30
	Female: (open) 2:36:12; (masters) 2:54:11
Elite Athlete Programs:	Yes
Cost:	$29/39
Age groups/Divisions:	≤19, 20-24, 25-29, 30-34, 35-39, 40-44, 45-49,
	50-54, 55-59, 60-64, 65-69, 70+
Walkers:	No
Requirements:	None
Temperature:	50° - 63° (10°C - 17°C)
Aid/Splits:	20 / every mile

HIGHLIGHTS Once referred to as "hell with the lid off" because its billowy smoke-stacks produced a perpetual dusk, Pittsburgh bears little resemblance to that description today, and the City of Pittsburgh Marathon showcases much of the city to prove it. Starting in shiny downtown with its numerous architectural landmarks, the race crosses the Allegheny, Monongahela, and Ohio Rivers before the striking finish at the three rivers' nexus. On the way, runners encounter Pittsburgh's diversity, from the Golden Triangle, to working-class Lawrenceville, to well-to-do Shadyside. Community support of the marathon has grown tremendously, so that now, with marathon organizers' assistance, each community holds a unique, marathon-day festival to commemorate the race and support the runners. The Pittsburgh Marathon also appeals to runners looking to improve their time, and the race will use the ChampionChip timing system in 1998 and 1999. In 1998, many of the United States' elite runners will be on hand as Pittsburgh hosts the USA Track and Field Men's National Marathon Championship for the second consecutive year.

RACE HISTORY The brainchild of Larry Kuzmanko, the Pittsburgh Marathon started in 1985 with about 1,800 runners. Over the years, the primary sponsorship has changed from USX, to Giant Eagle food stores, to the current University of Pittsburgh Medical Center. In 1988, the marathon served as the U.S. Women's Olympic Marathon Trials won by Margaret Groos in 2:29:50. The City of Pittsburgh took over the event in 1990, and its mayor, Tom Murphy, regularly participates.

COURSE DESCRIPTION The Pittsburgh Marathon's near loop course crosses the city's famous three rivers cutting through 12 distinct and diverse neighborhoods. The convenient new layout, revised in 1996, places the start and finish within a half mile of each other. The race starts in front of the City-County Building in the midst of downtown's gleaming high rises. The course, completely closed to traffic, heads along Grant Street (passing the well-known USX tower), then onto Liberty Avenue for the first mile. A slight upgrade faces the runners at mile 2 as they pass through the Strip District, a historic waterfront area of fresh produce, vegetables, and seafood. Running into the working-class community of Lawrenceville, the course passes the neighborhood's tribute to WWI, the Doughboy statue, before returning to the Strip District for miles 3 and 4. The runners cross the Allegheny River by way of the 16th Street Bridge, passing the fabled Heinz Factory at mile 5. Upon turning off the bridge, runners go through the flat North Side for miles 6 and 7, passing the famous Mexican War streets. A slight downgrade greets runners as they prepare to leave the North Side. Runners encounter a spectacular view of the Golden Triangle as they cross the Ohio River via the West End Bridge. As they turn off the bridge, runners have a slight downgrade for .25 miles until mile 8 on Carson Street. On this street, runners go through Pittsburgh's South Side for miles 8 to 11, passing historic Station Square at mile 9. They encounter boisterous spectators at the array of antique shops, bookstores, coffee houses, neighborhood bars, and restaurants along Carson Street between miles 10 and 11. Leaving the South Side, runners cross the last of the city's three rivers, the Monongahela, by way of the Birmingham Bridge. At the end of the bridge, runners face their one significant hill, climbing about 200 feet over .75 miles along Forbes Avenue leading to Oakland. At the top of the climb, they find a flat stretch for miles 12 to 13 as they pass the University of Pittsburgh Medical Center and the university. The runners travel on relatively flat Fifth Avenue entering unique Shadyside with its huge Victorian mansions, art galleries, and upscale restaurants and shops. The course passes by Mellon Park turning onto Penn Avenue. Relatively flat from miles 15 to 19, the course travels through the neighborhoods of Point Breeze, historic Homewood/Brushton, and East Liberty. Facing some slight rolling hills, runners pass through Highland Park from miles 19 to 22. At mile 22, runners receive an overwhelming greeting from the citizens of Bloomfield, who traditionally have a weekend-long series of events culminating with the race. The large, predominantly Italian, community fills the streets to encourage runners on their final stretch. The course returns to Lawrenceville and the Strip District for miles 23 to 25 with a gradual downgrade. At mile 25, runners enter the Golden Triangle via Penn Avenue, passing historic Heinz Hall and the Benedum Center. The turn onto Liberty Avenue leads to the finish at scenic Point State Park at the confluence of Pittsburgh's three rivers.

CROWD/RUNNER SUPPORT Enjoying the warm support of the city's residents, the Pittsburgh Marathon traditionally draws between 100,000 to 200,000 spectators around the course. Prior to 1996, a few of the neighborhoods the course bisects would schedule a festival to coincide with marathon race day. Marathon organizers have since developed a matching funds program to assist all twelve communities in hosting a race-day festival to showcase their individual neighborhood and to support the runners. In another nice touch, the Pittsburgh Post-Gazette includes all race registrants in the race-day newspaper. Many spectators attend the race with the list in hand and look for the names of the approaching runners to yell their encouragement.

Pittsburgh also boasts some of the top medical assistance of any race, with approximately 800 to 900 medical volunteers. Medical personnel staff all 20 aid stations.

RACE LOGISTICS   The start and finish lie within a ten-minute walk of all major downtown hotels. Runners staying outside of downtown can find plenty of convenient parking in the area. Marathoners can shower at the Downtown YMCA for a $4 fee.

ACTIVITIES   On Friday and Saturday of marathon weekend, a Marathon and Fitness Expo is held in conjunction with packet pick-up and late registration. The expo takes place at the PPG Wintergarden on Stanwix Street between Third and Fourth Avenue, a five-minute walk from the Westin William Penn Hotel, the headquarters hotel. Although you may retrieve your packet on race morning, there is no race-day registration. The race hosts a pasta party the evening before the marathon for about $10. After the marathon, attend the post-race party at the Westin William Penn Hotel, starting at 1:00 p.m. The awards ceremony begins at 2:00 p.m. All race registrants are eligible for the prize raffle at the post-race party, including two complimentary airline tickets to Hawaii.

AWARDS   Every runner receives a marathon T-shirt, and finishers receive medallions and official results certificates (sent in mid-July). All registrants also receive souvenir program/results booklets in August. The top three runners in each age group are sent award plaques. Elite runners compete for approximately $100,000 in prize money.

ELITE RUNNERS INFORMATION   The City of Pittsburgh Marathon recruits elite runners (men under 2:20 and women under 2:45). Depending on their credentials, elites are eligible for travel, lodging, expenses, and race entry. The top 10 American male finishers earn the following prize money: $20,000, $10,000, $7,000, $5,000, $4,000, $3,000, $2,500, $2,000, $1,500, and $1,000. The top five women's finishers receive $6,000, $3,000, $1,500, $1,000, and $500. The top five masters runners and the top five Pennsylvania residents earn: $1,000, $500, $250, $150, and $100. The top three Pittsburgh residents receive: $1,000, $500, and $250. For the 1998 U.S. Men's Marathon Championship, the U.S. Champion will win $100,000 if he breaks the American race record (2:12:57). If he does not break the record, he receives $20,000. The prize money structure is likely to change if Pittsburgh does not serve as the national men's championship after 1998.

ACCOMMODATIONS   The Westin William Penn Hotel, 530 William Penn Place (800-228-3000), serves as the headquarters hotel ($100). The other downtown hotel that offers discounts to runners is the Ramada Plaza Suites at $85/95 (800-225-5858).

RELATED EVENTS/RACES   Race weekend kicks off with the Children's Mini-Marathon held at Point State Park on the day before the marathon. Events include a 6.2 yard Diaper Derby for tots aged 1 to 2; a Tot Trot (26.2 yards) for kids 3 to 6; and a Fun Run/Walk for children 7 to 12. All children's events require pre-registration. On marathon day, the race holds a 5K Run/Walk (the only 5K in the U.S. to use the ChampionChip). Teams of four runners can run the marathon relay, starting with the full marathoners, with 8.9, 5.3, 7.7, and 4.3-mile legs. Teams can participate in one of several divisions, Corporate, Neighborhood Groups, Running Clubs, College, or High School. Team members must provide their own transportation to the relay exchange points.

AREA ATTRACTIONS   While in Pittsburgh, catch a Pittsburgh Pirates baseball game at Three Rivers Stadium. Regular attractions include the view from Mount Washington up the Duquesne Incline; the Andy Warhol Museum; the Carnegie Art Museum and Natural History Collection; the hands-on Carnegie Science Center; the Children's Museum; the Pittsburgh Zoo; Station Square; and the National Aviary.

VANCOUVER INTERNATIONAL MARATHON

OVERALL: 91.4

COURSE BEAUTY: 9-

COURSE DIFFICULTY: 5- (SEE APPENDIX)

APPROPRIATENESS FOR FIRST TIMERS: 9

RACE ORGANIZATION: 9+

CROWDS: 6

RACE DATA

Overall Ranking: 26
Quality Ranking: 25
Quickness Ranking: 86
Contact: Vancouver International Marathon Society
P.O. Box 3213
Vancouver, B.C., Canada, V6B 3X8
Tel. (604) 872-2928
Fax (604) 872-2903
E-mail: vim@istar.ca
http://www.wi.bc.ca

Date: Generally first Sunday in May
Start Time: 7:15 a.m.
Time Course Closes: 12:15 p.m.
Number of Finishers: 2,585 in 1997
Course: Loop
Certification: B.C. Athletics & AIMS
Course Records: New course in 1998
Elite Athlete Programs: Yes
Cost: US$38/40/60/75
Age groups/Divisions: ≤19, 20-24, 25-29, 30-34, 35-39, 40-44, 45-49, 50-54, 55-59, 60-64, 65-69, 70+
Walkers: No
Requirements: None
Temperature: 44° - 65° (7°C - 18°C)
Aid/Splits: 13 / mile 1 & halfway

HIGHLIGHTS Spectacularly located, Vancouver seduces visitors with seafaring charm, natural beauty, and a risqué air. The Vancouver International Marathon, our highest-rated Canadian race, captures all this and more, wafting along parkland, skyline, and shoreline. A new course debuts in 1998, eliminating the big climbs up Lion's Gate Bridge and the Second Narrows Bridge and the unsightly areas in north Vancouver. Instead, the new course sticks to Vancouver proper and South Vancouver which provides a more attractive venue. Like many West Coast marathons, VIM attracts a large number of Japanese runners, lending an international complexion to the race.

COURSE DESCRIPTION Vancouver's partially closed course starts on Pacific Blvd. sandwiched between B.C. Stadium, Plaza of Nations, and General Motors Place, home of the NBA's Vancouver Grizzlies. The largely flat first 3 miles circumnavigate False Creek, traveling through mostly commercial South Vancouver, including the futuristic ball of Science World and bustling West 2nd Avenue. Runners cross the Burrard Street Bridge at 5K, rising just over 100 feet to the apex at 3.8 miles where the high-rise apartment buildings of downtown appear. The race now angles back to the start/finish, giving your entourage another chance to wish you luck. Then it's on to Chinatown, historic Gastown, and the cosmopolitan business district. With the Coast Mountains rising to the north, runners enter gorgeous Stanley Park, Vancouver's urban forest, near mile 12. Filled with fragrant cedars and the occasional sleepy raccoon, the park has several hills during the 3-mile loop through its leafy confines. The course exits onto downtown Vancouver's south side for an enjoyable flat, wide pass of beaches, parks, and ocean views. Near mile 16 you cross the Burrard Street Bridge for the second time. Now the race shifts gears, passing through West Coast neighborhoods for a 6-mile out and back of beautiful homes, funky shops, and more beaches and parks. After crossing the Burrard Street Bridge for the third and final time near mile 24, you are thankful for the nice downgrade to mile 25, and the flat final mile to the finish at B.C. Place.

CROWD/RUNNER SUPPORT Thirteen aid stations carrying water and electrolyte replacement drinks support the runners along the course. About 40,000 spectators dot the route, with the most dense concentrations at the start/finish area and Stanley Park. Runners enjoy on-course entertainment at several points during the race.

RACE LOGISTICS B.C. Place lies near 20 or more downtown hotels, so most visitors will not require transportation to the start/finish area. If you need to drive to the start, plenty of pay parking exists at B.C. Place Stadium and nearby streets. The race does not provide shuttle bus service, so plan ahead to ensure you are not scrambling on race morning.

ACTIVITIES Pick up your race packet at the City Square Shopping Centre, 12th Avenue and Cambie Street, on Friday or Saturday before the race. There is no race-day registration or packet pick-up. You can also stop by the Lifestyle and Fitness Expo. The traditional carbo-load dinner (US$10) starts at 4:00 p.m. Saturday afternoon at the Holiday Inn Downtown. After the marathon, head to the awards ceremony and post-race social.

AWARDS Each marathon finisher receives a T-shirt, medal and certificate. The top three age-group winners receive trophies. VIM offers $7,000 in prize money, and Canadian runners are eligible for travel awards.

ELITE RUNNERS INFORMATION On a case-by-case basis, VIM offers transportation, lodging, meal allowances, and/or entry fee waivers to top marathoners. Prize money goes to the top three finishers, with $2,000 for first, $1,000 for second, and $500 for third. Top Canadian and B.C. finishers may also earn awards to overseas sister events.

ACCOMMODATIONS The Holiday Inn Downtown, 1110 Howe Street (604-684-2151), serves as the headquarters hotel. The Hyatt Regency is also convenient at 655 Burrard Street (604-683-1234). Otherwise, call the Vancouver Housing Bureau (800-224-0659) for help in finding the right accommodations for your budget and taste.

RELATED EVENTS/RACES For those souls not ready to tackle the marathon, Vancouver offers a half marathon and a 5K walk. About 2,000 runners participate in the half marathon, which starts with the marathon.

AREA ATTRACTIONS Call Tourism Vancouver (604-682-2000) for information on what's going on in Vancouver around marathon time. Cosmopolitan Vancouver offers many sights and activities, including Stanley Park, Chinatown, Gastown, and Robsonstrasse for shopping.

VANCOUVER

BRITISH COLUMBIA, CANADA

First SUNDAY in MAY

MARATHON
HALF MARATHON
5K WALK/RUN

A NEW MARATHON COURSE FOR '98

A flatter, faster course surrounded by beautiful snow capped mountains,
lush parklands and the waters of the Pacific Ocean.
Starts and finishes in the heart of the finest city in North America.
The people of Vancouver are waiting to welcome you on the first Sunday in May.

1998 MARATHON ENTRY FEE: Postmarked before		1998 HALF MARATHON ENTRY FEE: Postmarked before	
Dec 31/97	$50Cdn./$38US	Dec 31/97	$30Cdn./$23US
April 1st/98	$55Cdn./$40US	April 1st	$33Cdn./$25US
April 25	$75Cdn./$60US	April 25	$40Cdn./$30US
After April 25	$99Cdn./$75US	After April 25	$50Cdn./$36US

Fees shown above are for May 1998 Vancouver International Marathon.
For 1999 and beyond, contact the marathon office at one of the addresses below.

For more information contact us at:
VIM, PO Box 3213, Vancouver, BC, V6B 3X8, Canada
or phone: (604) 872-2928, fax: (604) 872-2903
email: vim@istar.ca
See us on the web at: www.wi.bc.ca

NATIONAL CAPITAL MARATHON

OVERALL: 83.8

COURSE BEAUTY: 9

COURSE DIFFICULTY: 3+

APPROPRIATENESS FOR FIRST TIMERS: 9-

RACE ORGANIZATION: 9-

CROWDS: 4

RACE DATA

Overall Ranking:	69
Quality Ranking:	59
Quickness Ranking:	55
Contact:	National Capital Marathon
	P.O. Box 426 Station A
	Ottawa, Ontario, Canada, K1N 8V5
	Tel. (613) 234-2221
	Fax (613) 234-5880
	E-mail: ncm@synapse.net
	http://www.sirius.on.ca/running/ncm.html
Date:	Generally second Sunday in May
Start Time:	8:30 a.m.
Time Course Closes:	1:30 p.m.
Number of Finishers:	706 in 1997
Course:	Two loops
Certification:	Athletics Canada
Course Records:	Male: (open) 2:26:02; (masters) 2:30:39
	Female: (open) 2:52:03; (masters) 3:11:09
Elite Athlete Programs:	Yes
Cost:	$45
Age groups/Divisions:	≤19, 20-24, 25-29, 30-34, 35-39, 40-44, 45-49,
	50-54, 55-59, 60-64, 65-69, 70+
Walkers:	No
Requirements:	None
Temperature:	60° (16°C)
Aid/Splits:	16 / every 5K

HIGHLIGHTS Unless you run on your toes, you'll be "heel-toeing through the tulips" in Canada's capital city of Ottawa during the National Capital Marathon. The haven of the Dutch royal family during World War II, Ottawa was rewarded with 100,000 tulip bulbs in 1945 and 20,000 replenishments every year thereafter. On top of the thousands of colorful tulips, majestic parliament buildings, scenic parkways, and pristine neighborhoods characterize the two-loop course. Held on Mother's Day, NCM celebrates by presenting every woman finisher with a rose.

COURSE DESCRIPTION Starting near Ottawa's Confederation Park and RMOC Plaza, NCM's sparkling course wastes no time in passing some of the city's greatest landmarks. The route glides past the historic Lord Elgin Hotel and the architecturally impressive Chateau Laurier before swinging south on Colonel By Drive. Runners quickly reach the historic Rideau Canal, and continue along its edge for nearly 5 miles. This section essentially runs flat with the exception of small inclines at miles 4 and 5 where the course passes the canal's upper locks. Leaving the canal, runners head mostly downhill during mile 6 followed by a short rise into Vincent Massey Park. A quick loop through the wooded park brings you back to Heron Road and a gentle incline for about .2 miles before the route heads north on Prince of Wales Drive. The next mile runs flat as you travel through the Experimental Farm. A downhill near mile 9.25 brings runners to Dow's Lake. The course flows around the boat-swollen lake before returning to picturesque Rideau Canal. The next 3.5 miles hug the canal passing beautiful tulip displays before returning to the start of the second loop.

CROWD/RUNNER SUPPORT NCM attracts some 10,000 spectators throughout the course with most gathering around the start/finish area in downtown Ottawa. Participants from the other races and scores of aid station volunteers provide excellent encouragement for your effort.

RACE LOGISTICS You'll find NCM hassle-free on race morning if you stay at the official race hotel or one of several downtown hotels within walking distance of the start/finish. If you're driving to the race, parking is plentiful. Also, the race provides a sweats check at the start.

ACTIVITIES The pre-race check-in and race expo at RMOC Plaza, located between Laurier Street W and Lisgar Street at the Rideau Canal, takes place on Saturday 9:00 a.m. to 4:00 p.m. and Sunday 7:00 a.m. to 8:00 a.m. After the race, unless you're extremely thirsty, enjoy some solid refreshments before heading to the beer tent (sorry, not free). A Sports Active Expo is held for sponsors and merchants to exhibit and sell their products. An awards ceremony, live music and dance show round out the day's festivities.

AWARDS Every runner receives a T-shirt, while finishers receive medallions and certificates. The top three overall competitors receive prize money, $1,500, $750, and $500, respectively. Age-group awards extend three deep, with winners generally receiving merchandise. All female finishers receive roses for Mother's Day. The morning after the race, see your name published in the Ottawa Sun. Results are also mailed to marathon participants.

ELITE RUNNERS INFORMATION Previous winners and elite runners, at the discretion of the race director, may receive some expense money and accommodations.

ACCOMMODATIONS The Radisson Hotel, 100 Kent Street (800-333-3333), serves as the official race hotel offering a special marathon rate. Other nearby hotels include: Lord Elgin, 100 Elgin Street (613-235-3333); Journey's End Hotel, 290 Rideau Street (613-789-7511); Chateau Laurier, 1 Rideau Street (613-241-1414); Capital Hill Motel & Suites, 88 Albert Street (613-235-1413); Parkway Motor Hotel, 475 Rideau (613-232-3781); Days Inn Roxborough-Ottawa City Center, 123 Metcalfe Street (613-237-9300); Aristocrat Apartment Hotel, 131 Cooper Street (613-232-9471); and Chateau Cartier, Aylmer, Quebec (800-807-1088).

RELATED EVENTS/RACES NCM sees to it that everyone has a chance to exercise by hosting several events over the weekend. Saturday evening brings an 8K in-line skate race starting at 6:00 p.m. and a 10K run at 6:30 p.m. Point to point, both courses travel from the Central Experimental Farm to RMOC Plaza, site of the marathon finish. Race day includes an in-line skate marathon that takes skaters on the same course that runners later follow. A half marathon starts with the marathon at 8:30 a.m. Finally, a 5K and 2K run/walk leaves at 8:45 a.m. taking participants on Queen Elizabeth Driveway along the Rideau Canal.

AREA ATTRACTIONS North America's largest tulip display has turned into one of Ottawa's largest celebrations, the Spring Tulip Festival. Don't miss the festivities which include live music, street dancing, hot air balloon rides, craft fairs, boat rides, and fireworks. Other must sees are the collection of fine art at the National Gallery of Canada and the re-creation of a rain forest at the National Museum of Civilization.

VERMONT CITY MARATHON

OVERALL: 88.5

COURSE BEAUTY: 9

COURSE DIFFICULTY: 4+ (SEE APPENDIX)

APPROPRIATENESS FOR FIRST TIMERS: 9-

RACE ORGANIZATION: 9

CROWDS: 5-

RACE DATA

Overall Ranking:	41
Quality Ranking:	44
Quickness Ranking:	81
Contact:	Andrea Riha
	Key Bank Vermont City Marathon
	P.O. Box 152
	Burlington, VT 05402
	USA
	Tel. (800) 880-8149 or (802) 863-8412
	E-mail: RUNVT@together.NET
Date:	Sunday of Memorial Day weekend (last weekend in May)
Start Time:	8:05 a.m.
Time Course Closes:	1:00 p.m.
Number of Participants:	2,000 in 1997
Course:	Near loop
Certification:	USATF
Course Records:	Male: (open) 2:18:03; (masters) 2:22:52
	Female: (open) 2:38:32; (masters) 2:47:28
Elite Athlete Programs:	Yes
Cost:	$40/50/55
Age groups/Divisions:	16-24, 25-29, 30-34, 35-39, 40-44, 45-49, 50-54, 55-59, 60-64, 65-69, 70+
Walkers:	No
Requirements:	16 years old
Temperature:	48° - 68° (9°C - 20°C)
Aid/Splits:	17 / digital clocks at miles 1, 3, 9, halfway, and 16.5

HIGHLIGHTS Personal recommendations often lead to our greatest experiences — the corner Italian restaurant, that foreign film treasure from Mexico, and the Vermont City Marathon. The success of VCM is owed mainly to contented runners passing the word on to their friends. Word of mouth has created a 20% increase in participants each year. Not surprisingly, Vermont City boasts one of the highest repeat runner rates in North America. What's its secret? For starters, location. Burlington radiates beauty with the Adirondack Mountains reflecting off gorgeous Lake Champlain. The marathon skirts the shoreline for several miles, providing spectacular views. Also, very few cities embrace a marathon quite like Burlington. As the city's largest annual event, you may think that finding enough volunteers is a concern. Not so. VCM sports an incredible 1,200 volunteers for 4,800 runners, a number that translates into superb organization and happy participants.

RACE HISTORY Most people agree that autumn is the nicest time of year in New England. No mystery then why most marathon race directors in the area hold their race during this time. The trees radiate color, the weather usually cooperates, and Boston is long gone. Not deterred by Boston, VCM organizers believed that an alternative to Boston was just what the New England spring racing schedule needed. Therefore, in 1989, the VCM was born, its name reflecting that it is a city course rather than a race through the woods.

COURSE DESCRIPTION The marathon starts in Battery Park, the site of famous artillery exchanges in the Revolutionary War, and finishes at Waterfront Park on the shore of Lake Champlain. Run entirely within the city of Burlington, the course travels through the Downtown Marketplace, the surrounding Hill Section, and the Old and New North Ends. Beginning with a 3.3-mile loop around the downtown area, a gentle incline greets the runners between .8 and 1.3 miles. At 1.5, runners proceed down a sharp, short decline after a right turn on Beach Street. From here, the course returns to the downtown area and Church Street with a gradual hill from 2.5 to 2.9 miles. Upon leaving town, the route continues to a divided 6.6-mile, out-and-back section on the closed Northern Connector Highway (Beltline). Although still early in the race, this is a difficult section due to the severe camber of the road, absence of crowd support, and lack of protection from the elements. Moderate inclines and declines occur from 6 to 6.5 and from 9 to 9.5 miles. Returning downtown, the course heads south for a 6.6-mile loop through mostly residential Burlington, Oakledge Park and along the waterfront with the picturesque Adirondacks in the background. Runners are welcomed back to downtown by hundreds of spectators, the Taiko drummer corps, and a challenging hill between mile 16 and 16.5 which takes the runners conveniently past the Radisson Hotel. The race proceeds slightly downhill on North Avenue from mile 16.5 to 21.5 with a short, steep down and up from mile 17 to 17.5 and a sharp .125-mile downhill at mile 18. The final 4.7 miles trace the mostly flat to slightly downhill bike trail paralleling Lake Champlain to the finish in Waterfront Park. Overall, the course drops 100 feet.

CROWD/RUNNER SUPPORT For a town of Burlington's size (40,000), the marathon attracts an impressive crowd of 10,000 spectators. Most of the bystanders take advantage of the spectator-friendly course layout by hovering near Battery Park, which the race passes several times. Fifteen excellent aid stations are located throughout the course along with several musical groups providing entertainment along the way, most notably the Taiko drummers at the foot of the course's toughest climb.

RACE LOGISTICS The start and finish are close to each other and to the race hotel, so transportation is not a concern. We recommend staying at the Radisson due to its proximity to the start/finish and to capture more of the race flavor. If you arrive by car, ample free parking is available.

ACTIVITIES VCM hosts a two-day Sports & Wellness Expo and packet pick-up beginning on Friday from 4:00 p.m. to 9:00 p.m. and Saturday from 9:00 a.m. to 6:00 p.m. VCM also offers various seminars throughout the day on Saturday. Try not to miss the "Mile by Mile Preview," an excellent slide show and discussion of the course. Runners, family, and friends are invited to enjoy an all-you-can-eat pasta party for a modest price, featuring a special guest speaker. The party always sells out, so purchase your tickets early. If you miss the pasta party, don't worry; nearby Church Street is loaded with great restaurants to meet your carbo-loading needs. After the race, runners are treated to complimentary food, drinks, massages and live music. The awards ceremony is held in Waterfront Park at 1:00 p.m.

AWARDS Every marathon runner receives a T-shirt and hospitality booklet. Finishers are presented with uniquely Vermont medallions, certificates by professional calligraphers, and results booklets. Division awards of Vermont pottery extend three deep, and prize money is awarded to top open and masters runners. Additionally, the first Vermont resident to cross the finish line receives a cash prize.

ELITE RUNNERS INFORMATION VCM has a modest budget to recruit elite runners (men under 2:20 and women under 2:55). Transportation, hotel accommodations, entry and expenses are provided. Open prize money is offered to sixth place with the overall winner receiving $1,300, $650 for second, $325 for third, $200 for fourth, and $100 for fifth and sixth. Masters prize money extends to third place with $300 for the winner, $200 for second, and $100 for third.

ACCOMMODATIONS Try to stay at the Radisson Hotel Burlington which functions as VCM headquarters. The scenery from the upper lakeview rooms will make you loathe to leave. The Radisson is located at 60 Battery Street (800-333-3333). Other hotels offering special marathon rates include the Sheraton Burlington Hotel and Conference Center, 870 Williston Road (800-677-6576); and the Holiday Inn, 1068 Williston Road, South Burlington (800-799-6363).

RELATED EVENTS/RACES Runners not ready to tackle the marathon may consider the marathon relay, run simultaneously on the same course. The unique, 5-leg relay consists of 3.3, 6.6, 6.6, 4.1 and 5.6-mile legs, with teams consisting of 2 to 5 members with each member running at least one complete leg. Any one member may run up to four legs, in any order. In 1997, 609 teams entered the marathon relay, competing for the most creative team name.

AREA ATTRACTIONS Art loving runners will want to check out the Festival of Fine Art which coincides with race weekend. Over 25 Vermont artists open their studios to the public. Maps are available from Art's Alive (802-864-1557). History buffs may want to tour Revolutionary War hero Ethan Allen's homestead. For great lake views, take a scenic ride on Lake Champlain aboard the Ethan Allen, a 500-passenger, triple-deck cruise ship. Or spend a few hours strolling along Church Street with its trendy shops, nice restaurants, and street entertainers.

GRANDMA'S MARATHON

OVERALL: 86.6

COURSE BEAUTY: 9-

COURSE DIFFICULTY: 3-

APPROPRIATENESS FOR FIRST TIMERS: 9

RACE ORGANIZATION: 10-

CROWDS: 4

RACE DATA

Overall Ranking:	57
Quality Ranking:	28
Quickness Ranking:	27
Contact:	Scott Keenan
	Grandma's Marathon
	P.O. Box 16234
	Duluth, MN 55816
	USA
	Tel. (218) 727-0947
	Fax (218) 727-7932
Date:	Generally third Saturday in June
	(June 20, 1998; June 19,1999)
Start Time:	7:30 a.m.
Time Course Closes:	1:30 p.m.
Number of Participants:	5,468 in 1997
Course:	Point to point
Certification:	USATF
Course Records:	Male: (open) 2:09:37
	Female: (open) 2:29:36
Elite Athlete Programs:	Yes
Cost:	$30/35
Age groups/Divisions:	12-18, 19-34, 35-39, 40-44, 45-49, 50-54, 55-59,
	60-64, 65-69, 70+, grandmother, wheelchair
Walkers:	No
Requirements:	12 years old
Temperature:	50° - 65° (10°C - 18°C)
Aid/Splits:	15 / miles 5, 6.2, 10, halfway, 15, 20, 25 & 26

HIGHLIGHTS What's this? A race for all the blue-haired, little old ladies of the world? Not quite. You don't have to be a grandma to run, but if you are, you can vie for the top Grandma award. Grandma's has earned a reputation as fast, exceptionally well organized, and a celebration. The race has attained cult-like status among marathon runners, possibly because of the odd name and Duluth location. The community really gets behind the race making Grandma's a BIG DEAL. And, event organizers have plenty of other activities to keep the family occupied. Kids love the Aerial Lift Bridge, reputedly one of only two left in the world. Straight and scenic in many places, the course rolls along the shores of Lake Superior. Few races match Grandma's in overall excellence for the runners and their families.

RACE HISTORY Sadly, Grandma's is not named for that rocking chair planted, sweater-making, bespectacled woman we all remember so fondly. Rather, the race gets its name from its original sponsor, Duluth-based Grandma's Saloon and Deli. The race was started by a group of Duluth runners in 1977 and had 150 entrants. Since then, Grandma's has grown into one of the top races in the country, with more than 6,000 runners. Because of its popularity, organizers limit entries at 7,000.

COURSE DESCRIPTION Grandma's runs on a point-to-point course beginning in Two Harbors, MN and ending in Duluth's Canal Park. The completely closed course follows Old Highway 61 along the shore of Lake Superior, the largest freshwater lake in the world, rolling lazily most of the way over newly resurfaced asphalt. The rural start turns more residential around mile 2. On the right are heavy woods. The first real hill on the course hits from mile 5.3 to 5.6, then it's an easy downhill. The course soon loses its residential quality and by mile 9.5 you are running right next to Lake Superior. Houses still pop up, and by mile 12, you pass some envy-worthy homes. The course continues to roll until mile 22, location of infamous Lemon Drop Hill which is actually two short hills to mile 22.4. Though not particularly difficult, Lemon Drop Hill could hit tired runners hard. Luckily, the thick crowds push you up the hill, and as you veer onto Superior Street, downtown Duluth emerges. Entering downtown after mile 24, you run on cobblestones and bricked streets. Just after 25, you make the turn toward the harbor, trudge up an overpass, wind through renovated Canal Park, and finish within a stone's throw of the Aerial Lift Bridge.

CROWD/RUNNER SUPPORT The Duluth community looks forward to the Grandma's celebration every year. An old train runs parallel to the marathon course to help spectators follow the race. Onlookers are mostly scattered, though, until roughly the 19-mile mark as runners approach downtown. Then the crowds become quite sizeable growing thicker and thicker as you near Canal Park. While every race claims it has great volunteers, Grandma's truly does. The 15 aid stations are very ably handled. Water, electrolyte replacement drink, sponges, and ice are all available at the stations.

RACE LOGISTICS The race provides bus transportation to the start at Two Harbors. Buses leave from a number of area hotels and the Duluth Convention Center from 5:15 a.m. to 6:00 a.m. You could provide your own means to the start, but it is not recommended due to limited parking. The race gladly transports your belongings to the finish.

ACTIVITIES On Friday, the Health and Fitness Expo kicks off at the Duluth Entertainment Convention Center (DECC), where you pick up your race packet and attend the free presentations by noted running experts. Also on Friday afternoon, take a bus tour of the marathon course. Buses leave from the DECC at noon, 2:00 p.m., and 4:00 p.m. Friday evening, make sure you join in the all-you-can-eat Michelina's spaghetti dinner at DECC from 11:00 a.m. to 9:00 p.m. Afterward, get jazzed-up by the live entertainment under the Big Top in Canal Park. Following the marathon, relax at one of the most festive post-race parties around, with live entertainment, a beer tent, and awards ceremony. All-in-all, Grandma's has just about the best activities in the country.

AWARDS All marathon finishers receive T-shirts and medallions. The top three runners in most age groups win special awards, as do the top local runner and grandmother. There is also $64,500 in prize money up for grabs as well as incentives.

ELITE RUNNERS INFORMATION Speedsters can negotiate with the race director for entry, transportation, food expenses, and possibly lodging, depending on just how speedy you are. Prize money goes to the top ten male and female runners ranging from $7,000 for first to $500 for tenth. The top masters runners and wheelchair finishers also earn prize money. There are a number of incentive bonuses for open and masters men who run under 2:20 and women under 2:40. The incentive bonuses range from $500 to $10,000.

ACCOMMODATIONS The key to finding the right place to stay in Duluth is to start early. Seriously. If you procrastinate you may find yourself pitching a tent. It's probably easiest to first call the Visitors Bureau (800-4-DULUTH) since they act as Grandma's lodging clearinghouse. Most convenient to the finish area are: The Inn on Lake Superior (218-726-1111); Radisson (218-727-8981); Holiday Inn (218-722-1202); Canal Park Inn (218-727-8821); and Comfort Suites (218-727-1378). Other good bets are Fitger's Inn (800-726-2982); and the Best Western — Edgewater (800-777-7925).

RELATED EVENTS/RACES Grandma's offers two other top-flight races: the William A. Irvin 5K and the Garry Bjorklund Half Marathon. The extremely festive atmosphere surrounding the 5K held Friday evening is perfect for friends and family. On Saturday morning, the popular half marathon starts at the marathon halfway point. The half has become one of the most popular in the Midwest, reaching its 3,000 runner limit one week after entry forms become available.

ROCK 'N' ROLL MARATHON

OVERALL: 88

COURSE BEAUTY: 9+

COURSE DIFFICULTY: 2+ (SEE APPENDIX)

APPROPRIATENESS FOR FIRST TIMERS: 9+

ORGANIZATION: 9

CROWDS: 4

RACE DATA

Overall Ranking:	45
Quality Ranking:	51
Quickness Ranking:	17
Contact:	Rock 'n' Roll Marathon
	c/o Elite Racing
	10509 Vista Parkway, Ste. 102
	San Diego, CA 92121
	USA
	Tel. (619) 450-6510
	Fax (619) 450-6905
	http://www.rnrmarathon.com
Date:	Generally third Sunday in June
Start Time:	7:00 a.m.
Time Course Closes:	1:00 p.m. (finish line open for 8 hours)
Number of Participants:	12,000 runner limit in 1998
Course:	Near loop
Certification:	USATF
Course Records:	NA
Elite Athlete Programs:	Yes
Cost:	$55/65
Age groups/Divisions:	≤19, 20-24, 25-29, 30-34, 35-39, 40-44, 45-49, 50-54, 55-59, 60-64, 65-69, 70-79, 80+
Walkers:	Yes
Requirements:	None
Temperature:	62° - 70° (17°C - 21°C)
Aid/Splits:	26 / every mile verbally and digital clocks

HIGHLIGHTS The Rock 'n' Roll Marathon has runners around the world waiting like children before Christmas. While we normally exclude unproven marathons from our books, the immense potential of Rock 'n' Roll is reason enough for inclusion. In fact, the 12,000 runner race limit for the 1998 debut edition was reached in early January. Combining the worlds of running and music to create one of the largest and most publicized first-time marathons ever, Rock 'n' Roll promises to become not just an event but an unforgettable happening. Twenty-six rock 'n' roll bands wait like unopened packages along a fast near-loop course starting in beautiful Balboa Park and passing the historic districts and magnificent coastal areas of San Diego — "America's Finest City." Who says we can't have Christmas twice a year?

COURSE DESCRIPTION The Rock 'n' Roll Marathon begins in the west end of Balboa Park and goes north for 1 mile through the community of Hillcrest. Turning left on University, runners then head south on Fourth Avenue to downtown San Diego, gradually descending 200 feet from mile 2 to mile 5. Leaving downtown, the route veers right with a few mild upgrades as you run through Little Italy (mile 5) and Old Town (mile 8). Now on the Pacific Highway, the course hits Mission Bay (mile 9 to mile 18), passing Sea World, Crown Point, and east Mission Bay. The loop around Mission Bay runs mostly flat along the water with a few bumps on overpasses. Returning toward downtown on the Pacific Highway, the course now heads through the Naval Training Center (mile 21) to San Diego Bay. The remainder of the course parallels San Diego Bay until the final turn up Broadway (after mile 25) to the finish at Horton Plaza. The course features a net elevation loss of over 200 feet, but watch out for the 50-foot rise between mile 22.5 and mile 24.

CROWD/RUNNER SUPPORT If you fail to meet your finish-time goal, it won't be for lack of entertainment along the way. Each mile is accompanied by a rock band and cheerleading squad. This should attract some crowd support, and we also expect support at the four relay exchange points and from thousands of Team in Training supporters along the route. In fact, the marathon anticipates hosting the largest contingent of the Leukemia Society's Team of any race ever held.

RACE LOGISTICS Many hotels are located within walking distance of the start and finish areas. However, be aware that the start and finish lie about one-and-one-half miles from each other. Race organizers transport your sweats to the finish for you to claim, and provide buses to take relay runners to the various exchange points.

ACTIVITIES In conjunction with the packet pick-up, a Sports and Fitness Expo, featuring live rock 'n' roll music in the lobby, happens Friday 10:45 a.m. to 7:30 p.m. and Saturday 9:00 a.m. to 6:00 p.m. at the Golden Hall - San Diego Concourse, located at Third Avenue and B Street. Late registration is available at the expo if the runner limit has not been exceeded. After the expo, a star-studded carbo-loading dinner takes place at the Plaza Hall - San Diego Concourse with, you guessed it, live rock 'n' roll music. Though the finish line signals the end of your run, the beat goes on for the rock 'n' roll bands during the huge post-race celebration at Horton's Plaza. Billed as a hard day's night celebration, a concert with a headlining rock band puts the finishing chords on a memorable weekend.

AWARDS Every finisher receives a T-shirt and medal. Top runners split a total prize purse of $100,000. At the time of this writing, prize money breakdown and age-group awards had not been determined.

ELITE RUNNERS INFORMATION RNRM offers transportation and lodging to elite runners. Contact Mike Long at Elite Racing (tel. 619-450-6510; fax 619-450-6905).

ACCOMMODATIONS Several hotels near the start and finish offer special race rates. Among them are: U.S. Grant, 326 Broadway (800-237-5029); Hyatt Regency, 1 Market Place (800-233-1234); and Westin, 910 Broadway Circle (800-228-3000). For other hotel options call the marathon office at (619-450-6510).

RELATED EVENTS/RACES If you don't want to miss the Rock 'n' Roll Marathon, but aren't ready to tackle the full distance, consider joining a few friends for the marathon relay. Teams consist of five people, including at least one female, and compete in dozens of divisions.

AREA ATTRACTIONS After Richard Nixon shunned San Diego at the last minute and awarded Miami with the 1972 Republican National Convention, a few overly sensitive San Diegan's began an informal public relations campaign to protect the image of their beloved city. "San Diego - America's Finest City" became the rallying slogan. Most visitors won't argue; the city abounds with beautiful scenery and entertainment. San Diego boasts some of Southern California's best beaches including Mission Beach, Pacific Beach, and La Jolla Shores. You can see Shamu and his orca friends at Sea World, the city's most popular attraction. One of the best zoos in the world, the San Diego Zoo houses over 3,200 animals and 6,000 plant species. Thirty miles north of town lies the San Diego Wild Animal Park where an open-air monorail takes you past some of the 2,400 free roaming animals native to Africa and Asia.

CALGARY MARATHON

OVERALL: 81.9

COURSE BEAUTY: 8

COURSE DIFFICULTY: 3

APPROPRIATENESS FOR FIRST TIMERS: 8

RACE ORGANIZATION: 9

CROWDS: 3-

RACE DATA

Overall Ranking:	82
Quality Ranking:	66
Quickness Ranking:	42
Contact:	Heather McRae
	Stampede Run-Off
	P.O. Box 296, Station M
	Calgary, Alberta, CANADA T2P 2H9
	Tel. (403) 264-2996
	Fax (403) 265-0640
Date:	Generally first Sunday in July
Start Time:	7:00 a.m.
Time Course Closes:	12:30 p.m.
Number of Finishers:	650 in 1997
Course:	Loop
Certification:	Athletics Alberta
Course Records:	Male: (open) 2:23:49
	Female: (open) 2:45:59
Elite Athlete Programs:	Yes
Cost:	$50/65/75
Age groups/Divisions:	18-29, 30-34, 35-39, 40-44, 45-49, 50-54, 55-59, 60-64, 65+
Walkers:	No
Requirements:	18 years old
Temperature:	50˚ - 57˚ (10˚C - 14˚C)
Aid/Splits:	14 / every mile and every 5K; projected finish times at 15K and 30K

HIGHLIGHTS Lovers of things Western will want to consider the Calgary Marathon. Held during the world-famous Calgary Exhibition and Stampede, the marathon assumes much of its cowboy flavor — the Carbo Chow Down, Post Race Whoop Up, and white cowboy hats for the winners. Mostly flat, the marathon takes in the wonderful Calgary Zoo, the Bow River and a number of residential communities.

RACE HISTORY The Calgary Marathon carries through a long tradition in Calgary, site of the 1988 Winter Olympics. In 1963, the nascent Calgary Marathon — then-named the Alberta and Western Canada Marathon Championship — hosted a meager nineteen participants. Its fate was forever changed, however, in the following year when Calgary hosted the Canadian Marathon Championship and the trials for the Tokyo Olympics. The Calgary Marathon joined the Stampede 10K and the Mayor's Fun Run/Walk in 1989 to become the Stampede Run-Off. To date, the event has raised over $200,000 for the Alberta Children's Hospital Foundation.

COURSE DESCRIPTION Calgary's relatively flat, out-and-back course runs through the scenic Bow River Valley; the only changes in elevation occur at roadway overpasses and underpasses. The race starts in downtown Calgary on 11th Street and 7th Avenue SW, immediately in front of the Calgary Science Centre and historic Mewata Armoury, and heads east through the city center. The course crosses the Bow River and continues east to loop through the Calgary Zoo. Runners go up a short rise (about 50 feet) to cross Memorial Drive and swing through Bridgeland, Calgary's Italian district. At 5 miles, the course heads west on Memorial Drive, paralleling the tree-lined Bow River, and takes a short loop through the West Hillhurst community. Crossing over the Crowchild Trail near 10 miles, runners loop through Parkdale, a quiet, shady community, before passing under the TransCanada Highway and through the community of Montgomery. At the halfway point, the course crosses the Bow River into Bowness, heading down the main avenue through this former suburb. The race loops past the old Bowness High School and then takes in the western section of the community below Canada Olympic Park. With the ski jumps of the 1988 Winter Olympics looming overhead, runners turn for home on a straight, flat stretch along the Bow River to 14th Street. An overpass draws runners to the finish line in Mewata Stadium, one block west of the start line.

CROWD/RUNNER SUPPORT Most spectators congregate near the bridge at 10K, in the neighborhoods at four relay exchange points on the marathon course, and at the finish.

ACTIVITIES The Calgary Marathon holds the Runners' Fitness Fair the two days preceding the race at the Eau Claire YMCA. There, you have an opportunity to visit health and fitness-related exhibits, purchase merchandise, pick up your race package, or register late. Course tours are available on Saturday at 9:00 a.m., noon, and 3:00 p.m., for a $1 fee. Another event you shouldn't miss is the all-you-can-eat Carbo Chow Down ($20), a buffet held Saturday evening at the Southern Alberta Institute of Technology. All finishers can gather at the Stampede Breakfast for a monumental pancake spread, a part of Calgary's great Stampede tradition. A number of activities are available to entertain participants of all ages. Additional tickets are available at the breakfast for $3. Post-race awards begin at 2:00 p.m., closing out the weekend of activities.

AWARDS In the finish area, the first overall finishers are honored. In keeping with its Western theme, marathon winners are crowned with a white cowboy hat! Prize draws are held, including the drawing for a trip to Vancouver. Each runner receives a long-sleeve T-shirt, and all finishers are awarded medals at the finish line. Certificates for all finishers, as well as age-group medals, trophies, and draw prizes are presented at the Post Race Whoop Up. Trophies are awarded to the fastest overall, first-time marathoners, masters overall (40-49), masters B (45-49), and seniors (50-59).

ELITE RUNNERS INFORMATION Complimentary entry and some expense coverage are available for those with PRs faster than the course record. Fastest overall runners receive $500 for first place, $250 for second, and $175 for third. A $500 bonus is handed out to the first runner to break the existing course records.

ACCOMMODATIONS Limited low-cost accommodation is available at the Southern Alberta Institute of Technology. Call Linda (403-284-8012) to book a room. You can also contact the Calgary Convention & Visitors' Bureau (800-661-1678) for more information regarding accommodations. Book early as this is the peak tourist season in Calgary, and rooms fill quickly.

RELATED EVENTS/RACES If you have family or friends who aren't prepared for 26.2 miles, the flat 10K Road Race and 5K Family Walk are options.

AREA ATTRACTIONS You'll have no problem finding activities at the Calgary Exhibition & Stampede. Food, entertainment, rodeos, and chuckwagon races are among the possibilities. If you seek the outdoors, Calgary lies one hour away from the majestic Canadian Rockies.

SAN FRANCISCO MARATHON

OVERALL: 90.3

COURSE BEAUTY: 10-

COURSE DIFFICULTY: 5+ (SEE APPENDIX)

APPROPRIATENESS FOR FIRST TIMERS: 9-

RACE ORGANIZATION: 8+

CROWDS: 5+

RACE DATA

Overall Ranking:	30
Quality Ranking:	68
Quickness Ranking:	89
Contact:	San Francisco Marathon
	120 Ponderosa Court
	Folsom, CA 95630
	USA
	Tel. (916) 983-4622
Date:	Generally second Sunday in July (July 12, 1998)
Start Time:	7:00 a.m.
Time Course Closes:	1:00 p.m.
Number of Participants:	4,300 in 1997
Course:	Point to point
Certification:	USATF
Course Records:	Male: (open) 2:17:34
	Female: (open) 2:40:32
Elite Athlete Programs:	No
Cost:	$45/55/65
Age groups/Divisions:	≤18, 19-24, 25-29, 30-34, 35-39, 40-44, 45-49,
	50-54, 55-59, 60-64, 65-69, 70+
Walkers:	No
Requirements:	None
Temperature:	50˚ - 60˚ (10˚C - 16˚C)
Aid/Splits:	12 / every mile

HIGHLIGHTS Held in one of the world's great cities and starting on earth's most famous span, the San Francisco Marathon should be the top destination marathon in North America. Yet it continues to underachieve, mostly due to the lack of a big-time sponsor and some lingering organizational issues. Despite these hurdles, the San Francisco Marathon sports an exciting and spectacular course over the Golden Gate Bridge, through the Presidio, Marina District, Fisherman's Wharf, North Beach, Chinatown, Financial District, Haight-Ashbury, Golden Gate Park, and Sunset District — the ultimate tour of San Francisco! While challenging, the course avoids many of the city's most egregious hills.

COURSE DESCRIPTION San Francisco's beautiful, point-to-point course begins on the Marin County side of the Golden Gate Bridge. With only two of the bridge's six lanes dedicated to the runners, anticipate a crowded and slow first mile. On a clear morning, the bridge offers incomparable views of San Francisco's skyline ahead and Alcatraz to the left. Upon crossing the bay, the course drops 225 feet in 2.25 miles, going through the scenic Presidio, a 200-year-old former military base. Runners then enter the Marina District, passing the Palace of Fine Arts, the

Exploratorium, and the red-brick buildings of Ghirardelli Square. The course climbs approximately 50 feet between mile 4 and 5 and drops 50 feet from mile 5 to 6. At mile 6, you head up Columbus Street, the heart of North Beach, home to many of the city's great Italian restaurants, rising another 50 feet to mile 7. Telegraph Hill and Coit Tower sit to your left. Heading straight into bustling, vibrant Chinatown, the course falls 50 feet once again to mile 8. The route then quickly touches the Financial District before proceeding down the Embarcadero, temporary home to the large ships docking in the harbor. Around mile 11, the course goes past the warehouses and cheap clothing outlets of the Mission District. At the half-marathon point, runners hit the toughest part of the course — a 200-foot climb in just over a mile. Coming in stages, the climb begins on Guerrero and ends on Haight Street. Here, runners pass sidewalk cafes and bargain shopping in the world's hippie capital. You then start downhill into gorgeous Golden Gate Park, one of San Francisco's true wonders. The downhill trek through the park reaches land's end at the Great Highway near 18.5 miles. After a short jaunt along the ocean just before the 19-mile mark, the course begins to climb about 100 feet to 20 miles at Sunset Boulevard. The race then leaves the park to go up and back for 3 miles on Sunset, giving you a nice, flat break before completing the climb through Golden Gate Park (another 100 feet) to the finish inside Kezar Stadium, former home of the San Francisco 49ers. Watch out for that last hill just before the stadium. While not long or difficult in normal circumstances, it has caused more than a few tears in the past.

CROWD/RUNNER SUPPORT   Perhaps the most important way a large sponsor could contribute to the race lies in promotion. In 1998, the race will hang banners throughout the city for the first time. This is an important element toward building community awareness and support for the event, and we hope that it will have a positive impact on spectator turnout. In the past, the San Francisco Marathon has been like an orphan on race day. In fact, you'd never know there was a marathon unless you happened to stumble right on top of it. Despite the limited past promotion, city dwellers, with and without homes, and tourists provide pockets of support along the course, particularly in the Marina District, along Columbus, in Chinatown, and in Haight-Ashbury.

RACE LOGISTICS   The fantastic Golden Gate Bridge start means that all runners must use the race-provided transportation. No cars or spectators are allowed at or near the starting line. Buses leave from the race headquarters hotel and from Kezar Stadium in Golden Gate Park beginning at 5:00 a.m. The race provides shuttle service from the finish back to the race hotel, but this service has been very limited and there were very long waits in 1997.

ACTIVITIES   On Friday and Saturday of race weekend you can attend the Sports and Fitness Expo held with packet pick-up and late registration at Pier 35, a large warehouse near well-known Pier 39 on Fisherman's Wharf. You may not register on race day. The pasta dinner dishes out on Saturday evening. After the race, struggle up the stairs to reach the refreshments and snacks in Kezar Stadium.

AWARDS   Every entrant gets to wear home a San Francisco Marathon T-shirt, and finishers also get to drape a nice medal around their neck. Age-group awards (generally engraved marble paperweights) go three deep in each division with special awards going to the overall winners.

ACCOMMODATIONS   The San Francisco Marriott at 4th and Mission Street (415-896-1600) serves as the headquarters hotel. Other convenient hotels include: The Parc Fifty Five Hotel, Market at Fifth (415-392-8000); Hyatt Regency San Francisco, 5 Embarcadero Center (415-788-1234); the Grand Hyatt San Francisco on Union Square (415-398-1234); Ramada Limited Downtown, 240 7th Street (415-861-6469); Ramada Inn at Union Square, 345 Taylor Street (415-673-2332); Best Western Carriage Inn, 140 7th Street (415-552-8600); Best Western Canterbury Hotel, 750 Sutter Street (415-474-6464); Days Inn Downtown, 895 Geary Street (415-441-8220); Holiday Inn, 1500 Van Ness Avenue (415-441-4000); and Donatello Hotel on Post (415-441-7100).

RELATED EVENTS/RACES   Your non-marathoning family and friends can join in the San Francisco 5K which starts in Kezar Stadium and winds through Golden Gate Park, or organize a team for the marathon relay. San Francisco 5K runners may register on race day.

AREA ATTRACTIONS   One of the world's great destination cities, San Francisco beckons with its incredible setting, colorful neighborhoods, eccentric population, world-class dining, and activities to suit any taste. Don't miss Golden Gate Park, loaded with interesting things to do and see, such as the Japanese Tea Gardens, a romantic picnic, or an outdoor performance. After making the Fisherman's Wharf circuit, make sure you check out some of San Francisco's myriad neighborhoods — exclusive Nob Hill, the beautiful Marina District, Italian North Beach, frenzied Chinatown, Japantown, wacky Haight-Ashbury, or industrial/arty SOMA (south of Market). For a cross-cultural experience, or culture shock depending on your point-of-view, stroll the Castro District, center of San Francisco's infamous gay community. If you need a break, head across the Golden Gate Bridge to artistic Sausalito. If you really need a break, trek up gorgeous Mt. Tamalpais (about 20 minutes north of SF), hit the beach at Santa Cruz (about 90 minutes south of SF), hike at Point Reyes National Seashore (about 45 minutes north), or head to the wine region of Sonoma and Napa Valleys (about 45 minutes north). A visitor could literally spend weeks in the area and not come close to exhausting the possibilities.

PIKES PEAK MARATHON

OVERALL: 81.6

COURSE BEAUTY: 9

COURSE DIFFICULTY: 10

APPROPRIATENESS FOR FIRST TIMERS: 3

RACE ORGANIZATION: 9-

CROWDS: 1-

RACE DATA

Overall Ranking: 84
Quality Ranking: 83
Quickness Ranking: 98
Contact: Pikes Peak Marathon
P.O. Box 38235
Colorado Springs, CO 80937
USA
Tel. (719) 473-2625

Date: Third Sunday in August (August 16, 1998)
Start Time: 7:00 a.m.
Time Course Closes: 5:00 p.m.
Number of Participants: 800 limit, filled by late May
Course: Out and back
Certification: None
Course Records: Male: (open) 3:16:39; (masters) 3:56:18
Female: (open) 4:15:18; (masters) 4:26:59
Elite Athlete Programs: No
Cost: $35/40/45
Age groups/Divisions: 16-19, 20-24, 25-29, 30-34, 35-39, 40-44, 45-49,
50-54, 55-59, 60-64, 65-69, 70-74, 75-79, 80-84,
85-89, 90+
Walkers: No
Requirements: NA
Temperature: 42° - 80° (6°C - 27°C)
Aid/Splits: 6 / at summit

HIGHLIGHTS Once considered an impossibility by its namesake Zebulon Pike, ascending and descending Pikes Peak has become a mid-August tradition for the 800 adventurists in the Pikes Peak Marathon. Known as "America's Ultimate Challenge," our most difficult destination marathon climbs an imposing 7,815 feet in 13.4 miles from Manitou Springs to the summit (14,110 feet). Once there, the thin air and glorious view of Kansas, the Sangre de Cristo Mountains, and the Continental Divide leave you breathless. The very same view inspired Kathy Lee Bates to write "America the Beautiful" with "Purple Mountain's Majesty" referring to Pikes Peak. If you're thinking about running Pikes Peak, don't delay your entry. With its cult-like following, the race fills extremely early.

RACE HISTORY The first annual race up and down Pikes Peak occurred on August 10, 1956. Race originator Dr. Arne Suominen, of Del Ray Beach, Florida, had two distinct reasons for establishing the event. First, he wanted to commemorate the 150th anniversary of the discovery of America's most famous mountain by Zebulon Montgomery Pike. Second, as a former Finnish marathon champion and harsh critic of tobacco, he wanted to prove that smoking reduced one's physical endurance. By challenging smokers and nonsmokers to race Pikes Peak, he was confident of proving his point. With the assistance of race director Rudy Fahl, who continued as the race director until 1980, thirteen runners including Suominen accepted the challenge. As it turned out, not one of the three smokers who entered the race finished. Suominen, indeed, proved his point, and in so doing, started one of the most infamous marathons in the world.

COURSE DESCRIPTION Although the average grade to Pikes Peak summit is 11%, it varies drastically including, believe it or not, some downhill portions. Don't get too excited on the downhills though, as the rule of the trail states that for every downhill section there is an immediate steep climb. Most runners can expect to come within a few minutes of their best road marathon time during the 13.4-mile ascent. Adding 25% to your best road half-marathon time gives you a good estimate of your time for the 12.9-mile descent.

Starting in front of the Manitou Springs City Hall (elevation 6,295 feet), the course travels along Manitou Avenue before turning left on Ruxton Avenue at approximately .5 miles. After passing Miramont Castle on the right, the route continues up a small hill. At the Cog Railway around 1.5 miles, a gravel road replaces the asphalt, marking the beginning of the steepest section of the course lasting almost a half mile before hitting the wild flowers and switchbacks of Barr Trail. Known as the Ws, the 13 switchbacks on Mount Manitou turn more than 90°, and the last rewards you with the first view of Pikes Peak since the start. The Ws end around 3 miles, but more switchbacks and a short downhill lead you to a natural rock arch at about 5.5 miles. Just beyond the arch, another short but steep section awaits you, followed by two switchbacks to the Manitou Incline Trailhead. The Manitou Incline Trail quickly drops down to a brief flat section and then rises steeply to French Camp around 6 miles. Six steep switchbacks bring you to a welcomed flat to downhill stretch as you leave Mount Manitou for Barr Camp (mile 7). The downhill ends at the "1/2 Mile to Barr Camp" sign, and that half mile is extremely challenging. Barr Camp (10,200 feet) marks the beginning of what many runners describe as the toughest section of the course; from here it's all uphill. The terrain soon turns rocky as you make your way to the Bottomless Pit at the 8-mile mark. From here, 15 switchbacks, each one longer than the last, take you to the A-Frame (11,500 feet) at 10.5 miles. The "3 Miles to Summit" sign signals you will soon be above tree line. Several switchbacks take you to the east face of Pikes Peak. With two miles to go, the trail ascends straight to The Cirque (13,200 feet) at nearly 12 miles. Becoming quite rocky, the course winds to the Sixteen Golden Stairs — the 16 rocky switchbacks near the summit. After scrambling up the stairs, you head right to a short flat to downhill section before hitting the next series of switchbacks. These take you past a sign honoring the memory of Fred Barr, the builder of the Barr Trail. Two switchbacks and a few rocky zigzags after the sign and you've made it to the summit! Now it's time to catch your breath and retrace your steps to the finish on Manitou Avenue in front of Soda Springs Park just beyond the corner of Ruxton Avenue.

CROWD/RUNNER SUPPORT Since few spectators are crazy enough to climb the mountain to cheer you on, most of the crowd support is limited to the start and finish areas. Additional support comes in the form of aid stations along the route and race personnel at the summit. Six aid stations cling to the mountain at the following locations: Manitou Incline — 2.4 miles; French Creek — 4.3 miles; Barr Camp — 7.6 miles; A-Frame — 10.2 miles; The Basin — 12.8 miles; and the summit — 13.4 miles. The rest of the time it's just you, nature, and 799 other runners challenging the mountain.

RACE LOGISTICS If you want a hassle-free race morning, try to stay in Manitou Springs. Most motels are within walking distance to the start line, affording you a satisfying shower soon after finishing. Pikes Peak maintains several time cutoffs at specific points on the route. Runners must reach these points by the indicated times or they will be pulled from the race:

Barr Camp by 10:15 a.m., A-Frame by 11:30 a.m., and the summit by 1:30 p.m.

ACTIVITIES Race packets are available for pick-up the week of the race at Runners Roost, 107 E. Bijou Street in Colorado Springs. On Friday and Saturday nights, the Manitou Springs Kiwanis Club holds a pre-race pasta party in Schryver Park for $10 per person. The awards ceremony begins at 2:00 p.m. in Soda Springs Park.

AWARDS All entrants receive T-shirts, and finishers receive medallions. The top three male and female runners receive belt buckles and bracelets, respectively. The top ten male and female finishers receive rock Kokopellis (an Indian artifact depicting fertility). Age-division winners receive entry into the next year's race. Two special awards named after Walt Stack, legendary San Franciscan peak climber, and Rudy Fahl, longtime Pikes Peak race director, are awarded to two inspirational competitors.

ACCOMMODATIONS Although Pikes Peak has no official race hotel, accommodations abound in the Manitou Springs area. But, don't procrastinate; August is high-tourist season so rooms go fast. Some options near the race include: Santa Fe Motel, 3 Manitou Avenue (719-475-8185); Red Wing Motel, 56 El Paso Blvd. (719-685-9547); Park Row Lodge, 54 Manitou Avenue (719-685-5216); and El Colorado Lodge, 23 Manitou Avenue (719-685-5485).

RELATED EVENTS/RACES On Saturday, the day before the marathon, the Pikes Peak Ascent is held. The race is limited to 1,800 runners and, like the marathon, fills early.

AREA ATTRACTIONS If you're impatient and don't want to wait for race day to admire the summit view, reserve a seat on the Pikes Peak Cog Railway, the effortless way to the top. Another natural wonder, Garden of the Gods City Park, contains 300-million-year-old natural formations accessible by a 45-minute tram tour. The U.S. Olympic Training Center provides a different kind of wonder in the form of state-of-the-art athletic training techniques and equipment, with athletes to match. A 75-minute tour of the Center will fuel your training fire. If you're not toured out, head to the United States Air Force Academy and jaunt through its grounds.

MONTREAL MARATHON

OVERALL: 77.8

COURSE BEAUTY: 8-

COURSE DIFFICULTY: 4-

APPROPRIATENESS FOR FIRST TIMERS: 8

RACE ORGANIZATION: 8

CROWDS: 4

RACE DATA

Overall Ranking: 97
Quality Ranking: 81
Quickness Ranking: 67
Contact: Marathon de l'ile de Montreal
Le club des coureurs sur route de Montreal
C.P. 1383, Succ. Place d'Armes
Montreal, Quebec, Canada H2Y 3K5
Tel. (514) 284-5272
Fax (514) 284-5323

Date: Generally second Sunday in September
Start Time: 9:00 a.m.
Time Course Closes: 3:00 p.m.
Number of Participants: 3,000 in 1996 (race canceled in 1997)
Course: Loop
Certification: Athletics Canada & AIMS
Course Records: New course in 1998
Elite Athlete Programs: Yes
Cost: US$50
Age groups/Divisions: 18-39, 40-49, 50-59, 60+
Walkers: No
Requirements: 18 years old
Temperature: 50˚ - 65˚ (10˚C - 18˚C)
Aid/Splits: 15 / none

HIGHLIGHTS Experience unique Montreal, an island of French civilization in the New World, by running Marathon de l'ile de Montreal (The Island of Montreal Marathon). The city itself entices out-of-towners to make the trip. Urbane, lively, and slightly foreign to non-French speakers, Montreal offers a great deal to the visitor — sport, culture, beauty, and entertainment. Unfortunately, organizers were forced to cancel the race in 1997. However, they plan to bring the race back in the future, with a brand new course. The marathon courses through Montreal and its suburbs, rolling past downtown (near mile 3), Old Montreal (mile 24) and finishes in beautiful LaFontaine Park. Relatively fast, the race offers a good introduction to the city and boasts one of the few free pasta dinners in North America.

RACE HISTORY The Montreal Marathon began in 1972 with 150 runners to commemorate the coming 1976 Olympic Games. The race started on the future Olympic Stadium site but over the years has undergone a number of facelifts (there were even two races annually from 1979 to 1981), name changes, and a cancellation in 1997. The current name — which refers to the three cities the marathon bisects — was affixed in 1992. Resurrected, the race debuts another new course in 1998. The marathon has grown by approximately 15% every year and attracted 3,000 runners in 1996.

COURSE DESCRIPTION The Montreal Marathon starts and finishes in lovely LaFontaine Park near downtown Montreal. The first 1.5 miles run around the park before heading west through downtown (mile 3). Now runners angle for the town of LaSalle, and from mile 8 to mile 13 they run along the Lachine Canal. By 13.5 miles, the course reaches the scenic St. Lawrence River, which it follows until mile 22, passing through the town of Verdun near mile 15. Runners hit beautiful Old Montreal near 24 miles, pass Montreal City Hall, and then return to LaFontaine Park for the finish.

CROWD/RUNNER SUPPORT Aid stations, located every 2.5 km (about 1.5 miles), carry water, electrolyte replacement drinks, energy bars, portable toilets, and minor first aid. Locals come out in clumps, with onlookers particularly dense at the start, in downtown Montreal, and the final half mile to the finish.

RACE LOGISTICS With limited parking and shuttle bus service to the start, race organizers strongly urge runners to take the subway to the Sherbrooke Station, which lies about a quarter mile from the start line.

ACTIVITIES On Thursday, Friday, and Saturday before the race, attend the Health and Fitness Expo to retrieve your race packet. You may not register or pick up your packet on race day. On Saturday evening, carbo load at the free Pasta Party beginning at 5:00 p.m. The first-come, first-served dinner fills quickly, so arrive early. For $7.50, friends and family may join you for dinner. After the race, runners enjoy food and drink at the post-race party in the finish area.

AWARDS Every runner receives a T-shirt and a pass to the pasta dinner. Runners who complete the race also earn finisher's medals and certificates. There are no age-group awards, although top runners vie for $20,000 in prize money.

ELITE RUNNERS INFORMATION Montreal offers special inducements to elite runners, which the race considers to be men under 2:16 and women under 2:39. The race could offer a combination of transportation, lodging, entry, and other expenses.

ACCOMMODATIONS Montreal has not determined its host hotel for future races. Contact the marathon office for the latest information on accommodations.

RELATED EVENTS/RACES Companion events to the marathon include a marathon relay, half marathon, and an in-line skating half marathon. The marathon relay consists of four-runner coed teams in open and corporate divisions. In-line skaters roll down the final half of the marathon course starting at 8:30 a.m.

PORTLAND MARATHON

OVERALL: 87

COURSE BEAUTY: 8

COURSE DIFFICULTY: 4- (SEE APPENDIX)

APPROPRIATENESS FOR FIRST TIMERS: 10

RACE ORGANIZATION: 10

CROWDS: 6

R A C E   D A T A

Overall Ranking:	51
Quality Ranking:	17
Quickness Ranking:	59
Contact:	Portland Marathon
	P.O. Box 4040
	Beaverton, OR 97076
	USA
	Tel. (503) 226-1111
	Fax (503) 224-8851
	E-mail: pdxmar@teleport.com
	http://www.portlandmarathon.org
Date:	Generally first Sunday in October (October 4, 1998)
Start Time:	7:00 a.m.
Time Course Closes:	3:00 p.m.
Number of Finishers:	3,860 in 1997
Course:	Near loop
Certification:	USATF
Course Records:	Male: (open) 2:17:21; (masters) 2:26:03
	Female: (open) 2:36:39; (masters) 2:54:57
Elite Athlete Programs:	No
Cost:	$50/85
Age groups/Divisions:	≤19, 20-24, 25-29, 30-34, 35-39, 40-44, 45-49, 50-54, 55-59, 60-64, 65-69, 70-74, 75-79, 80-84, 85-89, 90+, Clydesdale (185+ lbs.) and Bonnydale (145+ lbs.)
Walkers:	Yes
Requirements:	None
Temperature:	50° - 56° (10°C - 13°C)
Aid/Splits:	19 / every mile including pace

HIGHLIGHTS   With Portland known as the City of Roses, it's appropriate that the Portland Marathon never fails to come off smelling as sweet as a rose. Boasting twenty-six years of experience, the race is one of the premier marathon events in the United States. No stranger to adulation, Portland annually hosts the National Race Director's Conference during race weekend. What better way to learn how to produce a successful event than to watch first hand Portland's masterful organization. And, with Portland offering more running and non-running events over race weekend than any other marathon in North America, effective organization is a must. The second largest non-prize money marathon in the country (Marine Corps is larger), Portland definitely believes in its motto "Everybody is a winner." This fact is, undoubtedly, the reason why 70% of participants come from points 100 miles or further; 46 states and 15 countries in all. The race also offers

friendliness all-year round. What other marathon sends Christmas cards to past participants?

RACE HISTORY   One of the many races under the auspices of the Oregon Road Runners' Club, the Portland Marathon premiered in 1972 with 173 runners. However, due to rapid growth, the marathon was forced to change courses numerous times in its formative years. Add to this the frequent shifting of the race date and race director, and Portland topped out in the late seventies with 1,219 runners, then declined to a five-year low of 481 in 1981. Ironically, that same year marked the first time the course entered the downtown area, a dream of the race's founding fathers but continually squelched by city officials. That year also signaled the beginning of a new era for the Portland Marathon. As strange as it may sound, it started when one of the 481 runners quit mid-race. Runner Les Smith, president of the ORRC, did not quit from exhaustion. He quit because he felt that race management could be doing much more for the runners. He spent the next few hours assisting at an undermanned aid station and cheering on his fellow runners all the while visualizing the transformation of Portland into a world-class marathon. After assuming the position of race director in 1984, Les completely overhauled the race. Fifteen years later, Les continues at the helm of the race that treats every runner like a champion.

COURSE DESCRIPTION   The Marathon and Marathon Walk begin and end at charming Chapman/Lownsdale/Schrunk Parks, which are actually one big park in downtown Portland. Starting at the corner of SW Madison and Fourth, the course traces a route that embraces the many faces of a beautiful and friendly city, including the scenic riverfront, historic Old Town, and various residential neighborhoods. Broad panoramas of the city and dramatic views of the Cascade Mountain Range (Mt. Hood and Mt. St. Helens) and the St. Johns Bridge, one of the most beautiful suspension bridges in the world, inspire runners. Well-marked, the race provides large signs covered by balloons to signal each mile. The first 5 miles of the course are downtown. A gentle 1-mile downhill starts the race, with the next 2.5 miles gradually gaining 140 feet. An immediate, 2-mile downhill takes runners along the waterfront. The next section, from mile 5.5 to 12, travels through the industrial northwest section of town. You hardly notice this least scenic area of the course since the music and the adrenaline rush from eyeing other runners approaching from the opposite direction easily divert your attention. Making another gradual downhill, the course heads along the flat border road of the Forest Park area through mile 15. The principal elevation gain on the course occurs over the next two miles as runners climb nearly 150 feet leading to the beautiful St. Johns Bridge. Thereafter, you run along Portland's spectacular east bluff that faces the Willamette River from mile 18 through 24. There is an elevation loss of approximately 140 feet from mile 22 to 24.5, with a slight rise as runners go over Portland's Steel Bridge. You then turn back down to Marathon Avenue which leads to Front Avenue along the waterfront to the finish. Entirely run on well-maintained asphalt, the majority of the course is closed to vehicular traffic. Because the course records are relatively slow, you might surmise that the course is slow. But, remember, fast times are partly a function of prize money, one of the few things Portland doesn't offer. Make no mistake about it, Portland is a potential PR course.

CROWD/RUNNER SUPPORT   Enthusiastic spectators, numbering upwards of 50,000, line the streets throughout the course with the greatest percentage in the downtown area for the first 5 miles and for the last 1.5 miles. Large neighborhood crowds gather between 18 and 21 miles. Various musical groups and street performers entertain along the course and appear to enjoy the event as much as the runners. Les Smith no longer has to work an aid station for the race as Portland fashions 19 of them manned by volunteers from businesses and organizations around the city. The stations compete for awards, including best organized, best decorated, and most enthusiastic. The aid stations are tremendous (some have cups with lids and straws), and depending on the weather, sponge and spray stations are also available.

RACE LOGISTICS   Because the race starts and ends near all the hotels in downtown Portland, transportation is not a concern. Clothing storage is provided starting at 6:00 a.m.

and closing at 3:00 p.m. in the basement area of the Portland Building.

ACTIVITIES Featuring more pre-race activities than any marathon in North America, the Portland Marathon offers something for the whole family, including: a golf tournament, Big Band Jazz Night, Pasta Party, National Race Director's Conference (2 days), and a Sports and Fitness Expo. A post-race party for finishers takes place in the finish area. Portland offers a novel approach to the post-race food frenzy. Instead of shepherding the finishers along in extended lines through various food tables, large, sealed plastic bags containing a plethora of goodies are handed to each runner. Massage practitioners provide foot/leg massages in the finish area for a nominal donation. A party open to all entrants, volunteers and their guests begins at 1:00 p.m. at the Portland Hilton, with the awards ceremony at 3:00 p.m.

AWARDS Each finisher receives a long-sleeve T-shirt, finisher medallion, race pin, Pacific Redwood sapling, and red rose. Race certificates and post-race results are mailed to finishers at a later time. Awards go as deep as 15 depending on the number and percentage of entrants in each age division.

FIRST TIMERS INFORMATION The large field, broad crowd support, outstanding aid stations, plentiful entertainment, usually good weather, and scenic course with only one significant hill, translate into a superb race for a maiden voyage. While the course closes at noon, runners can proceed on well-marked sidewalks. Aid stations continue to provide aid to those within an 8-hour pace.

ACCOMMODATIONS The Portland Hilton, 921 SW 6th Avenue downtown (503-226-1611), serves as race headquarters. Specially priced rooms are reserved for marathoners and their guests at $145 per night. Other hotels in the area include: Days Inn, 1414 SW Sixth Avenue (503-221-1611); Marriott, 1401 SW Front Street (503-226-7600); Heathman Hotel, 1009 SW Broadway (503-241-4100); and the Benson Hotel, 309 SW Broadway (503-228-9611).

RELATED EVENTS/RACES Portland features six separate events in addition to the marathon. The fun includes a Marathon Walk, Niketown 5-miler, 10K Mayor's Walk, and Marafun Kids' run (2 miles), all of which take place on race Sunday. The Run & Shoot Summer Biathlon and 24-Hour Track Ultra Run take place on Saturday.

AREA ATTRACTIONS Portland is a great destination city. If you have a few extra days, we recommend embarking on a trip to Mt. Hood, Mt. St. Helens or the beautiful Oregon coast. Additionally, you can view the spectacular waterfalls of the Columbia Gorge only thirty minutes east of Portland on I-84. Oktoberfest at Oak Park is another entertainment option.

PORTLAND MARATHON

ENTRY FORM

Be a part of "the best organized marathon in America"!
— *The Ultimate Guide to Marathons*

Future Dates: October 4, 1998 • October 3, 1999 • October 1, 2000

Please read carefully before completing form. Please print clearly. Please note deadlines for sending applications and late fees. Marathon and Marathon Walk entries by mail ($50) must be postmarked on or before midnight, Sept. 10 for 1998, Sept. 9 for 1999, and Sept. 11 for 2000. Note: runners and walkers may enter in person for all events at a late fee rate at the Marathon Expo held at the Portland Hilton on the two days before the event.

(No refunds, exchanges or transfers)

(Please begin your name in the large box)   Check one box: ☐ Marathon Run ☐ Marathon Walk

1. Last Name _____   First Name _____   M.I. ☐

2. Address _____

   City _____   State ☐☐   Zip Code _____   Country _____
   (If other than U.S.)

3. Age ☐☐   4. Sex M ☐ F ☐   5. Total years of school ☐☐

6. Shirt size: S ☐   M ☐   L ☐   XL ☐   XXL ☐   (100% cotton)

7. Phone (work) ☐☐☐ — ☐☐☐ — ☐☐☐☐   (home) ☐☐☐ — ☐☐☐ — ☐☐☐☐

8. Best Previous Marathon Time: ☐☐ hr. ☐☐ min. ☐☐ sec.

9. Predicted Time: ☐☐ hr. ☐☐ min. ☐☐ sec.

Office Use Only
UGM 1/98

10. Completed Marathons: ☐☐☐

11. Completed Portland Marathons: ☐☐

Entry Fee ($50)	$_____
"Training For" Shirt ($15/$20)	$_____
Souvenir Shirt ($15/$20/$35)	$_____
Postage & Handling (see chart)	$_____
Total Enclosed:	$_____

(US Dollar amounts only: No foreign checks or money orders)

TRAINING FOR PORTLAND MARATHON SHIRTS
(check size)

A. S ☐ M ☐ L ☐ XL ☐   **Short Sleeve $15.00**

B. S ☐ M ☐ L ☐ XL ☐   **Long Sleeve Crew Neck - T-Shirt $20.00**

PORTLAND MARATHON SOUVENIR SHIRTS
(check size)

A. S ☐ M ☐ L ☐ XL ☐   **Short Sleeve $15.00**

B. S ☐ M ☐ L ☐ XL ☐   **Long Sleeve Crew Neck - T-Shirt $20.00**

C. S ☐ M ☐ L ☐ XL ☐   **Sweatshirt $35.00**

Shirt Postage & Handling Fees (Allow 5-6 weeks for delivery)	US/Canada	Foreign
$15-$25	$5	$7
$26-$40	$6	$9
Over $40	$7	$11

**Make checks payable to: Portland Marathon;
Mail to: P.O. Box 4040, Beaverton, OR 97076**

Signature _____   Date _____

This form may be reproduced, duplicated or enlarged.

MARATHON HOTLINE: (503) 226-1111
e-mail: pdxmar@teleport.com
Or visit our websites: http://www.teleport.com/~pdxmar
http://www.portlandmarathon.org

DON RASMUSSEN   The Portland Hilton Hotel

*IF YOU WOULD LIKE A COPY OF OUR 16 PAGE MARATHON ENTRY BOOKLET OR AN ENTRY BOOKLET THAT ALSO DESCRIBES THE FIVE-MILER, THE MAYOR'S WALK, THE MARAFUN KIDS' RUN OR THE 26.2-MILE MARATHON WALK, PLEASE SEND A LEGAL SIZE SELF ADDRESSED STAMPED ENVELOPE (55¢) TO THE ABOVE ADDRESS.

St. George Marathon

Overall: 93

Course Beauty: 9

Course Difficulty: 4 (see appendix)

Appropriateness for First Timers: 8

Race Organization: 10-

Crowds: 4

R A C E   D A T A

Overall Ranking:	21
Quality Ranking:	28
Quickness Ranking:	71
Contact:	St. George Marathon
	Leisure Services
	86 South Main Street
	St. George, UT 84770 USA
	Tel. (801) 634-5850
	Fax (801) 634-0709
Date:	Generally first Saturday in October
Start Time:	6:45 a.m.
Time Course Closes:	12:45 p.m.
Number of Finishers:	3,174 in 1997
Course:	Point to point
Certification:	USATF
Course Records:	Male: (open) 2:15:16; (masters) 2:22:52
	Female: (open & masters) 2:37:13
Elite Athlete Programs:	Yes
Cost:	$30
Age groups/Divisions:	Male: ≤12, 13-14, 15-18, 19-24, 25-29, 30-34, 35-39, 40-44, 45-49, 50-54, 55-59, 60-64, 65-69, 70-74, 75+, Heavyweight (200+)
	Female: ≤18, 19-24, 25-29, 30-34, 35-39, 40-44, 45-49, 50-54, 55-59, 60-64, 65-69, 70+, Heavyweight (140+)
Walkers:	No
Requirements:	None
Temperature:	37° - 80° (3°C - 27°C)
Aid/Splits:	13 / every 2 miles

HIGHLIGHTS   St. George has garnered quite a reputation recently as the fastest marathon in the United States (to its credit, St. George never billed itself as such). Whoever said that probably has not run the course. For the vast majority of runners, St. George is not the fastest U.S. marathon, probably not even in the top 20. A couple of long, taxing uphills and sharp, quad-killing downhills see to that. But that shouldn't detract from what it is — a distinctively beautiful, well-organized, fun community event within an easy drive of some of America's top destinations (see Area Attractions). The race provides unique touches that runners love, such as bonfires at the start for warmth. Race organizers go all out to accommodate everyone's needs, as many runners can attest. Sunrise over the barren mountains, the brilliant red rock formations of Snow Canyon, and several ancient volcanos make the scene spectacular in places. All of these combine to place the St. George Marathon at the top of many runners' lists.

Andre Tocco of San Pedro, California says, "*I have been going to this race for the past 14 years, and I have seen it grow .... But every year the quality of the race was never affected.*"

C O U R S E   D E S C R I P T I O N   The St. George Marathon runs point to point on Highway 18 from Pine Valley Road near Central, UT, to Worthen Park in St. George. Entirely closed to traffic with excellent asphalt, the course begins at an elevation of 5,240 feet and ends at 2,680 feet, an elevation loss of 2,560 feet. This impressive figure excites everyone about the speed of the race. However, the course contains two significant hills at miles 7 and 21.5, slowing down most runners.

The first small rise on the course occurs at .7 miles, then it levels out for a half mile. Runners hit a noticeable .33-mile hill, then it's mostly flat or gently downhill (except 3.2 to 3.7) to mile 5.6. You descend quickly into the town of Veyo at the 7-mile mark. Upon leaving Veyo, a challenging 1-mile climb (about 500 feet) awaits you, making you doubt talk of fast, downhill courses. The hill crests near 8 miles. You then have some time to recover on flat to slightly downhill roads to mile 9, where the road inclines gradually with some intermittent bumps to mile 12.3. The next essentially flat 2 miles become a sharp downhill from mile 13.7 to 15.4. Hope you did your downhill training! At 14.4, you negotiate a right curve and come face to face with interesting rock formations. The course flattens out from mile 15.4 to 16.7 and then declines just perceptively to 18.2. Another hill looms between mile 18.2 and 18.6, and then it's mostly downhill with a few bumps from mile 18.6 to 21.5. Just before the 20-mile mark, notice the beautiful rock formations to your right. Yet another strenuous, steep climb must be conquered between mile 21.5 and 22.1. Your legs are then hit immediately with a sharp downhill for .25 miles that eases slightly for the rest of the way to St. George at mile 23.4. Here, Highway 18 becomes Bluff Street, the main drag in St. George. Enjoy the sound of the crowds as you check out the impressive red rock bluffs overlooking the town. Bluff Street provides a nice, easy slope for a downhill finish. Before mile 25 you can see the white tip of the Mormon Temple against the red rock backdrop. At mile 25, you make a sharp left onto 300 South Street straight into Worthen Park for the finish.

C R O W D / R U N N E R   S U P P O R T   The marathon is the community event in St. George. Over 1,400 volunteers cater to the runners, while the locals turn out in droves in downtown St. George. Due to limited access, relatively few spectators perch along Highway 18. The two exceptions are at Veyo, where a large and supportive crowd turns out, and at Snow Canyon (mile 15). Aid stations stock water, electrolyte replacement drink, petroleum jelly, sponges, and first aid supplies; nurses are available for medical aid. Approximately 80 portable toilets dot the course.

R A C E   L O G I S T I C S   All runners must take the buses from Worthen Park to the start, unless camping in the Pine Valley area. Buses begin departing at 4:30 a.m. with the last bus leaving around 5:40 a.m. The race must bus 4,000 runners to the start, so arrive early. And remember, if you are staying in Nevada, St. George's clocks are one hour ahead. The bus ride provides an excellent opportunity to get an idea of what you're in for since it drives the course in reverse, although you can only see so much in the dark. Of course, the race transports your personal belongings from the start to the finish.

A C T I V I T I E S   St. George sponsors a race expo on Friday, from 9:00 a.m. to 9:00 p.m. at the Smith's Auditorium, Dixie Convention Center. A pasta feed with entertainment and all-you-can-eat food and drink is also at the Convention Center ($6). The race hosts a number of running clinics, including "Marathon 101" offering advice on how to run the St. George course. Runners keep warm by bonfires near the start in the morning chill and darkness. St. George hosts an excellent post-race party in Worthen Park. Good food, fresh fruit, drinks and entertainment preface the awards ceremony. Runners can relax with a complimentary 15-minute massage after the race before viewing the results at the Recreation Center.

A W A R D S   All entrants receive T-shirts and race posters. Finishers earn special medallions to commemorate their achievement. Age-group awards go up to ten deep. Overall and mas-

ters winners typically receive an all-expenses paid trip to run in the Ibigawa Marathon in Japan. A Special Achievement Award recognizes a particularly exceptional effort. After completing 10 St. George marathons, you are eligible for the Ten-Year Club. Club members are entitled to special T-shirts, photos, discounts on entry fees, and a post-marathon party.

FIRST TIMERS INFORMATION St. George offers a couple of challenges for the first timer — a demanding course (see Course Description) at moderate altitude and few spectators over the first 25 miles (except for miles 7 and 15). These factors are tempered by a supportive race organization with excellent aid stations, a scenic course, a sizeable field of runners, and usually good weather conditions. Prepare yourself for the course by doing plenty of hill training (both up and down). In one of St. George's many distinctive touches, first timers are given special T-shirts, products and prizes.

ELITE RUNNERS INFORMATION St. George provides limited assistance to elite runners, possibly including entry, transportation, lodging, and/or expenses. Funds are limited, so contact Kent Perkins for more information on obtaining elite status.

ACCOMMODATIONS For accommodations in St. George, call (800-259-3343). Entry forms also have a complete listing of lodging in Washington County. Hotels in St. George fill extremely early, so many runners stay in Nevada, a 45-minute drive from St. George (remember the time difference). You shouldn't have much trouble obtaining a reservation there.

RELATED EVENTS/RACES A 2-mile Mayor's Walk from Bluff Street Park to the marathon finish line begins at 7:00 a.m. Walkers receive T-shirts, walker numbers, and post-walk refreshments, and are eligible for random drawings. The walk draws over 1,200 participants.

AREA ATTRACTIONS St. George sits within a modest drive of two completely dichotomous attractions — Zion National Park and Las Vegas. Definitely worth the short trip from St. George, Zion offers some spectacular hiking, camping, and just plain sight-seeing. Also nearby is Cedar Breaks National Monument. If you have an extra couple of days, you can also visit Bryce Canyon National Park, which lies just beyond Zion. If you feel like a little more city action, Las Vegas lies just 2 hours away. Make the drive during the daylight, if you can, to admire the stunning gorge just outside of St. George on Interstate 15. The incredible bluffs envelope you in their majesty. Unforgettable!

TWIN CITIES MARATHON

OVERALL: 98.4

COURSE BEAUTY: 10

COURSE DIFFICULTY: 3- (SEE APPENDIX)

APPROPRIATENESS FOR FIRST TIMERS: 10

RACE ORGANIZATION: 10

CROWDS: 9-

RACE DATA

Overall Ranking: 8
Quality Ranking: 5
Quickness Ranking: 19
Contact: Twin Cities Marathon
708 North First Street, Ste. CR-33
Minneapolis, MN 55401
USA
Tel. (612) 673-0778
Fax (612) 673-0780
E-mail: tcm26pt2@aol.com
http://www.doitsports.com/marathons/twincities
Date: Generally first Sunday in October
Start Time: 8:00 a.m.
Time Course Closes: 2:00 p.m.
Number of Participants: 5,318 in 1997
Course: Point to point
Certification: USATF
Course Records: Male: (open) 2:10:05; (masters) 2:15:15 (U.S. Masters Record)
Female: (open) 2:27:59; (masters) 2:35:08 (U.S. Masters Record)
Elite Athlete Programs: Yes
Cost: $35/40/50
Age groups/Divisions: ≤19, 20-24, 25-29, 30-34, 35-39, 40-44, 45-49, 50-54,
55-59, 60-64, 65-69, 70+
Walkers: No
Requirements: None
Temperature: 43° - 64° (6°C - 18°C)
Aid/Splits: 12 / digital clocks at miles 1, 2, 3, 4, 10, halfway, 15, 20 & 25

HIGHLIGHTS "Beautiful" and "urban" are two words that cannot often be used together to describe marathons. When applied to the Twin Cities Marathon (TCM), however, beautiful and urban are as harmonious as Minneapolis and St. Paul — they have blended into a single, inseparable phrase. More than just another pretty race, TCM is one of America's finest marathons. Gorgeous, fast, flawless, and loud, over 200,000 spectators surround the route. Toss in all of the amenities of the Twin Cities area and you have an irresistible destination marathon. Few races should be on every marathoners' must-run list; TCM is one.

RACE HISTORY The Minnesota Distance Running Association created the Land of Lakes Marathon, Twin Cities' antecedent, in 1963. The first race had a rather modest three finishers. Over the next several years Land of Lakes was held at various locations in the Twin Cities. In 1976, the race was recast as the City of Lakes Marathon and moved to a four-lap course around

Lakes Calhoun and Harriet. It had 178 finishers. Then came the running boom. In 1981, City of Lakes reached its 1,700 runner limit in only one month. That same year, St. Paul held its own marathon, the St. Paul Marathon, which attracted nearly 2,000 runners. Organizers soon realized that a race which spanned the two cities straddling the Mississippi River would be a much greater attraction than two separate events. In 1982, the modern Twin Cities Marathon was born, drawing more than 4,500 entrants — a then-record for a first-time marathon. Since then, Twin Cities has blossomed into one of America's premiere races. It has been the site of numerous national marathon championships, and is the site of the U.S. Masters Marathon Championship until 2000. More U.S. records have been set on its course than any other marathon.

C O U R S E   D E S C R I P T I O N   The bulk of TCM traces parkways in bursting autumn brilliance, passing four lakes, a creek, and the Mississippi River on its trek from Minneapolis to St. Paul. The course is nothing short of spectacular. The race is run entirely on asphalt and is completely closed to vehicle traffic. TCM starts at the Hubert H. Humphrey Metrodome, home of the Minnesota Twins (MLB) and Vikings (NFL). The first 1.5 miles course through downtown Minneapolis, where you encounter the world renown Guthrie Theater and the Walker Art Center and Sculpture Garden. You complete one of the route's biggest inclines, an 80-foot climb in a half mile, as you reach the first aid station at 2.5 miles. Then it's slightly downhill until just past mile 3, where you come to the first lake on the course: Lake of the Isles, site of some of the finest homes in the Twin Cities. It's also the first step on the cities' parkway system, where you will run the next 19 miles of the race. After leaving Lake of the Isles behind, you soon reach Lake Calhoun (miles 4 to 6). The sun's reflection off the lake creates an inspirational setting. Shortly after the 6-mile point, a quick 20-foot climb brings you to Lake Harriet, where you pass the Rose Garden, a popular area for spectators and the media. As you depart Lake Harriet at 7.5 miles, you may feel a bit envious knowing that the three lakes are the most popular training sites for area runners. But try to remember that they have to endure the local winters. See, it all works out in the end!

With a smile on your face, the course turns east, starting a 4.5-mile stretch on Minnehaha Parkway, a tree-lined boulevard along beautiful Minnehaha Creek. This gently rolling piece (including a good 40-foot drop) leads to lake number four on the course: Lake Nokomis. After circling Nokomis, you pass the 13.1-mile mark — you're halfway home! Then it's back to Minnehaha Parkway for the next two miles before turning north to run along the Mississippi River (miles 15 to 19).

Crossing the Mississippi at mile 19, runners may be tempted to stop to view the bank of trees in full fall colors along the river. You then head south for two miles on the river road to begin the toughest part of the course — an incline of 130 feet over a two-mile stretch up Summit Avenue and its stately mansions (miles 21 to 23). You may see the governor as you puff past his mansion; he's usually out there watching the race. It's mostly downhill from this point to the finish, with a small rise at mile 25.

Seeing St. Paul Cathedral means you've done it. As you turn the corner at mile 26, the finish line, with the state capitol as a backdrop, is an awesome and welcomed sight. Bask in the glory the last two tenths of a mile as some of the 200,000 spectators cheer your arrival.

C R O W D / R U N N E R   S U P P O R T   Over 200,000 Twin City residents come out to cheer on the runners, quite a large turnout for communities of this size. TCM is not big on hoopla, the loud and crazy entertainment that lines so many courses these days. But it is big on volunteers, with more than 4,000 people helping out along the way. Twelve aid stations speckle the course at miles 2.5, 5, and every two miles thereafter, carrying water, electrolyte replacement drink, portable toilets, and medical aid. In addition, first aid is available at every mile marker. Medical personnel will be wearing red shirts, and communications personnel (should you need a ride to the finish) will be decked out in yellow shirts. Digital clocks which show the elapsed time are located at miles 1, 2, 3, 4, 10, 13.1, 15, 20, and 25.

RACE LOGISTICS Race organizers provide shuttle bus service to the starting line from official race hotels, and then from the finish area back to the hotels. Transportation is also available from the finish to the start following the race. The race transports your belongings from the start to the finish area.

ACTIVITIES TCM sponsors the large, two-day (Friday and Saturday) Marketplace and Fitness Fair that attracts 20,000 people to the headquarters hotel. The fair has more than 80 exhibitor booths with hands-on exhibits, free health screenings, great deals on running gear, and hourly drawings for free merchandise and services. You must pick up your race packet at the fair as there is no race number pick-up on race day. On Saturday, attend seminars on a variety of running topics presented by Running Times magazine. On Saturday evening, devour all the pasta you can at the carbo-load party (about $10). The post-race party and awards ceremony begin at 11:30 a.m. near the finish line.

AWARDS Every entrant receives a TCM Results Book. Finishers also receive T-shirts, medallions, and official results cards. TCM offers approximately $155,000 in prize money to at least 22 division winners. Division winners also receive merchandise awards. Masters runners make out particularly well at TCM. The first three finishers in each five-year age group, starting at age 40, receive prize money — $250 for first, $100 for second, and $50 for third — a nice, and rare, little bonus for many masters runners.

FIRST TIMERS INFORMATION Twin Cities is one of the best marathons in the country for first timers (our only nit-pick is there could be more than 12 aid stations), with about 2,000 in the race each year. All of the conditions are optimal for a positive experience: usually cool weather, abundant company, gentle course, supportive crowds, exceptional scenery, and top-flight organization.

ELITE RUNNERS INFORMATION TCM extends several benefits to elite runners (men under 2:20, women under 2:40), including hotel, transportation, expenses, free entry, and generous prize money. Priority is given to previous TCM participants. Open division prize money is offered to tenth place, with overall winners earning $20,000, then $12,000 for second, $7,000 for third, $5,000 for fourth, $4,000 for fifth, $3,000 for sixth, $2,000 for seventh, $1,500 for eighth, $1,000 for ninth, and $500 for tenth. The top five masters runners receive prize money from TCM ($5,000; $3,000; $2,000; $1,000; $500), and the top three masters also win prize money as part of the USATF American Masters Championship ($2,000; $1,000; $750). Contact the marathon office for more information.

ACCOMMODATIONS The headquarters hotel for the 1998 race is the Minneapolis Hyatt Regency, 1300 Nicollet Mall (800-233-1234). In 1999, the Radisson St. Paul, 11 E. Kellogg Blvd. (800-333-3333) serves as the race headquarters hotel. Both offer special rates to marathon runners, but you must book extremely early. Several other hotels in St. Paul give runners special rates, including: Days Inn Civic Center, 175 W. Seventh Street (800-325-2525); The Saint Paul Hotel, 350 Market Street (800-292-9292); the Radisson Inn, 411 Minnesota Street (800-333-3333); and Embassy Suites, 175 E. Tenth Street (800-EMBASSY). If you prefer to stay near the start in Minneapolis, the following offer special rates: Regal Minneapolis Hotel, 1313 Nicollet Mall (800-522-8856); Doubletree Guest Suites, 1101 LaSalle Avenue (800-662-3232); The Marquette, 710 Marquette Avenue (800-328-4782); Minneapolis Hilton Hotel, 1001 Marquette Avenue (800-HILTONS); and Marriott City Center, 30 S. 7th Street (800-228-9290).

RELATED EVENTS/RACES On Saturday, the day before the marathon, organizers hold a 5K Race/Walk, Kids' Half-Mile Fun Run, and Toddlers' Trot. The 1998 version will be at Lake Nokomis in Minneapolis. Every participant receives a T-shirt and post-race refreshments. In addition, every child who enters receives a "Number 1" bib and ribbon. You may register at the Fitness Fair, or on race day.

AREA ATTRACTIONS If you need more sports while in the Twin Cities, attend a Minnesota Vikings game. It is possible that the Twins will still be playing, if they make the playoffs. On the cultural side, see the Guthrie Theater, Walker Art Center, Minnesota Orchestra, St. Paul Chamber Orchestra, or the St. Paul Science Museum. Or, if you need to shop, check out the country's largest shopping center, The Mall of America, about 20 minutes from either city.

It's the annual running of the most scenic 26.2 urban miles in the country

It's more than 6,000 runners coursing along 26.2 miles of winding parkways, stunning foliage, blue lakes, and the majestic Mississippi River. It's a weekend packed with events, including a health and fitness expo, a 5K race, and a Kids' Half-Mile Fun Run. It's the lightning-fast course for the USA Track & Field Masters' Championship. It's over 200,000 colorful fans and 4,000 volunteers.

It's the Annual Twin Cities Marathon.

Minneapolis–St. Paul, Sunday, October 4, 1998, 8:00 A.M.
Minneapolis–St. Paul, Sunday, October 3, 1999, 8:00 A.M.

The Most Beautiful Urban Marathon in America©

For more information, contact TCM, 708 N. 1st Street, Minneapolis, MN 55401 (612) 673-0778.

http://www.doitsports.com/marathons/twincities

ROYAL VICTORIA MARATHON

OVERALL: 88.6

COURSE BEAUTY: 9

COURSE DIFFICULTY: 4 (SEE APPENDIX)

APPROPRIATENESS FOR FIRST TIMERS: 8+

RACE ORGANIZATION: 9-

CROWDS: 4

RACE DATA

Overall Ranking:	39
Quality Ranking:	59
Quickness Ranking:	75
Contact:	Victoria Marathon Society
	c/o #182-911 Yates Street
	Victoria, B.C. Canada V8V 4X3
	Tel. (250) 382-8181
Date:	Generally second Sunday in October
Start Time:	8:00 a.m.
Time Course Closes:	12:00 p.m.
Number of Finishers:	2,100 in 1997
Course:	Out and back
Certification:	B.C. Athletics
Course Records:	Male: (open) 2:19:31
	Female: (open) 2:42:32
Elite Athlete Programs:	No
Cost:	$55
Age groups/Divisions:	≤29, 30-34, 35-39, 40-44, 45-49, 50-54, 55-59,
	60-64, 65-69, 70+
	Teams: Open, Masters, Husband & Wife
Walkers:	Yes
Requirements:	None
Temperature:	50° - 65° (10°C - 18°C)
Aid/Splits:	17 / miles 1, 5, 10K, halfway, 15, 30K, 20 & 25.2

HIGHLIGHTS A truly unique marathon experience in North America awaits you on Vancouver Island, northwest of Seattle by car and ferry. The elegant and beautiful Royal Victoria Marathon, held in quaint, seaside Victoria, British Columbia, will delight and transport you to the Old World's heart. Victoria, a British enclave of pubs and afternoon tea, enchants visitors with its immaculate gardens, monumental air, and English manner. That marvelous setting, a healthy dose of ocean views, and typical Canadian hospitality unite to produce one of marathoning's rising stars.

COURSE DESCRIPTION Containing no serious hills, RVM's modified out-and-back course rolls for much of its 26.2 miles posing a challenge for many runners. The race starts alongside the B.C. Parliament Building, a monumental, gray stone structure that lends a decidedly British air to the city. After a downhill start passing famous, stately Empress Hotel, the course heads along Wharf Street, bordering Victoria's beautiful harbor. The first 2.3 miles proceed through downtown Victoria, passing shops, restaurants, and hotels with some long, gentle ups and downs. Runners then come up behind Beacon Hill Park, enter it by mile 2.8, and enjoy the gardens while passing through it. As you leave the park (mile 3.5), the ocean greets you until mile 4.3 when you traverse residential Oswego Street to the scenic Inner Harbor at mile 5. Following the line of hotels around the point, runners hit the shoreline at mile 6 and hug the coast for 2.3 miles. About mile 6.2, runners begin a gentle 60-foot incline to the 7-mile mark and then descend to mile 8. Ross Bay at mile 7.8 offers a great vantage to Hollywood Cove's hillside homes overlooking the ocean. Winding through residential Oak Bay from mile 8.3 to 11.4, the course rolls, rising about 50 feet. You're back along the water by 11.5 miles, passing expensive houses and entering the exclusive and scenic Royal Victoria Golf Course at mile 12.2. Runners roll through the golf course and reach RVM's halfway point at the marina on Oak Bay. The next five miles are mostly flat through an upscale neighborhood until you return to the marina (mile 18) and face the 50-foot climb to the golf course. Runners retrace their steps the rest of the way and finish in front of the Parliament Building at the Inner Harbor.

CROWD/RUNNER SUPPORT As the race grows, Victorians turn out in larger numbers to cheer the runners. While onlookers still speckle most of the route, the start/finish area and Oak Bay attract good crowds. Runners pass aid stations 17 times. Besides carrying the usual water and electrolyte replacement drink, aid stations, after mile 16, also provide energy bars to tiring runners.

RACE LOGISTICS The small downtown area and the proximity of several hotels to the Inner Harbor make race-morning transportation unnecessary for many runners. If you stay further out, you must provide your own means to the start, but abundant, free parking exists in the area.

ACTIVITIES On Friday or Saturday, runners may pick up their race packets at the headquarters hotel. Otherwise, retrieve your packet on the legislative grounds near the start on race morning. Bus tours of the marathon course depart Saturday afternoon and cost $5. On Saturday evening, attend the pasta dinner for about $20. After the marathon, stop by the free post-race social at the Harbour Towers, featuring a video of the race, finishers' certificates, and race results.

AWARDS Early registrants receive original design sweatshirts, with finishers earning RVM medals engraved with the shirt design and certificates. Age-group awards go up to 10 deep depending on the number of entrants in each category. All runners are eligible for several raffle prizes, including a trip to the London Marathon. A one-ounce gold coin goes to the runner who sets a new course record.

ACCOMMODATIONS Located about four blocks from the RVM start, the Harbour Towers, 345 Quebec Street (800-663-5896), serves as the sponsoring hotel, offering marathoners special rates of about $95 per night. Other lodging possibilities include: Ocean Point Resort, 45 Songhees Road (800-667-4677), about $100 a night; The Coast Victoria Harbourside Hotel, 146 Kingston Street (800-663-1144), about $110; Clarion Hotel Grand Pacific, 450 Quebec Street (800-663-7550), about $110; Quality Inn Harbourview, 455 Belleville Street (800-663-7550), about $90; Dashwood Seaside Manor, #1 Cook Street (800-667-5517); Dominion Hotel, 759 Yates Street (800-663-6101); Hotel Douglas, 1450 Douglas Street (800-332-9981); Strathcona Hotel, 919 Douglas Street (604-383-7137); and Green Gables Inn, 850 Blanshard Street (800-661-4115). For cheaper accommodations, try one of Victoria's many bed & breakfast inns, most of which lie outside downtown.

RELATED EVENTS/RACES RVM welcomes walkers to stride the full marathon. Royal Victoria sponsors a 10K run beginning at 8:30 a.m. on Sunday. Early registered 10K runners receive original shirts, and all 10K entrants participate in the random drawing for a trip for two on Air BC. Kids may do the Children's 1K Run for Charity, beginning at 9:30 a.m.

AREA ATTRACTIONS A great tourist city, charming Victoria contains numerous attractions for marathoners. Flower lovers will delight in the hanging flower baskets throughout the city and world-renowned Butchart Gardens. The British-like Old Town area contains scores of pubs, shops, and restaurants. Join in an English tradition and take afternoon tea at the Empress Hotel, or stroll the Inner Harbor and Beacon Hill Park.

CANADIAN INTERNATIONAL MARATHON

OVERALL: 83.4

COURSE BEAUTY: 7+

COURSE DIFFICULTY: 3-

APPROPRIATENESS FOR FIRST TIMERS: 9-

RACE ORGANIZATION: 9

CROWDS: 5-

RACE DATA

Overall Ranking:	75
Quality Ranking:	44
Quickness Ranking:	29
Contact:	Jay W. Glassman
	The Canadian International Marathon
	240 Heath Street West, Suite 802
	Toronto, Ontario, Canada M5P 3L5
	Tel. (416) 972-1062
	Fax (416) 972-1238
	E-mail: marathon@netcom.ca
	http://www.RunToronto.com
Date:	Generally third Sunday in October (October 18, 1998)
Start Time:	9:00 a.m.
Time Course Closes:	2:00 p.m.
Number of Finishers:	3,123 in 1997
Course:	Point to point
Certification:	AIMS, Athletics Canada, and Ontario Roadrunners Association
Course Records:	Male: (open) 2:20:33; (masters) 2:27:45
	Female: (open) 2:37:52; (masters) 2:52:06
Elite Athlete Programs:	No
Cost:	US$35/45/55; $45/55/70 Cdn.
Age groups/Divisions:	18-29, 30-39, 40-49, 50-59, 60+
Walkers:	Yes (but must finish in 5.5 hours)
Requirements:	18 years old
Temperature:	50° - 60° (10°C - 16°C)
Aid/Splits:	14 / mile 1 & every 5K

HIGHLIGHTS The maturing Canadian International Marathon offers a relatively quick course through perhaps Canada's most exciting city, Toronto. The race features a new route for 1998, cutting off about 4 miles from the loop at its top end, and then detouring through mostly residential areas in its middle section. The course still travels down Yonge Street, Toronto's main thoroughfare, for several miles. Runners take in Toronto's financial district, St. Lawrence Market, and the Ontario Legislature toward the end of the race. The recent upheaval in the Canadian marathon scene (with the demise of the Toronto Marathon in 1995 and the cancellation of Montreal in 1997) only bolsters CIM's future.

COURSE DESCRIPTION CIM's new course starts with an 8-mile loop through North York. Like before, the race begins on Yonge Street (reputed to be the longest street in the world) just north of Mel Lastman Square. Runners head south .6 miles to Sheppard Avenue and turn right, rolling through residential streets before heading north on Dufferin Street through G. Ross Lord Park. At Steeles Avenue, the course turns back toward Yonge Street, passing parks interspersed with shopping malls and apartment complexes. Back on Yonge Street, the route gradually descends past Mel Lastman Square (8 miles) continuing under the Highway 401 overpass. At Hogg's Hollow, near the halfway point, runners face the largest hill on the course, a tough 100-footer. Once over the hump, the course turns downhill once again. As the race continues on Yonge Street, it turns west on Chaplin to Oriole Parkway. Here it passes Upper Canada College, one of Canada's most exclusive boy's schools, before scurrying through upscale Forest Hill. Following Winston Churchill Park, runners go by pre-WWI Casa Loma, Canada's largest home. After proceeding down Davenport to Belmont (which turns into Aylmer Avenue), the course follows the scenic and forested Rosedale Valley Road to Bayview Avenue. The course meanders along the Don River Valley, before turning onto Front Street, marked by abandoned factories and warehouses. As the city approaches, runners pass the historic St. Lawrence Market, Gooderham, Worts Flatiron Building, and the trendy stores and restaurants of the area. Front Street gives way to Wellington Street through the heart of Toronto's financial district. Turning on University Avenue, you encounter cheering crowds while passing stately Osgoode Hall Provincial Courts, hospitals, and finish after a brief loop around the top of Queen's Park, home to the Ontario Legislature.

CROWD/RUNNER SUPPORT Approximately 35,000 supporters come out for the marathon. You also receive a warm reception by the 20 to 30 entertainment stations stretched along Yonge Street. The new 9:00 a.m. start should even boost audience attendance. You won't go unassisted at aid stations as typically over 800 volunteers offer their help, handing out water, sports drink, fruit, medical assistance, and transportation every 5K, then more frequently in the last 15K of the race. The course is marked every kilometer and every 5th mile.

RACE LOGISTICS Public transportation starts at 9:00 a.m. on Sundays so you need to find some other way to the start. Parking is provided if you plan to drive. Otherwise, shuttle buses depart the host hotels starting at 7:00 a.m. Take the bus from the finish area back to your hotel or to Mel Lastman Square. The marathon also provides a bag check at the start; your bag will be waiting for you at the finish.

ACTIVITIES Pick up your race packet, register, and attend the Runners' Expo on Thursday, Friday or Saturday preceding the marathon at the Delta Chelsea Inn (see below for address) from 10:00 a.m. to 7:00 p.m. Out-of-town runners may retrieve their packets on race morning at Mel Lastman Square. A free feast is provided for runners the evening before the marathon (non-runners may attend for $10). A workshop is also held to orient newcomers to the course and to talk about running generally. Food and refreshments are plentiful at the finish line in Queen's Park, and showers and a changing room are available at nearby Hart House.

AWARDS Every entrant takes home a Canadian International Marathon T-shirt. All full and half marathoners receive medals as they cross the finish line, and certificates of completion are mailed later. Overall winners receive merchandise.

ACCOMMODATIONS The official race hotels are the Holiday Inn On King, 370 King Street West (tel. 800-263-6364); and The Delta Chelsea Inn, 33 Gerrard Street West (tel. 416-595-1975; fax 416-585-4366). Reserve your room early because it can be difficult to find last-minute accommodations in Toronto on race weekend. Other hotels to try include: Sheraton Centre Toronto Hotel & Towers, 123 Queen Street West (tel. 416-361-1000); Toronto Hilton, 145 Richmond Street West (tel. 416-869-3456); or Royal York, 100 Front Street West (tel. 416-386-2511).

RELATED EVENTS/RACES Also featured are a half marathon, the Canadian Wheelchair Marathon Championships, and a corporate/school/military marathon challenge (for teams of up to eight runners). The fast half marathon runs along the lower part of the marathon course.

AREA ATTRACTIONS Renowned as one of the most culturally diverse cities on the planet, Toronto offers a dizzying array of activities, including an extremely active theater scene and excellent museums. Catch the tremendous view from the 553-meter CN Tower, the tallest freestanding building in the world. Hockey fans should visit the Hockey Hall of Fame and then catch a Maple Leafs game. Even if the Blue Jays are not playing, check out the amazing Sky Dome with its retractable roof.

Run Chicago

Save the Date

Sunday, October 11, 1998

Call today for your guaranteed entry
(312) 243-0003 or Toll-Free at 1-888-243-3344 (U.S. only)
or write The LaSalle Banks Chicago Marathon
P. O. Box 10597
Chicago, IL 60610-0597 USA

Visit us online at www.chicagomarathon.com

Start/Finish centrally located in downtown Chicago

Khalid Khannouchi 2:07:10 (1997 World's Best Time)
Jerry Lawson 2:09:35 (American Record)
Joan Benoit Samuelson 2:21:21 (American Record)

The LaSalle Banks

Chicago Marathon

American Airlines

BALLY TOTAL FITNESS

Gatorade
Thirst Quencher

new balance

Drivers wanted.

CHICAGO
Hilton
and Towers

CHICAGO MARATHON

OVERALL: 98.1

COURSE BEAUTY: 8+

COURSE DIFFICULTY: 1+

APPROPRIATENESS FOR FIRST TIMERS: 10

RACE ORGANIZATION: 10

CROWDS: 9-

RACE DATA

Overall Ranking:	9
Quality Ranking:	5
Quickness Ranking:	1
Contact:	The LaSalle Banks Chicago Marathon
	P.O. Box 10597
	Chicago, IL 60610-0597
	USA
	Tel. (888) 243-3344 or (312) 243-3274
	Fax (312) 243-5652
	http://www.ChicagoMarathon.com
Date:	Generally third Sunday in October (October 11, 1998)
Start Time:	7:45 a.m.
Time Course Closes:	1:15 p.m.
Number of Participants:	16,372 in 1997
Course:	Loop
Certification:	USATF
Course Records:	Male: (open) 2:07:10
	Female: (open) 2:21:21
Elite Athlete Programs:	Yes
Cost:	$50/60
Age groups/Divisions:	≤19, 20-24, 25-29, 30-34, 35-39, 40-44, 45-49, 50-54, 55-59, 60-64, 65-69, 70+
Walkers:	Yes
Requirements:	None
Temperature:	53° (12°C)
Aid/Splits:	12 / digital clocks every mile and at 10K, 20K & halfway

HIGHLIGHTS Chicago's dead population notoriously arises at opportune times; John F. Kennedy could have attested to that after the 1960 presidential election! Not limited to Chicago politics, however, resurrection extends to Chicago sports — Michael Jordan, the Bulls, and the Chicago Marathon. Sponsorship problems forced the cancellation of the 1987 race, but Chicago has regained its place as one of the country's top, big-city marathons; and if you like big cities, Chicago is a must. The city of big shoulders' impressive architecture, skyline, lakefront, sports, entertainment, history, and culture make it a destination town *par excellence*. Our fastest-rated race, Chicago's lightning course (North American records for male and females have been established here) tours numerous ethnic neighborhoods that most visitors never see. With the exception of the disqualified women's winner from 1992, rarely will you hear a negative comment about the extremely well organized Chicago Marathon. Alive and well, Chicago is yours to enjoy.

COURSE DESCRIPTION Taking runners through many of the city's most historic and diverse neighborhoods, the Chicago Marathon's loop course passes through Lincoln Park, Old Town, Greektown, Little Italy, Pilsen, Chinatown, Bridgeport and the Gap District. Starting in Grant Park, site of famous Buckingham Fountain, near the shore of beautiful Lake Michigan, runners head north traveling past the Hard Rock Café, Planet Hollywood and other chic restaurants and night spots during the three miles in the River North area. Continuing north, the route heads through Lincoln Park past the Lincoln Park Zoo and Diversey Harbor. Coffee shops, bookstores, and restaurants characterize the Lakeview area between miles 4.5 and 6. Heading south from Lakeview, runners return to Lincoln Park passing the world-renowned dance and blues clubs and international restaurants on Clark Street. Still early in the race, your sense of humor should still be intact as you pass the great comedy clubs in Old Town Chicago around 8 miles. After cruising past The Loop (shoppers' paradise), Merchandise Mart, City Hall, and Sears Tower near mile 10, the course heads west, crossing the Chicago River into Greektown. After hitting the halfway point in Little Italy, expect great spectator support, including music and dancing as the route enters Pilsen, Chicago's largest Hispanic area, around mile 15. The rainbow tour proceeds, cutting through Chinatown's Lion and Dragon dancers at mile 17. Bridgeport, the mayor's neighborhood, Comiskey Park, home of the White Sox, and the Southside, home of Bad Bad Leroy Brown, lie between miles 18.5 and 20. Heading east toward Lake Michigan, runners enter the supportive Gap District, a large black community, near the 23-mile mark. The next two miles head north on Lakeshore Drive and pass McCormick Place before hitting Columbus Drive. The beautiful view of the Chicago skyline should ease your effort up the short climb at mile 25. After passing Soldier Field and the Field Museum, you finish down the broad lanes of Columbus Drive in Grant Park.

CROWD/RUNNER SUPPORT Chicago's legendary sports-town image extends to the marathon; over 200,000 onlookers line the streets or hang out of apartment windows encouraging the marathoners. The twelve aid stations stretch an entire block in places, while numerous musical groups entertain. The course layout makes it very easy for spectators to view the race from several spots along the way. In fact, onlookers can watch the start, saunter six blocks, and cheer at the ten-mile mark.

For the long run.

Running. It's what you do.

And your body knows it. In any weather, over all kinds of terrain, and in spite of all biomechanical shortcomings, you run because you must.

And **FLEET FEET** exists because you run. As the nation's only group of locally owned and operated running stores, we're here to help you with the world's finest running shoes, apparel and accessories.

If you know **FLEET FEET**, you know running.

FLEET FEET Sports

Nationally known.
Locally owned.

Call us at 1-800-959-3004
or visit our web site at www.fleetfeet.com

If you are interested in franchise information, please call Julie at 800-959-3004

RACE LOGISTICS Convenient Grant Park makes arriving at the start relatively hassle free with the major hotels nearby. If you're arriving by car, you'll find ample parking in the area.

ACTIVITIES Chicago features a two-day Health and Fitness Expo and race registration at the Chicago Hilton & Towers. The expo includes over 100 exhibitors displaying the latest products and services from the sports, health and fitness industries. Runners may register or pick up their packets at the expo on Friday between 11:00 a.m. and 8:00 p.m. and Saturday from 9:00 a.m. to 6:00 p.m. A spectacular pasta carbo-load dinner is held on Saturday night from 6:00 p.m. to 8:00 p.m. at the Chicago Hilton. The dinner includes a three-course, sit-down meal, special guest appearances by celebrity runners, and a drawing for prizes. Runners, family, and friends are welcome, but the limited $15 tickets sell quickly. After the race, a great post-race finishers party takes place at a local hot spot with free food, wine, and beer. The overall winners' checks are presented along with a raffle for exciting prizes.

AWARDS Every marathoner receives a race T-shirt, goody bag, official race results booklet and entry into the post-race party. Participants finishing under 5:30 receive medallions, results cards and finisher's certificates. Age-group winners receive special prizes which are mailed soon after the event. Elite runners compete for $300,000 in prize money.

ELITE RUNNERS INFORMATION Chicagoan's have come to expect big-time sports with big-time players. Chicago Marathon organizers realize this and actively recruit some of the top names in marathoning. The race executive director holds complete discretion in conferring elite status. To be considered for expense money, you must contact Carey Pinkowski between January 1st and September 15th. A fast course and $300,000 in prize money, including generous time incentive bonuses, do not hurt Chicago's recruitment efforts. Prize money goes 10 deep in Open Divisions and five deep in Masters Divisions. Open winners earn $50,000, $25,000 for second, $20,000 for third, $15,000 for fourth, $10,000 for fifth, $5,000 for sixth, $4,000 for seventh, $3,000 for eighth, $2,000 for ninth, and $1,000 for tenth. The top American receives an additional $5,000. Masters winners take home $1,250, down to $350 for third. Time bonuses are awarded to any male runners under the qualifying times, ranging from $1,000 for a sub 2:13 to $100,000 for a world record. For women, the times range from sub 2:33 ($1,000) to a world record ($100,000).

ACCOMMODATIONS The Chicago Hilton and Towers, 720 S. Michigan Avenue (800-445-8667), only two blocks from the start/finish line, acts as the official race hotel. It offers special rates to marathon runners, but don't procrastinate. Other convenient hotels with special marathon rates include: Best Western Grant Park, 1100 S. Michigan Avenue (312-922-2900); Holiday Inn Chicago City Center, 300 E. Ohio Street (312-787-6100); River North Hotel, 125 W. Ohio Street (312-467-0800); Ramada Congress, 520 S. Michigan Avenue (312-427-3800); and the Sheraton Chicago, 301 E. North Water Street (312-464-1000).

RELATED EVENTS/RACES Race weekend begins Saturday with the Youth Mile Run open to children 5 to 14 years of age. Starting at 11:00 a.m. in Grant Park, the course loops Buckingham Fountain on Chicago's spectacular lakefront. For those not bitten by the marathon bug, Chicago offers a popular 5K starting at 8:15 a.m. on race day. If you're running the marathon, consider recruiting a few friends or co-workers and enter the Team Challenge. For an extra fee, corporate or open teams of three to five members compete in this uniquely scored event. Team members are scored according to their place within their age group, relative to the number of finishers in that division. The top three performances are then added together, and the team with the lowest total points wins.

AREA ATTRACTIONS Spicy Chicago offers something for everyone: architecture, art galleries, museums, fine restaurants, Chicago Pizza, theaters, night clubs, blues music, sports, ethnic neighborhoods, shopping, and the lakefront beach. Save a little race energy, and allow time to take in some of the attractions.

HUMBOLDT REDWOODS MARATHON

OVERALL: 83.5

COURSE BEAUTY: 10

COURSE DIFFICULTY: 2+ (SEE APPENDIX)

APPROPRIATENESS FOR FIRST TIMERS: 8+

RACE ORGANIZATION: 8+

CROWDS: 1-

RACE DATA

Overall Ranking: 73
Quality Ranking: 92
Quickness Ranking: 23
Contact: Humboldt Redwoods Marathon
P.O. Box 4989
Arcata, CA 95518-4989
USA
Tel. (707) 443-1220
Fax (707) 443-2553

Date: Generally third Sunday in October
Start Time: 9:00 a.m.
Time Course Closes: 2:00 p.m.
Number of Finishers: 349 in 1997
Course: Two out and backs
Certification: USATF
Course Records: Male: (open) 2:27:28
Female: (open) 2:46:16
Elite Athlete Programs: No
Cost: $30/40
Age groups/Divisions: ≤18, 19-24, 25-29, 30-34, 35-39, 40-44, 45-49,
50-54, 55-59, 60-64, 65-69, 70-74, 75-79, 80-84,
85-89, 90-94, 95-99, 100+
Walkers: No
Requirements: None
Temperature: 45° - 60° (7°C - 16°C)
Aid/Splits: 10 / miles 1, 5, 10, 15, 20 & 25

HIGHLIGHTS Noble, old growth redwood groves provide a protective canopy almost every step of the way in one of North America's best small races, the Humboldt Redwoods Marathon. The ultimate nature lover's race, Humboldt's fast course offers the perfect setting for inspired running and tranquil introspection as you weave among the creaking giants. The filtered light cascades down runners like worshipers in an outdoor cathedral. After the race, explore the rugged beauty of California's northern coast and surrounding parks.

COURSE DESCRIPTION The Humboldt Redwoods Marathon starts and finishes at the Dyerville Bridge on the Avenue of the Giants (a Hwy. 101 alternative scenic route). After crossing the south fork of the Eel River, the race immediately enters a canopy of centuries-old redwoods that recedes only for a quarter mile at 2.2 and 10.6. The mostly flat, extremely fast, completely closed first half contains some gentle ups and downs that impart an interesting illusion. *"The first half seems downhill both out and back! Really fast,"* says Jeff Hildebrandt of Roseville, California. Returning to the Dyerville Bridge at mile 13, runners proceed left down Bull Creek Road for the second out and back passing through Rockefeller Forest. Monitored by CHP pilot cars, this section of the course is narrower, quieter, and more winding and rolling, gaining about 150 feet from mile 14 to 20 and losing the same amount from mile 20 to the finish.

CROWD/RUNNER SUPPORT Other than the thousands of ancient redwoods witnessing your quest, spectators are pretty much limited to the start, halfway, and finish. In addition to the usual water and electrolyte replacement drink, the aid stations near miles 17 and 22 carry energy bars and fruit to help get you through the final miles. Portable toilets are located at every aid station.

RACE LOGISTICS The undeveloped race site in Redwoods State Park means facilities in the area are fairly limited. You will need to drive to the start since lodging is scattered throughout the area. If you are traveling north on Highway 101, take the Founder's Tree exit, while southbound travelers should take the second Redcrest exit. You immediately hit upon the staging area and monitors will direct you to the parking location. Try to arrive before 8:00 a.m. to avoid traffic hassles.

ACTIVITIES Runners can register late on Saturday afternoon at the Burlington Campground Visitor's Center or on race day near the start area. On late Saturday afternoon, attend a slide show and discussion of the course at the Visitor's Center. Saturday evening you can choose between the Weott American Legion's Spaghetti Feed ($5) or the Scotia Inn's pasta dinner (about $11), both all-you-can-eat affairs. After the race, there are refreshments, a raffle, and awards ceremony.

AWARDS Marathon entrants receive T-shirts, finishers earn medallions, and the top three in each age group receive special medals. The overall winners are awarded merchandise prizes, and the top three overall, top two masters, and top seniors take home commemorative awards.

ACCOMMODATIONS The two race sponsor hotels are the Scotia Inn, 100 Main Street, Scotia (about 15 miles from the start) (707-764-5683); and Hotel Carter, 301 L Street, Eureka (about 40 miles from the start) (707-445-1390). Possibilities in Fortuna (about 24 miles from the start) include: the Best Western Country Inn, 1528 Kenmar Road (800-528-1234); Holiday Inn Express, 1859 Alamar Way (800-465-4329); and Super 8 Motel, 1805 Alamar Way (800-800-8000). In Eureka (about 40 miles from the start) try the: Eureka Inn, 7th and F Streets (707-442-6441); Comfort Inn, 2014 4th Street (800-424-6423); Red Lion Inn, 1929 4th Street (800-547-8010); Carson House Inn, 4th and M Streets (800-772-1622); and Motel 6, 1934 Broadway (707-445-9631). See the Avenue of the Giants Marathon entry for more accommodations.

RELATED EVENTS/RACES You may want to run in the super-fast Humboldt Redwoods Half Marathon which covers the first half of the full marathon course. The popular half, the USATF Pacific Association Half Marathon Championship, regularly attracts over 1,000 entrants and runs concurrently with the marathon. In addition, $4,000 in prize money is offered to the top half marathon finishers (must be USATF Pacific Association members to receive prize money).

AREA ATTRACTIONS Spend some time wandering amongst the redwoods, such as the Founder's Grove Nature Trail for starters. If you have the energy and time, we highly recommend driving north to Prairie Creek Redwoods State Park (south of Klamath) and hiking the incomparable Fern Canyon Trail with 50-foot precipices covered by immense ferns.

MARINE CORPS MARATHON

OVERALL: 95.7

COURSE BEAUTY: 10-

COURSE DIFFICULTY: 3+

APPROPRIATENESS FOR FIRST TIMERS: 10

RACE ORGANIZATION: 10-

CROWDS: 5-

RACE DATA

Overall Ranking: 13
Quality Ranking: 24
Quickness Ranking: 48
Contact: Marine Corps Marathon
P.O. Box 188
Quantico, VA 22134-0188
USA
Tel. (800) RUN-USMC or (703) 784-2225
Fax (703) 784-2265
E-mail: marathon@quantico.usmc.mil
http://issb-www1.quantico.usmc.mil/marathon
Date: Generally fourth Sunday in October (October 25, 1998; October 24, 1999)
Start Time: 8:30 a.m.
Time Course Closes: 3:00 p.m.
Number of Participants: 16,000 in 1997
Course: Loop
Certification: USATF
Course Records: Male: (open) 2:14:01
Female: (open) 2:37:00
Elite Athlete Programs: No
Cost: $40
Age groups/Divisions: ≤19, 20-24, 25-29, 30-34, 35-39, 40-44, 45-49, 50-54, 55-59, 60-64, 65-69, 70+
Walkers: No
Requirements: None
Temperature: 49° - 68° (9°C - 20°C)
Aid/Splits: 20 / miles 1, 3, 5, 10, 15, 20, 22 & 24

HIGHLIGHTS Nicknamed "The People's Marathon®" and "Marathon of the Monuments," the Marine Corps Marathon has established itself as one of the country's finest marathons. As the name implies, the U.S. Marine Corps hosts this Washington, D.C. classic, drawing about 16,000 runners, about half of whom are first timers. The Marines execute the race splendidly, from race organization to providing encouragement along the course. Topping most other marathons in North America for first timers (Oprah ran her first marathon here), Marine Corps also provides a great race for veterans. The course tours the nation's capital, passing Arlington Cemetery, Georgetown, the Kennedy Center, Lincoln Memorial, Jefferson Memorial, U.S. Capitol, Washington Monument, Union Station, and Smithsonian Museums. The Washington, D.C. location and the Marines' dedication combine for an unbeatable destination marathon.

COURSE DESCRIPTION MCM's closed course starts and finishes near the Marine Corps War Memorial marked by the Iwo Jima Monument in Arlington, VA. The marathon first passes through sobering Arlington National Cemetery where many of the nation's great soldiers and John F. Kennedy are buried. Then it's past the Pentagon, the world's largest office building (after mile 1), Pentagon City, a large shopping mall (mile 2), and the mostly commercial surrounding areas between miles 2 and 3. During miles 4 to 6, runners wind around the Pentagon before returning to Arlington Cemetery (near mile 7). The course passes the starting area and the high-rise office buildings of Rosslyn, VA, at mile 8. At this point, the heart of the MCM course begins. Runners enter Key Bridge after mile 8 on a slight incline. Crossing the bridge, the stone spire of prestigious Georgetown University looms above you. Runners exit Key Bridge onto M Street, one of fashionable Georgetown's main thoroughfares. The course then cuts down to scenic Rock Creek Parkway, skirting the Potomac River, and passing the bright white Kennedy Center just after mile 10. Around 10.7 miles, the course turns left past the Lincoln Memorial to the famous Mall (miles 10.7 to 13 and 14.7 to 17.7). At about 11.5 miles, runners can glimpse the White House beyond the Ellipse on the left and the towering Washington Monument on the right. During mile 12, the course heads by many of the Smithsonian Museums, and mile 13, runners have an excellent view of the U.S. Capitol. Then, with a slight incline, it's on to Union Station (about 13.5 miles) before circling the Capitol and returning down to the Mall on the opposite (south) side. At mile 17.5, look across the Tidal Basin for a nice view of the Jefferson Memorial. Completely flat, miles 18 to 22.5 are run in scenic East Potomac Park, around Hains Point. The course crosses the 14th Street Bridge (mile 23) with a gentle incline, and then it's past the now very familiar Pentagon as runners retrace their steps to finish, on an incline, at the Iwo Jima Monument.

CROWD/RUNNER SUPPORT Most of MCM runs in the historic sections of Washington, so the course doesn't pass through many residential neighborhoods. Despite this, local spectators turn out in surprisingly good numbers at several points. Nearly 10,000 spectators pack the start/finish area, and large numbers also turn out along the Key Bridge. Particularly strategic, the Mall attracts many onlookers as they can cheer for their favorite runner three times. Right before the 14th Street Bridge is another prime spectator spot, since it is scenic and near accessible parking. Friends and family can take the Metro to several of these and other points on the course to support their runner. Helpful, polite, and enthusiastic, the Marines along the course provide the best inspiration (besides your fellow runners). Tall, 12-foot yellow poles with large mile indicators mark the course.

RACE LOGISTICS Several hotels have shuttle buses to the start. Check with race officials for the most recent list. If you have a car, you can park in the Pentagon's North and South parking lots and then take a shuttle from there to the start (6:30 a.m. to 8:30 a.m.). Unfortunately, the Metro does not run early on marathon day, so it is not a solution to make it to the start. However, runners could take a taxi to the start and take the Metro from Rosslyn Station or Arlington Cemetery Station after the race. The race has a bag drop for your belongings. After the race, meet your family in the post-race linkup area, marked by red banners indicating first letters of your last name.

ACTIVITIES Runners can pick up their race packets at the Hyatt Regency Crystal City Hotel on Thursday from 4:00 p.m. to 8:00 p.m., Friday from 10:00 a.m. to 10:00 p.m., or Saturday from 8:00 a.m. to 10:00 p.m. There is no race-day packet pick-up or registration. On Friday and Saturday, attend the runner's expo and symposium. On Saturday night, the Hyatt hosts a pasta dinner (about $10). After the race, hang out at the post-race party with refreshments, drink, and fruit. The awards ceremony is held on the west steps of the War Memorial at 1:00 p.m.

AWARDS Every entrant receives a T-shirt, and finishers receive medals, certificates and results books. Over 400 trophies are awarded in individual and 11 team categories. MCM presents Middendorf Trophy replicas to the overall winners. Among the categories of awards are: age-groups (men up to 10 places and women up to 5 places), wheelchair, first Virginia, Maryland, and Washington, D.C. residents, U.S. military, U.S. Marine Corps, Canadian military, Clydesdale, and retired military.

ACCOMMODATIONS   The Hyatt Regency Crystal City Hotel, 2799 Jefferson Davis Highway (703-418-1234), serves as the race headquarters hotel (about $110). Also convenient are the: Holiday Inn Key Bridge, 1850 N. Fort Myer Drive, Rosslyn (703-522-0400); Sheraton Crystal City, 1800 Jefferson Davis Hwy., Arlington (800-862-7666); Sheraton National Hotel, Columbia Pike & Washington Blvd. in Arlington (703-521-1900); and the Courtyard Marriott, 2899 Jefferson Davis Hwy. (800-847-4775). The race provides a complete list of hotels offering special rates to MCM runners.

RELATED RACES   MCM sponsors the Special Olympics Mini Marathon, where athletes from around the country compete in 5K, 10K, and unified road races after the marathon start.

NEW YORK CITY MARATHON

OVERALL: 99.3

COURSE BEAUTY: 8

COURSE DIFFICULTY: 4+ (SEE APPENDIX)

APPROPRIATENESS FOR FIRST TIMERS: 10

RACE ORGANIZATION: 10

CROWDS: 10+

R A C E   D A T A

Overall Ranking:	4
Quality Ranking:	1
Quickness Ranking:	70
Contact:	New York City Marathon
	New York Road Runners Club
	9 E. 89th Street
	New York, NY 10128
	USA
	Tel. (212) 423-2249
	Fax (212) 348-9614
	E-mail: susana@nyrrc.org
	http://www.nyrrc.org/mar.htm
Date:	Generally first Sunday in November
Start Time:	10:50 a.m.
Time Course Closes:	NA
Number of Finishers:	30,427 in 1997
Course:	Point to point
Certification:	USATF
Course Records:	Male: (open) 2:08:01
	Female: (open) 2:24:40
Elite Athlete Programs:	Yes
Cost:	$35/45 plus USATF membership
Age groups/Divisions:	18-19, 20-29, 30-39, 40-49, 50-59, 60-69, 70-79, 80+
Walkers:	Yes
Requirements:	18 years old & USATF membership
Temperature:	42° - 55° (6°C - 13°C)
Aid/Splits:	24 / digital clocks every mile

HIGHLIGHTS   Perhaps the most exciting marathon in the world, the New York City Marathon overwhelms the senses with its sights, smells, sounds, and energy. Over 60,000 runners vie for the 29,000 slots each year. The first Sunday each November, the lucky winners fill the upper and lower spans of the Verrazano-Narrows Bridge anxiously awaiting their trek through the five boroughs that comprise New York City and over the five bridges that connect each borough to the next. Over 2 million cheering spectators surround the course, buoying your every step.

RACE HISTORY   The New York City Marathon's humble beginnings may surprise runners new to the sport. Legendary runner Fred Lebow, who died of brain cancer in 1994, founded the marathon in 1970. Held entirely within Central Park, the race vanquished 72 of its 127 starters. One hundred hard-core spectators witnessed Gary Muhrcke's victory in 2:31:38, with the

top finishers earning cheap wrist watches and recycled bowling trophies. With grueling 80° temperatures, the survivors rushed to the waiting cans of soda only to find there were no can openers! In 1976, the race finally left Central Park for the five boroughs of the city. To keep things interesting, however, organizers threw in a flight of stairs on the course. Bill Rodgers won his first of four in a row that year, only to discover afterward that his car had been towed. In 1979, Grete Waitz of Norway entered her first marathon here, the start of her nine victories in eleven years. In 1981, both the men's and women's winners broke the then-world marathon record, with Alberto Salazar finishing in 2:08:13 and Allison Roe recording a 2:25:29. In 1994, eventual winner German Silva of Mexico nearly blew it at the end when he took his eye off the blue line and took a wrong turn in Central Park. He quickly recovered and snatched the victory in the closest finish in NYC's history. Things are never dull in New York.

COURSE DESCRIPTION Located on Staten Island, the marathon's three starting lines lie at the Verrazano-Narrows Toll Plaza. Runners use both the upper and lower spans of the bridge, the longest single suspension bridge in the world. Elite men and men under 3:30 start at the blue line on the Brooklyn-bound, right-side upper level. Local elite men and men over 3:30 start at the green line on the Staten Island-bound lower level. All women start at the red line on the Staten Island-bound upper level. After going up the bridge, about a 180-foot climb, runners hit the first mile mark at its midpoint and the second mile mark at the exit ramps. Miles 3 through 13 course through Brooklyn, passing Bay Ridge at mile 3, Fort Greene at mile 8, Bedford-Stuyvesant at mile 9, and Williamsburg at mile 11. The half-marathon point lies on the Pulaski Bridge (about a 40-foot incline) connecting Brooklyn and Queens (mile 13.1 to 15.5). The course heads through Long Island City, a manufacturing area since the industrial revolution and now home to the Silvercup Studios, often referred to as Hollywood East. At mile 15, runners climb 130 feet up the Queensboro Bridge, spanning the East River and Roosevelt Island, bringing them to Manhattan (mile 16 to 20). North on First Avenue, you pass through the Upper East Side, known as the silk stocking district; Yorkville in the East 80s, formerly a thriving German community; and then Spanish Harlem. Just before mile 20, you encounter the challenging Willis Avenue Bridge over the Harlem River. At mile 20, you make a quick trip through the ethnically diverse Bronx before hitting the final bridge, the Madison Avenue Bridge, leading back into Manhattan. The next two miles traverse Harlem, the center of black culture famous for its dance and music. The final miles tour rolling, challenging Central Park, one of the world's great urban retreats, finishing at Tavern on the Green.

HOW TO ENTER The New York City Marathon has instituted new entry procedures starting in 1998, including requiring an unfortunate (in our opinion) application fee. United States residents outside New York should request an entry form by sending a self-addressed, stamped, business-sized envelope and a $7 non-refundable handling fee (check payable to NYRRC or credit card information) to: Marathon Entries, P.O. Box 1388, G.P.O., New York, NY 10116. You can also request your form by e-mail using the electronic application request form in the NYRRC's web site (and including your credit card information). You may request your entry form at any time, but you may not return it to the New York Road Runners Club until the day after the Central Park Marathon Line-Up (noted in the race brochure). New Yorkers can attend the annual Central Park Marathon Line-Up to pick up their entry form. Standing in this line gives you slightly better odds of being accepted than receiving your entry by mail. Make sure to bring your $7 check. The first 17,000 runners are accepted on a first-come, first-served basis, with 7,500 from the Marathon Line-Up, 2,500 others drawn from New York, New Jersey, and Connecticut, and 7,000 drawn from the rest of the country. The next 3,000 runners are determined by a lottery held in July or August. The last 10,000 entries are reserved for international runners based on a quota system by country. Accepted runners are notified within about four weeks. The race maintains a wait list to fill spaces vacated by runners who are forced to cancel. Note that runners must belong to USATF to enter the race. For the latest entry information, check out the New York Road Runners Club's web site (see contact information).

CROWD/RUNNER SUPPORT Banners hang prominently along the race course and in midtown Manhattan, gearing up community support for the marathon. On race day, spectators turn out in tremendous numbers, with approximately 2 million viewing the race. More than 40 bands of all flavors speckle the course, providing a lift to tired runners. Twenty-four water stations line the course every mile starting at mile 3, with electrolyte replacement drink available every two miles beginning at mile 4 and every mile beginning at mile 22. A sponge station lies just after mile 18; sponges can be replenished in the kiddie pools from miles 19 to 25. Digital clocks indicate the elapsed time every mile, and several video checkpoints ensure race integrity.

RACE LOGISTICS Since the Verrazano-Narrows Bridge closes at 9:00 a.m., we recommend taking the race buses to the start area. Although unfortunately an expensive ride at $7 a head, it will eliminate much worry and aggravation on race morning. Buses pick up runners at the New York City Public Library at Fifth Avenue and 42nd Street between 5:30 a.m. and 7:30 a.m. You must purchase a ticket ahead of time at the Runner's Expo. The race will transport your warm-ups to the finish area.

ACTIVITIES On Wednesday through Saturday before the marathon, you can attend the marathon expo at the New York Coliseum. Bring your registration card and a photo ID to retrieve your race packet, and check out the approximately 80 exhibitor booths. You can also buy NYC Marathon souvenirs at the marathon gift shop in the Coliseum. The race holds a number of clinics and seminars which may interest you. See your information package for this year's topics. On Saturday evening from 4:30 p.m. to 9:30 p.m., join 17,000 other runners and guests at the pasta party at Tavern on the Green under the big tent. On race morning, munch on bagels at the start area to fuel your journey. After your race, meet your family and friends at the Family Reunion Festival on Central Park West from Columbus Circle to 72nd Street. The festival features food, beverage, music, and a giant screen projecting the race. An awards ceremony is held inside the Sheraton Hotel at 7:30 p.m., followed by the Celebration Party at 8:30 p.m. in the Roseland Ballroom and Disco, 239 West 52nd Street.

AWARDS Every NYC Marathon entrant receives an official race T-shirt and poster. Those who complete the race also receive finisher medals, and women receive a red rose. Age-group winners receive Tiffany trophies as do the top runners from each New York borough. Awards also go to the top three international teams, USATF-sanctioned teams, top five NYRRC local runners, and the oldest male and female to finish the race.

ELITE RUNNERS INFORMATION As expected, the NYC Marathon actively recruits the top runners from around the world. Elites are offered transportation, lodging, expenses, and the chance to take home a sizeable paycheck. The top six overall finishers respectively earn: $50,000 plus a new automobile, $25,000, $12,500, $7,500, $5,000, and $2,000. American citizens who finish in the top five earn double the above amounts. The race has established time bonuses for runners breaking 2:13 for men and 2:30 for women ($3,000) up to $65,000 for sub 2:07 and 2:22 times. The top three masters are awarded $3,000, $2,000, and $1,000. Prize money also goes to the top local teams and individuals, including time incentives.

ACCOMMODATIONS Two hotels serve as the NYC Marathon co-headquarters, the New York Hilton and Towers, 1335 Avenue of the Americas, between 53rd and 54th Streets (212-586-7000); and the Sheraton New York Hotel & Towers, 811 Seventh Avenue, between 52nd and 53rd Streets (212-581-1000). Runners who would like to stay at either hotel must complete an application provided with their acceptance notification. The race also provides a Hotel Guide listing scores of other possible lodgings.

RELATED EVENTS/RACES The race sponsors the International Friendship Run, a four-mile fun run held the day before the marathon at 8:00 a.m. Exclusively for international runners and their families, runners follow their country's flag from the United Nations to Tavern on the Green in Central Park. After the jaunt, runners swap T-shirts and pins with fellow marathoners from around the world.

COLUMBUS MARATHON

OVERALL: 88.2

COURSE BEAUTY: 8+

COURSE DIFFICULTY: 3- (SEE APPENDIX)

APPROPRIATENESS FOR FIRST TIMERS: 10-

RACE ORGANIZATION: 10-

CROWDS: 7+

R A C E   D A T A

Overall Ranking:	43
Quality Ranking:	16
Quickness Ranking:	21
Contact:	Columbus Marathon
	P.O. Box 26806
	Columbus, OH 43226 USA
	Tel. (614) 433-0395
	Fax (614) 433-0330
	http://www.columbusmarathon.com
Date:	Generally second Sunday in November
	(November 8, 1998; November 14, 1999)
Start Time:	9:00 a.m.
Time Course Closes:	2:30 p.m.
Number of Finishers:	3,067 in 1997
Course:	Loop
Certification:	USATF
Course Records:	Male: (open) 2:11:02; (masters) 2:20:23
	Female: (open) 2:30:54; (masters) 2:38:07
Elite Athlete Programs:	Yes
Cost:	$35/45
Age groups/Divisions:	18-19, 20-24, 25-29, 30-34, 35-39, 40-44, 45-49,
	50-54, 55-59, 60-64, 65-69, 70+
	Clydesdales (males 200+, females 140+): 18-39, 40+
Walkers:	No
Requirements:	18 years old
Temperature:	42° - 53° (6°C - 12°C)
Aid/Splits:	19 / digital clocks every mile & 5K, including pace
	& projected finish

HIGHLIGHTS   Fast, detailed, and runner-friendly, the Columbus Marathon regularly attracts 4,000 runners, many looking to improve their marathon mark. Columbus' excellent reputation led to its designation as the U.S. Men's Olympic Marathon Trials in 1992. The unique course design, called a cloverleaf by organizers, resembles the profile of a roadrunner, with the three loops depicting its tail, body/head, and leg. The layout allows runners to cover many of Columbus' most interesting neighborhoods, such as Short North, Ohio State University, Bexley, and German Village. Those not familiar with the city may be pleasantly surprised at what it offers, including museums, theaters, shopping, and diverse dining. Weather, the biggest variable, can range from cold and blustery to unseasonably warm.

COURSE DESCRIPTION Columbus' layout makes it spectator friendly, easy for tired runners to drop out, and more scenic than many loop courses. Completely closed to traffic, the race begins on High Street, the city's main drag, in front of the Nationwide Insurance Building. After a gentle down and up start through the Short North, with its galleries, trendy shops, and restaurants, the race turns flat until about 2.5 miles. A short rise, followed by a quick downhill leads to 3.7 miles. The runners pass the Ohio State agricultural areas here as they prepare for the 85-foot ascent into Upper Arlington, a quiet suburban community with tree-lined streets and some interesting homes. Beginning at mile 4, the climb concludes at mile 6.2. After a few minor ups and downs, the course descends gradually to the Ohio State University, passing Ohio Stadium, home of perennial Big Ten power Ohio State Buckeyes football team, at 10 miles. Leaving the campus, runners traipse down Neil Avenue and Victorian Village, with its renovated, turn-of-the-century homes. Passing by shady Goodale Park, the course returns to High Street, retracing its path through the Short North. Runners return downtown at mile 13.5 and turn east for a peek into the original Wendy's restaurant, followed by the Columbus Museum of Art. At mile 16, runners make a circuit around Franklin Park, home of the beautifully restored 1895 conservatory. Affluent Bexley, site of the Ohio Governor's Mansion and other distinguished homes, awaits at mile 17. The course from downtown to Bexley is generally flat with a few minor grades. Runners exit Bexley at mile 20. From here, the race features long, gentle rolls. At mile 22, the course passes Olde Towne East, one of Columbus' oldest neighborhoods, and Topiary Garden on East Town Street, reaching German Village at mile 23. The largest privately-funded restoration project in the country, German Villages' cobbled streets (none on the runners' route), beer halls, and proud brick homes will beckon your return after the race.

CROWD/RUNNER SUPPORT Columbus' course gives downtown onlookers a chance to catch their favorite runner four times during the race — the start, mile 13.5, mile 23, and the finish — by walking only a few blocks. Crowd support at other sections of the course is also surprisingly strong, with approximately 100,000 people cheering the runners.

Runners also find entertainment, including professional and high school bands, at a number of areas, especially at Schiller Park. Many of Columbus' 2,400 volunteers man the 19 aid stations, which stock water and electrolyte replacement drink, and the 13 portable toilet stations at even miles. Columbus' enthusiastic helpers consistently receive high marks from runners year after year. Among the race's other notable details are the digital clocks located every mile and 5K, including overall time, pace, and projected finish.

RACE LOGISTICS Columbus' compact downtown means most hotels lie near the race staging area, making transportation to the start unnecessary. However, a shuttle bus from the finish area will return you to the Hyatt Regency (pick-up at Broad and High Streets). For those driving into town, there is plenty of inexpensive, convenient, garage parking.

ACTIVITIES Packet pick-up and late registration are located at the Marathon Expo in the Hyatt Regency Ballroom. Runners may retrieve their packets on Friday, 4:00 p.m. to 9:00 p.m., Saturday, 9:00 a.m. to 8:00 p.m., and Sunday, 6:00 a.m. to 8:00 a.m. There is no race-day registration. On Saturday, attend clinics on a variety of subjects, including the popular Columbus Marathon 101 which gives advice to Columbus first-timers on how to run the race. Saturday night, the race holds a pasta party (about $10) in the Nationwide Insurance Cafeteria, connected by walkway to the Hyatt Regency.

AWARDS Every marathon entrant receives a high-quality, embroidered T-shirt, results magazine, and official race program, and finishers also earn medals. Age-group awards go mostly five deep. Finally, about $70,000 in prize money is up for grabs.

ELITE RUNNERS INFORMATION Male runners under 2:20 and female runners under 2:45 may qualify for elite status at Columbus. Elites may be offered travel, accommodations, and free entry. Promising young runners may also receive a complimentary entry. In addition, Columbus offers prize money totaling approximately $70,000, doled out to the top 5 overall finishers, top five Ohioans, and top five masters. Specifically, the top 5 finishers (male and female) earn $5,000, $2,500, $1,250, $750, and $500, respectively. Masters winners and top Ohioans receive $500, $300, $200, $150, and $100. A runner who sets a new course record receives $25,000. There are also time bonus incentives for men under 2:13 and women under 2:34.

ACCOMMODATIONS Conveniently located at the start and a few blocks from the finish, the Hyatt Regency, 350 North High Street (614-463-1234), serves as the host hotel. Also convenient are the Hyatt on Capitol Square, 75 East State Street (614-228-1234); Holiday Inn City Center, 175 E. Town Street (614-221-3281); Holiday Inn Crowne Plaza, 33 E. Nationwide Blvd. (614-461-4100); Hojo Inn Downtown, 1070 Dublin Road (614-486-4554); Courtyard by Marriott, 145 N. High Street (614-228-2244); Sheraton Suites Columbus, 201 Hutchinson Avenue (614-436-0004); Holiday Inn, 175 Hutchinson Avenue (614-885-3334); and Hampton Inn, 1100 Mediterranean Avenue (614-848-9696). Alternatively, call Peoples Travel (800-336-7662) for hotel accommodations at a special marathon rate.

RELATED EVENTS/RACES Two or three runners can band together to form a marathon relay team in either corporate or non-corporate divisions. Teams may be male, female, or coed. Relay legs run 13.9, 9.3, and 3 miles. Others may choose to run in the 5K, which starts immediately after the marathon/marathon relay. Kids may want to join in the Fun Run following the marathon start. Register at the marathon expo.

AREA ATTRACTIONS A clean, wholesome city, Columbus contains lots of museums, theaters, shopping, and other places of interest. Among them are the Columbus Museum of Art, 480 E. Broad Street; Wexner Center for the Arts on the Ohio State University campus at North High Street and 15th Avenue; the hands-on Center of Science and Industry, 280 E. Broad Street; a replica of Christopher Columbus' Santa Maria at the Riverfront; German Village south of Capitol Square; Short North; and the State Capitol building.

HONOLULU MARATHON

OVERALL: 92.8

COURSE BEAUTY: 9

COURSE DIFFICULTY: 4+ (SEE APPENDIX)

APPROPRIATENESS FOR FIRST TIMERS: 8

RACE ORGANIZATION: 9+

CROWDS: 6

RACE DATA

Overall Ranking: **22**
Quality Ranking: **25**
Quickness Ranking: **77**
Contact: **Honolulu Marathon Association**
3435 Waialae Avenue, Room 208
Honolulu, HI 96816
USA
Tel. (808) 734-7200
Fax (808) 732-7057
E-mail: info@honolulumarathon.org
http://www.honolulumarathon.org/
Date: **Generally second Sunday in December**
Start Time: **5:00 a.m.**
Time Course Closes: **Last finisher**
Number of Finishers: **26,495 in 1997**
Course: **Near loop**
Certification: **USATF**
Course Records: **Male: (open) 2:11:43; (masters) 2:17:24**
Female: (open) 2:31:01; (masters) 2:48:00
Elite Athlete Programs: **Yes**
Cost: **$30/40/50**
Age groups/Divisions: **≤14, 15-19, 20-24, 25-29, 30-34, 35-39, 40-44,**
45-49, 50-54, 55-59, 60-64, 65-69, 70-74, 75-79,
80-84, 85-89, 90-94, 95-99, 100+
Walkers: **Yes**
Requirements: **None**
Temperature: **65° - 85° (18°C - 29°C)**
Aid/Splits: **17 / every mile, clocks every 5 miles**

HIGHLIGHTS Like the swallows' yearly pilgrimage to San Juan Capistrano, runners from East and West flock to Hawaii for the burgeoning Honolulu Marathon. In 1997, nearly 33,000 runners made the flight to the tropics, perhaps to escape the pre-winter cold or to place the ultimate bookend on their marathon year. The painfully early 5:00 a.m. start, necessary because of the impending heat and humidity, is tempered by the most entertaining staging area of any marathon. Each year, upwards of 20,000 Japanese runners add a colorful flair to the race, providing more vitality than a hummingbird on honey as they proudly sport their brightly colored running club duds, wave club banners and bellow club chants. If this spectacle doesn't get you going, the gust of fireworks will surely put some bounce in your stride as you embark on a course that includes the world-famous sights of Waikiki Beach, Diamond Head and Koko Head Crater.

COURSE DESCRIPTION Most runners congregate in the darkness of Ala Moana Beach Park or the Ala Moana Shopping Center, listening to the lively military band. Amidst a torrent of fireworks and a Howitzer cannon blast, the 30,000+ runners stampede west toward downtown and Aloha Tower. Runners enter the Capitol District (miles 2 and 3) on South King Street, passing the Kamehameha Statue, Alliolani Hale (the Judiciary Building), Iolani Palace, the Hawaii State Library, Kawaihao Church, and Honolulu Hale (City Hall). With Christmas only weeks away, local businesses and merchants get into the marathon spirit by leaving on their Christmas lights to illuminate this predawn section of the course. Returning near the start after 5K, runners cross the Ala Wai Canal into the world-famous Waikiki strip just after 4 miles. The Hilton Hawaiian Village and Fort DeRussy lie on the way to your first glimpse of the balmy Pacific waters at Kuhio Beach (mile 5). Leaving the ocean behind, the course makes its first trip through Kapiolani Park, the eventual finish, six miles into the race. Virtually flat up to this point, the course begins ascending Diamond Head Road at 7.25 miles and peaks just past the lighthouse near mile 8 (93 feet). At

8.6 miles, the course veers left of Ft. Ruger Triangle Park, climbing to its highest point (108 feet) at 15K. A quick turn onto 18th Avenue leads runners past the Diamond Head Film Studio, home of Hawaii Five-O and Magnum P.I. The lonely next 3 miles on Kalanianaole Hwy., although barely 10 feet above sea level and absolutely flat, afford only a few places to see the ocean. Your spirits soon rise as you reach the half-marathon point just before the Aina Haina Shopping Center. After passing the Niu and Kuliouou Valleys around 14 miles, the course turns off the highway into residential Hawaii Kai, christened by a 200-yard climb over a short bridge. After retracing your steps on the lonely highway, a slight incline occurs past the Waialae Country Club (21.5 miles) before the course descends toward the ocean. At the bottom of the short decline sits the Aloha Gasoline station, site of a Hawaiian band and hula dancers in grass skirts. At mile 23, the course turns right onto Kahala Avenue, better known as the Million Dollar Mile because of the high value of its real estate. By mile 23.8, you begin the 1-mile climb up Diamond Head, gaining a modest 50 feet. From the cliffs to your left, watch the surfers and windsurfers in the water below. A 3-mile downhill from Diamond Head and you're in the homestretch — only flat Diamond Head Road (mile 25) and Kalakaua Avenue remain before the finish in Kapiolani Park.

CROWD/RUNNER SUPPORT Over 30,000 fellow runners and 50,000 spectators do their best to give you company on the course. The thousands of spouses, friends and other spectators left behind at the start get their next chance to cheer their runner at the 5K mark when the course returns near the start. Here, cheering sections from the Japanese running clubs shout, chant, blow whistles, sound horns, and jingle bells. Others cheer from their high-rise condos and hotel lanais along Ala Moana and Kalakaua Avenue in Waikiki. Not only do they cheer you on, but their camera flashbulbs light up your predawn path. More applause and encouragement come from residents of Hawaii Kai (15-18 miles) and the Million Dollar Mile (23-24 miles). As the day grows older and the temperature rises, each of the 17 aid stations becomes more of a welcomed sight. You'll especially enjoy the enthusiastic stations in Hawaii Kai around miles 15 and 17.

RACE LOGISTICS Free bus service from Kapiolani Park to the start begins at 2:00 a.m. The last bus leaves at 4:00 a.m. Kapiolani Park is located within walking (hobbling for the return) distance of major hotels along Waikiki Beach.

ACTIVITIES Early arrivers to Honolulu have first pick at arguably the best collection of souvenirs (most display Honolulu's signature Polynesian runner) of any North American marathon. An all-in-one Sports Expo, souvenir sale and packet pick-up extends from Wednesday to Saturday 10:00 a.m. to 6:00 p.m. There is no race-day registration for the marathon. Souvenir sales also take place at Kapiolani Park, Thursday through Saturday from 11:00 a.m. to 6:00 p.m. and race day from 6:00 a.m. to 4:00 p.m. On Friday evening, join runners from around the world at the carbo-loading and international T-shirt exchange party at the Waikiki Shell from 5:30 p.m. to 9:00 p.m. Bring a few of your race T-shirts to exchange for foreign ones that will truly impress your running buddies. After the race, speed your recovery with post-race refreshments and a well-deserved massage as you await the awards ceremony, starting at 1:00 p.m., at the Kapiolani Park Bandstand.

AWARDS Every finisher receives a T-shirt, shell lei, and medallion. Finisher certificates are also awarded and available the day after the race at marathon headquarters. Elite runners compete for several thousand dollars in overall prize money, while the top three in each age group receive trophies. Additionally, the top 5% of each age division receive medals.

ELITE RUNNERS INFORMATION The race maintains no official criteria establishing elite status. Instead, race organizers determine elite status and appropriate expenses on an individual basis. The usually substantial prize money purse fluctuates annually depending on sponsorship commitments.

ACCOMMODATIONS The Outrigger Reef Hotel, 2169 Kalia Road (800-688-7444) generally serves as the host hotel. Additional nearby hotels include: Sheraton Waikiki, 2255 Kalakaua Avenue (800-325-3535); Hyatt Regency Waikiki, 2255 Kalakaua Avenue (800-233-1234); Royal Hawaiian Hotel, 2259 Kalakaua (800-325-3535); Hawaiian Waikiki Beach Hotel, 2570 Kalakaua Avenue (800-877-7666); and Continental Surf Hotel, 2426 Kuhio Avenue (808-922-2755).

RELATED EVENTS/RACES To insure that you're not overly peaked for the marathon, run the Diamond Head Duet couples run. This is a free, 4.2-mile run on Thursday at 8:00 a.m. in Kapiolani Park. On race day, family and friends braving the early marathon start may consider participating in the 10K Mayor's Walk, benefitting Hawaii's Special Olympics, held immediately following the start of the marathon. The walk course covers the first 10K of the marathon and finishes in Kapiolani Park in plenty of time to watch the marathon finish.

AREA ATTRACTIONS While catching some rays will surely be near the top of your "to do" list, wait until after the race for sun worshiping on famous Waikiki Beach or snorkeling at nearby Hanauma Bay. In the meantime, take in the Kodak Hula Show at the Waikiki Shell Amphitheater in Kapiolani Park on Tuesday, Wednesday or Thursday at 10:00 a.m., or head to the U.S.S. Arizona National Memorial in Pearl Harbor. Although you'll pass Diamond Head Crater during the marathon, take time to hike the one mile in to the crater for a gorgeous sunrise or sunset and spectacular view of Waikiki.

KIAWAH ISLAND MARATHON

OVERALL: 84.7

COURSE BEAUTY: 9+

COURSE DIFFICULTY: 3-

APPROPRIATENESS FOR FIRST TIMERS: 9-

RACE ORGANIZATION: 9

CROWDS: 2

RACE DATA

Overall Ranking:	64
Quality Ranking:	70
Quickness Ranking:	35
Contact:	Dylan Jones
	Kiawah Island Resort
	12 Kiawah Beach Drive
	Kiawah Island, SC 29455
	USA
	Tel. (803) 768-2780
	Fax (803) 768-6022
Date:	Generally second Saturday in December
Start Time:	8:00 a.m.
Time Course Closes:	3:00 p.m.
Number of Finishers:	845 in 1997
Course:	Loop
Certification:	USATF
Course Records:	Male: (open) 2:21:24
	Female: (open) 2:52:08
Elite Athlete Programs:	Yes
Cost:	$27
Age groups/Divisions:	13-17, 18-23, 24-29, 30-34, 35-39, 40-44, 45-49, 50-54, 55-59, 60-69, 70+
Walkers:	Yes
Requirements:	None
Temperature:	45° - 60° (7°C - 16°C)
Aid/Splits:	12 / every 2 miles

HIGHLIGHTS   Chances are you have never heard of the Kiawah Island Marathon. Until now. Offering one of the most unique marathon experiences in North America, the race runs entirely on this 10,000 acre resort barrier island off the coast of South Carolina. Using just about every inch of road on the isle, the winding course passes salt marshes, semitropical wilderness, breathtaking golf courses, and maybe even an alligator! The elegant, post-race banquet knows no equals. And after the marathon, Kiawah Island is a terrific place to relax and savor your accomplishment. So if you want to escape the December frost, the Kiawah Island Marathon may be the best destination you've never heard of.

COURSE DESCRIPTION   Covered by salt marshes, wilderness, beaches, and golf courses, environmentally sensitive Kiawah Island consists entirely of a world-class resort and exclusive residential communities. The controlled marathon course, open to limited residential traffic, consists of a series of inventive loops and out and backs up and down the island. Since the barrier isle has relatively few roads, the race covers many twice, providing ample opportunity to view the other runners. The course has many curves and turns which could annoy faster runners. However, runners should love the excellent footing and the flat route (the highest elevation on the island is 14 feet), with the largest grades consisting of golf cart paths. If you want it any flatter you'd have to send out for it!

The marathon starts and finishes in front of the East Beach Conference Center. The first six miles of the course cover the western end of the island passing 21-acre Night Heron Park, the Cougar Point Golf Course, and the tree-lined roads of Kiawah's first residential area. The following 10 miles weave through the middle and eastern sections of the island, now comprised of second and third growth maritime forest and quintessential Southern Living homes. Indigo and cotton fields covered this area over 150 years ago. The next four miles (16-20) take runners down and back on spectacular Ocean Course Drive, providing vistas of marshland, salt water creeks, gracious oaks, and the famous Ocean Course where America claimed the 1991 Ryder Cup. The final stretch guides marathoners down beautiful Flyway Drive with ponds and gators motivating runners to the East Beach Conference Center finish line.

CROWD/RUNNER SUPPORT   Kiawah Island has a small local population so most of the crowds consist of runners' families and friends. An excellent spectator course, the runners pass most points at least twice. Located every 2 miles, aid stations offer runners the choice of water, sports drink and fruit. Splits are called roughly every two miles.

RACE LOGISTICS   There is a free shuttle service to the start area for those runners staying on the island. If you are staying in Charleston, there is plenty of parking near the conference center, but as always, you should arrive early.

ACTIVITIES   On Friday evening, attend the Pasta Bash at the East Beach Conference Center. The resort catering staff does a superb job with the dinner (about $13). Kiawah Island hosts an excellent awards ceremony and party following the marathon. A generous buffet of hot and cold food and beverage highlights the festivities.

AWARDS   Each pre-registered marathon entrant receives a long-sleeve T-shirt, with finishers earning medals. Kiawah "Proud Pelican" awards go to the top five open males, top three open females, and the male and female masters winners. Age-group awards are also given to the top three finishers in each age division. Ten percent of all pre-registered runners receive awards.

ELITE RUNNERS INFORMATION   Kiawah Island Marathon does not actively recruit elite runners, nor does it offer prize money. The race will, however, assist with on-site expenses such as lodging and entry fees on a case-by-case basis. Contact the race director for more information.

ACCOMMODATIONS   The Kiawah Island Inn offers special accommodation packages for marathon runners and their families. The resort also offers numerous villa and home options, starting at about $50 per person, per night. For resort reservations call (800-654-2924). Other companies also offer home and villa accommodations, including Ravenel Associates (800-845-3911); Pam Harrington Exclusives (800-845-6966); Benchmark Rentals (800-992-9666); Beachwalker Rentals (800-334-6308); and Charleston Resort Properties (800-845-7368). Budget lodging can be found in Charleston a short drive away.

RELATED EVENTS/RACES   Kiawah Island also sponsors a half marathon (with 1,329 finishers in 1997) and 5K, both held on the same day as the marathon.

AREA ATTRACTIONS   A true resort, Kiawah Island offers four world-class golf courses ranked among the top in the country, numerous tennis courts, ten miles of beach, and an outstanding children's program, Kamp Kiawah.

EUROPE

PREVIOUS PAGE: JUNGFRAU MARATHON

VALENCIA MARATHON

OVERALL: 80.7

COURSE BEAUTY: 7+

COURSE DIFFICULTY: 3-

APPROPRIATENESS FOR FIRST TIMERS: 7+

ORGANIZATION: 9+

CROWDS: 5-

RACE DATA

Overall Ranking: 86
Quality Ranking: 34
Quickness Ranking: 27
Contact: Marathon Popular de Valencia
S.D. Correcaminos
Arzobispo Fabian y Fucro 14b
46009 Valencia
Spain
Tel. +34/6-346-0707
Fax +34/6-346-3635

Date: Generally first Sunday in February
Start Time: 9:00 a.m.
Time Course Closes: 2:00 p.m.
Number of Finishers: 1,477 in 1997
Course: Near loop
Certification: AIMS
Course Records: Male: (open) 2:14:01
Female: (open) 2:34:08
Elite Athlete Programs: No
Cost: 5,000 ptas.
Age groups/Divisions: None
Walkers: No
Requirements: 18 years old
Temperature: 46˚ - 59˚ (8˚C - 15˚C)
Aid/Splits: 8 / every 5K

HIGHLIGHTS   You know how oranges are usually bright in color, but the taste may be sweet in good oranges or slightly sour in the bad ones. The Valencia Marathon is like a home-grown orange. Maybe not the prettiest on the exterior, but the inside tastes consistently sweet. The almost loop course goes mostly through the outskirts of Valencia (Spain's third-largest city), and although there are no major hills, there are five 180 degree turns. Overall, the race is very well organized, if not terribly scenic, and Valencia makes a good base for exploring southern Spain. In recent years, Valencia has been one of the few age-handicapped races among the major marathons. Although organizers dropped this format for 1998, they have left open the possibility of handicapping runners in the future, giving every runner the opportunity to taste the sweet finish line first.

COURSE DESCRIPTION   The Valencia Marathon starts in the middle of an industrial zone in northern Valencia and crosses the river into the main part of the city on fairly wide Avenida Del 9 de Octubre. The course circles around a mostly commercial area, returning to Avenida Del 9 de Octubre near 2.5K. A slight incline near 3K takes you through more commercial parts of town. After 8K the course follows Túria Riverbed Park. This pleasant stretch soon gives way to more commercial and industrial areas at 10K. The route reaches the Valencia Port, heads north for 1K, where the runners complete their first turnabout, and then travel south along the port for about 2K. Here you turn around again, retracing your steps until 17K where you plunge into one of the port's tentacles into the sea for a 3K out and back. You now begin perhaps the most pleasant section of the race, a 2.5-K dash on a wide esplanade along the Mediterranean Sea (20K to 22.5K). The following 18 kilometers go through mostly commercial and residential parts of Valencia on wide avenues. Just after 41K, the course returns to Túria Riverbed Park, going away from the stadium, completes a quick turnaround, and heads down to the riverbed. Runners follow the trail into the stadium where they complete three-quarters of a lap to reach the finish line.

CROWD/RUNNER SUPPORT   About 20,000 spectators come out on race day with another 5,000 or so in the stadium for the finish. The greatest crowd support comes between 30K and 35K, and from 40K to the finish. The Valencia Marathon features aid stations with water and sports drink every 5K. A solid blue line takes runners around the course.

RACE LOGISTICS   Race organizers do not provide transportation to or from the marathon. Runners staying at the host hotel generally walk. The hotel is located about 500 meters from the start and 1,500 meters (about one mile) from the finish.

ACTIVITIES   You may collect your race package on Friday or Saturday before the marathon at the race headquarter hotel, Hotel NH Center, next to the bus station. On Saturday, the race typically holds a conference on medical issues. That evening there is a pasta party in the restaurant Rosiña, carrera Fuente de San Luis, 72. Runners who want to carbo-load correctly should eat paella, which was created in Valencia. Finally, a painting competition for children determines the marathon poster for the following year.

AWARDS   Every runner receives a T-shirt, running bag, and program. Those who finish under 5 hours also receive a medal and certificate. The top 15 men and women receive prize money: 300,000 ptas. for first, 150,000 for second, 75,000 for third, 50,000 for fourth, 30,000 for fifth, and 20,000 for sixth through fifteenth. The person who sets a new course record also receives a 500,000 ptas. bonus.

ACCOMMODATIONS   The official race hotel is the Hotel NH Center, c/ Ricardo Micó 1 (tel. +34/6-347-5000; fax +34/6-347-6252). All of the NH Hotels have special marathon rates. Alternatively, you can call the marathon's travel agent, Zeus Tracel (tel. & fax +34/6-352-1142).

AREA ATTRACTIONS   Even though it is a rather large city, Valencia may surprise you by its grace. Among the attractions are the IVAM Modern Art Museum, the 14th-century cathedral, Museum of Fine Art (Museo de Bellas Artes), and Parque Gulliver. Valencia also lies quite near to some of the country's finest coastline and beaches.

SEVILLE MARATHON

OVERALL: 88.5

COURSE BEAUTY: 9-

COURSE DIFFICULTY: 3+ (SEE APPENDIX)

APPROPRIATENESS FOR FIRST TIMERS: 8+

ORGANIZATION: 9

CROWDS: 5-

RACE DATA

Overall Ranking: 41
Quality Ranking: 44
Quickness Ranking: 52
Contact: Marathon Ciudad de Sevilla
Instituto Municipal de Deportes
Avenida Kansas City s/n
41007 Sevilla, Spain
Tel. +34/5-459-6800
Fax +34/5-467-5524

Date: Generally fourth Sunday in February
Start Time: 9:00 a.m.
Time Course Closes: 2:00 p.m.
Number of Participants: 1,900 in 1997
Course: Loop
Certification: AIMS
Course Records: Male: (open) 2:11:21
Female: (open) 2:28:59
Elite Athlete Programs: Yes
Cost: 5,000 ptas.
Age groups/Divisions: 18-34, 35-39, 40-44, 45-49, 50-54, 55-59, 60+
Walkers: No
Requirements: 18 years old
Temperature: 41° - 54° (5°C to 12°C)
Aid/Splits: 8 / digital clock at halfway

HIGHLIGHTS Spain's many legacies come together in Seville. But with the bull-fighting, flamenco dancing, whitewashed buildings and orange trees stands a lesser known, but growing city tradition — the Seville Marathon. Starting near the Plaza de Espana in Parque Maria Luisa, the race covers over 100 streets and avenues during its winding city loop. Over 100,000 spectators line this marathon fiesta that takes runners past many of the city's famous Moorish and Baroque architectural treasures including the Maestranza Bullring, Torre del Oro, and the Cathedral and its bell tower, La Giralda.

COURSE DESCRIPTION The Seville Marathon features a flat, convoluted loop through the city and its suburbs. Although the city is known for its narrow streets and alley ways, the race predominantly runs on wider avenues. Beginning in the grassy grounds of Parque Maria Luisa, the race goes south for a 5-K loop past Benito Villamarin Stadium and Collegio Mayor University before crossing the Guadalquivir River into Triana. The next 5K cut through this old Sevillian barrio, famous for producing great bullfighters, flamenco artists and beautiful potteries. Returning to the eastern side of the Guadalquivir River, lovely views arise along the river's edge while heading south on Paseo de Cristobal Colon. The dazzling white bullring, Plaza de Toros de la Maestranza, appears on the left near 10K while the Torre del Oro, created as a defensive lookout in 1220, follows on the right. Turning left on Avenida de Roma, the route skirts the famous Tobacco Factory (11K), whose women workers inspired the opera Carmen. It then heads onto Avenida de la Constitucion, downtown Seville's principal avenue. Near 11.5K on Constitucion, the route passes Reales Alcazares, the city's striking palace, and the huge Seville Cathedral (where Christopher Columbus is reputedly entombed) and La Giralda. Leaving the city center, the route travels through La Macarena, Seville's northern barrio, known for its many beautiful churches. Arising at 15K, the Basilica de la Macarena, a shrine to Seville's much-venerated Virgen de la Macarena, affords you an opportunity to pray before tackling the remainder of the course. After paralleling the Guadalquivir River between 16K and 17K, runners meander through mostly residential and industrial areas of Seville's eastern suburbs for the next 21 kilometers. Near the finish at 38K, the route goes south for 1.5K, past the Residencia Sanitario G. Morato before turning onto Avenida de la Palmera for the final 2.5K to the finish on semicircular Plaza de Espana.

CROWD / RUNNER SUPPORT   The marathon attracts approximately 100,000 spectators with most congregating near the start, finish, and between 10K and 12.5K. The spectator-friendly course allows onlookers to view the race from several convenient locations: the 5-K mark near the Guadalquivir River, Avenida de la Constitucion at 11K, and the 34-K and 38-K marks near Plaza de Espana. Aid stations supplying water, electrolyte replacement drink, and sponges sit every 5K.

RACE LOGISTICS   Convenient Parque Maria Luisa makes arriving at the start relatively hassle free for runners staying in one of the many hotels nearby.

ACTIVITIES   Beginning on Friday, a two-day expo takes place at San Bernardo Station (Avenida de Cadiz s/n) from 10:00 a.m. to 2:00 p.m. and 5:00 p.m. to 9:00 p.m. Here you can pick up your race packet and attend the pre-race pasta meal on Saturday afternoon. After the race, return to San Bernardo Station for a luncheon that accompanies the awards ceremony.

AWARDS   Every marathoner receives a T-shirt, and finishers receive medals and certificates. The top 10 runners (male and female) earn prize money ranging from 500,000 ptas. for first to 10,000 ptas. for tenth. Extra money is awarded to course-record breakers. Age-group winners receive trophies.

ELITE RUNNERS INFORMATION   Elite runners (males under 2:11 and females under 2:28) may qualify for travel, accommodation, and meal expenses. Contact the marathon office for consideration.

ACCOMMODATIONS   The race has no official hotel. Several excellent hotels are located near the start including: Hotel Alfonso XIII, Calle San Fernando 2 (tel. +34/5-422-2850; fax +34/5-421-6033); Ciudad de Sevilla, Avenida Manuel Siurot 25 (tel. +34/5-423-0505; fax +34/5-423-8539); Hotel Giralda, Calle Sierra Nevada 3 (tel. +34/5-441-6611; fax +34/5-441-9352); Hotel Nuevo Lar, Piazza Carmen Benitez 3 (tel. +34/5-441-0361; fax +34/5-441-0452); and Hotel Melia Sevilla, Calle Dr. Pedro Castro 1 (tel. +34/5-442-2611; fax +34/5-442-1608). Also nearby and less expensive are Hostal Goya, Mateo Gago 31 (tel. +34/5-421-1170; fax +34/5-456-2988); and Hosteria del Laurel, Plaza de los Venerables 5 (tel. +34/5-422-0295; fax +34/5-421-0450).

AREA ATTRACTIONS   Many visitors to Spain rank Seville as one of their favorite cities. The quintessential Spanish city, Seville's narrow streets and beautiful buildings charm the running shorts off you. The sights are numerous and beautiful. For shopping and people watching, head to Sierpes Street in Barrio Santa Cruz, the old Jewish quarter. Of course, Spanish nightlife is legendary, and Seville does nothing to dispel the image. If you can extend your stay, bullfighting typically starts in March, and Semana Santa (Easter Week), is a week-long street celebration with a spiritual theme.

VIGARANO MARATHON

OVERALL: 82

COURSE BEAUTY: 8-

COURSE DIFFICULTY: 2- (SEE APPENDIX)

APPROPRIATENESS FOR FIRST TIMERS: 8

ORGANIZATION: 9+

CROWDS: 5-

RACE DATA

Overall Ranking: 81
Quality Ranking: 34
Quickness Ranking: 7
Contact: Vigaranomaratona
Via Municipio, 1
I-44049, Vigarano Mainarda (FE)
ITALY
Tel. +39/532-43196
Fax +39/532-436563
E-mail: fe0036k1@fe.nettuno.it
http://www.nettuno.it/fiera/vigaranomaraton/

Date: Usually in March (March 1, 1998)
Start Time: 9:30 a.m.
Time Course Closes: 3:30 p.m.
Number of Finishers: 1,000 in 1997
Course: Loop
Certification: AIMS
Course Records: Male: (open) 2:14:10
Female: (open) 2:34:11
Elite Athlete Programs: Yes
Cost: Lit. 45,000
Age groups/Divisions: Male: open, 50+
Female: open
Walkers: No
Requirements: 18 years old, medical certificate
Temperature: 48° - 63° (9°C - 17°C)
Aid/Splits: 8 / 10K, halfway, 30K

HIGHLIGHTS A city of two facades, one medieval and one renaissance, Ferrara splits down its middle with Viale Cavour separating the two. Likewise for the Vigarano Marathon (Vigaranomaratona in Italian). The Vigarano Marathon splits its course between the farms surrounding the towns and the ancient center of the cities. The loop route starts and finishes in the small town of Vigarano, with the city of Ferrara as the marathon's center and heart. Exceptionally flat, the route contains only two noteworthy rises, both small bridges. The extremely friendly race organizers devote significant personal attention to the runners, from finding hotels to aid stations. And after you've exhausted Ferrara's sights, the city is well located near many other tour-de-force cities, including Venice, Bologna, Florence, and Verona.

COURSE DESCRIPTION Starting in the center of Vigarano, the course quickly moves into farm areas before reaching a small residential community after 2K. From 3K to 12K, runners return to the farm, passing the 16th-century villa Diamantina at 5K. Although this first section contains a few minor bumps, the first real incline occurs at 11K when the race crosses over the A13 highway. You pass through some industrial areas near 12K as you hit the outskirts of Ferrara. Here you must keep to the right for about 1K before moving to the left side of the road. Between 14 and 15K, the course detours through a traffic-free industrial park (watch out for the railroad tracks near 15K). Just prior to 16K, houses begin to appear and the course traces the town's medieval brick walls. The city's former cathedral sits to the left just after halfway. Then from 22.75K to 24.5K, the route takes in old Ferrara, entering under the original city gates. On the right lies the beautiful current cathedral (12th century), and to the left rise Palazzo Ducale and Este Castle. Across the way, you find the bishop's residence. After turning on Viale Cavour, shops in old buildings constitute most of the sights. Of course, old means cobblestones, but there are less than 1K of them. The race turns on shady Viale IV Novembre at 24.5K, and you can just make out more sections of the town walls. Another bump hits at Via Bologna (26.5K), with shops and restaurants lining the route. After you turn off Via Bologna at 28K, a bank of trees offers shade, cooling you for the climb up the bridge at 29K. You are then rewarded with a nice 1K downhill through rural residential/industrial areas. By 31K, it's back through the orchards, winding through the village of Porotto from 32.25K to 34K. A particularly nice path lies just before 35K, where the orchard trees sit right up against the road. The road winds quite a bit between 33K and 37K, and then it straightens slightly. From 36K to 37K, runners pass through the village of Borgo Scoline. The race reaches the outskirts of Vigarano after 39K, and following a brief rural section on Via Rondona, the course turns right for the final stretch to the finish in Vigarano's center.

CROWD/RUNNER SUPPORT You find most of the crowd support at the start/finish, in the center of Ferrara, and in the villages along the course. There is also a dancing group and Palio group in medieval costumes to entertain you while you run. Aid stations are located every 5K (with water and sports drink at 5K and 10K and fruit, biscuits, salt, and candy, in addition to the fluids, from 15K), and in between you find sponge stations. You can also give your personal drinks to race officials at the expo before 8:00 a.m. on race morning, marked with your name, start number, and the aid station to which it should be taken.

RACE LOGISTICS The race provides shuttle bus service from race hotels to the start, and back to the hotels and train station after the race. Showers and changing facilities are located in the nearby gymnasium.

ACTIVITIES Pick up your race packet and breeze through the small expo in the tent on Vigarano Mainarda's central square on Saturday or Sunday before the race. Buses may be available for transporting runners to the race expo from their hotels in Ferrara. The week before the marathon, the race typically offers training advice from Orlando Pizzolato. Contact the race for more details. If you don't feel like finding your own carbo-load dinner, organizers offer a pasta party on Saturday evening.

AWARDS Every entrant receives a daypack, T-shirt, and special prices for various museums, sights, and restaurants in Ferrara. Finishers under 6 hours also receive a medal, certificate, and results booklet. Male open runners from 51st to 100th place, female runners from 11th to 15th, and male masters runners from 6th to 10th receive a track suit. Male open runners from 101st to 200th place, female runners from 16th to 20th place, and male masters runners from 11th to 20th place receive a special sweatshirt.

ELITE RUNNERS INFORMATION Male runners under 2:20 and females under 2:40 may qualify for elite status, with such perquisites as complimentary accommodations, expenses, entry, and possibly some appearance money. Prize money varies depending on the runner's time and place. The top 50 male open runners and top 10 female runners receive either prize money or expense reimbursement. The male winner receives Lit. 12,000,000, and bonus money if he sets a new course record. The amount of his bonus depends on his time, ranging from Lit. 1,000,000

for a 2:14, to Lit. 10,000,000 for a sub-2:10 time. The female winner receives Lit. 1,000,000, in addition to bonuses for a new course record.

ACCOMMODATIONS   Organizers will suggest accommodations for you depending on your needs. Contact the marathon office directly for hotels with special rates.

RELATED EVENTS/RACES   Other races offered include a noncompetitive 7K walk and a Mini Baby 2K Run.

AREA ATTRACTIONS   Historic Ferrara contains numerous medieval and renaissance attractions, including the Este Castle, Palazzo Municipale, the 12th-century cathedral, and Piazza Trento e Trieste.

CATALUNYA-BARCELONA MARATHON

OVERALL: 90.7

COURSE BEAUTY: 8+

COURSE DIFFICULTY: 4- (SEE APPENDIX)

APPROPRIATENESS FOR FIRST TIMERS: 8+

ORGANIZATION: 9

CROWDS: 6

RACE DATA

Overall Ranking: 29
Quality Ranking: 32
Quickness Ranking: 60
Contact: Marathon Catalunya
c/ Jonqueres 16, 9. C
08003 Barcelona
Spain
Tel. +34/3-268-0114
Fax +34/3-268-4334
E-mail: marathon_cat@redestb.es
http://www.redestb.es/marathon_cat/index.htm

Date: Generally third Sunday in March
Start Time: 9:30 a.m.
Time Course Closes: 2:30 p.m.
Number of Finishers: 2,970 in 1997
Course: Point to point
Certification: AIMS
Course Records: Male: (open) 2:11:04
Female: (open) 2:30:06
Elite Athlete Programs: Yes
Cost: 3,000/5,000 ptas.
Age groups/Divisions: 18-22, 23-29, 30-34, 35-39, 40-44, 45-49, 50-54, 55-59, 60-64, 65-69, 70+, wheelchair
Walkers: No
Requirements: 18 years old
Temperature: 57° - 64° (14°C - 18°C)
Aid/Splits: 13 / digital clock at halfway

HIGHLIGHTS Christopher Columbus needed to know what lay beyond the line of horizon. He thought India, but he had to find out for certain. Despite naysayers and countless obstacles, he boldly mounted a voyage into the unknown. Just like marathoners. Marathoners need to know how their bodies will react at 22 miles. They need to prove the naysayers wrong; it is not insanity to run 26.2 miles in one day. Heck, maybe even in under 4 hours. In Barcelona, these kindred spirits meet. Just before 40K, the Monument a Colom, with Christopher Columbus pointing confidently to the New World, rises into the air. This sight should propel many of you to the finish, because if Columbus can sail into the end of the map for week stacked upon week, you surely can run another 2 kilometers. If you don't share this admiration of Columbus' vision and tenacity, the Catalunya (Barcelona) Marathon still has plenty to offer. The marathon covers about 80% of the route taken by the 1992 Olympic marathon runners. It carries runners from the town of Mataró, along the Mediterranean coast, to the center of Barcelona, finishing in the Olympic complex at Pl. Marqués de Foronda. It is well supported in the many villages fronting the sea and in downtown Barcelona. And perhaps most of all, the race takes place in one of the greatest cities in the world. Columbus would be proud.

COURSE DESCRIPTION   The point-to-point marathon course contains very few turns since it follows the line of the sea for about 25 kilometers. Starting in Mataró at the Plaça Espanya, the course goes mostly on a gentle downgrade for the first 5K (with small bumps near 1K and 5K) as it threads its way toward the Mediterranean. Runners reach Carretera Nacional II, which they follow for the next 20K. Around 6K runners pass through the town of Cabrera, passing the beach near 7K. Pinched between the sea and numerous small towns as it approaches Barcelona, the course goes through Vilassar (9K), Premià (12K), El Masnou (16K), Montgat (19K), and Badalona (23K). Just prior to Montgat, the route rises about 65 feet over 2K, dropping down again near sea level by 20K. In Badalona (23K), the course gradually takes runners away from the sea through the commercial districts in Sant Adrià, climbing almost 65 feet on Avenida Guipúscoa (27K). Reaching Barcelona near 30K, you run behind the beach (Platja de la Mar Bella) at 31K. Before you pass between the large city park (Parc Ciutadella) and concrete Barceloneta after 35K, you have a 45-foot rise and fall, briefly viewing the harbor before turning into the beautiful city. Runners reach the city's most popular street, pedestrian La Rambla, with flower stalls filling its median, near 38K. Rounding La Rambla at stately Plaça Catalunya, runners head down the opposite side on a gentle decline, reaching the port and the statue of Christopher Columbus (Monument a Colom) before 40K. You now face undoubtedly the most difficult stretch of the race. With Montjuïc rising to your left, the course climbs over 100 feet up Avenida Del Paral-lel, turning toward the Olympic complex, and finishing in Pl. Marqués de Foronda.

CROWD/RUNNER SUPPORT   The marathon attracts solid crowds along its route, particularly in the towns along the Mediterranean and in central Barcelona. You find 13 aid stations during the marathon. The stations roughly alternate between water and sponges, and water and sports drink. Medical services also can be found along the course.

RACE LOGISTICS   Runners take special trains from Barcelona-Sants station to Mataró. From there, the start is about a ten-minute walk. The race provides the train schedules and ticket in your runner's packet. Leave your warm-ups in Mataró's Central Park, and pick them up in the finish area. After the race you need to find your own way back to your hotel. Poop-out vans take those runners unable to complete the race to the finish.

ACTIVITIES   Beginning Thursday evening and running all day Friday and Saturday, the race expo and packet pick-up takes place in Palau 12 in the Olympic complex. The pasta party is held at the expo on Saturday.

AWARDS   Every runner receives a T-shirt, and finishers receive nice paperweight-type figurines, certificates, and results books. The top three runners in each age group receive trophies, as do the top 15 overall men and top 10 overall women.

ELITE RUNNERS INFORMATION   Male runners with times under 2:15 and females under 2:45 may qualify for elite status at Barcelona. Elites typically enjoy free accommodations and travel expenses. Appearance money may be available for the best athletes.

ACCOMMODATIONS   You can reserve your hotel room through the race entry form. A wide range of hotel classes and prices are available (from about 8,000 ptas. to 19,000 ptas. per night for two people in a double room). For more info, call +34/3-304-3232 or fax +34/3-304-3326.

RELATED RACES   Barcelona also hosts a Mini Marathon on race morning.

AREA ATTRACTIONS   One of the world's most "in" cities, Barcelona offers something for everyone's taste and disposition. For a relaxing getaway from the hectic city, take a short train ride to the beach town of Sitges to the southeast of Barcelona.

LISBON HALF MARATHON

OVERALL: 89.9

COURSE BEAUTY: 9

COURSE DIFFICULTY: 2-

APPROPRIATENESS FOR FIRST TIMERS: NA

ORGANIZATION: 9

CROWDS: 6

RACE DATA

Overall Ranking:	34
Quality Ranking:	32
Quickness Ranking:	NA
Contact:	Lisbon Half Marathon
	Rua André Gouveia
	Lote A - Loja A/B
	1750 Lisbon, Portugal
	Tel. +351/1-757-2517
	Fax +351/1-757-0569
Date:	Generally third Sunday in March (March 15, 1998)
Start Time:	10:00 a.m.
Time Course Closes:	1:30 p.m.
Number of Participants:	16,000 in 1997
Course:	Point to point
Certification:	AIMS
Course Records:	Male: (open) 1:00:17
	Female: (open) 1:07:12
Elite Athlete Programs:	Yes
Cost:	US$15
Age groups/Divisions:	Open, 40-44, 45-49, 50-54, 55+
Walkers:	No
Requirements:	None
Temperature:	50° - 59° (10°C - 15°C)
Aid/Splits:	4 / digital clocks every 5K

HIGHLIGHTS   While this is predominantly a marathon book, we do include a few non-marathons, and we couldn't resist the Lisbon Half Marathon. At more than 15,000 runners, it is Portugal's largest long-distance race and its most significant draw for foreign runners. After taking the ferry over to the start, you join the thousands of other runners inching your way over the Ponte 25 de Abril ("April 25th Bridge") in a spectacular procession toward Lisbon. The race finishes at the Mosteiro dos Jerónimos, a gorgeous 15th-century monastery. If you are fast and can position yourself near the front of the pack, the course can produce some quick times.

COURSE DESCRIPTION   The Lisbon Half Marathon consists of an out and back to Baixa from Ponte 25 de Abril, and then an out and partial back to Belém. The race starts at the toll plaza of the Ponte 25 de Abril. Relish the spectacular view of Lisbon as you slowly make your way over the bridge. Upon entering Lisbon-proper, runners find themselves in Alcântara, winding their way to Avenida da India (which turns into Avenida 24 de Julho). Heading toward Baixa (the Lower City), Lisbon's center, the course passes the National Museum of Ancient Art as it follows the Tejo River. Just after the Triumphal Arch and Monument of José I on the Praça do Comércio, the route turns into Baixa on the lively Rua da Prata. Upon hitting Praça da Figueira (Fig Tree Square), runners quickly turn to beautiful Rossio (Square), with the classical Donna Maria II National Theater. Back down toward the river, runners retrace their steps to Alcântara, looping the

Doca da Alcântara (including crossing the metal bridge). Returning to Avenida da India, the course passes under the Ponte 25 de Abril, tracing the river the entire way to Belém. Among the points of interest on this part of the course: the Lisbon Fair, Electricity Museum, Praça Afonso de Albuquerque, and the Tower of Belém. The race now turns up and back to the finish at the stunning Jerónimos Monastery.

C R O W D / R U N N E R   S U P P O R T   The race estimates that 20,000 to 30,000 spectators line the half marathon route. The four aid stations (every 5K) provide water and sports drink. In addition, digital clocks give the elapsed time every 5K.

R A C E   L O G I S T I C S   You need to take a ferry from Belém's River Station to the race start at the head of Ponte 25 de Abril. Ferries leave every half hour from 7:00 a.m. to 9:00 a.m. Get there early because you do not want to hassle with the crowds trying to pry their way onto the final boat. After the race, you must take public transportation or a taxi back to your hotel, if it is not within walking distance of the monastery in Belém.

A C T I V I T I E S   There are plenty of race-related activities here. Pick up your race number at the expo held in the Electricity Museum in Belém, across from Belém's train station. If the race is not full, you can register there as well. The expo runs from Wednesday to Saturday before the race. Also at the expo, on Thursday, Friday, and Saturday evening is a pasta party. The race usually holds a concert on Friday night in the Electricity Museum. Warm up with the "Discoveries Route" breakfast run on Saturday morning. This 4K jaunt through Belém starts at Padrao dos Descobrimentos (Monument to the Discoveries). A mimosa breakfast in Mosteiro dos Jerónimos follows the run.

A W A R D S   Each runner receives a T-shirt and other goodies when they pick up their race packet. Finishers also corral a medal. The top 30 master men (40-44) receive prize money ranging from 150,000 escudos to 3,000 escudos. Men in each of the other masters categories (45-49, 50-54, and 55+) compete for 50,000 escudos for the winner, down to 2,000 escudos for 21st to 30th place.

E L I T E   R U N N E R S   I N F O R M A T I O N   If you are an Olympic medalist, World Champion, European Champion, or have similar credentials, you may be awarded elite status at the Lisbon Half Marathon. Among the possible perquisites are transportation, appearance money, lodging, entry, and prize money (including time bonuses). The top thirty men and women receive prize money. Males receive 1,000,000 escudos for first, 600,000 for second, 400,000 for third, 300,000 for fourth, 200,000 for fifth, 150,000 for sixth, 100,000 for seventh, 80,000 for eighth, 70,000 for ninth, 60,000 for tenth, 50,000 for eleventh, 40,000 for twelfth, 30,000 for thirteenth, 20,000 for fourteenth, 15,000 for fifteenth, 10,000 for sixteenth through twentieth, and 5,000 for twenty-first to thirtieth. Females receive 800,000 escudos for first, 300,000 for second, 200,000 for third, 150,000 for fourth, 100,000 for fifth, 60,000 for sixth, 40,000 for seventh, 30,000 for eighth, 20,000 for ninth, 15,000 for tenth, 10,000 for eleventh through twentieth, and 5,000 for twenty-first to thirtieth. Time bonuses tend to be paid in US$, ranging from $200 to $5,000 (men under 1:02:30 and 1:00:00 respectively) and $200 to $3,000 (women under 1:10:30 and 1:08:00 respectively).

A C C O M M O D A T I O N S   The host hotel for the Lisbon Half Marathon is the Meridian Hotel Park Atlantic, Rua Castilho 149 (tel. +351/1-381-8700; fax +351/1-387-0472).

R E L A T E D   E V E N T S / R A C E S   There are a galleon full of races on the Lisbon Half Marathon weekend. In addition to the Discoveries Route breakfast run mentioned above, there is a Mini-Champions Competition on Saturday afternoon for youngsters ages 8 to 14 at the Electricity Museum. A Mini-Marathon of about 7K starts with the half marathon.

A R E A   A T T R A C T I O N S   Lisbon (and Portugal) rewards visitors with a wide variety of attractions. Portugal is quite proud of its nautical explorations in years past, and some of the best places to see this pride are Mosteiro dos Jerónimos, Padrão dos Descobrimentos, and Torre de Belém. Lisbon has plenty of old neighborhoods that are wonderful to explore, including Alfama, Bairro Alto, Rossio, Baixa, Chiado, and Mouraria.

ROME CITY MARATHON

OVERALL: 97.6

COURSE BEAUTY: 10

COURSE DIFFICULTY: 5-

APPROPRIATENESS FOR FIRST TIMERS: 10-

ORGANIZATION: 9-

CROWDS: 9+

RACE DATA

Overall Ranking:	11
Quality Ranking:	22
Quickness Ranking:	84
Contact:	Rome City Marathon
	Italia Marathon Club
	Via Michelangelo Poggioli, 3
	I-00161 Rome
	Italy
	Tel. +39/6-445-6626
	Fax +39/6-446-2552
	E-mail: italiamarathon@geco.it
Date:	Generally third or fourth Sunday in March (March 29, 1998)
Start Time:	9:30 a.m.
Time Course Closes:	4:00 p.m.
Number of Finishers:	4,166 in 1997
Course:	Loop
Certification:	AIMS
Course Records:	New course in 1998
Elite Athlete Programs:	Yes
Cost:	US$50
Age groups/Divisions:	NA
Walkers:	No
Requirements:	18 years old & medical certificate
Temperature:	50° (10°C)
Aid/Splits:	7 / every 5K, halfway

HIGHLIGHTS The Rome City Marathon may be the greatest running tour in the world. Starting near the broken outline of the Colosseum, this tour includes the Forum, Trevi Fountain, Piazza Navona, Spanish Steps, Villa Borghese, and the Pantheon. Simply some of the greatest achievements of the past 2,000 years. Of course, they didn't have asphalt when these great monuments were built. Consequently, cobblestones litter this course like sand at the beach — they're practically everywhere. Everyone romantically speaks of Rome's original seven hills, and this course finds at least one of them, although you probably won't be feeling very frisky at that point (around 28K). Be aware, however, that at our press time, the Rome City Marathon is in turmoil from a hostile takeover. The new organizers changed the date at the last minute, leaving many foreign runners in the lurch. There are also rumors that they are working to change the course by removing the section through Villa Borghese, making it faster, but less touristic. We strongly suggest you contact the race for the latest information. If they can overcome their current struggles, the Rome City Marathon certainly has all of the raw materials necessary to surge to the top of the international marathon heap.

COURSE DESCRIPTION Entirely closed to traffic, Rome's loop course begins in the shadow of the Colosseum, one of man's most recognized monuments. Runners head down Via dei Fori Imperiali, passing the ruins of the Roman Forum on the left, and rounding Piazza Venezia and its massive lily-white monument to Vittorio Emanuele II (often referred to as the "wedding cake"). Now runners skirt Campidoglio (Capitoline Hill) and Palatine Hill (2K) before embarking on two out and backs, passing the Baths of Caracalla between 4K and 5K. The course circumnavigates the Colosseum at 8K, goes by Piazza Venezia at 9K, and heads down the shopping street of Via del Corso. The race dips into the side streets, taking runners past the incredible Trevi Fountain at 10K, returning to Via del Corso. After circling Piazza del Popolo (with its 3,200-year-old Egyptian obelisk of Ramses II), the course rounds the Augusteum and the Ara Pacis (Peace Alter) between 12K and 13K before lining the Tiber River until 16K. Crossing the Tiber River over the Milvio Bridge, runners now head toward green Villa Ada (20K). Just after 22K, you wind through the Olympic Village (22K to 25K), seeing the Flaminio Stadium just before 25K. The course now goes down Via Flaminia from 25.5K to 27K before turning into the beautiful Villa Borghese. Here, runners must surmount the largest climb of the race, about 180 feet over 2K. Runners savor the beautiful park until 30K, followed by the Villa Medici and the church of the Trinita dei Monti at the top of the Spanish Steps. Running down fashionable Via Sistina until Piazza Barberini, site of Bernini's graceful Tritone fountain, you make two right turns, and go through the Piazza di Spagna and its famous meeting place of Rome, the Spanish Steps (32K). Runners make another circuit around the Piazza del Popolo and Augusteum before trekking to gorgeous Piazza Navona before 35K. After looping around the wonderful plaza with its Fountain of the Four Rivers, you wind through the neighborhood and past the Pantheon between 35K and 36K. Piazza Venezia signals the start of a slightly shorter version of the first loop of the race. The Rome City Marathon finishes near the start under the steady gaze of the Colosseum.

CROWD/RUNNER SUPPORT In addition to the monuments pushing you along, approximately 700,000 Romans come out for the race. There are also orchestras, bands, theater groups, and other entertainment at various locations along the route. The aid stations start at 10K, and then occur every 5K thereafter. The stations normally provide water and sports drink. Sponging stations every 5K also help you keep your cool. Note that the split times likely will be given in Italian (as opposed to digital clocks), so bring your own watch.

RACE LOGISTICS You need to find your own way to the Colosseum for the race start, and from the finish back to your hotel. Public transportation includes the bus and subway.

ACTIVITIES You must collect your race packet at the Marathon Center in the Ostiense Air Terminal during the week before the race. The terminal is located at Piazza 12 Ottobre 1492. To retrieve your number you must bring your medical certificate, identification card, and your entry card (provided by the race after registration). The race often sponsors a number of cultural events the week leading up to the marathon. Check with the marathon office for more details. On Saturday evening, the marathon hosts a pasta party (not that you'll have trouble finding great pasta in Rome), and on Sunday night, attend the post-race party with live music and dancing (if you can walk).

AWARDS Each marathon entrant receives a T-shirt and other commemorative gift, while finishers also garner medals and certificates.

ELITE RUNNERS INFORMATION The top 30 men and top 20 women finishers earn prize money ranging from L15,000,000 to L100,000.

ACCOMMODATIONS There are thousands of places to stay in Rome, ranging from small pensione to luxury hotels. The race does not have an official headquarters hotel, so contact your travel agent for your lodging arrangements.

RELATED EVENTS/RACES Rome also runs a non-competitive Mini Marathon (7K) that goes over the first loop of the marathon route.

CHAMBORD MARATHON

OVERALL: 84

COURSE BEAUTY: 9

COURSE DIFFICULTY: 2

APPROPRIATENESS FOR FIRST TIMERS: 8

ORGANIZATION: 9-

CROWDS: 1-

RACE DATA

Overall Ranking: 68
Quality Ranking: 83
Quickness Ranking: 14
Contact: Marathon de Chambord
Christian Hurson
9 rue du Commerce
41000 Blois, FRANCE
Tel. +33/2-54 20 51 03
Fax +33/2-54 55 30 09

Date: Generally first Sunday in April
Start Time: 9:00 a.m.
Time Course Closes: 2:30 p.m.
Number of Finishers: 1,123 in 1997
Course: Two loops
Certification: F.F.A.
Course Records: Male: (open) 2:23:26
Female: (open) 2:54:10
Elite Athlete Programs: No
Cost: 120FF (Payment by Eurocheque)
Age groups/Divisions: ≤39, 40-49, 50-59, 60-69, 70+
Walkers: No
Requirements: Medical certificate
Temperature: 50° - 68° (10°C - 20°C)
Aid/Splits: 9 / none

HIGHLIGHTS Underneath it all, beneath your knit shirt and khakis, you yearn for a fairy tale, to live in a castle surrounded by forests, perhaps riding horses in your leisure time (which is always), or maybe even going on a hunt with 80 hounds. Let's face it though; you're a runner. So you do the next best thing and run the Marathon de Chambord, centered around the Loire Valley's most important château, Chambord. If you prefer fresh air and pastoral settings, the Marathon de Chambord is a great alternative to the Paris Marathon, usually held on the same day. Fairly fast, the two-loop course gently rolls through forests and contains about 10K on packed trails. Remember, course records are often a function of prize money. After the marathon, you can dream until dawn as you visit the Loire Valley's many châteaux tucked in the hills and along the bends of valley rivers.

COURSE DESCRIPTION This two-loop course starts and finishes behind the Château Chambord, a spectacular venue. Runners head to Route Charles X, a very gently undulating road that is lined by oaks and Norway pine on both sides. Near 6K, the course reaches the village of La Chaussee-Le-Comte, with its brown stucco houses and narrow lanes. After winding around the village until 7.5K, the route reaches waving farm fields, green and beautiful, with the wall of Chambord to the left. At 8.5K, runners enter the forests surrounding the area. Here the surface turns from paved to packed trail, mostly even, with only a few patchy spots. The course cuts through the forests for approximately 5K, first on Allee Jehan de Chatillon, and then on Allee de Boulogne, and finishing on Allee du roi de Pologne, where the road once again becomes paved. Near 13.5K, runners turn onto Route de la Bracieux, heading back to the château on a gently rolling lane. The castle suddenly bursts upon you as you exit the trees, but you must first make a brief loop to the right before you can actually reach the château. Runners then complete a second loop that differs only slightly at the start from the first.

CROWD/RUNNER SUPPORT Of course, in your fairy tale you don't imagine suffocating crowds of subjects, or you wouldn't have built your castle in the country. So don't expect huge bands of spectators here. There is some entertainment around the start/finish area, however, and the families of runners provide encouragement. Water stations are located every 5K, and sponge stations sit in between the water stations.

RACE LOGISTICS It is probably easiest to have a car in the Loire Valley. A good deal of parking exists around the château, where all race activities center.

ACTIVITIES Retrieve your race packet at the marathon village in Chambord on Saturday, 3:00 p.m. to 8:00 p.m., or Sunday from 6:30 a.m. to 8:30 a.m. The race hosts a pasta party at the château on Saturday evening, with two sittings. The dinner costs 50FF for adults and 20FF for children. After the race, enjoy jazz music and other entertainment.

AWARDS Each runner receives a T-shirt and special gift, while finishers also receive medals. Other prizes are raffled. Results are provided in the Nouvelle Republique, which participants receive. The top three age-group finishers also take home awards.

ACCOMMODATIONS In the past, three hotels have given special rates for marathon runners: Climat de France, 48 rue des 4 vents, 41350 Vineuil (tel. +33/2-54 42 70 22; fax +33/2-54 42 43 81); Tour Hotel, Sortie Blois rue de Montprofond (access from RN 152 route d'Orleans), 41260 La Chaussee ST Victor (tel. +33/2-54 78 48 98; fax +33/2-54 74 30 32); and Manoir Bel Air, 41500 Saint-Die-sur-Loire (tel. +33/2-54 81 60 10; fax +33/2-54 81 65 34).

AREA ATTRACTIONS The Loire Valley is a spectacular tourist area, particularly for the romantic. Scores of châteaux, ranging from fortresses to opulent hunting retreats, nestle the valleys, and many of the most spectacular are open to the public. The region also overflows with vineyards and wineries that you can tour and sample their product. And if you tire of the rural life, Paris bustles less than two hours away by either train or car.

PARIS INTERNATIONAL MARATHON

OVERALL: 94.8

COURSE BEAUTY: 10-

COURSE DIFFICULTY: 3+ (SEE APPENDIX)

APPROPRIATENESS FOR FIRST TIMERS: 10-

ORGANIZATION: 9+

CROWDS: 5-

RACE DATA

Overall Ranking: 16
Quality Ranking: 34
Quickness Ranking: 51
Contact: Marathon International de Paris
A.M.S.P.
8 rue Crozatier
75012 Paris, FRANCE
Tel. +33/1-53 17 03 10
Fax +33/1-53 17 03 13

Date: Generally first Sunday in April
Start Time: 9:00 a.m.
Time Course Closes: 2:40 p.m.
Number of Participants: 21,400 in 1997 (Limited to 22,000)
Course: Near loop
Certification: AIMS
Course Records: Male: (open) 2:10:03
Female: (open) 2:27:55
Elite Athlete Programs: Yes (contact race)
Cost: US$45/75/95 or 220FF/370/450
Age groups/Divisions: NA
Walkers: No
Requirements: 20 years old, medical exam within past year
Temperature: 50°F (10°C)
Aid/Splits: 8 / 1K, every 5K, halfway

HIGHLIGHTS   Before the swarm of tourists, and at the beginning of spring's refreshment, Paris celebrates with a marathon. Run entirely on the Right Bank of Paris, the Paris International Marathon takes full advantage of the city's natural beauty. Nearly 8 miles of the race hug the Seine River, while about 6 miles and 4 miles traipse through the city forests of Bois de Vincennes and Bois de Boulogne, respectively. Along the way, the course passes many of Paris' most familiar landmarks: the Arc de Triomphe, Louvre, Notre Dame, and Eiffel Tower. Although the crowds are a bit disappointing for a race of this size, the Paris International Marathon remains an exciting event in one of the world's most exciting cities.

COURSE DESCRIPTION   Not quite a loop course, the Paris International Marathon starts on the Champs-Elysees near rue Balzac. Behind you looms the Arc de Triomphe, and ahead of you lies a nice downgrade over worn cobblestones that shouldn't pose too much difficulty footing wise. If you can see over the people, place de la Concorde and the Louvre sit before you. Lined with cafes and shops and people, the Champs-Elysees is a fairly wide street, especially by Parisian standards. Near the 1K mark to the right are Le Grand Palais and Le Petit Palais. Going around the throbbing place de la Concorde, with its ancient obelisk heart, the Orangerie Museum is to the right. You exit the square at the 2K mark onto stylish rue de Rivoli, passing the Jeu de Paume and skirting the gold-tipped fence of the Jardin des Tuileries en route to the Louvre (3K). The cobblestones end here (although you have some brief encounters in other spots). The course turns right after the Louvre and then left onto the Quai Louvre along the Seine River where you have a small rise.

Here you pass Pont Neuf, the oldest bridge in Paris, while soon the twin towers of Notre Dame appear on your right. The 5K mark sits past the ornate Hotel de Ville. The race soon moves away from the river, up a gradual incline to the Bastille (6K), marked by the towering monument ahead. The Bastille Opera lies on your left as you descend on rue de Lyon. The course enters perhaps its least attractive section on Avenue Daumisnil (6.5K to 10K), rising about 45 feet to place Felix Eboue (near 8.5K), where the scenery improves somewhat. You now enter the beautiful Bois de Vincennes (10K to 20K), passing idyllic lakes and green expanses. From 14K to 16K there is a very gentle rise (about 35 feet), while the course falls about 60 feet from 17K to 19K. After exiting the park, the course continues to descend gently as it makes its way back to the riverfront (just after 23K). You now trace the Seine using the lower expressway directly on the river's edge, passing once again Hotel du Ville at 25K. You pass under Pont Neuf at 26K, admiring the Eiffel Tower and the Gare d'Orsay in the distance before you enter the Tuileries Tunnel. You emerge from the tunnel at 27K with the Gare d'Orsay immediately to your left and place de la Concorde to your right. This stretch includes a few tough, short bumps as you exit various underpasses. You come directly and dramatically opposite the Eiffel Tower at 30K. As the course moves onto Avenue du President Kennedy, you move slightly away from the Seine River to complete the 5K to Bois de Boulogne (35K to 41K). The race exits the park on Avenue Foch in spectacular fashion with the Arc de Triomphe towering ahead. The finish line lies about halfway up the avenue. You've come almost full circle, and hopefully you can exult in the spirit of the Arc de Triomphe and celebrate your great victory (unless the Paris International Marathon turned out to be your Waterloo).

CROWD/RUNNER SUPPORT The marathon attracts decent, but not great, crowds, particularly in the first 10K, along the Seine River, and at the finish. Aid stations are located only at every 5K (3.1 miles) so make sure you take aid at every stop. Kilometers are marked on the ground, and split times are indicated by digital clocks at 1K, every 5K, and the half marathon.

RACE LOGISTICS Paris is an extremely easy city to get around in, and you can exploit this fact to get to the Paris International Marathon. Use the Metro (subway) for your marathon travels. You can get to the race expo by using either the Trocadero stop or the Pont de l'Alma stop. The small, crowded (did somebody say smelly?) expo sits in the tent at the edge of the Seine River near the Eiffel Tower. Get to the race start using the George V, Charles de Gaulle-Etoile RER, or Kleber stops. You can easily figure this out once you get there using the ubiquitous Metro maps.

ACTIVITIES Not big on accompanying activities, the Paris International Marathon hosts only the small expo and a mediocre (but big) pasta party. This doesn't pose much problem, however, since the city offers plenty of bustle.

AWARDS All entrants receive a marathon T-shirt. Runners who finish under 5:40 also earn a medal and a certificate (which will be mailed following the race).

ACCOMMODATIONS A great "budget" area to stay near the Eiffel Tower and the race expo is rue Cler and its immediate surroundings (Metro: Ecole Militaire). Perhaps the best, most inexpensive place is the one-star Grand Hotel Leveque, 29 rue Cler (tel. +33/01-47 05 49 15; fax +33/01-45 50 49 36). Other options include: Hotel Mars (2 stars), 117 avenue de la Bourdonnais (tel. +33/01-47 05 42 30; fax +33/01-47 05 45 91); Hotel Bourdonnais (3 stars), 111 avenue de la Bourdonnais (tel. +33/01-47 05 45 42; fax +33/01-45 55 75 54); Hotel du Centre (2 stars), 24 bis, rue Cler (tel. +33/01-47 05 52 33; fax +33/01-40 62 95 66); and Hotel du Champs de Mars (2 stars), 7 rue du Champs de Mars (tel. +33/01-45 51 52 30; fax +33/01-45 51 64 36).

AREA ATTRACTIONS Simply one of the world's greatest cities, this section is completely superfluous for this race. Let's leave it at this: April is a wonderful month to visit Paris. Flowers bloom in the gardens, and the tourist population is comparatively light.

ANTWERP MARATHON

OVERALL: 87.9

COURSE BEAUTY: 9-

COURSE DIFFICULTY: 2-

APPROPRIATENESS FOR FIRST TIMERS: 8+

ORGANIZATION: 9

CROWDS: 5+

R A C E   D A T A

Overall Ranking:	47
Quality Ranking:	41
Quickness Ranking:	7
Contact:	Antwerp Marathon
	Schoebroekstraat 8
	3583 Paal-Beringen
	Belgium
	Tel. +32/11-45 99 81
	Fax +32/11-45 03 55
	E-mail: bverbeeck@cis.be
Date:	Generally second or third Sunday in April (April 19, 1998)
Start Time:	1:00 p.m.
Time Course Closes:	6:00 p.m.
Number of Finishers:	1,700 in 1997
Course:	Two separate loops
Certification:	AIMS
Course Records:	Male: (open) NA
	Female: (open) NA
Elite Athlete Programs:	Yes
Cost:	BF 1,000 / 1,300
Age groups/Divisions:	Male: 18-39, 40-44, 45-49, 50-54, 55-59, 60-64, 65+
	Female: 18-34, 35-39, 40-44, 45-49, 50+
Walkers:	No
Requirements:	18 years old
Temperature:	50˚ - 59˚ (10˚C - 15˚C)
Aid/Splits:	8 / digital clocks at 1K, 2K, 3K, 4K, every 5K, halfway, 41K

HIGHLIGHTS   Diamonds and shipping have established Antwerp as one of Europe's richer cities, and it shows. The marathon shows it off to you as you dash on the 11K loop through the downtown and the city's most spectacular square, gilded Grote Markt. The final 31K of the route go through the suburbs. As you might expect of a low country, the course is very flat and contains relatively few turns (31 to be exact) for a European race. Furthermore, the relatively small size of the field, combined with excellent organization, means you won't get stuck behind the herd. This translates into tremendous potential for good times, in both senses of the phrase.

COURSE DESCRIPTION   Runners complete two separate loops, an inner 11K loop through central Antwerp and an outer 31K loop through the suburbs. The race starts on broad, grand Frankrijklei, turning left (away from the center) on Maria Henriettalei. Skirting the triangular park, the race continues on main avenues as it heads south on Charlottalei, Belgiëlei, Koningin Elisabethlei, Jan Van Rijswijcklaan, and Binnensingel. Near 4K, runners angle for the Schelde River. The route follows the river for about 2K, and then turns into the old city center. Runners pass through Antwerp's most beautiful square, Grote Markt, after 7K, eventually reaching Italiëlei (which turns into Frankrijklei). After passing the start (near 10K), the course retraces its route past the park to finish the initial 11K loop. Instead of heading south, runners now go straight on wide avenues that parallel the highway ringing the city for about 5K (including a second stretch on part of Binnensingel). It is here (about 18K) where runners tour various Antwerp suburbs for 20K. Around 38K, runners turn right onto Binnensingel, and retrace their steps (from 10 to 15K) to the finish on Frankrijklei.

C R O W D / R U N N E R   S U P P O R T   The race brings out about 50,000 city residents to cheer on the runners. The strongest crowd support lies in the city center and on Frankrijklei, with scattered support in the suburbs. The aid stations (every 5K) offer water, sports drink, and Lipton ice tea. In addition, the race will place your personal bottle at the aid station you designate. Just bring your marked bottle to the designated stand in the Stadsfeestzaal on Sunday morning. In warm weather, sponge stands are added at several points along the way. Starting at 10K, medical posts are situated every 5K along the route should you have any physical problems. Each kilometer is clearly marked with large signs at each digital clock location or on the ground.

R A C E   L O G I S T I C S   The race does not provide any transportation to the start, but many downtown hotels are located within walking distance of the start and finish area. If you are staying outside of town, the start lies not too far from the train station. You can leave your warm-ups in the start area and then retrieve them after the race. Dressing rooms are available inside the Handelsbeurs (Meir), about a half mile from the start/finish. Following the marathon, shuttle buses take runners to the Wezemberg Swimming Pool where they can shower and swim if they like. Buses also return runners to the finish area.

A C T I V I T I E S   Each runner receives two tickets to the pasta party on Saturday evening in the Stadsfeestzaal Meir (Meir municipal banquet hall). You can pick up your race packet while there, or you can return on Sunday morning. After the race, massage and medical services are available in the finish area and at the Wezemberg Swimming Pool.

A W A R D S   Every runner gets a marathon T-shirt, while finishers also earn medals. The top ten men and women finishers receive special prizes, as do the top two men and three women in each of the masters categories. There is also a prize drawing for all of the participants.

E L I T E   R U N N E R S   I N F O R M A T I O N   Fast runners could be eligible for transportation expenses, accommodations, and appearance money (depending on your credentials) at the Antwerp Marathon. In addition, the race generally offers some prize money.

A C C O M M O D A T I O N S   DEMA Hotels usually offer special rates for marathon weekend (tel. +32/3-227-3829; fax +32/3-231-6707), many of which are located near the start and finish area. Other convenient hotels are: Hotel Colombus, Frankrijklei 4 (tel. +32/3-233-0390); Tower Hotel, Van Ertbornstraat 10 (tel. +32/3-234-0120); Hotel Terminus, Fr. Rooseveltplaats 9 (tel. +32/3-231-4795); Residence 1, St. Jacobsmarkt 85 and Residence 2, Molenbergstraat 9 (tel. +32/3-232-7675); and Hotel de Rosier, Rosier 23 (tel. +32/3-225-0140).

R E L A T E D   E V E N T S / R A C E S   Your family and friends can participate in the 11K Mini-Marathon, which takes runners on the scenic first loop of the marathon course.

A R E A   A T T R A C T I O N S   A beautiful, sophisticated city, Antwerp is the diamond center of the world, and home to Peter Paul Rubens. Be sure to check out the beautiful Onze Lieve Vrouwekathedraal, containing two of Ruben's better works. Also see the Koninklijke Musea voor Schone Kunsten (for more Rubens) and the Provinciaal Diamantmuseum (for your diamond viewing). The city center is full of beautiful buildings and pleasant cafes, particularly the area around spectacular Grote Markt.

HAMBURG MARATHON

OVERALL: 98.7

COURSE BEAUTY: 9+

COURSE DIFFICULTY: 3+ (SEE APPENDIX)

APPROPRIATENESS FOR FIRST TIMERS: 10

ORGANIZATION: 10

CROWDS: 9-

R A C E   D A T A

Overall Ranking:	6
Quality Ranking:	5
Quickness Ranking:	38
Contact:	Shell Marathon Hamburg
	Postfach 60 62 20
	D-22254 Hamburg
	GERMANY
	Tel. +49/40-61 67 73
	Fax +49/40-61 49 78
	E-mail: HLV.Shell_Marathon@t-online.de
	http://www.championship.de/shell_Marathon
Date:	April 19, 1998; April 25, 1999; April 16, 2000
Start Time:	9:00 a.m.
Time Course Closes:	2:00 p.m.
Number of Finishers:	10,006 in 1997
Course:	Loop
Certification:	AIMS
Course Records:	Male: (open) 2:09:57
	Female: (open) 2:27:24
Elite Athlete Programs:	Yes
Cost:	DM65/75/80
Age groups/Divisions:	≤30, 31-35, 36-40, 41-45, 46-50, 51-55, 56-60, 61+(W),
	61-65, 66-70, 71+ (M), wheelchair, In-line skaters
Walkers:	No
Requirements:	18 years old
Temperature:	45˚ - 61˚ (7˚C - 16˚C)
Aid/Splits:	15 (every 2.5K after 5K) / digital clocks every 5K

HIGHLIGHTS   Hamburg may not be on Germany's beaten tourist path; it is a large port city known for commerce not sight-seeing. Perhaps that is what makes the Hamburg Marathon such a pleasant surprise. Well known in Germany as one of the country's finest marathons, Hamburg follows a beautiful route through many of the city's nicest neighborhoods. The course includes the infamous Reeperbahn, the city lakes, and of course the port. Although not terribly difficult, the course nevertheless contains some hills, mostly concentrated in the first third of the race, and several sharp turns. Hamburg deserves its German reputation for excellent organization, which you can feel starting from the large sports expo to the race-day services. All-in-all, the Hamburg Marathon is one of Europe's best. Maybe one day, the tourists and foreign runners will figure it out.

C O U R S E   D E S C R I P T I O N   The race maintains three starts at the Hamburg Messe (Convention Center). The loop course heads straight for the Reeperbahn, one of the world's most famous red-light districts, on a very slight incline. Once on the Reeperbahn, runners have a gentle downgrade as they pass the sex shops and restaurants. At about 2K, runners face a good incline of 60 feet to 3K. The race passes through beautiful neighborhoods in Altona, Ottensen, and Othmarschen, turning on small, narrow Schlagbaumtwiete (about 6.25K) to head back toward downtown on Elbchaussee. Tree-lined Elbchaussee takes you along the water where you can soon see Hamburg's large container facility. Turning a pleasing mixture of residential and commercial, the street goes mostly down to 11K, passing the St. Pauli Fish Market (just after 9K). Paralleling the port and harbor, the route ascends slightly from 11K to 12K and then back down to 13K. Passing the main train station, you enter a tunnel for a short period. Around 18K, the course reaches its most stunning section: 3 kilometers along Außenalster, a city lake lined with gorgeous homes and buildings and filled on sunny days with sailboats. In the background on the left, the Hamburg skyline appears as you move around the lake. Before 20K, runners move away from the lake into a mostly residential area. Near 23K, you reach the Stadpark (city park). The race turns up again from 24K to 25K on Alte Wöhr and then another small bump over a railroad crossing. After a brief tour of a commercial park, the race once again turns into pleasant residential and park-like areas, including a small river (after 29K). Alsterkrugchaussee (33K to 35K) contains nice older buildings, as do the streets that follow until you reach the opposite side of Außenalster near 38K. With the lake on your left and gorgeous houses and foreign consulates to your right, this section makes for inspired running in the race's final stages. This helps because from 40K, the race heads mostly on an upgrade until 42K, where the last stretch goes slightly downhill into the finish at the Messe.

CROWD/RUNNER SUPPORT   Bring your earplugs if you do not like noise while you are running. The German spectators, boisterous and numerous, cheer you on with gusto, banging on pots and blowing in noisemakers. In all, about 250,000 exuberant Hamburgers come out for the marathon. Along the way, you have good support in the form of aid and water stations, manned by local firemen. Every 5K brings aid stations with water, some food, tubs for sponges, and bananas (after 20K). In between, starting at 7.5K, water stations supply water and tubs for sponges. In addition, each kilometer is clearly marked, and digital clocks show the elapsed time every 5K. The race uses the ChampionChip for race timing, so participants must either purchase, rent, or have their own chip.

RACE LOGISTICS   All three start lines are located near the Hamburg Messe, which contains a subway station for easy access. (Entrants receive a free ticket for public transportation on the Hamburger Verkehrsverbund.) There is some parking in the area around the Messe, but it may require some searching on race day. The race offers a baggage area for your warm-ups, and you can shower and change after the race in Hall 8 of the Messe.

ACTIVITIES   Race activities start with the large, excellent, three-day race expo at the Hamburg Messe. You also pick up your race package there. On Saturday morning there is an organized jog, followed by a breakfast buffet, free to marathon entrants. Saturday afternoon, you can carbo-load at the potato party at the Messe. Also on Friday and Saturday, you can preview the marathon route for DM10. Sign up at the marathon expo.

AWARDS   All marathon entrants receive a program and clothing bag, while finishers under 5 hours also receive a medal, certificate, and results book. You can purchase T-shirts at the expo. Special awards go to the top 6 overall male and female runners and the top 3 in each age group.

ELITE RUNNERS INFORMATION   Male runners with times better than 2:16 and females under 2:38 can try to get elite status at Hamburg. Among the perquisites for elites are free accommodations, travel expenses, and the chance to win prize money, including DM15,000 for first place and DM10,000 for a new course record.

ACCOMMODATIONS   Runners can book hotels through their race entry form. The race offers lodging in 4-star hotels (DM240 - DM280), 3-star hotels (DM140 - DM180), 2-star hotels (DM75 - DM100), private accommodations (DM45), and youth hostels (DM35).

RELATED EVENTS/RACES   On Saturday, in-line skaters can participate in a number of skating events. An in-line skating expo also runs concurrently with the marathon expo.

AREA ATTRACTIONS   A large, cosmopolitan city, Hamburg contains the usual big-city attractions like museums, shopping districts, cathedrals, and night life. For those who want to travel, Berlin lies a few hours to the east.

ROTTERDAM MARATHON

OVERALL: 88.6

COURSE BEAUTY: 7+

COURSE DIFFICULTY: 1+ (SEE APPENDIX)

APPROPRIATENESS FOR FIRST TIMERS: 10

ORGANIZATION: 10

CROWDS: 8

RACE DATA

Overall Ranking: 39
Quality Ranking: 10
Quickness Ranking: 2
Contact: Stichting Rotterdam Marathon
Postbus 9412
3007 AK Rotterdam
THE NETHERLANDS
Tel. +31/10-417 28 86
Fax +31/10-432 50 50
http://www.rotterdammarathon.nl

Date: Generally third Sunday in April
Start Time: Noon
Time Course Closes: 5:00 p.m.
Number of Finishers: 9,000 in 1997
Course: Loop
Certification: AIMS
Course Records: Male: (open) 2:06:50 (World Best)
Female: (open) 2:22:07
Elite Athlete Programs: Yes
Cost: Dfl. 82.50
Age groups/Divisions: Male: 18-39, 40-44, 45-49, 50-54, 55-59, 60+
Female: 18-34, 35-39, 40-44, 45+
Walkers: No
Requirements: 18 years old
Temperature: 54˚ - 59˚ (12˚C - 15˚C)
Aid/Splits: 16 / digital clocks at 1K, 2K, 3K, 4K, every 5K,
halfway and 1000 and 500 meters to go

HIGHLIGHTS The Rotterdam Marathon attracts runners with its fast course (the world's best time was set here in 1988), excellent race organization, and strong community support. These factors combine to make Rotterdam our second-fastest-rated race in the world. Rotterdam fills up on race weekend, and the city practically closes on Sunday for the race. The route itself is unremarkable, although it contains a few highlights such as the Erasmus Bridge and the waterfront. Probably most appropriate for those who want to focus on running a fast time, the Rotterdam Marathon uses the ChampionChip which helps reduce the time lost at the narrow start.

COURSE DESCRIPTION The Rotterdam Marathon's loop course starts and finishes in front of Stadhuis (City Hall), one of the few old buildings in central Rotterdam, on the city's main street, Coolsingel. The course heads toward the water on a slight incline, crossing the ultra-modern Erasmus Bridge, which resembles a sailing ship, at 1.2K. Runners have nice views while crossing the bridge, old houses to the left and the very industrial port to the right. Once you scream down the bridge at 2K, you follow the port until nearly the 5-K point. The course here is almost entirely flat and commercial until skirting a densely wooded park from 6K to 11K, passing the AHOY complex near 9K. After 11K, apartment complexes and commercial areas characterize the route (passing through the park near 13K) until 19K. Runners have a very slight upgrade on the out portion of the brief out and back on Olympiaweg, and a slight downgrade on the back portion. The route passes the stadium near 20K, rises slightly up a small bridge to 21K, and falls nicely after the peak to near the halfway point. At 22K, runners have a .5K rise of about 40 feet as they race through the grit to the Erasmus Bridge at 23K with downtown ahead. Upon crossing the bridge, the race heads to the right along the waterfront to 26K, passing the red Willems Bridge. After 26K, runners head away from the water toward the race hotel. The course begins circumnavigating a large, pretty park near 29K until 36K when the course retraces its steps past the race hotel, along the water, and up Coolsingel to the finish. This fairly scenic section is good as you pass fellow runners opposite you.

CROWD/RUNNER SUPPORT Rotterdam comes out for the marathon. Banners hang throughout the city proclaiming the coming of the race, and the city practically closes on race day. A mini festival pops up around the start/finish area with food, drink, and music. Not surprisingly, the crowds along the course are strong, if not swarming. You will find water stations about every 2.5K, with the stations every 5K offering sports drink in addition to water. A brass band and other groups entertain runners at several points along the route.

RACE LOGISTICS The start/finish sits near many of the downtown hotels, and is 550 yards from the main train station and bus station. If you are staying away from downtown, the Metro (subway) may be your easiest route to the start. You could also drive and park near the start if you can negotiate the closed streets. The race utilizes the ChampionChip for race timing; you may purchase or rent chips from the race, or you may bring your own.

ACTIVITIES Runners pick up their race packets on Friday, Saturday or Sunday before the race in a large tent at AHOY, the exposition and concert venue across the river from downtown. You may get to AHOY either by car or Metro. A fairly large race expo runs in conjunction with packet pick-up. The race is exploring the possibility of having a pasta party. Check with the race organization for the latest information.

AWARDS Every runner receives a T-shirt and program book, while finishers also receive medals and certificates. The top three finishers in each age group receive a cup and some prize money.

ELITE RUNNERS INFORMATION Rotterdam strongly recruits elite athletes. At the race's discretion, male runners with times under 2:13 and female runners with sub-2:30 times could be offered elite status. If you are given elite status, you will be taken care of, including accommodations. The race offers prize money and time incentive bonuses to top finishers.

ACCOMMODATIONS The Novotel Rotterdam Brainpark, K P vd Mandelein 150 (tel. +31/10-453 07 77; fax +31/10-453 15 03), serves as the race headquarters hotel. More convenient to the start/finish are: Hilton Rotterdam, Weena 10 (tel. +31/10-414 40 44; fax +31/10-411 88 84); Hotel Central, Kruisk 12 (tel. +31/10-414 07 44; fax +31/10-412 53 25); Inntel Hotel, Leuvehaven 80 (tel. +31/10-413 41 39); Scandia Hotel, Willemspln 1 (tel. +31/10-413 47 90; fax +31/10-412 78 90); Golden Tulip Rotterdam (Atlanta Hotel), A v Nesstr 4 (tel. +31/10-411 04 20; fax +31/10-413 53 20); Holiday Inn Centre, Schouwburgpin 1 (tel. +31/10-433 38 00; fax +31/10-414 54 82); and Savoy, Hoogstr 81 (tel. +31/10-413 92 80; fax +31/10-404 57 12).

RELATED RACE A large 10K, limited to 5,000 runners, runs after the marathon.

AREA ATTRACTIONS Rotterdam is not terribly interesting from the tourist's point of view. Bombing destroyed much of the city in World War II, and a boring, modern skyline replaced the old buildings. Happily, the Netherlands is a very small country, and Amsterdam lies a short distance to the north, and Antwerp and Brugge in Belgium are nearby in the south.

BELGRADE MARATHON

OVERALL: 80

COURSE BEAUTY: 8-

COURSE DIFFICULTY: 3+ (SEE APPENDIX)

APPROPRIATENESS FOR FIRST TIMERS: 8

ORGANIZATION: 9

CROWDS: 4

RACE DATA

Overall Ranking: 90
Quality Ranking: 51
Quickness Ranking: 54
Contact: Belgrade Stark Marathon
Humska 1
11000 Beograd
YUGOSLAVIA
Tel. +381/11-648-266
Fax +381/11-651-328
E-mail: maraton@beograd.com
http://www.beograd.com/marathon

Date: Generally fourth Saturday in April (April 25, 1998)
Start Time: 10:00 a.m.
Time Course Closes: 3:00 p.m.
Number of Participants: 200 in 1997
Course: Near loop
Certification: AIMS
Course Records: Male: (open) 2:12:27
Female: (open) 2:33:07
Elite Athlete Programs: Yes
Cost: US$25 (paid in cash when you pick up race number)
Age groups/Divisions: Male: Open, 40-49, 50-59, 60-69, wheelchair
Female: Open, 35-44, 45-54, 55-64, wheelchair
Walkers: No
Requirements: 18 years old
Temperature: 55° - 73° (13°C - 23°C)
Aid/Splits: 15 (every 2.5K after 5K) / none

HIGHLIGHTS   Many readers may think of Belgrade as a war-ravaged city to be avoided at all costs. Ripped asunder by civil strife. The current reality, however, does not support this view. Rest assured, Belgrade stands intact, and its marathon is internationally recognized. The varied course gives an interesting perspective on Belgrade and the Balkan region. Split between the old and new sections of the city, the route spends a fair amount of time along the Sava and Danube Rivers. Until very recently, this race was organized under incredible duress. The United Nations imposed strict sanctions against Serbia and Montenegro (the Federal Republic of Yugoslavia) because of their support of ethnic Serbs in the terrible war in Bosnia and Croatia. Among other things, the sanctions restricted international air traffic into Belgrade. As a result, foreign runners had to fly into Hungary, Romania, or Bulgaria, and make their way to Belgrade by bus. Happily, you can now fly directly to Belgrade and feel for yourself the intact city's warm welcome.

C O U R S E   D E S C R I P T I O N   Runners congregate in downtown Belgrade, between the City Assembly and the Federal Assembly buildings. The first 6K of the race course through old Belgrade, including a stretch on the city's longest street, Revolution Boulevard. Runners face a 100-foot upgrade between 1K and 2K, followed by a 260-foot decline from 3K to 5K. After this trip through the pleasant old city, you cross the Branko Bridge over the Sava River between 6K and 7K. The race now completes two laps of a 16.5K loop through new Belgrade. This basically flat (with a few overpasses), triangular-shaped loop consists of a mixture of suburban residential areas, and modern commercial buildings and hotels. It is run between the confluence of the Sava and Danube Rivers, mostly on wide avenues and boulevards. This section also affords great views of Belgrade's unique fortress, Kalemegdan. After completing the second 16.5K loop through new Belgrade (near 39K), you again cross the Branko Bridge into old Belgrade. The final 2K are fairly hilly, ending with a patch through a shopping district, and finishing in front of the venerable Moskva Hotel in Terazije Square. Note that the course is completely closed to traffic.

C R O W D / R U N N E R   S U P P O R T   The race supports runners with 15 aid stations along the route, each with water, sports drink, and first aid. Every 5 kilometers is marked by a large sign until 35K, after which every kilometer is marked. Bring your own watch since there are no digital clocks on the course. Most of the spectators gather in the neighborhoods in new Belgrade and in the old part of the city.

R A C E   L O G I S T I C S   Runners staying at the host hotel (the Hyatt Regency) are provided transportation to the race start and back to the hotel after the finish. The other recommended hotels (see below) are all within walking distance of the finish (about 50 yards) and the start (about 550 yards).

A C T I V I T I E S   You may pick up your race packet from the Registration Booth at the host hotel in the four days preceding the race. A small expo takes place next to the Registration Booth. A local restaurant hosts a pasta party on Friday evening, and a concert is typically held as well.

A W A R D S   Every entrant receives a race T-shirt, and finishers also receive medals. Prize money goes to the top 10 males and top 8 female finishers. The top 10 men generally receive:

US$10,000 for first, $6,000 for second, $4,500 for third, $3,300 for fourth, $2,200 for fifth, $1,200 for sixth, $800 for seventh, $600 for eighth, $500 for ninth, and $400 for tenth. The top 8 women currently receive: US$6,000 for first, $3,600 for second, $2,400 for third, $1,300 for fourth, $900 for fifth, $600 for sixth, $500 for seventh, and $400 for eighth.

ELITE RUNNERS INFORMATION Male runners with PRs of 2:15 or under, and female runners with times under 2:45 receive consideration for elite status. Elites may be offered travel expenses, hotel accommodations, appearance money, and/or free entry, depending on their credentials.

ACCOMMODATIONS The Hyatt Regency Belgrade, Milentija Popovica 5 (tel. +381/11-311-1234; fax +381/11-311-2234) serves as the official host hotel. Other convenient hotels include the A-class Moskva Hotel, Balkanska 1 (tel. +381/11-327-312); Hotel Balkan (B-class), Prizrenska 2 (tel. +381/11-687-466; fax +381/11-687-543); and Kasina Hotel (B-class). Contact the Kasina Hotel through the marathon office.

RELATED EVENTS/RACES Two other races run in conjunction with the marathon, both of which attract far more participants. The half marathoners run with the full marathon runners until 11K, where the half marathon course splits off and completes one shorter loop through new Belgrade before finishing in front of the Moskva Hotel. About 2,000 runners finished the half marathon in 1997. There is also a huge 5K Fun Run which attracts about 30,000 participants.

AREA ATTRACTIONS You definitely want to wander through the bohemian quarter of Skadarlija, perhaps Belgrade's most popular attraction. Steep Skadarska Street has preserved its authentic Old World look. Here painters sell their canvases, and Skadarlija actors, fortune-tellers, and musicians wearing straw boaters mill about. The area contains many well-known restaurants with traditional music and Serbian cuisine. Kalemegdan Fortress is Belgrade's oldest historical site and its largest city park. The name Kalemegdan refers to the large plateau surrounding the actual fortress. Located in the park are the Statue of Victor (Belgrade's symbol), the Military Museum, Forestry and Hunting Museum, Cvijeta Zuzoric Art Pavilion, several churches, a children's amusement park, sports grounds, restaurants, and the city zoo. Between Kalemegdan Fortress and Terazije Square (the marathon finish line) runs Knez Mihajlova Street, a pedestrian mall filled with shops and galleries. Finally, runners may be interested in spending some time in Ada Ciganlija, the island in the Sava River. This green retreat offers good running possibilities and a pebble beach for relaxing in warm weather.

This is the truth.

Some shoes are harder to take off than others. There comes that point, after 500 miles, or 600 miles, when you and your shoes have run your last mile together. And it's time to retire them to lawnmowing duty or weekend shopping errands. Some shoes are harder than others to take off that last time. Because, very simply, some shoes bring you better runs, better experiences, better memories. And if that sounds corny to you, it may be because you've never been in love with a pair of shoes.

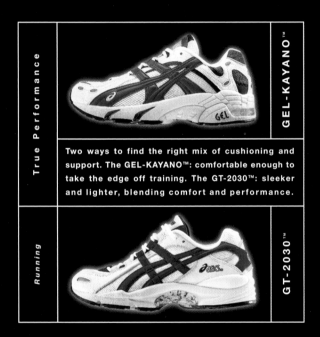

LONDON MARATHON

OVERALL: 99.7

COURSE BEAUTY: 8+

COURSE DIFFICULTY: 2- (SEE APPENDIX)

APPROPRIATENESS FOR FIRST TIMERS: 10

ORGANIZATION: 10

CROWDS: 10

RACE DATA

Overall Ranking:	2
Quality Ranking:	3
Quickness Ranking:	4
Contact:	The London Marathon
	PO Box 1234
	London SE1 8RZ
	United Kingdom
	Tel. +44/171-620-4117
	Fax +44/171-620-4208
Date:	April avoiding Easter (April 26, 1998)
Start Time:	9:30 a.m. (9:00 a.m. for elite women)
Time Course Closes:	2:30 p.m.
Number of Participants:	30,000 in 1997
Course:	Point to point
Certification:	AIMS
Course Records:	Male: (open) 2:07:55
	Female: (open) 2:21:06 (World Best)
Elite Athlete Programs:	Yes (contact the race)
Cost:	£55
Age groups/Divisions:	None
Walkers:	No
Requirements:	18 years old
Temperature:	50° - 54° (10°C - 12°C)
Aid/Splits:	23 / digital clocks every mile, every 5K, and halfway

HIGHLIGHTS   A huge and brilliant spectacle, the London Marathon brings out the best in London with its colorful runners and enthusiastic supporters. It is also one of the best organized marathons on earth, from aid stations to start procedures to transportation. Mostly run on fairly narrow two-lane roads, the course contains bright bursts of scenery, passing the Cutty Sark, Tower Bridge, Tower of London, House of Parliament, Big Ben, and Buckingham Palace. In between these sights, the course reminds runners of London's strong industrial past and present and the sometimes gritty reality of life in and around the city.

COURSE DESCRIPTION   One part spectacular tourist route and three parts other, the London Marathon boasts a very fast course. But mid- and back-of-the-packers may be slowed by the enormous crowd of runners on the narrow roads and tight turns, particularly in the first several miles, despite the three separate starts in Blackheath. The relatively few inclines and declines are gradual, with only a couple short exceptions. Beware of some speed bumps in the

early sections that may be difficult to spot amongst the throng. The first six miles go through mostly industrial/residential areas and a few village centers, dropping about 130 feet from mile 1 to 4. The lone scenic landmarks during this stretch are: the Woolwich Royal Artillery Barracks (which possesses the largest Georgian facade in Europe) before mile 3; and after mile 6, the Royal Naval Hospital, designed by Christopher Wren, and Queen's House, erected for Anne of Denmark in 1616. Near mile 6.5, runners circumnavigate the beautiful Cutty Sark, the 1869 tea clipper which held the record for the fastest loaded voyage from Australia to London. After a nice trip through attractive Greenwich, the route again becomes mostly residential/industrial, going through the Surrey Docks area from mile 9.5 to 11. The race now heads to the beautiful, brown-stoned Tower Bridge (mile 12.5), built in 1894. From mile 13 to 14, the course proceeds down gritty Cable Street, scene of clashes between the Blackshirts and Socialists during the 1930s. Just after mile 14, runners pass St. Anne's Church, built between 1712 and 1730. After cutting through residential Poplar, the race climbs a short hill to the Isle of the Dogs (miles 16 to 20), a business/industrial complex containing one of the tallest buildings in Europe in Canary Wharf. At South Quay, runners pass through the area damaged by an IRA bomb in 1996. Two more short hills await during mile 19, followed by a nice downhill entering a quarter-mile tunnel to mile 20. Tobacco Dock and St. Katherine's Dock mark miles 21 and 22, respectively; watch for the speed bumps which may be difficult to pick out. The course becomes quite narrow as it navigates around the race headquarters hotel. By mile 22.5, runners reach the famous Tower of London, home to English monarchs in past centuries. Race officials lay 6 feet-wide carpet for the quarter mile of cobbles as runners pass Traitor's Gate and The Tower. Be very careful, though, because many runners have tumbled in the Tower's shadow. Now the race prepares for its grand finale, getting progressively more scenic as tired runners head for the finish. Miles 23 and 24 pass through the City of London and the Billingsgate Market, the former fish market which still contains three feet of perma frost after centuries of cold storage on the site. Just prior to mile 24, the course heads down another quarter-mile tunnel, the Blackfriars Underpass, with a good hill leading up. Here the course turns extremely nice, with the River Thames to the left of the tree-lined road along the Embankment. By this time, Big Ben and the House of Parliament come into view, and as you turn on Great George Street and Birdcage Walk, there is one mile to go. At mile 26, runners round The Mall in front of Buckingham Palace, finishing on London's great ceremonial avenue on a slight upgrade.

CROWD/RUNNER SUPPORT The London Marathon is quite a sight. Noisy, enthusiastic crowds line most of the course and are especially thick in the small towns, around the Tower Bridge and The Tower of London, certain sections of the Isle of Dogs, and the last 4 miles. The race also contains great characters among its runners. Hundreds of participants raise money for charity by dressing up in outlandish costumes, such as Big Ben, a rhinoceros, sunflowers, cave men, and the opposite sex. If the crowds and the running entertainment aren't enough, live music pumps you up at several points of the race. The excellent aid stations, found every mile between miles 3 and 25, dole out entire bottles of water, and additional stations (at every 5 miles) also give out electrolyte replacement drink. Sponges are available at several spots. The mile marks are quite tall and readily visible, as are the 35 or so digital clocks around the course.

RACE LOGISTICS You can take the Tube (subway) to the Earls Court stop to reach the packet pick-up site and large race expo. While you could get dropped off near the race start on marathon morning, it is probably easiest to board the specially scheduled trains which take you within a ten-minute's walk of the various start lines. Pay careful attention to the train schedules for your particular start, contained in the information packet, since the last train leaves London about an hour before the race start. You can deposit your warm-ups in the race bag for pick-up after you finish.

ACTIVITIES The race hosts a large, four-day expo at Earls Court. You must retrieve your race packet during the expo. There is no official pasta dinner, but London contains plenty of eateries so carbo-loading should not be difficult.

AWARDS Every finisher receives a T-shirt and a medal. The race awards $295,000 in prize money, plus time and record bonuses. Veterans (men 40+ and women 35+) receive: $1,000 for first, $500 for second, and $250 for third. Prize money goes 12 deep for overall men and 10 deep for overall women with: (men) $55,000 for first, $30,000 for second, $22,500 for third, $15,000 for fourth, $10,000 for fifth, $7,500 for sixth, $5,000 for seventh, down to $1,000 for twelfth; (women) $55,000 for first, $30,000 for second, $22,500 for third, $10,000 for fourth, $7,500 for fifth, $5,000 for sixth, down to $1,000 for tenth. Men under 2:13 and women under 2:33 also receive a time bonus ranging from $1,000 to $100,000 for a world record. Runners setting new course records receive an additional $25,000.

HOW TO ENTER Each year over twice as many runners apply to enter the London Marathon as there are places. You must apply for entry before the end of October prior to the following year's race. For details on overseas entries call Sports Tours International (tel. +44/161-703-8161).

ACCOMMODATIONS The Tower Thistle Hotel, St. Katherine's Way (tel. +44/171-481-2575; fax +44/171-488-4106) near the Tower Hill Tube station, serves as the race headquarters. However, the hotel fills up incredibly fast. For alternative accommodations runners can call the marathon's travel agency, Sports Tours International (tel. +44/161-703-8161).

RELATED EVENTS/RACES London also runs a Mini Marathon (2.5 miles) for youngsters from London boroughs aged 11 to 17.

AREA ATTRACTIONS London contains scores of great tourist sights, but many find the best of London can be found in the various neighborhoods, such as Covent Garden, Picadilly, Soho, and Mayfair.

MADRID MARATHON

OVERALL: 95.7

COURSE BEAUTY: 8

COURSE DIFFICULTY: 4

APPROPRIATENESS FOR FIRST TIMERS: 9+

ORGANIZATION: 9+

CROWDS: 9+

RACE DATA

Overall Ranking: 13
Quality Ranking: 15
Quickness Ranking: 64
Contact: Marathon Popular de Madrid (MAPOMA)
c/ Linneo, 4
28005 Madrid
Spain
Tel. +34/1-366-9701
Fax +34/1-364-0313
E-mail: mguillem@stnet.es
http://www.mapoma.es

Date: Generally last Sunday in April (April 26, 1998)
Start Time: 9:30 a.m.
Time Course Closes: 3:00 p.m.
Number of finishers: 5,057 in 1997
Course: Near loop
Certification: AIMS & RFEA
Course Records: New course in 1998
Elite Athlete Programs: Yes (contact the race)
Cost: 5,000 ptas.
Age groups/Divisions: 18-22, 23-29, 30-34, 35-39, 40-44, 45-49, 50-54, 55-59, 60-64, 65-69, 70+, wheelchair
Walkers: No
Requirements: 18 years old
Temperature: 55° (13°C)
Aid/Splits: 8 / every 5K

HIGHLIGHTS Traditionally Spain's top marathon, both in terms of the number of runners and organization, the Madrid Marathon is unveiling a new course for 1998. The apparent goal of the change is to smooth some of the race's more difficult hills. Whether they are successful or not remains to be seen because the course had yet to be finalized by our deadline. Organizers assure us that the new course will follow about 85% of the old one, but just which 85% is unclear. The ratings above, therefore, are based on the old course, and given the apparent similarity between the two, we do not expect much difference. The overall high quality of the race and the strong support by Madrid's residents should remain constant.

COURSE DESCRIPTION Race organizers do know that the new course will start on Alcala Street (near the Alcala Door) and finish on Castellana Street by La Cibeles. These

areas are within walking distance of each other and lie near Parque del Retiro, Madrid's most popular city park. Like before, we expect most of the race to remain in the center city and through urban residential areas. Among the highlights of the old course (which may or may not remain) were Palacio Real (the Royal Palace), Puerta del Sol (the city's central plaza), and the sprawling park, Casa de Campo.

CROWD/RUNNER SUPPORT The new course should not affect the strong crowd turnout. Historically about 800,000 Madrid residents cheered runners on; quite a good showing. The runner support remains the same, however. Aid stations occur every 5K, with sponging points in between. The course is well marked with a dotted-blue line, and each kilometer is indicated by a tall sign at the side of the road.

RACE LOGISTICS You will likely have to find your own way to the start. The Metro stop Retiro is most convenient to the race start. The marathon provides a dressing area, including showers, and a warm-up drop-off spot. Note that Madrid uses the ChampionChip race timing system so you must pay a deposit of 2,000 ptas. when you pick up your race number and chip (unless you own your own).

ACTIVITIES Pick up your race number at the "Feria del Corredor" (Fair of the Runner) located at the host hotel, Hotel Convencion. The expo starts on Thursday evening and runs through Saturday night. Note that the expo takes a siesta from 2:00 p.m. to 5:00 p.m. The pasta party (free to runners) takes place on Saturday evening. You can buy additional dinner tickets at the expo. A post-marathon party rocks at a local disco on Sunday evening.

AWARDS Every runner receives a marathon T-shirt, and each finisher under 5.5 hours receives a medal and certificate. You can purchase the results magazine for 600 ptas. The top 3 runners in each age division take home trophies, as do the first 200 open men and the first 25 open women. The top 20 runners overall also earn prize money, provided they run under 2:30 for males and 2:50 for females. Prize money breaks down as follows: 100,000 ptas. for first, 75,000 for second, 50,000 for third, 30,000 for fourth, 20,000 for fifth, 10,000 for sixth through tenth, and 5,000 for eleventh through twentieth. An additional bonus goes to the runner who sets a new race record.

ACCOMMODATIONS The Hotel Convencion, c/ O'Donnell 53 (tel. +34/1-574-8400; fax +34/1-574-5601) serves as the official host hotel. A double room runs about 10,800 ptas. per night, while a single room costs about 9,525 ptas. per night.

AREA ATTRACTIONS Madrid is primarily known for two things: incredible museums and high-intensity night life. The most prominent museums are the world-renown Museo del Prado, Centro de Arte Reina Sofia (modern art), Museo de la Real Academia de Bellas Artes de San Fernando, Museo Thyssen Bornemisza, and Museo de la Ciudad. When you need a break, people watch at the Plaza Mayor or relax in Parque del Retiro.

TURIN MARATHON

OVERALL: 84.1

COURSE BEAUTY: 8

COURSE DIFFICULTY: 2+

APPROPRIATENESS FOR FIRST TIMERS: 8+

ORGANIZATION: 9+

CROWDS: 5-

RACE DATA

Overall Ranking: 66
Quality Ranking: 34
Quickness Ranking: 16
Contact: Turin Marathon
Via Ventimiglia, 145
10127 Torino
Italy
Tel. & Fax +39/11-663-1231
E-mail: turinmarathon@comune.torino.it

Date: Generally first or second Sunday in May
Start Time: 9:30 a.m.
Time Course Closes: 4:00 p.m.
Number of Finishers: 2,400 in 1997
Course: Loop
Certification: AIMS
Course Records: New course in 1998
Elite Athlete Programs: Yes
Cost: L80,000
Age groups/Divisions: 18-29, 30-34, 35-39, 40-44, 45-49, 50-54, 55-59, 60-69, 70-74, 75+ (M), 60-64, 65+ (F), wheelchair
Walkers: No
Requirements: 18 years old & medical certificate
Temperature: 52° - 59° (11°C - 15°C)
Aid/Splits: 8 / none

HIGHLIGHTS The Turin Marathon, Italy's oldest, assumes the often contradictory characteristics of the city and area, and is a pleasant surprise for many international runners. The race unveils a new course in 1998, a loop that takes the marathon back to its early days. The course passes through surrounding towns and the old city center, never letting you forget that Turin is one of Italy's most important industrial cities and also a great city of art and history. The race is well known as one of the fastest in Europe (the new course should not change that designation) and benefits from its friendly and professional race organization.

COURSE DESCRIPTION The marathon starts in southeastern Turin at the Palavela, a former sports arena. The race heads south to the edge of the suburb Moncalieri and then goes west. Passing through the towns of Nichelino, Borgaretto, Beinasco and Orbassano, the route turns north through Rivalta to Rivoli. Up to this point the race consists mostly of commercial areas, mixed with residential spots and countryside. Now runners turn east toward the city of Turin, entering it on Corso Francia. In the distance, runners can see Superga, site of the plane crash that claimed the Turin soccer team in 1949. Cutting through the city, the course enters one of Turin's four monumental entrances in Piazza Statuto. Closed on three sides by porticoes, the square features a monument commemorating the piercing of the Frejus Tunnel, a major feat of civil engineering. After passing through the square, runners head down shop-filled Via Garibaldi which connects Piazza Statuto with Piazza Castello. Runners skirt Piazza Castello, anchored by the imposing Palazzo Madama, and enter Via Roma, Turin's most famous street. Entirely rebuilt during the Fascist period, Via Roma's spacious porticoes are lined with elegant shops. The highlight of the course comes at Piazza San Carlo, often described as the "drawing room of Turin." This beautiful square is centered by the famous equestrian monument known as the bronze horse. Continuing through Piazza Carlo Felice (near the central train station), the course turns left on wide Corso Emanuele II to pleasant Valentino Park, one of Turin's favorite running spots. After the park, the race turns right on Corso Bramante, and then left on Via Genova on the way to the finish at the Palavela.

CROWD/RUNNER SUPPORT Historically, Turin has not drawn hordes of spectators like London or Berlin, but it is impossible to tell how the new course will affect crowd support. Expect decent crowds in the small towns and at different points in the city itself. The race offers aid stations every 5K and sponging points in between each aid station. Most aid stations hand out water and sports drink, while the final two also offer fruit candies.

RACE LOGISTICS You likely will need to get to the Palavela start on your own, although there may be shuttle buses from the train station. After the race, shuttle buses take runners from the finish at Palavela to the train station. For those runners who are unable to finish the race, shuttle buses are available at two spots to transport them to the finish area.

ACTIVITIES Runners must pick up their race packets at the marathon expo in the Palavela. The expo typically runs from Thursday to Saturday. On Saturday evening, the race has hosted a Marathon Show in San Carlo Square, featuring entertainment in a great setting. After the race, refuel at the runners' lunch inside the Palavela. You can also shower, have a massage, and obtain medical assistance.

AWARDS Each marathon entrant receives a T-shirt and other race goodies. Finishers earn a medal or some other souvenir.

ELITE RUNNERS INFORMATION The race offers A-level elite runners (2:12 for men and 2:33 for women) such enticements as transportation, hotel, expense, and possibly appearance money. B-level recruits (2:15 for men and 2:35 for women) typically receive hotel accommodations and free entry. Everyone has a chance to win some prize money. The top 10 men earn prize money ranging from L30,000,000 for first to L2,000,000 for tenth. Prize money for the top 6 women ranges from L15,000,000 for first to L1,000,000 for sixth. A L100,000,000 bonus goes to the runner who sets a new world record. Male and female masters runners over 40 earn L3,000,000 for first, L2,000,000 for second, and L1,000,000 for third. Top wheelchair athletes also win prize money.

ACCOMMODATIONS Most international runners go through the race staff to arrange accommodations in Turin. The race staff can secure lodging in a variety of hotels, ranging from youth hostels to 4 star luxury hotels. Double rooms typically range from L122,000 to L250,000. Staying near the central train station on Corso Vittorio Emanuele may make your race day logistics much simpler.

AREA ATTRACTIONS Turin may surprise the first-time visitor. It houses numerous important museums, including the well-known Egyptian Museum, and the Motor Museum which contains one of the most extensive automobile collections in the world. The Savoy Residences and many other buildings of historical and artistic interest embody the city and surrounding countryside.

COPENHAGEN MARATHON

OVERALL: 84.6

COURSE BEAUTY: 9-

COURSE DIFFICULTY: 2+

APPROPRIATENESS FOR FIRST TIMERS: 7+

ORGANIZATION: 8+

CROWDS: 4-

RACE DATA

Overall Ranking: 65
Quality Ranking: 75
Quickness Ranking: 20
Contact: Copenhagen Marathon
Århusgade 85
DK-2100 Copenhagen
DENMARK
Tel. +45/31-38 74 48
Fax +45/31-38 69 03
E-mail: sparta@sparta.dk
http://www.sparta.dk

Date: Generally third Sunday in May
Start Time: 9:30 a.m.
Time Course Closes: 3:30 p.m.
Number of Finishers: 4,705 in 1997
Course: Loop
Certification: AIMS
Course Records: Male: (open) 2:14:16
Female: (open) 2:35:48
Elite Athlete Programs: No
Cost: DKR 250/280
Age groups/Divisions: ≤19, 20-24, 25-29, 30-34, 35-39, 40-44, 45-49,
50-54, 55-59, 60-64, 65-69, 70+
Walkers: No
Requirements: 18 years old
Temperature: 55° (13°C)
Aid/Splits: 10 / none

HIGHLIGHTS   With a name like the Wonderful Copenhagen Marathon you have high expectations. After all, wonderful is a pretty strong word. When you go to Copenhagen, however, you realize that "Wonderful Copenhagen" is the city's promotional slogan. Ah, that explains it! You see, wonderful describes the city, not the marathon. Scenic and flat, the course runs in diverse areas of the city — the old central district, residential communities, city parks, and the harbor. But you cover much of it in relative obscurity for a big-city marathon. The crowds lack in both number and enthusiasm. Presumably everyone partied a bit too hard the night before in this notoriously entertaining city. You may have a few cars for company, though. The well-meaning volunteers don't have the same clout or fortitude to block traffic on the course as the police. Unfortunately, the race competes with neighbors Hamburg, Germany (about three weeks earlier) and Stockholm, Sweden (about three weeks later), both much better marathons. Like the name says, the best thing about this race is Wonderful Copenhagen.

COURSE DESCRIPTION The Copenhagen Marathon's circuitous loop course starts on Vester Voldgade, near the historic city center. Turning left at Rådhusplats, Town Hall Square, runners course up Vesterbrogade, past Tivoli amusement park and into older commercial and residential areas for much of the first 15 kilometers. On this section of the route, the nicest part lies near 9K where the course passes through a green parkway dense with trees and shrubs. Runners cover some streets two or three times. At 16K, the course returns to the start area for the trip to the north side of the city, first reaching Ørsteds Park and then the wide, pretty canals streaming through the city. After the brief stretch from about 18K to 22K through residential and commercial areas, the route traces the canal until about 26K. Then runners head toward large, mostly flat Fœlled Park (site of the race expo), which they circumscribe until about 30K. A trip past Ostre Anlœg, followed by mostly commercial and apartment buildings leads to Strandboulevarden near 36K. This wide street with a green median goes down with a gentle grade toward Churchill Park. After crossing a pedestrian bridge, you have a slight up-and-down as you approach the industrial harbor. You pass the Little Mermaid, although you probably can't see it since the road elevation is low. Winding up and away from the water, the road runs past the fort-like Kastellet and descends. Runners pass over some cobblestones as they head toward the water, and then follow the harbor edge in a scenic patch of the race. You can soon spot Amalienborg Plads (the royal palaces) to your right, after which you cross beautiful, rowdy Nyhavn, and you have slightly less than 2K left until the finish on Vester Voldgade.

CROWD/RUNNER SUPPORT We've already mentioned the sparse and quiet spectators along the Copenhagen Marathon course. Aid stations sit every 4K or so, and a few carry fruit in addition to the normal water.

RACE LOGISTICS You need to find your own way to the start. Many of the downtown hotels are located within about 1 mile of Vester Voldgade. After the race, there is bus service to Tivoli for the awards ceremony, but Tivoli lies only a short distance from the finish area. Otherwise, you need to get back to your hotel on your own. The race does provide a baggage drop for your warm-ups at Christiansborg.

ACTIVITIES You must pick up your race packet at the meager sports expo held on Friday and Saturday before the race. This expo is located in the Sports Arena in Fœlled Park. Available parking in the park can be tight. The subway will drop you about a mile and a half from the arena, if you feel like stretching your legs. Should you feel so inclined, you can eat pasta during the evening at the expo. The awards ceremony takes place in Tivoli amusement park; runners receive free admission to Tivoli following the race.

AWARDS Each runner receives a marathon T-shirt and program book, and all finishers under 6 hours get medals and certificates. There are also age-group awards.

ACCOMMODATIONS The area surrounding the train station offers the largest concentration of reasonably priced lodging. The area is also relatively convenient to the race start and finish. The one downside is that it borders Copenhagen's red-light district. Among the possibilities are: Best Western Mayfair Hotel, Helgolandsgade 3 (tel. +45/31-31 48 01; fax +45/31-23 96 86); and Best Western Webers Hotel, Vesterbrogade 11B (tel. +45/31-31 14 32; fax +45/31-31 14 41). Cheaper, but less convenient (and much more sterile), is the Hotel CAB INN, Danasvej 32-34 (tel. +45/31-21 04 00; fax +45/31-21 74 09).

RELATED EVENTS/RACES If you bring along the kids, they may want to run in the kids' race held on Saturday in front of the sports expo site.

AREA ATTRACTIONS Well known for its night life, Copenhagen offers plenty of jazz bars, night clubs, restaurants and drunk Swedes, here for the cheap (comparatively speaking) beer. Kids and adults alike will enjoy charming Tivoli. There is some good shopping along the pedestrian-only streets near City Hall Square. Nyhavn harkens to the Copenhagen of its sea-faring past. If you go in the evening, be prepared for revelers packed like a tin of sardines in beer.

PRAGUE INTERNATIONAL MARATHON

OVERALL: 90.1

COURSE BEAUTY: 9+

COURSE DIFFICULTY: 2+ (SEE APPENDIX)

APPROPRIATENESS FOR FIRST TIMERS: 9-

ORGANIZATION: 9-

CROWDS: 4

RACE DATA

Overall Ranking:	31
Quality Ranking:	59
Quickness Ranking:	18
Contact:	Prague International Marathon
	Zahoranskeho 3
	120 00 Prague 2
	Czech Republic
	Tel. +420/2-299163
	Fax +420/2-298197
	http://www.vol.cz/pim
Date:	Generally fourth Sunday in May
Start Time:	9:00 a.m.
Time Course Closes:	3:00 p.m.
Number of Participants:	2,000 in 1997
Course:	Near loop
Certification:	AIMS
Course Records:	Male: (open) 2:09:07
	Female: (open) 2:32:58
Elite Athlete Programs:	Yes
Cost:	US$45/70
Age groups/Divisions:	Male: 18-40, 41-45, 46-50, 51-55, 56-60, 61+
	Female: 18-35, 36-40, 41-45, 46-50, 51-55, 56-60, 61+
Walkers:	No
Requirements:	18 years old
Temperature:	66° (19°C)
Aid/Splits:	8 / none

HIGHLIGHTS The invasion of Prague begins every spring these days. Only now, the incursion comes largely from the West. At the end of May, runners join the fray, massing to the Prague International Marathon. The marathon's rather unique course loops through the center city two-and-one-half times and contains one long out and back along the Vltava River. Runners see many of Prague's most noted landmarks — the Charles Bridge, National Theater, Jewish Quarter, Prague Castle, and Old Town Square. The course runs over a mixture of cobblestones (on the city laps) and asphalt (on the longer section by the river). The great thing about this spring invasion is that it truly benefits everyone, the city of Prague and the marauding runners.

COURSE DESCRIPTION The Prague International Marathon starts on Wenceslas Square, the city's primary commercial center. A slight downgrade past old commercial buildings takes runners to the Vltava River at 1K. With the Prague Castle perched on the hill across the river, runners pass the statue-lined Charles Bridge (about 1.5K). The course runs through 3 city

quarters before crossing the river via the Legie Bridge at 6K. Runners now commence the 30K out-and-back section with two turnaround points. Heading south, the route races through several kilometers of fairly unattractive commercial areas before reaching the city outskirts. This gently rolling section turns green as it passes along the Vltava River. Runners return to the city center around 36K, and are treated to a great view of the Prague Castle. The race now completes the city loop once again. The loop may prove more difficult this time since you pass the street to the finish at 37K, knowing you still have 5K to go. The race boasts a terrific finish inside gorgeous Old Town Square, filled with people celebrating the runners.

CROWD/RUNNER SUPPORT Runners find most expressions of support during the center city loops, particularly along the river and on Parizska Street, the final stretch to the finish. The aid stations, located every 5K, offer water, tea, sugar, salt, and fruit. Every kilometer is marked by a sign along the roadside. Buses pick up those runners who must drop from the race.

RACE LOGISTICS The start and finish are within hobbling distance of each other. Runners must find their own way to the start, although many city center hotels sit nearby. Public transportation is free to runners on race day.

ACTIVITIES Pick up your number or register in the tent on Wenceslas Square during the week leading up to the marathon. The race currently does not have an expo or organized pasta party.

AWARDS Marathon entrants receive a T-shirt and magazine, and finishers earn a medal and certificate. Full results are available at an additional fee. The first European Union finisher receives a trophy from the EU. The top 3 masters runners (men over 40 and women over 35) receive prize money: US$1,000, $600, and $400 for men, and $600, $300, and $200 for women.

ELITE RUNNERS INFORMATION The race offers special inducements to male runners under 2:16 and female runners under 2:36, such as travel, expenses, lodging, and appearance money. Prize money totals about US$80,000, with the top 10 men earning from $18,000 to $500. The top 5 women receive from $6,000 to $1,000. An additional US$100,000 in performance bonus money is available, ranging from $1,500 for men under 2:12 and women under 2:32 to $50,000 for a world record.

ACCOMMODATIONS The race headquarters hotel is the Mövenpick Hotel Prague, Mozartova 1 (tel. +420/2-5715-1111; fax +420/2-5715-3131). Other possibilities include the moderately-priced and very convenient Evropa Hotel, Vaclavske Namesti 25 (tel. +420/2-2422-8117; fax +420/2-2422-4544); AXA Hotel, Na Porici 40 (tel. +420/2-2481-2580; fax +420/2-232-2182); and Harmony Hotel, Na Porici 31 (tel. +420/2-232-0016; fax +420/2-231-0009).

RELATED EVENTS/RACES Prague also offers shorter runs for the fitness minded. A 9K Fun Run starts at 9:45 a.m. on Wenceslas Square, and the 4.5K Children's Fun Run begins at 9:30 a.m. Both races finish in Old Town Square.

VIENNA CITY MARATHON

OVERALL: 86.1

COURSE BEAUTY: 8+

COURSE DIFFICULTY: 4-

APPROPRIATENESS FOR FIRST TIMERS: 8+

RACE ORGANIZATION: 9

CROWDS: 5-

R A C E   D A T A

Overall Ranking:	59
Quality Ranking:	44
Quickness Ranking:	62
Contact:	Vienna City Marathon
	Enterprise Sport Promotion
	Senefeldergasse 11 / DG / 15
	A-1100 Wien
	Austria
	Tel. +43/1-606-9510
	Fax +43/1-606-9540
	E-mail: vcm@asn.or.at
	http://www.asn.or.at/vienna_marathon
Date:	Generally last Sunday in May (May 24, 1998)
Start Time:	9:00 a.m.
Time Course Closes:	2:00 p.m.
Number of Finishers:	6,000 in 1997
Course:	Point to point
Certification:	AIMS
Course Records:	Male: (open) 2:09:28
	Female: (open) 2:30:49
Elite Athlete Programs:	Yes
Cost:	AS440/480/520
Age groups/Divisions:	18-29, 30-34, 35-39, 40-44, 45-49, 50-54, 55-59, 60-64, 65-69, 70+
Walkers:	No
Requirements:	18 years old
Temperature:	46˚ - 57˚ (8˚C - 14˚C)
Aid/Splits:	8 / every 5K by digital clocks

HIGHLIGHTS Long straddled between East and West, Vienna continues its balancing act to this day. The Vienna City Marathon straddles two of the city's waterways, the Vienna River and the Donau Canal, and takes in the downtown in between. The course landmarks give good insight into the nature of the race and the city. Not too long after running through the amusement park in Leopoldstadt, past the Ferris wheel and roller coaster, runners finish the race along the central Ring which contains many of the city's most grandiose buildings, including the City Hall, Opera House, Museum of Fine Arts, the university, Hofburg (the Hapsburg Palace), and Parliament. The solid race organization and the city's central location make it a good spring marathon bet for runners from the East and West.

COURSE DESCRIPTION   The race begins in front of the Schönbrunn Palace, a long yellow place with enormous grounds. Following the Vienna River, runners primarily pass old buildings as they head on a mostly flat road for the first 2K. The buildings become newer and the course becomes an easy downgrade near 3K, and then a slight upgrade near 4K. Runners cross the river before 5K and head back toward the city on the opposite bank on a very gently rolling road. The race passes the Schönbrunn Palace at 8.8K before crossing back over the river on its way to the downtown Ring. The course cuts through shopping districts from 9K to 13K, with a slight upgrade for the last 1K of this section. An easy decline leads runners to the Ring near 13.6K. Here you pass the Parliament, beautiful City Hall, Hofburg, the university, and Voltivkirche (Cathedral) in the nicest patch of the race. You turn right on Liechtenstein Strasse on a downgrade past old buildings (16K). Reaching 17K on Alserbach Strasse on a slight incline, the race turns right along the shady and pleasant Donau Canal. Runners cross the canal over the Urania Bridge just before 20K, continuing on the opposite bank. Near 23K, the course ducks into Leopoldstadt Park on Stadion Allee. This large green park is the site of many locals' daily run, an amusement park, stadium, and conference center. You head down Haupt Allee through the trees, going by 25K and reaching the amusement park near 26K. A nice jaunt amongst the roller coasters is followed by a trip around the Vienna conference center (Messe) complex, returning to Haupt Allee after 30K. The route now follows Haupt Allee through the trees in the other direction until it reaches the circle at Lusthaus. Runners circumnavigate the circle and retrace their steps to Stadion Allee (around 36K). Crossing the Stadion Bridge, you make your way toward the Ring and finish in front of gorgeous City Hall.

RACE LOGISTICS   The best way to reach the start is by public transportation (which you must pay for). Take subway line U4 to the Schönbrunn station. There is little or no parking near the start line. You may deposit your warm-ups in the marked vehicles for retrieval after the race. If you must have your own liquid concoction, the race will transport it to the aid station of your choice. Bring your clearly marked bottles to the BP station in the start area between 7:00 a.m. and 8:00 a.m. There is no organized transportation from the race finish to the start line. You must either use public transportation or rely on your friends or family.

ACTIVITIES   On Friday or Saturday before the race you must pick up your race packet in the tent near Rathausplatz (City Hall Square), where you can also browse the small expo. On Saturday evening the race holds a carbo-load party in the Festival Hall of the Vienna City Hall. After the race you may get a massage or take a shower in the tents past the finish area. The awards ceremony takes place in the expo tent at 4:00 p.m. Note that awards will not be mailed, so if you did well, attend the ceremony.

AWARDS   All finishers receive T-shirts and medals. Each finisher also receives a results book and certificate by mail. The top three male runners receive prize money: US$13,000 for first, $8,000 for second, and $5,000 for third. The top three women earn $6,000 for first, $3,000 for second, and $1,500 for third. The top 3 age-group finishers receive trophies.

ELITE RUNNERS INFORMATION   The race recruits elite runners on an individual basis. Interested runners should contact the Elite Runners Coordinator, Mr. Johannes Langer (tel. & fax +43/6245-76733).

ACCOMMODATIONS   Each year the marathon works with a number of hotels to provide special rates for marathon weekend. Contact the race directly for the latest information, or check out their web page.

RELATED EVENTS/RACES   If you happen to be in Vienna around marathon time, but are not quite in marathon shape, you may want to consider the 14.5K race. Kids aged 6 to 15 can enter the 2.5K Mini Marathon. Four friends can band together for the marathon relay with legs of 15K, 4.7K, 11.8K, and 10.695K.

STOCKHOLM MARATHON

OVERALL: 100

COURSE BEAUTY: 10-

COURSE DIFFICULTY: 4 (SEE APPENDIX)

APPROPRIATENESS FOR FIRST TIMERS: 10-

ORGANIZATION: 10-

CROWDS: 8

RACE DATA

Overall Ranking:	1
Quality Ranking:	13
Quickness Ranking:	65
Contact:	Stockholm Marathon
	Box 10023
	S-10055 Stockholm
	Sweden
	Tel. +46/8-667-1930
	Fax +46/8-664-3822
	E-mail: info@marathon.se
	http://www.marathon.se
Date:	Generally first Saturday or Sunday in June
Start Time:	2:00 p.m.
Time Course Closes:	8:00 p.m.
Number of Finishers:	11,000 in 1997
Course:	Two loops
Certification:	AIMS & Swedish Athletic Association
Course Records:	Male: (open) 2:11:37
	Female: (open) 2:28:24
Elite Athlete Programs:	Yes
Cost:	SEK 375
Age groups/Divisions:	17-39, 40-44, 45-49, 50-54, 55-59, 60+
Walkers:	No
Requirements:	17 years old
Temperature:	62° (17°C)
Aid/Splits:	14 / digital clocks at 5K, 10K, 15K, 20K, halfway, 25K, 30K, 35K, 40K

HIGHLIGHTS Scandinavia is a land of extremes — extremely dark and chilly in the winter and a sun that fires well into the night during the summer months. A land of high costs and high beauty, and Sweden is no exception. Therefore, it should come as no surprise that the Stockholm Marathon is exceptional — gorgeous, well-organized, boisterous, and somewhat unique for its late afternoon hours — so exceptional in fact that it ranks as our top-rated destination marathon in the world. This large race serves as a remarkable tribute to the hearty people who must endure training in the long, dark winter, bursting out into the summer afternoon in celebration. The two-loop course (with a longer first loop) weaves mostly in the city center, taking full advantage of the city's spectacular location along the Baltic waters, passing buildings ranging from medieval to modern, and finishing on the track that has witnessed 81 world track records inside

the wonderful, low-slung, red-brick 1912 Olympic Stadium filled to its brim with spectators.

C O U R S E   D E S C R I P T I O N   The Stockholm Marathon starts adjacent to the 1912 Olympic Stadium on Lidingövägen. With the very large number of runners, expect delays crossing the starting line particularly if your group starts near the rear of the pack. The course quickly turns on Valhallavägen, a broad street with a wide median swath and lined with older apartment and commercial buildings. Runners have a nice gentle downgrade on Valhalla for the first 2K until the circle at Oxenstiersgatan. Here you head toward the imposing Kaknästornet (radio tower) which looms to your right. The course turns more open and winding, with a short hill at 3K, and a decline at 3.5K. As you enter the woods at 4K, a slightly longer hill greets you, followed by a downgrade as you turn toward the tower at 4.5K. With some undulation, you round the tower and then head left on Djurgårdensbronvägen toward the beautiful royal island park of Djurgården. After crossing a narrow bridge to the island, runners face the largest incline so far, about 30 feet over a kilometer (.62 miles). Enjoy the scenery while running through the parks and woods over rolling paths and roads. Along the way you drift by Skansen (the world's oldest open-air museum), the Gröna Lund amusement park, and the Wasa Museum (Sweden's number one tourist attraction). As you exit the island, the brownstone Nordic Museum stands to your left, and then you cross the short bridge back to Stockholm proper at 8K. The course now heads down elegant Strandvägen, home to the Royal Dramatic Theater and the National Museum. Off to the left, moored boats rock gently, and in the distance lie Gamla Stan (Old Town) and Skeppsholmen in a gorgeous stretch of running. The course passes the harbor, followed by the commercial heart of the city, taking runners to medieval Gamla Stan by 10K. Runners have terrific views of Strandvägen to their left and the Parliament and blockish Royal Palace on the right as they cross the flat bridge to Gamla Stan. The course skirts Gamla Stan along the water providing a glimpse of the narrow passages of medieval Stockholm. The route quickly reaches Slussen on Southern Stockholm, tracing the water's edge as it heads west. Söder Mälarstrand provides awesome views of Gamla Stan, the Cathedral, and red-brick City Hall across the water. Near 14K, runners face the largest hill (about 90 feet) on the course as they cross the tough Västerbron. Savor the incredible city to your right as you lug up and then fly down the bridge. Soon back along the water, you pass City Hall at 17K. Briefly traversing a bike path, the course turns mostly commercial on Fleminggatan, which contains a nice upgrade before the turn onto St. Eriksgatan. Runners then face another steady incline up Odengatan near 20K until Odenplan (20.5K) at the University of Stockholm. Now it's a sharp downhill for almost a half kilometer, leading to another good uphill as you approach the turn onto Valhallavägen reaching the Olympic Stadium around 22K. Runners now begin the shorter second loop, which is identical to the first except that it cuts off the jaunt through Djurgården. Instead, the race heads straight toward Strandvägen, passing Nobelparken, home to many of the foreign ambassadors who live in the city, and the American Embassy. After passing the embassy you have a nice downgrade onto Strandvägen where the course resumes its original path.

C R O W D / R U N N E R   S U P P O R T   Typically, about 200,000 Stockholmers come out into the summer afternoon to cheer on the runners, making the marathon Sweden's biggest sporting event. The crowds are concentrated in the downtown area and the finish where 15,000 fans pack the 1912 Olympic Stadium. The race also provides excellent runner support in the form of aid stations every 3K or so (about 2 miles) and digital clocks every 5K and at halfway. Aid stations offer water, sports drink, fruit, candy, portable toilets, and first aid, and a sponge station sits just before each aid stand. In hot weather, the race organizers place showers at several points along the route.

R A C E   L O G I S T I C S   Perhaps the best way to get to the race start is by subway. Runners ride for free on race day by showing their bib number. Take the Stadion station exit and proceed to Östermalms IP, a stadium near the Olympic Stadium. You need to arrive by 1:30 p.m. Once inside Östermalms IP you will find the exit for your start group, signified by the color of your bib. The race places runners in different groups based on their previous marathon times in order to allow for a more orderly start. You may drop off your warm-ups inside Östermalms IP for retrieval after the race. There are limited changing facilities and showers near the start/finish area. Slower runners will be removed from the race if they do not pass through a series of checkpoints within the following time limits: just after 22K in 3 hours, 29K in 4 hours, and 32K in 4.5 hours.

ACTIVITIES The race holds a medium-sized expo in conjunction with registration and packet pick-up on Friday and on race morning. In the past, the expo has been held at the Olympic Stadium, but the race is looking into the possibility of moving it to the elegant City Hall. The pasta party, free to all marathon entrants, is held on Friday evening near the expo site.

AWARDS Each runner who finishes in less than 6 hours receives a finisher's T-shirt, nice medal, and certificate. Special awards go to the top three finishers in each age group.

ELITE RUNNERS INFORMATION Fast runners may be offered elite status at the discretion of the race director. Elites could be offered complimentary transportation, lodging, entry, and the opportunity to win prize money. Interested runners should send their resume to Anders Olsson at the marathon office.

ACCOMMODATIONS Be aware that lodging is rather expensive in Stockholm. The Stockholm Globe Hotel, Arenaslingan 7 (tel. +46/8-725-9000; fax +46/8-649-0880) serves as the official race hotel. A double room at the special race rate costs about SEK 800 — a good deal in Stockholm. Closer to the city center and race start are: Best Western Mornington Hotel, Nybrogatan 53 (tel. +46/8-663-1240; fax +46/8-662-2179); BW Wellington Hotel, Storgatan 6 (tel. +46/8-667-0910; fax +46/8-667-1254); and BW Stockholm Plaza Hotel, Birger Jarlsgatan 29 (tel. +46/8-14 51 20; fax +46/8-10 34 92). Cheaper options include the excellent hostels Af Chapman and Skeppsholmen Vandrarhem (tel. +46/8-679-5015 or 679-5017). Reserve far in advance to have any hope of scoring a spot in one of these little gems. You may also utilize the marathon's accommodation service (tel. +46/8-21 22 30; fax +46/8-21 22 44).

RELATED EVENTS/RACES On race weekend youngsters aged 7 to 16 can participate in the Mini Marathon with about 8,500 other boys and girls. The race distances range from 1.2K for the youngest to 4.1K for the oldest.

AREA ATTRACTIONS A striking city, Stockholm offers a huge array of activities for all tastes and ages, ranging from wild nature and the 24,000 island archipelago to museums and medieval Gamla Stan (The Old Town). In addition, a popular festival of restaurants, offering a "smörgåsbord" of food and entertainment, typically occurs on race weekend.

Stockholm Marathon

First weekend of June

★ Biggest marathon race in any of the Scandinavian countries with 12000 runners from all over the world.

★ Scenic course through down town Stockholm, and the royal park Djurgården.

★ Finish in the 1912 Olympic Stadium.

★ Ideal weather conditions. Average temperature 18 degrees Centigrade. Humidity 60 percent.

★ T-shirt, certificate and an exclusive commemorative medal to all finishers.

★ Free carboloading party.

For entry forms and further information please contact Stockholm Marathon, Box 100 23, SE–100 55 Stockholm, Sweden. Telephone: 46 – 8667 1930. Fax: 46 – 8664 3822. E-mail: info@marathon.se Internet homepage: http://www.marathon.se

LOIRE VALLEY MARATHON

OVERALL: 85.9

COURSE BEAUTY: 9+

COURSE DIFFICULTY: 2+

APPROPRIATENESS FOR FIRST TIMERS: 7

ORGANIZATION: 9-

CROWDS: 1+

RACE DATA

Overall Ranking: 60
Quality Ranking: 79
Quickness Ranking: 21
Contact: Marathon du Val de Loire
Office de Tourisme de Tours
78, rue Bernard Palissy
BP 4201
F-37042 Tours Cedex
FRANCE
Tel. +33/2-47 70 37 37
Fax +33/2-47 61 14 22 or
Tel. & Fax +33/2-47 64 12 38

Date: Generally third Saturday in June (tentative)
Start Time: 9:00 a.m.
Time Course Closes: 2:30 p.m.
Number of Participants: Limited to 1,200 runners
Course: Point to point
Certification: NA
Course Records: NA
Elite Athlete Programs: No
Cost: 100 FF (payable by Eurocheck)
Age groups/Divisions: NA
Walkers: No
Requirements: 18 years old
Temperature: 52° (11°C)
Aid/Splits: 8 / none

HIGHLIGHTS Many visitors to the Loire Valley insist that biking from château to château best captures the tranquil spirit of the place. Others prefer to motor around in a horseless carriage. But once every year, runners descend upon the valley to tour it the really old-fashioned way — on foot — in the Loire Valley Marathon. The marathon takes runners past three of the area's most noteworthy châteaux: Villandry with its sculptured garden; fairy tale-like Ussé; and idyllic Azay-le-Rideau. The "V" course navigates by the Cher, Loire, and Indre Rivers, whose banks the runners follow for much of the way. Although the course officially remains open for 5.5 hours, very few runners finish in more than 4 hours, making the tour better suited for faster runners.

COURSE DESCRIPTION The Loire Valley Marathon's V-shaped course begins in the garden of the Château of Villandry, and makes a quick tour of the town before heading toward the little Cher River through a brief tent of short trees near 1K. Runners soon reach the river levee with tree-dotted fields to the left. At 3K, runners go down and up a rough cobblestone lane for .5K and then come to the joining of the Loire River with the Cher. After a brief dip and rise at 6K, the course goes under the highway past farmland, coming along the river again near 7K. The tiny village of Les Roberts greets runners near 8K, followed by La Chapelle-aux-Naux, a typical village of brown buildings, at 9.5K. Then it's through the surrounding farmland until meeting up with the Loire River again at 14.5K. The church spire of Bréhémont (15K) rises ahead as you run along the levee. You pass through the small town and then soon make your way back to the levee until 22K, where you turn left for a 4.5K loop around Ussé at the bottom of the "V". After turning (just before 23K), runners encounter the most inspiring scene of the race, Château Ussé floating ahead. Going straight for the château, the course traverses two narrow bridges before finally reaching Ussé at 24K. After running through the château grounds, you tour the town of Rigny-Ussé until 25K, where you veer into the surrounding farms (on a packed dirt road for about 1.5K). Runners return to the levee road at 27.5K for about .5K before veering toward the village of Rivarennes (32K) on the final leg of the "V", including another kilometer on dirt road, and then through Quinçay. At this point the roads become busier, and after the village of Marnay (34K), the foliage turns very green with ivy crawling over stone walls. Runners reach the outskirts of Azay-le-Rideau at 39K, run through the grounds of the château at 41K, and then finish in the town center at Place de la République.

CROWD/RUNNER SUPPORT   Although mostly a rural race, runners find whiffs of support in the villages and châteaux along the route. Aid stations sit every 5K.

RACE LOGISTICS   Many runners find a car is the easiest way to get around. However, the race does provide other options. Shuttle buses leave from the tourist office of Azay-le-Rideau to the start at Villandry from 7:00 a.m. to 8:15 a.m. on race morning. Later that afternoon, buses go from the campsite in Azay-le-Rideau to Villandry. On race morning, you can leave your warm-ups at the parking lot of Villandry Stadium, and the race will transport them to the finish for retrieval. Runners may shower after the race at the campsite in Azay-le-Rideau.

ACTIVITIES   Pick up your race number at the tourist office in the city of Tours on Thursday or Friday before the race from 10:00 a.m. to 6:00 p.m. You may also retrieve your number on race morning near the start. On Friday, enjoy the local market in Azay-le-Rideau featuring food and wine tasting.

AWARDS   Every entrant receives a T-shirt, and runners who finish the tour also receive medals. Following the race, there is a random drawing for a variety of prizes.

ACCOMMODATIONS   The city of Tours offers the widest variety of accommodations. Contact the tourist office (tel. +33/2-47 70 37 37; fax +33/2-47 61 14 22) for information. If you prefer the smaller towns or to be more in the country, contact the tourist office of: Azay-le-Rideau (tel. +33/2-47 45 44 40; fax +33/2-47 45 31 46); Rigny-Ussé (tel. +33/2-47 95 55 85; fax +33/2-47 95 45 33); or Villandry (tel. +33/2-47 50 02 08; fax +33/2-47 50 00 90).

AREA ATTRACTIONS   The Loire Valley is a spectacular tourist area, particularly for the romantic. Scores of châteaux, ranging from fortresses to opulent hunting retreats, dot the valleys, and many of the most spectacular are open to the public. The region is also filled with vineyards and wineries that you can tour and sample products. And if you tire of the rural life, Paris is less than two hours away by either train or car.

MIDNIGHT SUN MARATHON

OVERALL: 83.1

COURSE BEAUTY: 9-

COURSE DIFFICULTY: 4-

APPROPRIATENESS FOR FIRST TIMERS: 8-

ORGANIZATION: 9-

CROWDS: 3-

RACE DATA

Overall Ranking:	78
Quality Ranking:	74
Quickness Ranking:	67
Contact:	Midnight Sun Marathon
	P.O. Box 821
	N-9001 Tromsø
	Norway
	Tel. +47/77-68 40 54
	Fax +47/77-65 56 35
	E-mail: post@msm.no
	http://www.msm.no/
Date:	Generally first Saturday in July
Start Time:	10:00 p.m.
Time Course Closes:	3:30 a.m.
Number of Finishers:	250 in 1997
Course:	Two separate out and backs
Certification:	AIMS
Course Records:	Male: (open) 2:20:56
	Female: (open) 2:47:25
Elite Athlete Programs:	No
Cost:	NOK 325/375
Age groups/Divisions:	18-29, 30-39, 40-44, 45-49, 50-54, 55-59, 60-64,
	65-69, 70-74, 75+, wheelchair
Walkers:	Yes, but note maximum time.
Requirements:	18 years old
Temperature:	50° (10°C)
Aid/Splits:	8 / none

HIGHLIGHTS One of the world's most unique running experiences can be found at 70° North latitude, 250 miles north of the Arctic Circle at the Midnight Sun Marathon in Tromsø, Norway. Run under the glow of midnight (assuming the weather holds) over a course that essentially consists of two separate out and backs, one along the edge of Tromsøya island, and one along the mainland shore. The steep bridge connecting the two provides a good challenge that must be conquered twice during the race. In the background rise the mountains that frame the city, known as the "Gateway to the Arctic." After the race, take advantage of the small city's surprisingly active nightlife, or head up to Europe's northern edge.

COURSE DESCRIPTION The Midnight Sun Marathon starts at night in downtown Tromsø at Kulturhuset (the Concert House) on Grønnegatan. At .5K, runners turn left on Strandskillet, heading toward the sea (1K). The course then runs along the water, past the harbor, until the Polar Museum at 2K. Here runners circle around to access the Tromsø Bridge, a steep span that should get your legs nice and warm. On top of the bridge, runners have a great view of the mountainous mainland and the new, modern Arctic Cathedral. After a blistering downhill, you reach the mainland (3K), and embark on the first out and back (you actually run on two parallel roads) down Solstrandveien. Here you have nice views of Tromsøya, the sea, and the distant mountains, turning around at 10K. You return on RV 8, go under the Tromsø Bridge near 16K, and make a short loop through the mainland harbor. At 20K, you scramble up the bridge and scamper down to Tromsøya. You now loop around to the right, past the Polar Museum, and then back along the water in front of downtown as before. The final section consists of a U-shaped out and back, mostly along the island's perimeter (23K to 42K). The turn-around loop at the airport begins near 30K. The finish line sits in Stortorget (Main Square) in downtown Tromsø.

CROWD / RUNNER SUPPORT As you might expect of a race held at night, the crowds are modest, mostly gathering in downtown Tromsø where they can see the runners at least twice during the various races. The runners from the other larger events also cheer on the marathoners. Runners can hydrate and refuel at the 8 aid stations located every 5K. The aid stations carry water and sports drink.

RACE LOGISTICS Tromsø is a small city of 57,000 residents, so getting to the race start should not be difficult. In fact, most downtown hotels lie within an easy walk of the start line.

ACTIVITIES Pick up your race package at Kulturhuset on Stortorget on Friday or Saturday before the race. You can register on race day. On Saturday morning, hang out with other runners at the Breakfast Race which features a short run followed by a light breakfast. The awards ceremony kicks off at noon on Sunday in the small theater (Lillescenen) in Kulturhuset.

AWARDS Every finisher earns a medal. Three-time finishers receive a silver medal, while five-time finishers strike gold (a gold medal that is). The top 3 marathoners under 2:30 for men and 2:55 for women receive NOK 10,000, NOK 5,000, and NOK 3,000 respectively. A NOK 2,000 bonus goes to the runner who sets a new race record. The top 3 in each age group (or top one-third, whichever is less) receive special awards. Note that the race will not forward unclaimed prizes.

ACCOMMODATIONS The Scandic Hotel (tel. +47/77-67 34 00; fax +47/77-67 67 40) serves as the official race hotel. Or you can contact the local tourist information office, Tromsø Arrangement AS, P.O. Box 311, N-9001, Tromsø, Norway (tel. +47/77-61 00 00; fax +47/77-61 00 10) for other possibilities.

RELATED EVENTS / RACES You can enjoy the midnight sun in several shorter races if you prefer. The possibilities include a half marathon (11:30 p.m. start), 10K (9:00 p.m. start), 4.2K Mini Marathon with its costumes and carnival-like atmosphere (8:00 p.m. start), and the children's race (7:30 p.m. start). In all, the five events attract about 3,500 runners to the far north.

HELSINKI CITY MARATHON

OVERALL: 89.7

COURSE BEAUTY: 9+

COURSE DIFFICULTY: 4- (SEE APPENDIX)

APPROPRIATENESS FOR FIRST TIMERS: 9

ORGANIZATION: 9+

CROWDS: 5-

RACE DATA

Overall Ranking: 35
Quality Ranking: 34
Quickness Ranking: 61
Contact: Helsinki City Marathon
Radiokatu 20
FIN-00240 Helsinki
Finland
Tel. +358/9-3481-2405
Fax +358/9-3481-2367
E-mail: sul.harraste@sul.slu.fi
http://www.sul.fi/helsinkicity/
Date: Generally end of July or in August (July 25, 1998)
Start Time: 3:00 p.m.
Time Course Closes: 9:00 p.m.
Number of Finishers: 4,427 in 1997
Course: Part loop, part out and back
Certification: AIMS
Course Records: Male: (open) 2:12:47
Female: (open) 2:36:14
Elite Athlete Programs: Yes
Cost: FIM 250
Age groups/Divisions: Male: Open, 40-44, 45-49, 50-54, 55-59, 60+
Female: Open, 35-39, 40-44, 45-49, 50+
Walkers: No
Requirements: None
Temperature: 61° - 68° (16°C - 20°C)
Aid/Splits: 20 / 5K, 10K, 15K, halfway, 30K, 35K

HIGHLIGHTS If you want to stray from the worn European marathon track, you should consider the Helsinki City Marathon. The race builds on the historic footsteps of Finnish distance running legends, including Paavo Nurmi whose statue inspires the waiting marathoners at the starting line. The afternoon start also gives the race that off-the-beaten-track feeling. In return for your adventurous spirit, the marathon offers a lot — a beautiful, rolling course that views the dark Baltic Sea for much of the way. Especially gorgeous is the stretch from 9K to 12K as the course island hops with stunning views of downtown Helsinki. The race also boasts typical Scandinavian efficiency and friendliness in its organization, including 20 aid stations for the 5,000 or so runners who have found their way north.

COURSE DESCRIPTION The rolling Helsinki City Marathon starts beside the statue of Paavo Nurmi, near the Olympic Stadium. The first 2K of the race roll around the

Olympic complex, including the stadium, swimming hall, ice arena, and Eläintarha track and field area. By 3K, the course follows Helsinki's main street, Mannerheimintie, before heading toward the water. After 4K, runners go along the water for much of the remaining way. At 5K, the route features its second-highest climb, about 60 feet over 1K, and then it's a good downhill to 6.5K. After a brief (1K) period away from the water, the route begins its trek along the thin strips of land surrounding the city. Runners face a couple of 35-foot hills at 8K and 10K, as they embark on the most spectacular part of the race from 9K to 12K. Here, the route goes from island to island via a series of bridges with downtown Helsinki off to the left. After 12K, the race turns back toward the city, still following the sea for much of the time. The 22-K mark sits in the heart of Helsinki in beautiful Esplanadi Park. After looping through the center of Helsinki, the course follows much of the same route back (24.5K to 31K). After 31K, runners head to the city of Espoo, still tracing the sea (31K to 35K). Just past 35K, the course retraces its steps again toward the city as it heads for the finish in Olympic Stadium. En route, you must surmount another good climb (about 60 feet) from 38.5K to 39.5K, then you have a great downhill from 39.5K to 41K.

CROWD/RUNNER SUPPORT The Helsinki City Marathon draws decent crowds (usually ranging from 30,000 to 40,000 people) along its course. Most of the spectators congregate in the downtown area, along Mannerheimintie, Esplanadi Park, the market place, and Kaivopuisto. The race also boasts plentiful aid stations, one every 2 to 3K. Each aid station carries water, sports drink, and juice; later stations also offer some food. Entertainment exists at several points during the race.

RACE LOGISTICS Runners staying at the host hotel can walk to the race start (about .6 miles). Others may have to find their own way to and from the race, which should not pose any problems. The stadium sits along the city's main street and is served by bus and tram.

ACTIVITIES Pick up your race packet at the expo on Friday or Saturday morning. The expo is held at the Olympic Stadium. On Friday evening, join the rice party next to the stadium, featuring music, race videos, and guest speakers. After the race, partake in the food and drink in the finish area at Olympic Stadium. You can also shower, take a sauna, or even swim at the swimming pool located a couple of hundred yards from the Olympic Stadium.

AWARDS All marathon finishers under 6 hours earn a medal, T-shirt, and certificate.

ELITE RUNNERS INFORMATION Runners with times better than 2:16 for men and 2:38 for women may be offered elite status, including free airfare on Finnair, accommodations, and possibly expense money. The race also offers about US$16,500 in prize money, with FIM 42,000 earmarked for the men and FIM 18,000 allotted to the women.

ACCOMMODATIONS The Sokos Hotel Pasilia, Maistraatinportti 3 (tel. +358/9-148-841; fax +358/9-143-771) serves as the official race hotel. The hotel is only about 1K from the race start and finish. You can make a reservation at the hotel through the marathon entry form.

RELATED EVENTS/RACES The race offers several events along with the marathon, including a 10K race, 3K Fun Run for children and adults, and 7K in-line skating event.

SIBERIAN INTERNATIONAL MARATHON

COURSE BEAUTY: 8

COURSE DIFFICULTY: 3 (SEE APPENDIX)

APPROPRIATENESS FOR FIRST TIMERS: 7

ORGANIZATION: 8+

CROWDS: 7+

RACE DATA

Overall Ranking:	86
Quality Ranking:	49
Quickness Ranking:	37
Contact:	Konstantin Podbelski
	Siberian International Marathon
	P.O. Box 41, Glavpostamt
	Omsk, 644099
	Russia
	Tel. +7/3812-24-25-67
	Fax +7/3812-24-27-23
	E-mail: Root@sim.omsk.su
	http://www.cocos.ru/SIM/sim.htm
Date:	Generally first Saturday in August
Start Time:	8:30 a.m.
Time Course Closes:	1:30 p.m.
Number of Finishers:	778 in 1997
Course:	Two loops
Certification:	AIMS
Course Records:	Male: (open) 2:13:02
	Female: (open) 2:32:15
Elite Athlete Programs:	No
Cost:	US$15
Age groups/Divisions:	≤39, 40-49, 50-59, 60-64, 65-69, 70+
Walkers:	No
Requirements:	None
Temperature:	64˚ - 73˚ (18˚C - 23˚C)
Aid/Splits:	8 / every kilometer

HIGHLIGHTS   Welcome to the new Siberia. Once a land of mystery and trepidation, Russia's immense backyard is remaking itself into a land of adventure and openness. Eager to show the world its fresh face, Siberia and its residents welcome visitors, and the Siberian International Marathon is a very important means to dispel any lingering myths about the area. Held in Omsk, centrally located along the Trans-Siberian Railway, the marathon's mostly flat, two-loop course travels through city streets and along the bank of the Irtysh River. The importance of the race is underscored by the fact that participants in the inaugural event in 1990 were the first outsiders to step foot in the city since the end of the Soviet period. While a bit remote, three hours by air or 48 hours by train from Moscow, those who make the journey are rewarded with wonderful hospitality and a memorable weekend of activities, including a three-day sports expo and an elaborate opening ceremony complete with musical performances, pizza party, and fireworks. They also get huge bragging rights on the next group run back home. Need more evidence of your warm reception? How about thousands of townspeople cheering you and the other athletes competing in the marathon and accompanying relay, 5-miler and kid's fun run. And you can leave the earmuffs and snowshoes at home; typical August temperatures range from 64° to 73°. Put in historical context, the Siberian International Marathon is an important part of the new Siberia and should be especially appealing to runners seeking new running frontiers.

COURSE DESCRIPTION The Siberian International Marathon features a two-loop course (one inside the other) through the Omsk city center and along the Irtysh River, passing more Lenin monuments than any marathon in the world. Starting in Central Square in Omsk, bordered by a large, grey former KGB building on the right and a beautiful fountain on the left, the route goes slightly uphill on Krasnyi Put (Red Way). At 1K, the route skirts the Pushkin Library, the biggest library in Siberia. Between 4K and 5K, runners climb 35 feet while running through the outskirts of downtown. Mostly flat through 14K, the course then descends 35 feet, hitting the Irtysh River near 15K. The next 6K follow the outline of the river, returning to Central Square near halfway. Runners follow Luba's Avenue, the city's most historic road, from 21K to 23K passing the 100-year-old St. Nicholas Cathedral and a couple of Lenin period monuments. Except for two bumps near 22K and 29K the race runs mostly flat during the second half. From 23K to 31K runners complete the big loop, running through more city streets and along the Irtysh River before retracing their steps along Luba's Avenue for the return to Central Square. After the 11K inner loop through the city center, the race ends at Central Square.

CROWD/RUNNER SUPPORT Race organizers estimate that 300,000 spectators line the SIM course, with the greatest number near the central square. Extra motivation springs from several music bands splashed along the route playing rock and folk tunes. Aid stations sit every 5K and contain water, cold tea and electrolyte replacement drink.

RACE LOGISTICS There are several ways to get to Omsk. The most popular route is through Moscow, a 3-hour flight. If time is not an issue, and you would like to see some Russian countryside, catch a train. A two-day trip from Moscow, the train ride takes you through central Russia, Ural, and Western Siberia along the famous Trans-Siberian Railway. On marathon morning, race organizers provide bus transportation from the hotels to the start. Return trips are available after the finish.

ACTIVITIES Pick up your race number at the three-day sports expo starting on Thursday at the city's expo center. Saturday brings the elaborate opening ceremonies held at the Omsk Stadium. The festivities continue following the marathon, with an awards ceremony and concert held at the Sport-Concert Hall.

AWARDS Every finisher receives a T-shirt and medal; a results book and certificate are mailed later. Prizes run ten deep for top male and female finishers, with overall winners earning a Russian Lada car. Others receive prize money with US$3,000 for second, $2,500 for third, and down to $500 for tenth. A course record carries a $3,000 bonus. Age-group winners also receive cash awards. All finishers have a chance to win special raffle prizes.

ACCOMMODATIONS The Mayak Hotel, ul Lermontora 2 (tel. +7/3812-31-54-31) serves as the official race hotel and is centrally located to all race festivities. More options include: Hotel Tourist, ul Tito 2 (tel. +7/3812 31-64-14); and Hotel Sibir, ul Lenina 22 (tel. +7/3812-31-25-71).

RELATED RACES The events do not stop with the pre-race activities. Race day affords non-marathoners the chance to compete in a marathon relay, 5-mile run, or kid's fun run.

AREA ATTRACTIONS Visits to the Dostoevsky Museum (he spent four years in exile here) and the Kreposts 18th-century forts share top billing with boat excursions on the Irtysh River as the area's major tourist attractions. Since you've made it this far into the Siberian heartland, consider boarding the Trans-Siberian Railway to Irkutsk, once known as the "Paris of Siberia." Only 64 kilometers from Irkutsk is Lake Baikal, set amongst some of the world's most beautiful countryside. Hiking, mountain biking, and boating activities abound in this natural paradise.

REYKJAVIK MARATHON

OVERALL: 84.1

COURSE BEAUTY: 9

COURSE DIFFICULTY: 3-

APPROPRIATENESS FOR FIRST TIMERS: 8

ORGANIZATION: 9-

CROWDS: 4

RACE DATA

Overall Ranking:	66
Quality Ranking:	59
Quickness Ranking:	32
Contact:	Reykjavik Marathon
	Laugardal
	Engjavegur 6
	104 Reykjavik, Iceland
	Tel. +354/588-3399
	Fax +354/581-3686
	E-mail: rmar@toto.is
	http://www.toto.is/rmar
Date:	Third or fourth Sunday in August (August 23, 1998; August 22, 1999; August 20, 2000; August 19, 2001)
Start Time:	11:00 a.m.
Time Course Closes:	NA
Number of Finishers:	116 in 1997
Course:	Two loops
Certification:	AIMS
Course Records:	Male: (open) 2:17:06
	Female: (open) 2:38:47
Elite Athlete Programs:	Yes
Cost:	US$30
Age groups/Divisions:	Male: 18-39, 40-49, 50-59, 60+
	Female: 18-39, 40-49, 50+
Walkers:	No
Requirements:	18 years old
Temperature:	54° - 57° (12°C - 14°C)
Aid/Splits:	8 / none

HIGHLIGHTS High up in the Atlantic Ocean there is an island nation known for short summers, hot springs, and beautiful people. It lies well off of the trans-Atlantic tourist path, which only intensifies the attraction of Iceland for many people. The small city of Reykjavik, Iceland's capital, hosts a marathon each summer to celebrate the country's outdoor lifestyle, clean, brisk air, and the long summer days. The race sports a rolling, two-loop course around downtown Reykjavik and surrounding areas, passing along the harbor and much of the city's coastline. In the background, runners are treated to beautiful views of the mountain ranges which frame the city. The race has two distinct feelings about it — a medium-sized event during the first loop with the half-marathon runners, and a small, quiet affair during the second loop when only a few runners continue for the full marathon. In the days after the race, the area's many hot springs provide a perfect antidote to the marathon pounding.

COURSE DESCRIPTION   Reykjavik's two-loop course starts in the city center on Frikirkjuvegur. Runners head west out of the city center on rolling roads for about 3K, before turning east along the seashore. Mostly flat, the race briefly moves away from the water through the narrow neck of the city, reaching a golf course just after 5K where the route rises 33 feet. Back on the water's edge, runners have beautiful views of the mountains north of the city. Near 9K, the course goes between Reykjavik Harbor and downtown, pulling just away from the water around 13K. The course turns rolling again and near 16K, runners turn back toward the city center, reaching it near 20K. After a brief period along the water, the route returns to the race start for the beginning of the second loop.

CROWD/RUNNER SUPPORT   Reykjavik does not attract significant crowds to the race. Approximately 2,000 spectators cheer the runners, mostly congregating near the start/finish area. The marathon provides aid stations to runners every 5K, offering water and sports drink. In warm weather, the race also sets up sponge stations. Every 5K of the route is marked.

RACE LOGISTICS   The compact nature of the city means that runners should not encounter any difficulty in reaching the race start.

ACTIVITIES   Pick up your race packet on Saturday before the race in City Council Hall. On Saturday evening, the race hosts a pasta party open to all marathon entrants. Runners can request a course tour from the Iceland Tourist Bureau, Skogarhlio 18 (tel. +354/562-3300; fax +354/562-5895).

AWARDS   All marathon entrants receive race T-shirts, and each finisher also receives a medal. The top 3 runners in each age group earn prizes, and everybody is eligible for the raffle drawing.

ELITE RUNNERS INFORMATION   Marathoners with times under 2:20 for men and 2:40 for women could be offered elite status, possibly including transportation to Iceland, accommodations, expenses, and free entry. The top 3 male and female finishers receive round-trip tickets on Icelandair, worth up to US$1,000. In addition, the runner who sets a new course record earns US$1,000.

ACCOMMODATIONS   The Iceland Tourist Bureau, Skogarhlio 18 (tel. +354-562-3300; fax +354-562-5895) can handle your accommodation requirements for the marathon. Lodging options include rooms in private homes, guest houses, and hotels.

RELATED EVENTS/RACES   Along with the marathon, Reykjavik offers a half marathon (one loop of the marathon course), 10K, and 3K Fun Run. The four races together attract about 3,000 runners, most of whom run the 10K, half marathon, and Fun Run.

JUNGFRAU MARATHON

OVERALL: 93.7

COURSE BEAUTY: 10+

COURSE DIFFICULTY: 9 (SEE APPENDIX)

APPROPRIATENESS FOR FIRST TIMERS: 2

ORGANIZATION: 9

CROWDS: 4

RACE DATA

Overall Ranking: 20
Quality Ranking: 51
Quickness Ranking: 97
Contact: Vreni Schild
Jungfrau Marathon
P.O. Box 41
CH-3112 Allmendingen/Bern
Switzerland
Tel. +41/79-421-9500
Fax +41/31-951-7562
E-mail: marathon@uniplus.ch
http://www.jungfrau-marathon.ch

Date: Generally first Saturday in September
Start Time: 9:15 a.m.
Time Course Closes: 3:45 p.m.
Number of Finishers: 2,387 in 1997
Course: Point to point
Certification: AIMS
Course Records: Male: (open) 2:55:07
Female: (open) 3:22:50
Elite Athlete Programs: No
Cost: CHF 75 (DM 85)
Age groups/Divisions: 18-19, 20-39, 40-44, 45-49, 50-54, 55-59, 60-64, 65+
Walkers: No
Requirements: 18 years old and early registration.
Temperature: 54° - 69° (12°C - 20°C)
Aid/Splits: 12 / digital clocks every 10K and halfway

HIGHLIGHTS Remember the spectacular scenery in *The Sound of Music*? Rugged mountain peaks, pristine meadows of edelweiss and wild flowers, quaint chalets, glistening waterfalls. Add a smattering of bell-ornamented bovines and you have Switzerland's Jungfrau Marathon — our highest-rated European race for both scenery and difficulty. Named from the white-robed Augustinian nuns of Medieval Interlaken, the Jungfrau (Virgin) Range includes the famous Eiger, Monch and Jungfrau mountain faces that loom over the start in Interlaken. While meandering steadily up paved roads over the first thirty kilometers, runners tour the small alpine villages of Gsteigwiler, Zweilutschinen, Lauterbrunnen and Wengen. The final twelve kilometers over steep mountain trails take you through the white moraine of glaciers frozen into the peaks. You probably will not be hearing any blissful noises as you struggle against the pitch of the mountain and the paucity of air (unless you enjoy the sounds of wheezing lungs and groaning bodies). Safely at the finish line in Kleine Scheidegg, however, you may finally be able to appreciate the crisp beauty of the place and even hear a few notes of joy and relief.

COURSE DESCRIPTION The point-to-point course begins at 1,850 feet in Interlaken (Switzerland's most popular tourist area) and finishes at 6,842 feet in Kleine Scheidegg, a mere halfway up the Jungfrau Range. Starting in front of the famous five-star hotel Victoria Jungfrau, the race embarks on an initial 3K loop through Interlaken, then skirts the lovely shore of Lake Brienz (the cleanest lake in Switzerland) at 6K. Here, the race veers west heading gradually uphill to the villages of Wilderswil (10K) and Gsteigwiler (12.5K). While flat landers will decry the 800-foot climb over the first half of the course, the real climbing is only just beginning. Runners enter Lauterbrunnen at the halfway point. Unique for the towering (over 1,950-feet high) rock walls that surround its village, Lauterbrunnen hosts the largest and loudest group of spectators along the route. Reminiscent of Alp Duez in the Tour de France, zealous spectators allow barely enough room for runners moving through. From here, the course continues past Trummelbachfalle, home of the tremendous Trummelbach Falls and Wengwald while ascending to the mountain village of Wengen at 30K. Famous for hosting the Lauberhorn World Cup downhill ski race and a huge marathon party, Wengen lies at 4,203-feet, meaning the course gains 1,550 feet from 20K to 30K with most of it com-

ing in the second 5K. Changing from pavement to narrow trail in Wengen, runners enter the most scenic yet difficult section of the course. Rising nearly 3,275 feet from Wengen to the 40-K mark at Eigergletscher (7,218 feet), the route's highest point, the race quickly transforms into a power walk for a majority of the competitors. In the final 2K, the course finally descends (330 feet), before ending in Kleine Scheidegg (6,842 feet).

CROWD/RUNNER SUPPORT While you might imagine that the point-to-point and rural nature of the course preclude substantial crowd support, the Jungfrau Marathon actually coddles spectators. Rail lines conveniently follow most of the serpentine marathon route. The trains offer an ideal environment for following the race by stopping at several of the most attractive points along the course. After departing from the Ostabahnhof train station in Interlaken East, your first destination should be Lauterbrunnen (you must depart here to catch the train to Wengen-Kleine Scheidegg) where you can see two stages of the race (20K and 25K). Next, you'll head to Wengen

(30K), only 15 minutes away by train, and join in the town's big marathon party. Near the 38-K mark, you disembark and view the race from Wixi before heading to the finish in Kleine Scheidegg. A team of announcers provide loud speaker race updates at key points along the course. Twelve aid stations provide drinks, soup, and food. Over 600 race volunteers patrol the route.

RACE LOGISTICS The start of the race is conveniently located in the heart of Interlaken. If you're staying in Interlaken, you'll have no problem walking from your hotel to the start. Those arriving by car should follow signs to the Marathon Car Park and catch the shuttle bus service to the starting area. The service, including parking and a return trip, costs CHF 5. Race organizers transport one piece of baggage per competitor to the finish line. Be sure to pack some warm clothes as cooler weather usually accompanies the finish. The marathon uses a computer-chip timing strap worn on the left ankle of each runner. After finishing, runners can relive their marathon adventure (or nap) while riding for free on the train going down the mountain.

ACTIVITIES Race festivities start Friday afternoon with number distribution at Casino-Kursaal from 1:30 p.m to 6:30 p.m. Youth races take place near the starting area at 5:00 p.m. Beginning at 6:00 p.m., many of the finer restaurants in Interlaken, Lauterbrunnen and Wengen open their doors for a pasta festival offering various dishes at a special price. The official opening ceremony occurs at the starting area at 6:30 p.m. Body massages are available at the fin-

ish, and an awards ceremony begins at 1:30 p.m.

AWARDS Every finisher receives a T-shirt, medal, certificate and results booklet. Prize money totals CHF 35,250 (including a trip to Japan for the Mount Fuji Climbing Race for the top male and female). The winners of each of the 16 categories receive attractive natural prizes. All finishers qualify for a random drawing, including a trip for two to the New York City Marathon.

ACCOMMODATIONS Several hotels in Interlaken and Lauterbrunnen offer special marathon rates. Your best bet is to call the tourist offices: for Interlaken call +41/33-822-2154 and for Lauterbrunnen call +41/33-855-1955. If you don't mind the inconvenience of being away from the start area, you may find less expensive housing in one of the smaller villages on the way up the mountains. Try Wilderswil Tourist Office (+41/33-822-8455) or Wengen Tourist Office (+41/33-855-1414).

RELATED EVENTS/RACES On Friday, youth races (1 to 2 miles) take place at the start area beginning at 5:00 p.m.

MÉDOC MARATHON

OVERALL: 97.6

COURSE BEAUTY: 9+

COURSE DIFFICULTY: 3+

APPROPRIATENESS FOR FIRST TIMERS: 10-

ORGANIZATION: 9+

CROWDS: 8

RACE DATA

Overall Ranking:	11
Quality Ranking:	19
Quickness Ranking:	42
Contact:	A.M.C.M.
	Maison du Vin
	33250 Pauillac, FRANCE
	Tel. +33/5-56 59 17 20
Date:	Generally first Saturday in September
Start Time:	9:30 a.m.
Time Course Closes:	3:30 p.m.
Number of Participants:	Limited to 7,500
Course:	Loop
Certification:	NA
Course Records:	NA
Elite Athlete Programs:	No
Cost:	300FF
Age groups/Divisions:	NA
Walkers:	No
Requirements:	18 years old
Temperature:	50° (10°C)
Aid/Splits:	22 / none

HIGHLIGHTS   Mardi Gras in motion. A 26.2-mile wine tasting orgy. A three-day fiesta, squeezed around a marathon. All of these phrases describe le Marathon des Châteaux du Médoc et des Graves. Meekly. This roving party follows the rolling hills of Médoc through the world's most famous vineyards. You run in the middle of a human circus that would make Barnum and Bailey proud: towering windmills, King Tut, the Pink Panther, Viking longboats, cross dressers, clowns, and bumblebees are a sampling of who and what you meet en route. Have you chosen your costume? Over half of the runners wear or push something off-stride, and you don't want to be the only one at the Halloween party in street clothes! And if you feel a little less than frisky in your tutu around 24 miles, slide an oyster or two down your throat from the on-course oyster bar, and finish it with a vintage white wine. That is, if you can still see straight after the 21 wine stops that came before. (Are you the one that drank all of the Lafite-Rothschild at 23K?) Of course, this utter madness does have a purpose — the costume contest judged by the 1,000 children plucked along the way. Behind the costumes and the wines sit some of France's most stunning estates, carefully crafted, and knotted grapevines bursting with fruit near the annual harvest season. In short, this race has more distractions and temptations for marathoners than Las Vegas has for members of Gamblers Anonymous! To be a part of this organized mayhem, you must enter extremely early, as it is France's most popular marathon. If you go there hoping to set a PR, don't bother going. Okay, so you take home your weight in wine if you win the race, but you miss out on the ambiance, camaraderie, and plain fun of the one marathon in the world that is meant to be tasted in sips.

COURSE DESCRIPTION   The race starts and finishes in the narrow streets of Pauillac, northeast of Bordeaux. Lined by vineyards and more than 30 of the world's most famous wine estates, the rolling course passes Lynch-Bages, Lafite-Rothschild, Mouton-Rothschild, Clos d'Estournel, Latour, and Pontet-Canet. As you wind past cafes in the city after the race start, you may find yourself caught behind an incredible bottleneck caused by a fire engine, giant windmill, Egyptian Sphinx, or Viking ship. You finally emerge from the pack, and head south for the first 8K, passing, among other things, Château Lynch-Bages and Latour. On the curve where the course changes directions to the north, runners pass the front door of brick Château Branaire Ducru. Snaking its way north, the course goes by several more estates, coming parallel with Pauillac near 19K. In the next several kilometers you come across some of the most beautiful châteaux in the region: Château Mouton-Rothschild, Château Lafite-Rothschild, and Château Cos d'Estournel. Those at the back of the pack may miss out on the Lafite-Rothschild tasting since it is usually the most popular stop, and they uncork only so much wine. Just after 30K, the route begins its turn toward home with several more estates in front of you, including Le Bosco, Tronquoy-Lalande, Montrose, and Haut-Marbuzet. Around 37K, runners begin the long, straight stretch to Pauillac. The oyster bar at 39K comes at just the right time to give you that extra spunk to trudge, weave, or swim your way home.

CROWD/RUNNER SUPPORT   A boisterous party before, during and after the race, the Médoc Marathon start is one of the most uplifting in the world. There is singing, chanting, yelling, and just plain merrymaking as you crawl through the city of Pauillac. The town's 1,000 children double as aid givers and judges for the race costume contest, and the runners *cum* entertainers do their best to play to the kids. The wine, of course, doesn't hurt the exuberance. The race has 22 conventional aid stations with water, biscuits, dried fruit, oranges, and sponges. Then there are the 22 wine-tasting spots, with some of the world's best wines offered to the runners. Some have meats and cheeses to go along with the red and white stuff. Then, of course, is the infamous oyster bar at 39K. To help circulate all that wine through your system, there are 15 massage stations along the route. All in all, you have never experienced this kind of runner support during a marathon!

RACE LOGISTICS   A car will make your stay in the region much more convenient, particularly with all of the dinners and activities associated with the race.

ACTIVITIES   The Médoc Marathon is a three-day party. The packet pick-up location seems to change every year so contact the race for the latest information. At 6:30 p.m. on Friday attend the "Milles Pate" Dinner held at a different château each year. This pre-race party is more boisterous than most post-race celebrations and should not be missed. Throughout the day, there are free visits to the region's châteaux and tastings by appointment. After the race on Saturday, there is the prize giving where the winners are hoisted onto scales to determine their weight in wine. At 7:00 p.m. is the "Sans Pate" dinner in the tents along the banks of the Gironde in Pauillac. At 11:00 p.m. that night, everyone celebrates with a fireworks show. Most races call it quits at the end of race day, but not here. On Sunday, trot or walk in the 9K recovery run which includes more wine tastings. After all of this partying, you will need a month to regain your equilibrium.

AWARDS   Every finisher receives a T-shirt, medal, and bottle of wine. Prizes are awarded for the best costumes as well as for age-group finishers. And, of course, the winners receive their weight in wine to make up for all of the wine they skipped along the way. The biggest award here, however, is the race itself and the good feeling you will have when you leave.

ACCOMMODATIONS   Contact the race (early!) for the latest on hotels offering special marathon rates. Note that if you go with an organized tour, you may be stuck staying mostly in Bordeaux, when you would rather be in the wine country. The key is to plan ahead.

AREA ATTRACTIONS   Isn't it obvious?

OSLO MARATHON

OVERALL: 87

COURSE BEAUTY: 9

COURSE DIFFICULTY: 3 (SEE APPENDIX)

APPROPRIATENESS FOR FIRST TIMERS: 8

ORGANIZATION: 9

CROWDS: 5-

R A C E   D A T A

Overall Ranking:	51
Quality Ranking:	44
Quickness Ranking:	38
Contact:	Oslo Marathon
	P.O. Box 5889 Majorstua
	N-0308 Oslo
	Norway
	Tel. +47/22-59 17 59
	Fax +47/22-59 17 50
	E-mail: oslomaraton@bislettalliansen.no
	http://www.bislettalliansen.no
Date:	Generally second Saturday in September
Start Time:	2:05 p.m.
Time Course Closes:	7:35 p.m.
Number of Finishers:	1,000 in 1997
Course:	Two loops
Certification:	AIMS
Course Records:	Male: (open) 2:31:59
	Female: (open) 2:56:48
Elite Athlete Programs:	No
Cost:	NOK 340/390/440
Age groups/Divisions:	17-20, 21-34, 35-39, 40-44, 45-49, 50-54, 55-59,
	60-64, 65-69, 70-74, 75+
Walkers:	No
Requirements:	17 years old
Temperature:	54° (12°C)
Aid/Splits:	8 / none

HIGHLIGHTS   The land of seafaring Vikings and fjords hewn by ancient glaciers cuts a very different swath today. Now anything but rough and tawdry, Oslo beckons with its clean nature and cool demeanor. The Oslo Marathon shows much of it to you, from 13th-century Akershus Slott to the modern Bislett Stadium, from the water of Oslo fjord to the Vigeland's sculpture garden. The race has a rather unique course — it is two loops, but within each loop is a 7K circuit through downtown that runners complete twice, meaning you become very familiar with the area by the fourth time around. The course is rolling with no particularly big climbs (the largest altitude gain is about 130 feet over 2.5K, which runners have to surmount four times during the race), but their cumulation could prove a bit challenging toward the end.

COURSE DESCRIPTION The marathon starts near Bislett Stadium (site of numerous track and field world records) and heads toward downtown for a 7K loop through the city which runners complete twice, passing the Royal Palace Park (Slottsparken). A gentle downgrade until 2K, the course hits downtown after the park, reaching the water of the Oslo fjord at Rådhusplassen (City Hall Plaza). The route follows the water, going by 13th-century Akershus Slott, rounding the Vippetangen Pier, and turning left onto Rådhusgata. Runners surmount a 35-foot hill and then pass City Hall before turning right on Amundsens gate toward the National Theater. Runners veer right at Oslo's main street, Karl Johans gate, and go past Oslo University near 5K. You turn off of Karl Johans gate, weaving your way northwest to Parkveien on a gentle upgrade, just above the Royal Palace Park, where you begin the loop again. After the second loop (and the third swing by Royal Palace Park), runners go right on wide Colbjørnsens gate (near 15K) to Frogner Park. Enjoy the tens of statues by Gustav Vigeland in the open-air museum as you move through the park, spying his most famous creation, the 65-foot obelisk of seething human forms, to your left. You leave the park behind and travel down Gyldenloves gate, retracing your steps until the left turn at Skovveien (which parallels Parkveien) as the course heads straight for Bislett Stadium on a mostly flat road. Upon whizzing past the stadium, full marathoners make a quick detour and then begin the second loop, giving them a second chance to catch the scenery they may have missed the first time around. The race finishes on the lightning-fast surface of the Bislett track, although most runners may be going at something less than world-record speed at this point.

CROWD/RUNNER SUPPORT The nature of the course means you have plenty of opportunities to check out the other runners in the race. You find aid stations at 8 points along the course. There are actually just two stations, but their strategic placement means you will pass them eight times, or roughly every 5K. The aid stations offer the usual fluid replacements.

RACE LOGISTICS Perhaps the best way to get to the race start is on public transportation. Among your options are bus, subway, and city train.

ACTIVITIES Pick up your race package at the runners expo held in the Radisson SAS Scandinavia Hotel, Holbergs gate 30. The expo is open on Friday and Saturday morning before the race. You cannot retrieve your number at the start area. On Friday evening the marathon holds a rice party. Pick up your ticket at the expo.

AWARDS Every finisher garners a medal. The top 10 in each age division earn special awards (up to one-third of each division's runners).

ACCOMMODATIONS There are three official race hotels that offer great deals for marathon runners on race weekend (about NOK 500). The Radisson SAS Scandinavia Hotel, Holbergs gate 30 (tel. +47/22-11 41 00; fax +47/22-11 30 17) serves as the expo and packet pick-up location. Otherwise, try the Radisson SAS Plaza Hotel, Sonja Henie Plass 3 (tel. +47/22-93 87 95; fax +47/22-17 73 00); or Radisson SAS Park Hotel, Fornebuveien (tel. +47/67-12 02 20; fax +47/67-12 31 10).

RELATED EVENTS/RACES Oslo offers two other races for the marathon disinclined, a half marathon (consisting of one loop of the marathon course) and a 5K through downtown Oslo.

AREA ATTRACTIONS Perhaps Norway's greatest attraction is its nature, which you can hike, raft, boat, sail, and canoe through. Many people love to hop on a cruise ship and view Norway's spectacular fjords from the sea; others prefer to hop on a train to picturesque Bergen (often detouring on the Myrdal to Flåm route) for some gorgeous mountain scenery before arriving at one of the country's most popular small cities. Oslo itself offers many museums, including Vigeland's sculpture garden in Frogner Park.

BERLIN MARATHON

OVERALL: 99.7

COURSE BEAUTY: 8+

COURSE DIFFICULTY: 2- (SEE APPENDIX)

APPROPRIATENESS FOR FIRST TIMERS: 10

ORGANIZATION: 10

CROWDS: 10

RACE DATA

Overall Ranking:	2
Quality Ranking:	3
Quickness Ranking:	4
Contact:	Berlin Marathon
	Waldschulallee 34
	D-14055 Berlin
	GERMANY
	tel. +49/30-302 53 70
	fax +49/30-306 22 03
	http://www.berlin-marathon.com
Date:	Generally third or fourth Sunday in September (September 20, 1998)
Start Time:	9:30 a.m.
Time Course Closes:	3:00 p.m.
Number of Finishers:	18,514 in 1997
Course:	Near loop
Certification:	AIMS
Course Records:	Male: (open) 2:07:02
	Female: (open) 2:23:44
Elite Athlete Programs:	Yes
Cost:	DM80/90/120
Age groups/Divisions:	≤30, 31-35, 36-40, 41-45, 46-50, 51-55, 56-60, 61+ (W), 61-65, 66-70, 71+ (M), wheelchair
Walkers:	No
Requirements:	18 years old
Temperature:	50° - 73° (10°C - 23°C)
Aid/Splits:	14 / every 5K

HIGHLIGHTS Running the Berlin Marathon is like the best kind of history lesson — well organized, very fun, and informative. One of the feetful of marathons that are a study of efficiency, Berlin also boasts supportive crowds and tremendous excitement. The course takes runners on a tour of Germany's past, recent and not-so-recent. Most striking, perhaps, are the stark examples of socialist architecture in the Eastern section of the city — often grand boulevards or squares framed by austerity and conformity — and realizing that the course would have been impossible to run 10 years ago. Now the city is changing almost as quickly as the route takes runners from Charlottenburg Tor to Kurfurstendamm. Construction cranes clog the city, but they should not slow you down on the swift course, flat but for gentle inclines between 27K and 34K. In all, Berlin is undeniably one of the best races in the world, our 2nd-rated destination marathon, and the best history lesson you've ever had.

C O U R S E   D E S C R I P T I O N   Not quite a loop course, the Berlin Marathon starts on Straße des 17 Juni at the Charlottenburger Tor, two stone gates guarding this grand avenue. Soon the Tiergarten surrounds the tree-lined road. At 1.3K, runners round a circle with a golden winged lady atop a soaring pedestal. Now you can see the hugely symbolic Brandenburg Gate, and by 3K runners enter the former "no-man's land" of divided Berlin, passing through the gate's columns at 3.2K. Entering the former East Berlin, runners head down its ceremonial boule-vard, Unter den Linden, which contains Humboldt University and a cathedral among its attractions. Near 5K, the course turns left onto Karl-Liebknecht Straße which features the Rotes Rathaus (Red Town Hall) and the soaring Fernsehturm TV tower at its end on Alexanderplatz. Here, runners real-ly begin to get a great sense of dour socialist-style architecture (6K to 11K). At 7K, the route goes right on Lichtenberger Straße which contains mostly austere apartment buildings. This entire area is under so much construction that it is impossible to discern what will emerge. Near 13.5K, run-ners begin to parallel the Landwehr Canal (13.5K to 15K) in commercial Kreuzberg, a popular nightspot. This stretch contains the first minor undulations of the race, but you will hardly notice them. Sonnenallee (18K) contains many restaurants and trees, and then runners turn on narrow Innstraße, on their way to Karl Marx Straße (19.2K), a nice street of old commercial buildings. You have excellent, attractive running for the next 4K. Mostly commercial for 10K, the course begins a gradual incline around 27K. After a 1K dip near 30K, the course ascends again (about 45 feet) on Unter den Eichen (passing the Botanical Gardens) and continues on Habelschwerdter Allee until about 33.2K. This very posh residential area (33K to 36.5K) dips slightly before reaching the course's highest point at 177.8 feet near 34.3K. Except for a slight rise near 38K, the rest of the course is either flat or a gentle downgrade, making for a fast finish. At 36.5K, the route reaches swanky Hohenzollerndamm, a nice wide street. About the last 2K of the race run down flat Kurfurstendamm, a primary commercial street, finishing in the shadow of the WWII-scarred Kaiser-Wilhelm-Gedachtnis-Kirche, now serving as a memorial.

CROWD/RUNNER SUPPORT Approximately every 5K, runners find full-blown aid stations with water, bananas, tea, and first aid. Starting at 13.5K, water-only stations also lie about every 5K making for a total of 14 fluid stations along the course. Support also comes in the form of spectators, about 800,000 of them. And German fans are known for being loud!

RACE LOGISTICS You need to find your own way to the start, although it shouldn't be too difficult. Near many downtown hotels, the start also lies near two subway stops (Ernst-Reuter-Platz and Zoolog. Garten). Bring your ChampionChip or rent one from the race since Berlin uses them for race timing.

ACTIVITIES Pick up your race packet at Messehallen on Messedamm on Thursday, Friday or Saturday before the race. You may view the course on Saturday for a 25DM/30DM fee. The pasta party kicks off on Saturday evening adjacent to the race expo. Finally, the race organizes a variety of tours and activities on race weekend. Ask for more information.

AWARDS All finishers under 5.5 hours receive a medal, certificate, and results book. If you want a T-shirt, however, you likely will have to buy one. The race hands out generous prize money to the top finishers (see below).

ELITE RUNNERS INFORMATION At the race's discretion, male runners under 2:13 and females under 2:32 could be offered elite status. Elites generally garner complimentary accommodations and travel expenses. Elites also vie for prize money. The top fifteen men receive the following: DM30,000 for first, 20,000 for second, 12,000 for third, 10,000 for fourth, 8,000 for fifth, 6,000 for sixth, 4,000 for seventh, 3,000 for eighth, 2,500 for ninth, 2,000 for tenth, 1,500 for eleventh, 1,200 for twelfth, 1,000 for thirteenth, 800 for fourteenth, and 600 for fifteenth. The top 12 women earn: DM30,000 for first, 20,000 for second, 10,000 for third, 6,000 for fourth, 4,000 for fifth, 3,000 for sixth, 2,000 for seventh, 1,800 for eighth, 1,500 for ninth, 1,000 for tenth, 800 for eleventh, and 600 for twelfth. In addition, there are significant time bonuses for men finishing under 2:13 and women finishing under 2:35. The bonuses range from DM500 to DM100,000 for a world record.

ACCOMMODATIONS Runners can book hotels through their race entry form. The race offers lodging in 4-star hotels (DM240 - DM280), 3-star hotels (DM140 - DM180), 2-star hotels (DM75 - DM100), private accommodations (DM45), and youth hostels (DM35).

RELATED EVENTS/RACES On Saturday before the marathon, runners and their families can participate in the Breakfast Run, a 6K warm-up from Schloss Charlottenburg to Berlin Olympic Stadium. On marathon day, a Mini Marathon for local students starts from the 38K point on Hohenzollerndamm to the marathon finish. In 1997, organizers added an inline-skating marathon over the same route the runners take.

ROUTE DU VIN HALF MARATHON

OVERALL: 88.9

COURSE BEAUTY: 10-

COURSE DIFFICULTY: 1

APPROPRIATENESS FOR FIRST TIMERS: NA

ORGANIZATION: 9

CROWDS: 4

RACE DATA

Overall Ranking: 36
Quality Ranking: 51
Quickness Ranking: NA
Contact: Jozef De Clerck
Route du Vin Half Marathon
7, rue Michel Rodange
L-5252 Sandweiler
LUXEMBOURG
Tel. +352/4301-37240
Fax +352/4301-37317
E-mail: josef.declerk@eurostat.cec.be

Date: Generally fourth Sunday in September
(September 27, 1998; September 26, 1999)
Start Time: 3:00 p.m.
Time Course Closes: 5:30 p.m.
Number of Finishers: 1,500 in 1997
Course: Point to point
Certification: AIMS/IAAF
Course Records: Male: (open) 1:00:26
Female: (open) 1:08:12
Elite Athlete Programs: Yes (contact the race)
Cost: BEF/LUF 400/600
Age groups/Divisions: NA
Walkers: Yes, but no specific category. Note 2:30 time limit.
Requirements: None
Temperature: 58° - 79° (15°C - 26°C)
Aid/Splits: 4 / every 5K

HIGHLIGHTS The Route du Vin Half Marathon probably conjures images of running through the famous vineyards of Bordeaux, Burgundy, or the Loire Valley. If it does, you're in for a surprise — a pleasant one at that. This wonderful race shadows the lazy Moselle River in Luxembourg, just across from Germany. Run during the grape harvest, the race features hills swept with burnt-orange vines. In addition to beautiful, the Route du Vin Half Marathon boasts an exceptionally fast course — no hills or turns, just a few practically unnoticeable grades and curves as it follows the contours of the river. The Route du Vin Half Marathon may in fact be one of the best-kept running secrets in Europe.

COURSE DESCRIPTION This point-to-point course runs on excellent pavement, providing for a premiere running environment. Starting in the small town of Remich on the Esplanade, the race goes along the Moselle River for the entire 13 miles (21K). By 2K, you leave Remich and then enjoy the area countryside. Near 3.5K you reach the small town of Stadtbredimus. Here you really begin to see the lines of vineyards ahead of you. The scenery becomes even more dramatic near 5K as limestone cliffs provide the backdrop for the short rise of grape plants on your left. The rest of the way alternates between the rolling vineyards and the small towns overlooking the Moselle River: Ehnen (9K to 10K), Wormeldange (11K to 12K), Ahn (14K to 15K), and Machtum (18K to 19K). As the river bends to the right, you can just make out the town of Grevenmacher and you know the finish, at the local sports center, approaches.

CROWD/RUNNER SUPPORT   The race offers aid stations at 5K, 10K, 15K, and 18K, with bottles of water and sponges. You encounter good crowd support in the many small towns along the route.

RACE LOGISTICS   Staying in Remich eliminates any need for transportation to the start. All the hotels in the town are very near the Esplanade. If you're staying outside of Remich, you need to find your own way to the start, probably by car. After the race, organizers provide shuttle buses back to Remich. Changing facilities are located at the Remich swimming pool and at the Sports Centre and Technical College in Grevenmacher. Drop your clothing off at the Remich swimming pool for transport to the finish area.

ACTIVITIES   The Route du Vin Half Marathon does not offer related activities, such as a pasta party or race expo. The race sends pre-registered runners their numbers in the mail. Otherwise, you may register on the morning of race day (10:00 a.m. to noon) at the Remich swimming pool. Everyone is invited to the awards ceremony held in the large tent near the finish line. It's a great chance to swap running stories over a beer or two.

AWARDS   Each finisher receives a bottle of Moselle wine, and will receive the race results in the mail. T-shirts are available for sale in the finish area. Prize money for the top finishers totals about US$40,000.

ACCOMMODATIONS   For lodging information contact the local tourist office, Office National du Tourisme, P.O. Box 1001, L-1010, Luxembourg (tel. +352/40 08 08 20; fax +352/40 08 08 30).

AREA ATTRACTIONS   The race presents a good opportunity to explore the region's wineries during the harvest season. It is also a great chance to explore Luxembourg, a beautiful country often overlooked by tourists.

BUDAPEST MARATHON

OVERALL: 86.9

COURSE BEAUTY: 9+

COURSE DIFFICULTY: 3-

APPROPRIATENESS FOR FIRST TIMERS: 8+

ORGANIZATION: 9-

CROWDS: 4

RACE DATA

Overall Ranking: 54
Quality Ranking: 59
Quickness Ranking: 32
Contact: Budapest Marathon
Budapest Sport Office
PO Box 332
1438 Budapest, Hungary
Tel. +36/1-267-6560
Fax +36/1-267-6561
E-mail: bsi@mail.matav.bu
http://www.dataware.hu/bsi
Date: Generally first Sunday in October (October 4, 1998; October 3, 1999; October 8, 2000)
Start Time: 10:30 a.m.
Time Course Closes: 4:00 p.m.
Number of Finishers: 1,220 in 1997
Course: Loop
Certification: AIMS
Course Records: Male: (open) 2:22:02
Female: (open) 2:46:50
Elite Athlete Programs: Yes
Cost: US$40/50
Age groups/Divisions: Open, 36-40, 41-45, 46-50, 51-55, 56-60, 61-65, 66-70, 71-75, wheelchair
Walkers: No
Requirements: 18 years old
Temperature: 50° - 68° (10°C - 20°C)
Aid/Splits: 10 / none

HIGHLIGHTS   This charming marathon should be one of the most popular tourist marathons in Europe. Most of the race follows the quays along the Danube River, separating the hilly Buda side of the city from flat Pest. In the middle, the course meanders through Margaret Island, the city's urban playground. The gorgeous riverside route highlights Budapest's famous bridges, and runs past the city's most visited monuments, Castle Hill (Várhegy), Gellért Hill, and Parliament.

COURSE DESCRIPTION   The Budapest Marathon starts and finishes on Óbudai Island in the middle of the Danube River in north Budapest. Runners start through the park-like island before reaching the Buda (or western) side of the Danube where the course follows the Buda Quay south along the scenic river for the first 9K. While on this beautiful stretch, you pass Margaret Island, Margaret Bridge, Castle Hill and its royal palace, and the foot of Gellért Hill. Just after 9K, runners cross the Danube over the Szabadság ("Liberty") Bridge, reaching the Pest side of

the city. You now go north along the Pest Quay, giving you a new perspective on the ground you just covered. After passing the Hungarian Parliament building, you soon reach Margaret Island, the city's most beautiful refuge. From 15K to 17K you wander through the paths and parks filled with residents and tourists. Upon leaving the island the course crosses the Àrpàd Bridge to the Pest Quay, heading south back toward the city center, passing the Parliament building before reaching Szabadság Bridge. You again cross the bridge (going the opposite way) to the Buda side, and continue heading south (25K to 29K) into the southern section of Budapest. At 29K, the course does a sharp turn-around and retraces its path to Szabadság Bridge (35K). Here runners continue to head north on the Buda Quay, straight to Óbudai Island, where the race finishes in the middle of a meadow.

CROWD/RUNNER SUPPORT   The marathon coincides with a special festival, which draws about 10,000 people to the start/finish area on Óbudai Island. Pockets of spectators nestle along the Danube, especially in the heart of the city, and Margaret Island fills with people on nice days. Aid stations refresh you every 4K, with water, sports drink, bananas, grapes, and sugar.

RACE LOGISTICS Public transportation offers perhaps the best means to get to the race start. Óbudai Island is at the "Filatorigát" station of the suburban train line, HÉV. You can catch the HÉV at Batthány Square, which is off of the metro (subway) red line.

ACTIVITIES You can retrieve your race packet at the Race Center on Óbudai Island on Saturday, or on Sunday morning before the race. Going on Saturday would give you a stress-free opportunity to figure out how to get to the start on race day.

AWARDS Every participant receives a T-shirt, and if you finish the 26.2 miles, you also receive a medal, finisher's bag (loaded with food and goodies), certificate, and results list (the last two are sent by mail). The prize money changes from year to year, but hovers somewhere around the following: 120,000 HUF for first, 80,000 HUF for second, 50,000 HUF for third, 40,000 HUF for fourth, and 30,000 HUF for fifth and sixth.

ELITE RUNNERS INFORMATION The race recruits elite runners on an individual basis. Please contact the marathon office for consideration and more details.

ACCOMMODATIONS The Hotel Dunapart and Stadion Hotel serve as the official race hotels. Book through the marathon office to receive the special rate.

RELATED EVENTS/RACES Together with the marathon, there is a 7K Mini Marathon and a Fun Run for kindergarten children on Óbudai Island. A large festival, complete with concerts, fireworks, food and entertainment, perks you up in the finish area.

AREA ATTRACTIONS Budapest is clearly one of Europe's most beautiful cities, full of graceful, old buildings, charming bridges, and narrow, winding streets. By far the most visited site is Castle Hill (Várhegy). You may want to tour the damp, cool tunnels underneath the hill that have been used by several military forces over the centuries, including Germany in WWII. Also check out the ornately decorated, 13th-century Mattias Church (Mátyás Templom). Other popular attractions include Gellért Hill, Parliament, Great Synagogue, Hungarian National Gallery, Fine Arts Museum, National Museum, Budapest History Museum, and Margaret Island. After the marathon, make liberal use of Budapest's numerous natural hot springs bathhouses.

BUCHAREST MARATHON

OVERALL: 74.9

COURSE BEAUTY: 8-

COURSE DIFFICULTY: 2

APPROPRIATENESS FOR FIRST TIMERS: 7

ORGANIZATION: 8+

CROWDS: 2

RACE DATA

Overall Ranking: 102
Quality Ranking: 85
Quickness Ranking: 13
Contact: Mr. Silviu Dumitrescu
Bucharest International Marathon
Aleea Valea Florilor 1
Bloc Z7, # 33
77376 Bucharest - 6
Romania
Tel. & Fax +40/1-745-3602

Date: Generally second Saturday in October
(October 10, 1998; October 9, 1999)
Start Time: NA
Time Course Closes: 6 hours
Number of Participants: 350 in 1997
Course: Out and partial back
Certification: NA
Course Records: Male: (open) 2:25:56
Female: (open) 2:57:54
Elite Athlete Programs: No
Cost: US$15
Age groups/Divisions: NA
Walkers: No
Requirements: None
Temperature: 64° (18°C)
Aid/Splits: 8 / digital clocks every 10K

HIGHLIGHTS Runners in the Bucharest International Marathon who occasionally look up from their feet will be struck with the stark contrasts in this city. They start on broad avenues, here lined with sidewalk cafes and stately embassies, and there faced by socialist tragedies. At times, runners pass through pleasant parks, such as Herastrau Park and its boat-filled lake, and at other times they see reminders of Bucharest's not-too-distant upheavals, like Piata Universitatii. Bucharest is a city where sometimes frustrating hassles are tempered by the hospitable race organizers, who even will find you a room at a Romanian runner's house if you like. The flat marathon course hosts a relatively small number of runners. Those who prefer more company can compete in the popular 4K race that follows the first 4k of the marathon route.

COURSE DESCRIPTION Runners assemble in Bucharest's heart, Piata Universitatii, site of bloody demonstrations in 1989 and again in 1990. Surrounded by the university and the Intercontinental Hotel, runners proceed up Bulevardul N. Balcescu, a main avenue of sidewalk cafes and restaurants. The course passes through Piata Romana to Bulevardul Ana Ipatescu which leads to Piata Victoriei. Framed by the government of Romania building and the Natural History Museum, Piata Victoriei takes runners to Soseaua Kiseleff, another fashionable avenue lined with lime trees. These streets comprise the most elegant in Bucharest and are home to several foreign embassies. Reaching the Arcul de Triumf at 4K, the route then passes Herastrau Park and its popular Village Museum. With crowded Lake Herastrau off to the right, runners go by Casa Presei Libere (Press House) near 6K, after which they leave the city behind. Skirting the Baneasa Airport, the race now stays outside Bucharest, going through a quiet forest for over 11 kilometers. Around 40K, runners reenter Bucharest following the path they used earlier (passing Casa Presei Libere) and finish in the Youth Stadium (Stadionul Tineretului).

CROWD/RUNNER SUPPORT Crowd support focuses around central Bucharest, which means the first 6K and the last 2K of the marathon. The aid stations, every 5K, generally provide water, lemons, tea, and sponges.

RACE LOGISTICS If you stay at one of the several hotels lying near the starting area at Piata Universitatii, race morning should be hassle free. After the race, hop on the race-provided bus back to Piata Universitatii.

ACTIVITIES Race-related activities include a welcome banquet and folklore show. Details have yet to be settled.

AWARDS Each participant receives a T-shirt. Finishers receive diplomas and a chance to win random prizes. Top runners earn limited prize money and electronic equipment.

ACCOMMODATIONS Hotels near the start include: Sofitel, B-dul Expositiei 2 (tel. +40/1-212-2998; fax +40/1-212-0646); Bulevard, B-dul Kogalniceanu 1 (tel. +40/1-615-3300); Intercontinental, B-dul Balcescu 4 (tel. +40/1-614-0400; fax +40/1-312-0486); and Capitol, Calea Victoriei 56 (tel. +40/1-615-8030; fax +40/1-312-4169). You can also request to stay in the home of a local runner.

RELATED EVENTS/RACES Bucharest offers non-marathoners a chance to run 4K through the city streets. The popular race generally draws nearly 4,500 participants and runs along the nice first 4K of the marathon course before ending in the Youth Stadium.

AREA ATTRACTIONS Much of Romania's charm lies in its countryside and mountain scenery. The Carpathian Mountains, forming the frontier between the province of Transylvania and Moldavia and Wallachia, offer some of the most beautiful and least exploited hiking areas in Europe. Of course, the ominous Bran Castle of Count Dracula located in Brasov, stands as one of the most popular tourist attractions, but also worth seeing are some of the smaller Saxon settlements and quaint churches the area has to offer. Excursions to Romania's Black Sea beaches are also popular, though weather may be a bit chilly in October. The race organizers provide assistance in arranging many of these activities.

ISTANBUL EURASIA MARATHON

OVERALL: 81.9

COURSE BEAUTY: 8+

COURSE DIFFICULTY: 4 (SEE APPENDIX)

APPROPRIATENESS FOR FIRST TIMERS: 7

ORGANIZATION: 8-

CROWDS: 3-

RACE DATA

Overall Ranking: 82
Quality Ranking: 97
Quickness Ranking: 78
Contact: Istanbul Eurasia Marathon
Millet Cad. No. 109
34280 Capa Istanbul
Turkey
Tel. +90/212-587 05 44
Fax +90/212-587 42 74
E-mail: istspor@iris.com.tr
http://www.istbldspor.org.tr

Date: Generally second Sunday in October
Start Time: 9:00 a.m.
Time Course Closes: 2:00 p.m.
Number of Finishers: 1,500 in 1997
Course: Point to point
Certification: AIMS
Course Records: Male: (open) 2:17:56
Female: (open) 2:34:44
Elite Athlete Programs: Yes (contact the race)
Cost: US$30
Age groups/Divisions: M: 18-39, 40-44, 45-49, 50-54, 55+, wheelchair
F: 18-34, 35-39, 40-44, 45-49, 50+, wheelchair
Walkers: No
Requirements: 18 years old
Temperature: 58° (14°C)
Aid/Splits: 8 / none

HIGHLIGHTS If you're one of those people who want to run a marathon in each continent and you have an efficient nature, you may be inclined to run the Istanbul Eurasia Marathon. The only race in the world where you can notch two continents with one race, Istanbul starts on the Asian side of the city, crosses the Bosphorus Bridge, and lands in Europe where most of the race winds. Therein lies the race's novel attraction — bridging two continents and experiencing a city long torn between Europe and Asia. The result is that the city and the race are some of both — Asian frenzy and European structure. In all, the race crosses three bridges, one over the Bosphorus and two over the Golden Horn linking the European sections of Istanbul.

COURSE DESCRIPTION The Istanbul Eurasia Marathon begins on the Asian side of the Bosphorus Bridge. After a 165-foot downhill, which you may or may not be able to take advantage of due to the crowd of runners, you reach the Bosphorus Bridge by 2K. Crossing the bridge affords you spectacular views of the Bosphorus Straight and European Istanbul ahead and to your left. As you leave the bridge, the neo-Renaissance Ortaköy Camii mosque sits to the left. At 4K, runners face a very good climb of 330-feet over 3K through the suburbs. The course turns around in Maslak (11K) and heads back toward the heart of Istanbul, passing through Mecidiyeköy before arriving in Taksim. The race now passes through the "new" city, Beyoglu. After crossing the Atatürk Bridge, the race enters the Old City – the ancient city of Byzantium and Constantinople. You soon pass by the raised Aqueduct of Velens, possibly constructed in the 4th century. After going through mostly old commercial areas, the race heads south on an out-and-back stretch to the SSK Istanbul Hospital. Once back in the old city, the race skirts the Bosphorus, giving you awesome views of the waterway and the minarets of the Blue Mosque, Sancta Sophia, and Topkapi Palace. The course enters Eminönü, dominated by Yeni Cami ("New Mosque"), crossing over the Golden Horn by the Galata Bridge. Now back in the new city, you can see the ancient Galata Tower, a Genoese fortification. Still largely following the Bosphorus, runners reach the marble, 19th-century Dolmabahçe Palace. You now know the finish line, in Inönü Stadium, lies just a short distance away.

CROWD / RUNNER SUPPORT   Turkey is still fairly new to the idea of half-naked people in shorts and tank tops running through the city streets. As such, there are no New York-like crowds. Quizzical looks and honking horns predominate more than cheers and applause. The race provides water stations every 5K and sponging stations every 2.5K.

RACE LOGISTICS   Foreign runners can catch a special bus in front of City Hall (Municipality Building Sarachane) for the race start. After the race you can shower near the finish area.

ACTIVITIES   There is a pasta party the evening before the Marathon at City Hall (Municipality Building Sarachane).

AWARDS   Every finisher under 5 hours receives a medal and T-shirt. Age-group winners earn trophies. The top 20 men and top 15 women also receive prize money ranging from US$20,000 to $100. A US$5,000 bounty also goes to the runner who sets a new course record.

ACCOMMODATIONS   Runners can call the marathon's official travel agency, Sena Tour, for lodging information (tel. +90/212-513-3404 or 3505 or 3506; fax +90/212-511-1566). The luxury hotels tend to congregate near Taksim Square, while cheaper lodging can be found in the Old City.

RELATED EVENTS / RACES   The race also holds the much larger 8K Public Race in conjunction with the marathon. In 1997, the 8K supposedly had 100,000 runners.

AREA ATTRACTIONS   A city of minarets and domes, situated at the crossroads of history, Istanbul can captivate and frustrate. It contains numerous masterpieces, such as Hagia Sophia, Topkapi Palace, Blue Mosque, Suleymaniye Mosque, and Yerebatan Sarnici. It also houses incredible bazaars, including the Grand Bazaar (Kapali Carsi) and the Egyptian Bazaar (Misiv Carsisi). And of course you must sample a bona fide Turkish Bath.

ITALIAN MARATHON

OVERALL: 80.7

COURSE BEAUTY: 7+

COURSE DIFFICULTY: 2- (SEE APPENDIX)

APPROPRIATENESS FOR FIRST TIMERS: 8+

ORGANIZATION: 9+

CROWDS: 5-

RACE DATA

Overall Ranking:	86
Quality Ranking:	34
Quickness Ranking:	7
Contact:	Italian Marathon
	C.P. 330
	I-41012, Carpi (Modena)
	ITALY
	Tel. +39/59-65 02 97
	Fax +39/59-65 13 30
Date:	Generally second Sunday in October
Start Time:	9:30 a.m.
Time Course Closes:	2:30 p.m.
Number of Finishers:	1,955 in 1997
Course:	Loop
Certification:	AIMS
Course Records:	Male: (open) 2:09:43
	Female: (open) 2:28:22
Elite Athlete Programs:	Yes
Cost:	Lit. 70,000
Age groups/Divisions:	20-29, 30-34, 35-39, 40-44, 45-49, 50-54, 55-59, 60-64, 65-69, 70-74, 75-79, 80+, wheelchair
Walkers:	No
Requirements:	18 years old
Temperature:	57˚ - 61˚ (14˚C - 16˚C)
Aid/Splits:	8 / digital clocks every 5K

HIGHLIGHTS The Italian Marathon vies for Italy's fastest marathon award, especially with its circular course with only six overpasses for hills. Overall, the course rises about 15 feet for the first half and drops the same on the way back. The six overpasses are grouped toward the middle of the route, between 15K and 28K. Held smack in the middle of Northern Italy, only 37 miles from Bologna, the race venue is convenient to many of the country's most popular tourist spots: Florence, Venice, Verona, and the Italian Riviera. The race also doubles as the Italian National Marathon Championships which usually produces fast times on the quick course.

COURSE DESCRIPTION Starting in the city of Carpi in Piazza Martiri, one of Italy's largest squares, the course heads toward Soliera, a small town with a marvelous castle. Runners begin the trek through the mixture of Italian countryside, small towns, and commercial districts that characterize most of the race. You scale the first hill of the route at 15K, a 20-foot overpass. Then it's again essentially flat until the second overpass, a little higher and steeper than the last, at 19K. Here the course skirts the city of Modena, famous for its cathedral and tower. The third overpass occurs just before 22K. As you head back toward Carpi, three more overpasses await in relatively quick succession at 25K, 27K, and 28K. The course now runs mostly flat as it goes through the small towns of Lesignana, and Ganaceto. By 40K the course enters the outskirts of Carpi, goes through the town center, and finishes in the central square, Piazza Martiri.

CROWD/RUNNER SUPPORT Most of the crowd support is found at the start and finish, but there is also good support in Soliera, Modena and the other towns along the way, including bands and entertainment. Aid stations with water, sports drink, sugar, salt, and lemons are set up every 5K of the race. Your own special drink can be set out for you at the desired aid station by dropping it off at the designated spot in the start area at least two hours before the race. A sponge station cools off runners in between aid stations.

RACE LOGISTICS Piazza Martiri, the center of town, is only 330 feet from the train station and 500 feet from the bus station. Consequently, you should have little problem getting to the race start. A dressing area and showers are available at the finish in the Castello Dei Pio.

ACTIVITIES Runners who register at least one month prior to the race will be mailed their start numbers. Otherwise, you can retrieve your race packet at the marathon expo in the Castello Dei Pio (the Middle Ages Castle) in Piazza Martiri on Friday, Saturday, and Sunday before the race. While there is no official pasta dinner, the race generally gives vouchers for dinner at a restaurant near Piazza Martiri. On Saturday you can enjoy the concert at the Municipal Theater of Carpi near the start/finish area.

AWARDS Each entrant receives a T-shirt and a small gift. Finishers also receive medals and are mailed their finisher's certificate and results book. Age-group awards go five deep, with first place receiving a special T-shirt and gold medal. The second finisher earns a silver medal, and third place through fifth place receive bronze medals. Five-time age-group champions are awarded a parchment proclaiming this feat and a special gold medal.

ELITE RUNNERS INFORMATION The Italian Marathon recruits top runners on a case-by-case basis. Interested runners should contact the race organization for consideration. Overall prize money typically falls in the US$180,000 range.

ACCOMMODATIONS For race accommodations, contact C.T.M., Via Guido Fassi 48, Carpi (MO) 41012 (tel. +39/59-68 50 60; fax +39/59-65 21 75).

LAUSANNE MARATHON

OVERALL: 94.2

COURSE BEAUTY: 10-

COURSE DIFFICULTY: 4+

APPROPRIATENESS FOR FIRST TIMERS: 9-

ORGANIZATION: 9+

CROWDS: 5-

RACE DATA

Overall Ranking:	18
Quality Ranking:	34
Quickness Ranking:	80
Contact:	Lausanne Marathon
	Case Postale 31
	1162 Saint-Prex
	Switzerland
	Tel. +41/21-806-3016
	Fax +41/21-806-2548
Date:	Generally third Sunday in October (October 18, 1998)
Start Time:	9:15 a.m.
Time Course Closes:	NA
Number of Finishers:	1,400 in 1997
Course:	Out and back
Certification:	AIMS
Course Records:	Male: (open) 2:14:08
	Female: (open) 2:33:34
Elite Athlete Programs:	Yes
Cost:	Sfr 30/40
Age groups/Divisions:	14-29, 30-39, 40-49, 50+, wheelchair
Walkers:	Yes
Requirements:	None
Temperature:	52° - 59° (11°C - 15°C)
Aid/Splits:	8 / none

HIGHLIGHTS Switzerland seems to be one of those blessed countries. Heart-thumping beauty goes hand in pocket with Swiss-watch efficiency. All in a strong sports-minded culture forged by the crisp air and natural splendor. These elements come together in Switzerland's best city marathon held in Lausanne. The course kisses the lip of Lake Geneva and the foot of the Alps, passing through 10 towns on its way from Lausanne to Peilz and back. The rhythmic route rolls strongly as it curves along the foothills. If you like options, Lausanne offers a handful of races, including the marathon, wheelchair marathon, half marathon, quarter marathon, and mini marathon. Each benefits from the Swiss race organization, the Alpine fresh air, and blessed Switzerland.

COURSE DESCRIPTION The out-and-back course begins at Place de Milan, a large park in downtown Lausanne. A good downhill takes runners to the shore of Lake

Geneva (1K) as they begin their journey along the lake. You soon pass through Ouchy with the rippling blue waters of the lake just off to your right framed by the Alps in a stunning portrait. This tree-lined stretch has patches of cobblestones, but they should not pose any difficulties for runners. As you go through the village of Pully, the course leaves the lake for the shelter of the hillside. A rolling road takes you to Lutry (turnaround point for the quarter marathon) with more gorgeous views of the lake and mountains. The terraced hills provide runners with varied scenery. Still rolling, the course begins to climb a bit above the lake past the steepled hills of Cully in another stretch of incredible running. The turnaround for the half marathoners soon arrives, followed by a nice downgrade as you approach the town of Rivaz, and then a decent rise. Once out of Rivaz, the curvy, undulating course runs wedged between the terraced hills and Lake Geneva. Another gentle downgrade leads to attractive St. Saphorin with the Alps rising ahead. Runners now have a couple of good ups and downs between towns. Larger Corseaux leads quickly to Vevey as the route goes through the back of these towns, giving you a breather from the picturesque scenery. Runners turn around in Peilz after the tower, and retrace their steps toward Ouchy. Remember you have two good uphills between Corseaux and St. Saphorin. The race finishes at the Olympic Museum in Ouchy. Overall, you have lakeviews for about one-half of the race.

CROWD/RUNNER SUPPORT Most of the crowds gather along the lakefront in Lausanne and in the towns that the race passes through. The course layout gives you ample opportunity to view your fellow competitors. Aid stations lie every 5K along the route, with a few sponging stations thrown in. The aid stations provide water, fruit, and sugar.

RACE LOGISTICS Race organizers usually provide free bus transportation before and after the race. Details accompany your race packet.

ACTIVITIES Pick up your race packet at the marathon expo in front of beautiful Bellerive Beach and Pool along the lake in Ouchy. On Saturday evening enjoy the pasta party, also held at the Bellerive Beach.

AWARDS Runners generally receive a race T-shirt (although this isn't the case every year). Each finisher earns a medal after crossing the finish line. The race subsequently mails runners a finisher's certificate and full results. The top 3 runners in each age division receive special prizes.

ELITE RUNNERS INFORMATION Lausanne provides hotel accommodations and some expense money for runners it recruits. Contact the race directly for more information.

ACCOMMODATIONS The race does not have an official headquarters hotel. Runners can reserve rooms of various standards through the Lausanne Tourist and Congress Office (tel. +41/21-617-7321; fax +41/21-616-8647). Hotel rooms typically range from Sfr. 110 to Sfr. 390.

RELATED EVENTS/RACES Lausanne gives all runners the chance to participate and run along Lake Geneva. The half marathon and quarter marathon (about 6.5 miles) also start at Place de Milan in Lausanne and run along the highway toward Montreux, finishing in front of the Olympic Museum in Ouchy. There is also a mini marathon for the kids.

AREA ATTRACTIONS Steeply hilly Lausanne is a pretty town in and of itself. Lake Geneva is the main attraction here, together with the Olympic Museum. Since Switzerland is so small, practically any point in the country is only a short drive away.

ATHENS MARATHON

OVERALL: 74.9

COURSE BEAUTY: 8

COURSE DIFFICULTY: 4 (SEE APPENDIX)

APPROPRIATENESS FOR FIRST TIMERS: 5

ORGANIZATION: 6

CROWDS: 2

RACE DATA

Overall Ranking:	102
Quality Ranking:	104
Quickness Ranking:	83
Contact:	Athens Marathon
	c/o Apostolos Greek Tours Inc.
	Paul Samaras
	3145 S. Akron Street
	Denver, CO 80231
	Tel. (303) 755-2888
	Fax (303) 755-4888
	E-mail: Apostolo@iguana.ruralnet.net
	http://www.ruralnet.net/~apostolo/TheRun.html
Date:	Generally fourth Sunday in October (Note: November 1, 1998)
Start Time:	8:30 a.m.
Time Course Closes:	2:30 p.m.
Number of Finishers:	705 in 1997
Course:	Point to point
Certification:	IAAF
Course Records:	Male: (open) 2:11:07
	Female: (open) 2:31:10
Elite Athlete Programs:	No
Cost:	US$20
Age groups/Divisions:	Men: 18-39, 40-49, 50-59, 60-69, 70+
	Women: 18-29, 30-39, 40-49, 50+
Walkers:	No
Requirements:	18 years old
Temperature:	63° - 72° (17°C - 22°C)
Aid/Splits:	8 / none

HIGHLIGHTS   Most people know that the marathon race has something to do with a Greek messenger who, after running from Marathon to Athens to bring word of an Athenian victory over the Persians, reportedly collapsed and died after gasping out his news. To commemorate Pheidippides' heroic effort, the Greek Government holds the Athens Marathon at the end of October each year. Beginning at the site of the Battle of Marathon, the race follows nearly the same celebrated route that Pheidippides covered over 2,500 years ago, while finishing at the Olympic Stadium in Athens. Though not particularly scenic, the historical significance of the course, and Athens in general, is more than enough reason to travel to Athens. Marathoners in the first modern Olympic Games in 1896 journeyed along these roads; the same roads used by Plato, Sophocles, and Euripides. Be aware, however, that Athens is not known for its strong race organization. Aid stations running out of water has been a recurring problem, one that hopefully will be rectified in the future.

COURSE DESCRIPTION The Athens Marathon route remains similar to the one Pheidippides made famous. Though the road has improved, and small villages dot today's course, the bulk of the journey from Marathon to Athens runs unceremoniously through agricultural areas. A wide marble line, still in place from the 1896 Olympic Marathon, denotes the start along the main street in Marathon. Mostly flat for the first 12K, the course loops the Tomb of the Marathon Warriors at 9.7K, then cuts through the village of N. Makrl (10.3K). Gradually gaining over 400 feet through the rolling hills between 13K and 32K, the route passes the halfway point near Pikermi. After Palini (28K), the route courses through suburban Athens, dropping 350 feet over the final 10K to the dramatic finish in the Olympic Stadium.

CROWD/RUNNER SUPPORT Not much has changed since Pheidippides made his famous run. With the exception of a smattering of onlookers in the little villages along the course, the rural route affords little spectator support. Race support is also minimal. While it's unclear why Pheidippides died at the end of his heroic run, dehydration may have played a part. Lack of water along the route continues to be a problem today. While aid stations sit every 5K, they are notorious for running out of water. We advise slower runners to carry a water bottle. Although distance markers lie only every 5K, you may see other kilometer marks left over from the 1997 World Championships Marathon held over the same course. Remnants of the traditional blue line, used for the world championships, may be visible on the road, ensuring that no runner loses his way.

RACE LOGISTICS The race provides bus transportation from the finish at Olympic Stadium to the start in Marathon. Some hotels lie within walking distance to the stadium. Because very little parking exists at the start, race organizers highly encourage using the buses. The race usually falls on the day after the end of daylight savings. Remember to set your watch accordingly.

ACTIVITIES The pomp and circumstance prevalent in many marathons are conspicuously absent in Athens. In keeping with the ancient Greek ideals of pure athletic competition, the government-run race maintains no commercial sponsorship. No health and fitness expo, pre-race pasta party, or goody bag accompanies the event. Pick up your race number on Monday through Saturday before the event between 9:00 a.m and 3:00 p.m. at SEGAS offices, 137 Syngrou Avenue.

AWARDS Every finisher receives a certificate and medal. The top three male and female finishers receive trophies and olive wreaths. Age-division winners typically go home empty handed, though this may change in the coming years.

ACCOMMODATIONS While we generally don't recommend package tours, you may want to consider one for Athens. Europe's oldest city is now one of its most crowded, housing over 4.5 million people. It can be very difficult getting around, so before arriving be sure to have a plan. Some hotels lie within walking distance of the Olympic Stadium. However, if you arrive early and wish to get in a few runs prior to the race, you're better off staying outside of the downtown area. Contact Apostolos Greek Tours, Inc. in the U.S. (970-669-8377) for lodging options.

RELATED EVENTS An unofficial half marathon starts with the marathon and finishes near Pikermi. Contact Apostolos Greek Tours, Inc. for more information.

AREA ATTRACTIONS Athens' concentration of history and culture can keep you occupied for days. The hilltop Acropolis is the most spectacular attraction. One of the earliest settlements in Greece, the Acropolis houses many legendary monuments and temples including the Parthenon, Athena Nike, the Propylaia, the Erechtheion, and the Acropolis Museum. The National Archaeological Museum in Moussio contains the world's most important collection of ancient Greek art. Enjoy the fine shops and active nightlife of the Plaka on the north slope of the Acropolis. Not far from the city is Delphi, considered to be the center of the world by ancient Greeks. Delphi's museum is home to many classical and ancient sculptures, including the famous bronze The Charioteer and Sphinx of the Naxians. For a break from sight-seeing head to one of the excellent beaches in Vouliagmeni, a delightful coastal town only 24 kilometers from Athens.

ECHTERNACH MARATHON

OVERALL: 86.7

COURSE BEAUTY: 9

COURSE DIFFICULTY: 3-

APPROPRIATENESS FOR FIRST TIMERS: 8

ORGANIZATION: 9

CROWDS: 4

RACE DATA

Overall Ranking:	56
Quality Ranking:	51
Quickness Ranking:	30
Contact:	Euro-Marathon Echternach
	P.O. Box 96
	L-6401 Echternach
	Luxembourg
	Tel. +352/4379-7102
	Fax +352/340-667
	E-mail: marathon.echternach@hermesnet.com
	http://www.marathon-echternach.lu
Date:	Generally last Sunday in October
Start Time:	9:30 a.m.
Time Course Closes:	2:30 p.m.
Number of Finishers:	1,355 in 1997
Course:	Combination two loops & two out and backs
Certification:	AIMS
Course Records:	Male: (open) 2:13:28
	Female: (open) 2:33:05
Elite Athlete Programs:	Yes
Cost:	LF 800
Age groups/Divisions:	≤20, 21-29, 30-34, 35-39, 40-44, 45-49, 50-54, 55-59, 60-64, 65-69, 70+
Walkers:	No
Requirements:	None
Temperature:	50°F (10°C)
Aid/Splits:	8 / every 5K

HIGHLIGHTS   The tiny Grand Duchy of Luxembourg often gets overlooked on the European map, squashed between the powerhouses of Germany and France. Even the most thoughtful runner outside of Belgium may never even consider running in this islet of a nation. That is very unfortunate because the country hosts two outstanding long-distance races, and the Echternach Marathon is one. Held in the tiny village of Echternach, just across the thin Sûre River from Germany, the marathon combines a pleasing mixture of charming town and pretty countryside. The people there are super friendly. In fact, the course director, who also happens to be the town police chief, gave me a personal course tour complete with flashing red lights as we zipped down the pedestrian paths during the heat of the midday stroll. If this is any indication, this race is big on satisfying the runner and making sure you remember your stay in Luxembourg.

COURSE DESCRIPTION The Echternach Marathon consists of two loops around the town lake, followed by a short out and back west along the Sûre River, and then a final out and back east along the river to the town of Rosport. Entirely closed to traffic, the route contains some rolling countryside, but no major climbs. The start and finish lie in the beautiful town center, not far from the Sûre and the German border. The first bit goes through the restored town, including a brief stint on cobblestones, before heading through a residential section on its way to Lac See. Runners reach the lake near 1.5K, with round hills to the right and the water on the left. Leaving the small lake at 3K, the course winds through rolling country, traverses a brief commercial park at 5K, and goes through another residential area. Skirting the town, runners follow the river in a scenic stretch of running until 8.5K, where they dart back to town, pass the cemetery, and ready themselves for the second loop around Lac See. Near 15K, the course begins its out and back to Weilerbach along the pretty road. Runners have a very slight incline as they race the Sûre to the turnaround about 1,950 feet after the village of Weilerbach (just past 19K). The halfway point lies on the return trip to Echternach, and runners merge to the bike path clinging to the river providing some very nice views. Upon reaching Echternach, the race passes under the bridge near the start (about 23K), eventually going up a short hill to the road. You're now on your way to Rosport (25K to 40K), reaching the town of Steinheim near 28K and the outskirts of Rosport near 31.5K. The turnaround lies after the town near 32K. You are now in the homestretch — the final 9K to the center of Echternach. The race climaxes with a jaunt down the pedestrian-only street through the town center, finishing near the race start.

CROWD/RUNNER SUPPORT Runners find the locals come out in force in the small towns along the route. Aid stations are located every 5K. Each station offers water, sports drink, sponges, and fruit. Picky runners may drop off bottles of their own concoction at the race office at least 90 minutes prior to the race start with labels indicating the desired pick-up station.

RACE LOGISTICS Runners who stay in Echternach face a hassle-free race day. The town is quite small, meaning the start/finish is within easy reach of all central hotels. Showers are available at several areas near the finish. There is also a bus service from Echternach to a shower facility at Irrel.

ACTIVITIES Retrieve your marathon packet at the race office in Echternach on Saturday before the race from 2:00 p.m. to 8:00 p.m. or on race morning between 6:00 a.m. and 8:30 a.m. (Please note that participants will not receive confirmation of their entry.) A free pasta party kicks off on Saturday evening. Guests may attend for LF200.

AWARDS Each entrant receives a race T-shirt, gift bag, and entrance to the pasta party. Women runners also receive an assortment of cosmetics. All runners who finish the marathon earn medals. The top three finishers in each age group receive special prizes.

ELITE RUNNER INFORMATION The top 20 men and top 10 women receive prize money ranging from 100,000 LF to 2,000 LF. There are also bonus awards for the top runner who sets a new course record: 100,000 LF for men and 50,000 LF for women.

ACCOMMODATIONS For lodging information in Echternach you can contact the local tourist office, 9-10 parvis de la Basilique, L-6486, Echternach (tel. +352/720-230; fax +352/727-524). Runners may camp for free at the official campsite about 400 yards from the race start/finish on Route de Diekirch (tel. +352/720-272). Possible hotels include: Bel-Air, 1, route de Berdorf (tel. +352/729-383; fax +352/728-694); De La Basilique, 7-8, place du Marche (tel. +352/729-483; fax +352/728-890); Grand-Hotel, 27, route de Diekirch (tel. +352/729-672; fax +352/729-062); and Universel, 40, rue de Luxembourg (tel. +352/729-991; fax +352/728-787).

AREA ATTRACTIONS Echternach contains many points of historical interest and beauty, including the Basilique de St-Willibrord and the Eglise Sts-Pierre-et-Paul (8th to 12th century). Short drives will take you to many other spots in this beautiful country, including Vianden and the vineyards and wineries near Remich and Grevenmacher.

FRANKFURT MARATHON

OVERALL: 91

COURSE BEAUTY: 8+

COURSE DIFFICULTY: 2 (SEE APPENDIX)

APPROPRIATENESS FOR FIRST TIMERS: 10

ORGANIZATION: 10-

CROWDS: 9-

RACE DATA

Overall Ranking:	27
Quality Ranking:	11
Quickness Ranking:	10
Contact:	Frankfurt Marathon
	Postfach 700 709
	60557 Frankfurt am Main
	Germany
	Tel. +49/1805-25 87 35
	Fax +49/69-68 60 70 90
	E-mail: TCF-Info@frankfurt-main.de
	http://TCF.frankfurt.main.de
Date:	Generally last Sunday in October (October 25, 1998)
Start Time:	10:00 a.m.
Time Course Closes:	3:30 p.m.
Number of Participants:	8,000 in 1997
Course:	Loop
Certification:	AIMS
Course Records:	Male: (open) 2:10:59
	Female: (open) 2:26:48
Elite Athlete Programs:	Yes (contact the race)
Cost:	DM 75
Age groups/Divisions:	NA
Walkers:	No
Requirements:	18 years old
Temperature:	48° - 58° (9°C - 14°C)
Aid/Splits:	13 / digital clocks every 5K

HIGHLIGHTS The oldest city marathon in Germany, Frankfurt delivers a large, exceptionally well-organized race over a very flat course (there are no inclines here greater than 25 feet). With four trips over the Main River, runners pass through the modern city center, charming Höchst, and happening Sachsenhausen. The race is also convenient, with all race activities centered around the Frankfurt Messe (particularly if you stay in the nearby Marriott). Perhaps best of all is the extremely strong support given by the Frankfurters — entertainment and neighborhood festivals cram this route, giving you that extra knee lift for your PR chase.

COURSE DESCRIPTION The loop course starts (and finishes) at the Messe Tower, turning up Senckenberganlange. On this wide street with its broad median you pass Goethe University before turning right on tree-lined Bockenheimer Landstr. (1K). After 2K you wind along a pleasant park setting on a slight upgrade, which goes ever so slightly down from 3K. Becoming nicely commercial after 4K, runners head for their first crossing of the Main River on the Alte Bridge between

5K and 6K. Enjoy the views to the right as you run over the bridge. You have a brief stretch through the nightspot of Sachsenhausen on the south side of the river before crossing the Main via the Untermain Bridge as the towers of Frankfurt loom ahead of you (about 7K). The next 3K travel through commercial sections of the downtown, passing between the main train station and the Messe near 10K. Once on Frankenallee, runners embark on the quietest section of the course. Mostly lined by trees and apartment buildings, this area alternates between nice and less-nice sections. At 13K, runners reach Mainzer Landstr. during the least attractive part of the course. The scenery improves once on Oeser Str. (about 17K), becoming beautiful through the town of Höchst, with its cobblestones, quaint buildings, and color. After looping through the town, the course returns to Mainzer Landstr. at 21K on a nice downgrade. Veering right on Nieder Kirchweg, runners now look forward to the Schwanheimer Bridge (about 23K). After circling up and down the bridge, runners front the river for a brief period before heading into a residential area. This section becomes quite nice on Rheinlandstr. at 25K with pleasant homes to the left and forest to the right. The race remains residential until Goldsteinstr. (29K), where it turns commercial with an industrial park on Lyoner Str. (30K). Back into nice neighborhoods on Rennbahnstr. (33K), the course goes down wide Kennedyallee as it reenters Sachsenhausen. The route forges the Main River for the final time just before 38K, winding its way through downtown toward the finish in front of the Messe.

CROWD / RUNNER SUPPORT Come to Frankfurt prepared for some noise. Almost every kilometer runners come across some entertainment or neighborhood festival that celebrates the marathon. And the raucous supporters are not shy. Especially boisterous are the folks in the city center, Höchst, and Sachsenhausen. Every 5K the race offers full-blown aid stations with water, sports drink, and bananas. Starting at 12.5K and continuing every 5K thereafter you also have water-only stations.

RACE LOGISTICS There are two primary ways of getting to the race start. Runners with cars may park for free at the Frankfurt Messe grounds. Wheel-less runners have free-access to public transportation on race weekend. You can store your warm-ups in the staging area. Note that Frankfurt uses the ChampionChip, so you must rent or buy one if you do not already own one.

ACTIVITIES Early-registered runners receive their numbers in advance by mail. Otherwise, pick up your race package at the expo beginning on Friday afternoon at the Zierhof and forum, adjacent to the Festhalle in the Frankfurt Messe. If you need to get that last warm-up in, consider the 5K Breakfast Race on Saturday morning, which goes from the city center to the Messe. After the run, munch on a pretzel and sip apple juice, while wearing your free T-shirt (which also serves as your start "number"). Runners who would like to see what they are in for can take a marathon course tour on Saturday for about DM 5. Also on Saturday at the Festhalle inject some carbos at the potato party, free to marathon runners. After the marathon, replenish all of those lost carbos with the free beer (and food if you are also hungry).

AWARDS Each entrant is loaded down with a marathon program, jute runner's bag, and marathon training calendar. If you finish, you receive a medal, certificate, T-shirt, and results book. The top age-group finishers also receive prizes.

ACCOMMODATIONS Runners can make hotel reservations through the tourist office for special marathon weekend deals. These deals typically include a race T-shirt, entry fee, and other goodies. Contact the Tourism & Congress GmbH, Kaiserstraße 56, Frankfurt am Main 60329 (tel. +49/69-21 23 08 08; fax +49/69-21 24 05 12). Two people in a double room for two nights typically range from DM400 to DM600. The Marriott is particularly convenient to the race start and finish, as are the pensions in Westend.

RELATED EVENTS / RACES If you have the kids in tow, they can participate in the 4.2K Mini Marathon (ages 10-17), or the .42K or 2K run for those 9 and under.

AREA ATTRACTIONS Like any large, cosmopolitan city, Frankfurt offers an array of museums, nightlife and restaurants. Its central location makes it convenient to many other interesting places, such as the Rhine Valley, Heidelberg, and Strasbourg, France.

VENICE MARATHON

OVERALL: 98.5

COURSE BEAUTY: 9+

COURSE DIFFICULTY: 3+

APPROPRIATENESS FOR FIRST TIMERS: 10-

ORGANIZATION: 9+

CROWDS: 8

RACE DATA

Overall Ranking:	7
Quality Ranking:	19
Quickness Ranking:	42
Contact:	Venicemarathon Club
	Via Felisati, 34
	I-30171 Mestre Venezia
	Italy
	Tel. +39/41-940 644
	Fax +39/41-940 349
Date:	Generally fourth Sunday in October (October 25, 1998; October 24, 1999)
Start Time:	9:45 a.m.
Time Course Closes:	3:45 p.m.
Number of Finishers:	4,800 in 1996
Course:	Point to point
Certification:	AIMS
Course Records:	Male: (open) 2:09:26
	Female: (open) 2:29:11
Elite Athlete Programs:	Yes (contact the race)
Cost:	Lit.115,000/135,000
Age groups/Divisions:	M: 18-23, 24-39, 40-44, 45-49, 50-54, 55-59, 60+
	F: 20-29, 30-34, 35-39, 40-44, 45-49, 50-54, 55+
Walkers:	No
Requirements:	18 years old
Temperature:	57° (14°C)
Aid/Splits:	8 / 10K, halfway, 30K

HIGHLIGHTS   A floating city with thoroughfares of water, Venice and its web of narrow passages may not seem the ideal venue for a major international marathon. The crafty marathon organizers have solved this little problem by starting the marathon in Stra, reaching Venice proper near 37K. And if the appropriate route does not exist, the organizers create one, as in the unique pontoon bridge spanning the mouth of the Grand Canal. Created solely for the Venice Marathon, this floating bridge exists for less than 24 hours, choking off the city's primary lifeline on race day. Italy's largest marathon shadows the Brenta River under the gaze of historic *palazzi*, through industrial Marghera and Mestre before traversing the 3K-long bridge linking the mainland to Venice. The race benefits Unicef, the United Nations' children's fund.

COURSE DESCRIPTION   The Venice Marathon's point-to-point route begins at the central Piazza Marconi in Stra, a small town west of Venice. Runners soon meet the Brenta River, a small, quiet stream lined with weeping trees and at least 32 historic villas. Among them is the Villa Pisani, an 18th-century estate once occupied by Napoleon. The race then becomes a mixture of rural commercial and residential areas, passing through Fiesso from 3K to 4K and the nice village of Dolo from 5K to 7K. Then it's back in the curving countryside, through Mira (10K), and into a particularly pleasant section of the route, lined with trees and several noteworthy *palazzi*. Runners reach Oriago at 15K, and the gorgeous, 16th-century Villa Foscari at 18.7K. Here, the character of the course changes dramatically. Now dominated by industrial and commercial zones, runners plod through Marghera from 21K to 26K and Mestre from 27K to 34K. At 33K, runners face a good climb up an overpass as they head to Liberty Bridge (34K to 37K). After runners emerge from Marghera and Mestre, Venice floats ahead of them like a desert oasis. Liberty Bridge allows runners to savor their trek, knowing that rest and refreshment lie just ahead. Once in Venice, runners traipse through the harbor area (38K), cross the first of the race's 13 arched bridges, and then trace the edge of the Giudecca Canal. It is here that the race you have imagined materializes. After 41K, you run on water over the floating 160-meter bridge spanning the Grand Canal. As the little bridges grow more difficult, some of Venice's greatest attractions lie to your left: St. Mark's Square, the Doge's Palace, and the Bridge of Sighs. When you spy the giant red hand rising from the ground, you know the finish lies just ahead. Dig down for the final bridges prior to the finish on Riva dei Sette Martiri.

CROWD/RUNNER SUPPORT   Nearly 300,000 people crowd along the race route, mostly in the villages along the Brenta River and in historic Venice. The race provides aid stations every 5K, with water, sports drink, fruit, and sugar. Sponging stations sit in between the aid stations. Ailing runners can drop out at the 20K, 25K, and 32K points and hop on the bus/boat to the finish.

RACE LOGISTICS   The race provides bus transportation from Venice-Tronchetto and the Mestre Train Station to the race start in Stra. Buses begin leaving at 7:00 a.m. Transportation is also provided after the race from the finish area to the start, with service beginning at 2:00 p.m. Of

course, you can leave your bag of warm-ups at the start for retrieval after the race.

ACTIVITIES Pick up your race packet at the Exposport, located at the Tronchetto Terminal, on Friday or Saturday. The expo is also open on Sunday afternoon. Runners may not pick up their numbers on race day. A pasta party is held on Saturday evening in Marghera. However, runners should have no problem finding the pasta of their choice in one of the city's hundreds of restaurants. The awards ceremony kicks off after the race at 6:00 p.m. at the Exposport.

AWARDS All runners receive a Venice Marathon T-shirt and race program, while finishers also earn a commemorative medal. The race mails finisher certificates and results books to runners following the event. A total of ITL 85,000,000 in prize money goes to the top runners, with additional bonuses available for runners who break certain time standards.

ACCOMMODATIONS If you want to experience the Venice ambience, then stay in Venice proper. For cheaper lodging, but far less atmosphere, try Mestre. For accommodation information, contact Oltrex Viaggi, Pizzale Roma, S. Croce 466/F, Venice (tel. +39/41-570-9287; fax +39/41-522-1986).

RELATED EVENTS/RACES On Sunday morning, approximately 10,000 runners take part in the noncompetitive Unicef Welcome Run, a 5K race to promote the Unicef initiative.

DUBLIN MARATHON

OVERALL: 93.9

COURSE BEAUTY: 9-

COURSE DIFFICULTY: 4+ (SEE APPENDIX)

APPROPRIATENESS FOR FIRST TIMERS: 10-

ORGANIZATION: 9+

CROWDS: 7-

RACE DATA

Overall Ranking: 19
Quality Ranking: 23
Quickness Ranking: 76
Contact: Dublin Marathon
P.O. Box 1287
Dublin 2, Ireland
Tel. +353/1-670-7918
Fax +353/1-670-7921

Date: Generally fourth Monday in October
Start Time: 9:30 a.m.
Time Course Closes: NA
Number of Finishers: 4,065 in 1997
Course: Loop
Certification: Irish National Athletic Board
Course Records: New course in 1998
Elite Athlete Programs: Yes
Cost: US$50
Age groups/Divisions: M: <35, 35-39, 40-44, 45-49, 50-54, 55-59, 60+
F: <40, 40-44, 45-49, 50+
wheelchair, cerebral palsy and blind
Walkers: Yes
Requirements: None
Temperature: 54° - 57° (12°C - 14°C)
Aid/Splits: 8 / digital clocks every 5 miles

H I G H L I G H T S   We've all seen the worn phrase "runner friendly" on countless race entry blanks, but how many races actually live up to this self-described billing? The Dublin Marathon certainly does. Internationally known as the "Friendly Marathon," a tag bestowed by the world press and not the race, Dublin shows that proverbial Irish hospitality is not limited to the city's pubs. Every year over half the field comes from overseas, many returning for a second or third time. Held annually on a Monday bank holiday, Dublin emphasizes the community. Thousands of spectators line the winding loop that starts and finishes on O'Connell Street, the city's most famous thoroughfare. In between, runners take in many of Dublin's historic Georgian streets, passing Trinity College, Merrion Square, St. Stephen's Green and Phoenix Park along the way. The International Breakfast Run and a pasta party with traditional Irish music and coffee provide a nice race warm-up. Please do your best to save the Guinness and Irish whiskey for after the race.

COURSE DESCRIPTION The Dublin Marathon features a loop course with as many turns as the city has pubs. Starting on O'Connell Street, the race travels south over the Liffey River before passing the 43-acre grounds of Trinity College, the oldest university in Ireland and home to the Book of Kells. Bordered by fashionable brick-faced Georgian townhouses through Merrion Square and Ballsbridge, Dublin's most prestigious suburb, the course reaches the Montrose Hotel and National Television Headquarters when looping University College around 4 miles. With the exception of a 20-foot drop between mile 5 and 7, the route gradually rises 110-feet to the 16-mile mark, passing some of the city's finest restaurants and shops in St. Stephen's Green near mile 10 and the boisterous crowd in The Coombe historic area between miles 10.5 and 12. From The Coombe, the race goes southwesterly through suburbs before twisting north to the Walkinstown Roundabout near mile 18. Miles 19 to 22 run northwest and include a 250-yard steep downhill over the Old Salmon Leap Bridge into the Old Village near 22 miles. With the high stone wall of Phoenix Park on the left and the Liffey River to the right, runners now travel east on a slight downhill for the final 4 miles to the O'Connell Street finish.

CROWD/RUNNER SUPPORT Few marathons boast more enthusiastic crowd support than Dublin. While spectators are scattered along the whole course, areas of heaviest support include: the start and finish area on O'Connell Street, the Ballsbridge neighborhood around 3 miles, St. Stephen's Green near mile 10, and The Coombe historic area between miles 11 and 12. Onlookers can easily walk from the start to the 10-mile mark to support their favorite runners. Aid stations sit every 3 to 4 miles and contain water, candy, first aid, portaloos, and Irish cheer.

RACE LOGISTICS Runners must find their own transportation to the start, although several hotels lie within easy walking distance. City buses, taxis and Dublin Area Rapid Transit (DART) are readily accessible for those staying further away.

ACTIVITIES The race has not determined the site or time of packet pick-up. Contact the marathon office for the latest information. A pasta party with live, traditional Irish music happens Sunday night, time and location to be announced. Tickets for this popular event cost $8 and should be pre-booked on your entry form. The awards ceremony and post-race party typically take place at an area pub.

AWARDS   Every finisher receives a T-shirt and marathon souvenir. The top male and female runners receive a car and Dublin crystal, while second through sixth-place runners take home prize money and Dublin crystal. Master category winners receive prize money and Dublin crystal, while other category winners receive, you guessed it, Dublin crystal.

ELITE RUNNERS INFORMATION   Complimentary entry, travel expenses, and accommodations are often offered to fast runners. Contact the marathon office for consideration.

ACCOMMODATIONS   From concrete high rises to family-owned guesthouses and inns, Dublin offers a wide variety of lodging options. Accommodations closest to the start include: Royal Dublin, 40 Upper O'Connell Street (tel. 800-528-1234; fax +353/1-873-3120); and Gresham, 23 Upper O'Connell Street (tel. 800-44-UTELL; fax +353/1-878-7175). Also within 1 mile of the start are: Temple Bar Hotel, Fleet Street (tel. 800-44-UTELL; fax +353/1-677-3088); and Central, 1-5 Exchequer Street (tel. +353/1-679-7303; fax +353/1-679-7303). Those on a budget may consider Jurys Christchurch Inn, Christchurch Place (tel. 800-44-UTELL; fax +353/1-475-0488), lying approximately 1.25 miles from the start. Two guest houses a bit further away are Frankies Guest Hotel, 8 Camden Place (tel. +353/1-478-3087); and The Horse and Carriage Guest Hotel, 15 Aungier Street (tel. +353/1-478-3537; fax +353/1-478-4010).

RELATED EVENTS/RACES   On Sunday morning, the International Breakfast Run (included in the entry fee of foreign participants) helps runners release a few pre-race jitters. The approximately 3K race goes around a historic part of Dublin. Afterward, competitors exchange international race T-shirts and enjoy a breakfast in Dublin's Civic Offices with the sounds of local music echoing in the background.

AREA ATTRACTIONS   Allow plenty of time for your stay; there is much to see and do here, including visits to the National Gallery, National Museum, and Dublin Castle. See the Book of Kells at Trinity College and stroll through the shops or dine in one of the fine restaurants in Temple Bar or St. Stephen's Green. Head a dozen miles south of town to County Wicklow which features some of Ireland's best rural scenery. Glendalough, a beautiful monastery, and Powerscourt Waterfall and Gardens, are two leading area attractions. Of course, you can't go wrong simply sipping thick brown Guinness while listening to a good Irish yarn at the local pub.

VARDINOYIANNIOS MARATHON

OVERALL: 73.8

COURSE BEAUTY: 9-

COURSE DIFFICULTY: 2+ (SEE APPENDIX)

APPROPRIATENESS FOR FIRST TIMERS: 6

ORGANIZATION: 7+

CROWDS: 1+

RACE DATA

Overall Ranking: 104
Quality Ranking: 103
Quickness Ranking: 26
Contact: Vardinoyiannios International Marathon
OFI Amateur Sports Club
Isavron Street 93
Iraklion 71303 Crete
Greece
Tel. +30/81-259-850
Fax +30/81-261-860

Date: Generally first Sunday in November (November 1, 1998)
Start Time: 9:30 a.m.
Time Course Closes: 1:30 p.m.
Number of Finishers: 70 in 1997
Course: Point to point
Certification: AIMS
Course Records: Male: (open) 2:19:05
Female: (open) 2:43:57
Elite Athlete Programs: Yes
Cost: None
Age groups/Divisions: None
Walkers: No
Requirements: 18 years old
Temperature: 68° - 77° (20°C - 25°C)
Aid/Splits: 16 / verbal splits every 5K

HIGHLIGHTS   On the Greek island of Crete, birthplace of Europe, the marathon returns to its simple beginnings in the Vardinoyiannios International Marathon, the only marathon with prize money that does not have an explicit entry fee. Like in the old days, VIM is not meant for the slow of foot. You must run under 4 hours here. This small race (about 70 runners) is held in the memory of Paul Vardinoyiannis, race benefactor since its inception in 1986. The runners may be few, but they are exceptionally varied; in 1997, 21 countries were represented at the race. The point-to-point course starts at the Mallia Palace, and travels west along the built-up coastline to Iraklion, where it finishes in Iraklion Stadium.

COURSE DESCRIPTION   VIM's course starts outside the ancient, Minoan ruins of the Mallia Palace. Runners proceed west along the flat road, reaching the beach town of

Mallia near 5K. The course continues flat along the Sea of Crete to Stalida around 10K. Between 11K and 16K the route rises a very gradual 25 feet, passing through the old town of Hersonissos near the 15K mark. Runners stay along Crete's north coast, which tends to become increasingly built up with resort hotels the nearer you get to Iraklion, going by the U.S. air base (25K) and airport (35K). The only minor incline during this period is 30 feet between 28K and 30K. By now you reach the outskirts of Iraklion, passing by the port and along the city's original Venetian Walls from 38K to 42K. The marathon finishes on the track of the Iraklion Liberty Stadium.

CROWD/RUNNER SUPPORT Small events typically do not attract huge crowds, and VIM is no exception to that rule. Runners come across handfuls of support in the coastal villages, the harbor of Iraklion, and the finish. The race pampers runners with 8 full-blown aid stations and 8 water stations. The full aid stations contain water and sports drink. In between those are water and sponging stations. The race will set out your own drink bottles at the desired locations. Simply take your bottles to the race information desk in the official hotel on Saturday evening. You can receive medical assistance at 15K and 30K.

RACE LOGISTICS Unless you want to do some sight-seeing on your own, you do not need a car at the VIM. Race officials pick you up at the airport and whisk you to the race hotel. They also transport you from the hotel to the start line in Mallia and back to the hotel after the race. You may leave your warm-ups inside the bus.

ACTIVITIES Runners receive their race packages at the host hotel. On Saturday you can tour the course by bus, followed by the technical meeting which gives you last-minute details and instructions about the race. The awards ceremony takes place immediately after the marathon. On Sunday evening, runners meet for the farewell party at the host hotel.

AWARDS All runners receive T-shirts, sports bags, medals, and certificates. Trophies and prize money go to the top 6 male runners and top 3 female runners. Prize money can change from year to year, but typically ranges as follows for men: US$2,500 for first, $2,000 for second, $1,500 for third, $1,000 for fourth, $750 for fifth, and $500 for sixth. For women it goes $2,000 for first, $1,500 for second, and $1,000 for third. There are also bonuses for a new race record ($1,000) and for times under 2:17 for men and 2:35 for women.

ELITE RUNNERS INFORMATION VIM usually recruits two or three fast runners each year. Contact the race if you merit consideration for transportation, lodging, and board for the marathon.

ACCOMMODATIONS The Akti Zeus Hotel, located along the oceanfront about 8 kilometers east of Iraklion, serves as the official race hotel. Make your reservations through the marathon office.

AREA ATTRACTIONS Crete contains fabulous remains from the many civilizations that have occupied the island: Arabs, Venetians, Turks, and Greeks. One of Greece's best museums is the Archaeological Museum in Iraklion which contains artifacts from the ancient Minoan period. Near Iraklion are the famous Knossos palace ruins, around which the myth of the labyrinth and Minotaur swirl. Also nearby is the charming village of Bali. To escape the crowds, head to Crete's southern side.

MALTA CHALLENGE MARATHON

OVERALL: 82.3

COURSE BEAUTY: 9

COURSE DIFFICULTY: 5+

APPROPRIATENESS FOR FIRST TIMERS: 7

ORGANIZATION: 8

CROWDS: 4

RACE DATA

Overall Ranking:	80
Quality Ranking:	81
Quickness Ranking:	90
Contact:	Sportsmans Travel International
	Malta Challenge Marathon
	P.O. Box 112
	Valletta CMR 01
	Malta, Europe
	Tel. +356/34 43 78
	Fax +356/33 85 59
Date:	November 13-15, 1998; November 19-21, 1999
Start Time:	Stage 1: 3:00 p.m.; Stage 2: 11:00 a.m.; Stage 3: 9:00 a.m.
Time Course Closes:	Stage 1: 4:30 p.m.; Stage 2: 11:45 a.m.; Stage 3: 12:45 p.m.
Number of Finishers:	247 in 1996
Course:	Varies
Certification:	AIMS
Course Records:	Male: (open) 2:15:49
	Female: (open) 2:37:34
Elite Athlete Programs:	Yes (contact the race)
Cost:	LM 27.50
Age groups/Divisions:	Males: 17-19, 20-39, 40+
	Females: 17-19, 20-34, 35+
Walkers:	No
Requirements:	17 years old
Temperature:	57° - 68° (14°C - 20°C)
Aid/Splits:	5 / none

HIGHLIGHTS Off the toe of Italy, tiny Malta rests in the narrow of the Mediterranean Sea, pinched between Sicily and Tunisia. Three inhabited islands of various sizes comprise the country: Malta at 246 square km, Gozo at 67 square km, and Comino at 2.7 square km. Perhaps it is fitting that this former British colony stages a marathon in three stages of various lengths, mirroring in some way the size disparity of the three islands themselves. Stage 1 runs from the highlands of the interior to the coastal cliffs and back for a total of 11.195K. Stage 2 the following day consists of two challenging 3K loops in the fishing village of Kalkara. The final 25K in stage 3 follow the coastal road into the capital of Valletta. Running a marathon in stages may sound easy, but the three straight days of heavy exertion wear on the body. And the difficulty of the route could create sore legs going into the final day. Thus, an important factor is race strategy. Namely, how hard do you run the first two days, ensuring that you leave enough spring in your legs for the final, longest stage? Such novel factors, combined with Malta's pleasant winter weather, make this race a fun and interesting running experience.

COURSE DESCRIPTION Stage 1. The 11.195K first stage begins in the interior town of Rabat. The course heads to the sea, rising about 150 feet from .5K to 1.5K. Undulating to 3K, the race then climbs steadily (160 feet) to 5K. Runners pass through Buskett before reaching the Dingli Cliffs. You briefly skirt the cliffs and then loop back toward Rabat. The course loses about 325 feet from 5K to 10K, giving runners a good break for the final 100-foot climb to the finish in Rabat.

Stage 2. This two-loop stage starts in the quaint fishing village of Kalkara. Runners climb about 160 feet over the first kilometer. The second kilometer goes mostly down, with another incline from 2K to 2.5K. The final .5K screams downhill about 125 feet to where runners begin the second lap.

Stage 3. The point-to-point 25K final stage begins at the Coral Reef Restaurant in Qawra. Heading north, runners reach the coastal town of Bugibba, where the course merges onto the coast road. Skimming past the sea for a spell, runners veer inland at 8K across St. George's peninsula, beginning an arduous climb of 175 feet over 2K. At 10K, the course descends about the same elevation by 11.5K. Runners soon pass through animated St. Julian's Bay, where they again go mostly along the fortified coast. Essentially flat now, the course passes through Balluta Bay, Sliema, Tigne Fort, Gzira seafront, Ta' Xbiex and Msida Creek, Pieta Creek, and Floriana. Just before 21K, you face a short, tough hill of about 125 feet, followed by 1K of general downgrade. Runners reach the northern battlements of Valletta and, on a gentle upgrade, finish under the arches of Freedom Square.

CROWD/RUNNER SUPPORT The three stages combine rural and city running, which means the spectators vary accordingly. There are 5 aid stations along the three routes. During the first 11.195K stage you find one aid station at 5K. There are no aid stations during the tough 6K second stage. Organizers provide four aid stations (every 5K), two of which have sponges, along the 25K final stage. The aid tables have water and a sports drink.

RACE LOGISTICS Runners receive complimentary transportation from the race hotels to the start of each stage, and then back to the hotels after each race.

ACTIVITIES The Malta Challenge gives runners a course preview on Thursday, the day before the first stage. This should help finalize your last-minute race strategies. A pre-race pasta party and a post-race bash on Monday evening highlight race weekend festivities.

AWARDS Every runner receives a race program, commemorative pin, and T-shirt. If you finish the three stages, you also get a finish-line photo, 70 mm medal, minted at the Birmingham mint, certificate, and results. Top age-group finishers are awarded trophies and a sports voucher. The top three overall runners earn US$250, $200, and $150 respectively.

ACCOMMODATIONS The race has not finalized its official host hotels for future events. Runners generally stay in Sliema. Contact the race for the latest accommodations information.

RELATED EVENTS/RACES Runners can choose to run only the 6K second stage, if they don't feel like sandwiching two tough races around it.

AREA ATTRACTIONS Malta has a long history of domination by foreign powers. Consequently, the influence of many cultures is felt and seen throughout the tiny country. Among the treats are: Megalithic temples, the old city of Mdina (called the silent city), the picturesque "Luzzus" fishing boats, the Casino de Malte in St. Julians, scenic fishing villages, and the Blue Grotto.

FLORENCE MARATHON

OVERALL: 92.1

COURSE BEAUTY: 10-

COURSE DIFFICULTY: 4-

APPROPRIATENESS FOR FIRST TIMERS: 9

ORGANIZATION: 9-

CROWDS: 5-

RACE DATA

Overall Ranking:	25
Quality Ranking:	58
Quickness Ranking:	63
Contact:	Firenze Marathon Committee
	Casella Postale 597
	I-50100 Firenze
	ITALY
	Tel. & Fax +39/55-572-885
Date:	Generally last Sunday in November
Start Time:	9:00 a.m.
Time Course Closes:	3:00 p.m.
Number of Finishers:	3,257 in 1996
Course:	One-and-one-half loops
Certification:	AIMS
Course Records:	Male: (open) 2:14:02
	Female: (open) 2:32:53
Elite Athlete Programs:	Yes
Cost:	Lit. 70,000
Age groups/Divisions:	Open, walkers, wheelchairs
Walkers:	Yes
Requirements:	18 years old, medical certificate
Temperature:	46° - 54° (8°C - 12°C)
Aid/Splits:	8 / none

HIGHLIGHTS The Florence Marathon may be one of the ultimate tourist marathons. Of course, this implies two sides. On the one side, the flat course passes many of Florence's most important and beautiful sites — the Duomo, Piazza Signoria, the Uffizi Gallery, the Arno River, and the center city itself. But, like tourists, this beauty and flatness come at a price. In Florence's case the price being a winding route with more turns and shimmies than Michael Jackson, much of which you cover twice. In short, don't go to Florence to run fast or to experience a true "runner's" marathon. Like fine Tuscan wine, enjoy Florence slowly, lingering over its colors, smells, and textures, blending in like a native.

COURSE DESCRIPTION The Florence Marathon follows a circuitous, one-and-one-half loop route through mostly city streets. The race starts near the city stadium, site of local soccer matches. The first 2K circle the park bordering the stadium. Then the course turns mostly commercial, until the 4K point, where it turns urban residential. Here, runners face a very gradual 1K incline up Via Pier Carpponi until the left turn on Via Fra Bartolommeo which leads you

toward the historic center of Florence on a gentle downgrade. By 5K you are running in the old city, with Giotto's Campanile in the distance. (Much of the race in the center runs over thick-slab cobblestones which test the cushion of your shoes.) Near 5.5K, runners pass through Piazza San Marco and Piazza della SS. Annunziata, and then start veering toward the Arno River (about 7K), passing one of Florence's original city gates, Porta alla Croce. This begins some exceptionally scenic running along the Arno River with the hills beyond the flowing water to the left and graceful Florence to the right. The course quickly turns back toward the center, reaching Piazza San Croce and its beautiful 13th-century church at 8K. The next stop on this tour is the incredible Duomo (9K), Florence's masterpiece cathedral built with green, white, and pink marble and capped by a tremendous dome. The next kilometer or so offers great window shopping as you pass many of Florence's most exclusive stores, taking a "U" route through Piazza Della Signora, Florence's most beautiful square (and race finish), to the opposite side of the Duomo (10K). After circling Piazza Giovanni and passing through Piazza Republica, runners begin the 2K trek to Cascine Park (12K to the half-marathon point). This shady park makes for some pleasant running, particularly the asphalt streets. The only problem being that you cover almost every road in the park, going up and back, up and back again. (This can prove particularly demoralizing during the second loop through the park from 30K to 39K.) After halfway, you cross the Arno over Ponte Vittoria, with spectacular views of Florence to your left. The course then flows against the river for about 2K, before turning up commercial Via De Serragli, eventually U-turning at Piazza della Calza (near 24K) onto Via Romana. Runners pass the Pitti Palace as they approach the river and 25K. After again enjoying wonderful views of the city, you cross the river over Ponte alle Grazie. Here the course begins its second loop through the center using slightly different streets at times than the first loop, but passing many of the same sights (26K to 30K). After exiting Cascine Park for the second time, you follow the river on Lungarno Vespucci until Piazza de Giudici, where you head left on Via dè Castellani for the final 1K loop around the Duomo and back down to the spectacular finish in the Uffizi Gallery on Piazza Della Signoria.

CROWD/RUNNER SUPPORT One of the benefits of the labrynith course is that spectators can view the race at several points with minimal movement. Also, since this is Christmas shopping season, many Florentines browse the shops in the city center on race day. This spells good news for marathoners who will find fair numbers of supporters in the center as a result. The stretches through Cascine Park will be the loneliest, but then you will be too busy making sure you're going the right way to notice. The race organization provides aid stations every 5K, offering water, sports drink, fruit, and sugar cubes. Look for the kilometer markers on the ground.

RACE LOGISTICS Runners need to find their own way to the start. Options include public buses, trains, or taxis. The stadium does not lie far from the center (about 4 miles). You have access to changing facilities after the race. Hobble back to your hotel in the center from the finish, or take the public transportation.

ACTIVITIES Pick up your race packet and attend the expo on Friday and Saturday before the race at Centro Affari Firenze (convention center) at Piazza Adua near the Central Train Station. On Saturday morning, the race offers guided tours of Florence, and during the day you may attend the Technical Conference (subjects vary yearly). The pasta party dishes out on Saturday evening, but you are better off finding your own great restaurant.

AWARDS Every entrant receives a T-shirt or sweatshirt (depending on the year) and possibly some other race memento. Finishers under 5 hours also receive a medal and certificate. There are no age-group awards.

ELITE RUNNERS INFORMATION Fast runners could be offered elite status at the discretion of the race director. You would most likely be offered hotel and free entry. Modest prize money goes to the top 20 men and top 10 women. Men's prize money ranges from Lit. 3,000,000 for first, Lit. 1,500,000 for second, Lit. 1,000,000 for third, Lit. 800,000 for fourth, Lit. 600,000 for fifth, Lit. 500,000 for sixth, Lit. 400,000 for seventh, Lit. 300,000 for eighth, Lit. 250,000 for ninth, Lit. 200,000 for tenth, and Lit. 100,000 for eleventh through 20th. For women, prize money ranges from Lit. 3,000,000 for first, Lit. 1,500,000 for second, Lit. 750,000 for third, Lit. 300,000 for fourth, and Lit. 100,000 for fifth through tenth.

ACCOMMODATIONS Florence Marathon runners can get special rates at the various affiliated Florence Promhotels. For information and reservations, contact Florence Promhotels directly (tel. +39/55-570 481; fax +39/55-587 189).

RELATED EVENTS/RACES The marathon intends to add a half marathon race to its menu. Details are not yet available.

AREA ATTRACTIONS Florence needs no introduction with its international reputation for art and culture, despite its relatively small size. Headlining attractions include the incredible Duomo (cathedral), Uffizi Gallery, and Michelangelo's original David.

A FRICA / **M** IDDLE **E** AST

PREVIOUS PAGE: COMRADES MARATHON

TIBERIAS INTERNATIONAL MARATHON

OVERALL: 75.4

COURSE BEAUTY: 8

COURSE DIFFICULTY: 3

APPROPRIATENESS FOR FIRST TIMERS: 7-

ORGANIZATION: 8

CROWDS: 2

R A C E   D A T A

Overall Ranking:	100
Quality Ranking:	90
Quickness Ranking:	48
Contact:	Tiberias Marathon
	c/o Shartours
	6 Shmuel Hanaziv Street
	Netanya 42281 - Israel
	Tel. +972/9-862-1343
	Fax +972/9-862-3082
Date:	Generally first Wednesday in January
Start Time:	9:00 a.m.
Time Course Closes:	2:00 p.m.
Number of Finishers:	241 in 1997
Course:	Out and back
Certification:	AIMS
Course Records:	Male: (open) 2:14:02
	Female: (open) 2:34:17
Elite Athlete Programs:	Yes (contact the race)
Cost:	US$30
Age groups/Divisions:	M: 18-39, 40-44, 45-49, 50-54, 55-59, 60-64, 65+, wheelchair
	W: 18-34, 35-44, 45+, wheelchair
Walkers:	Yes (earlier start)
Requirements:	None
Temperature:	59° - 68° (15°C to 20°C)
Aid/Splits:	8 / none

HIGHLIGHTS   The lowest marathon in the world, averaging 650 feet below sea level, the Tiberias Marathon follows the footsteps of Jesus around the Biblical Sea of Galilee. Starting and finishing in Tiberias, known for its Byzantine churches, hot springs, and beachfront activities, the race hugs the shoreline passing the famous baptismal site of Yardenit as it crosses the Jordan River near 10K. With the steep, green hills of Golan Heights on the right, the course turns around at Kibbutz Ein Gev on the sea's east coast. Shartours, one of the event organizers, offers several touring options in conjunction with the race, taking in some of the legendary holy land sights such as Mt. Beatitudes, where Jesus delivered the Sermon on the Mount, and Capernaum, where he met his first disciples.

COURSE DESCRIPTION   Starting in downtown Tiberias, on the west shore of the Sea of Galilee, the marathon's mostly flat out-and-back course runs counter clockwise along the shoreline. With the tranquil sea (known by locals as Lake Kinneret) on the left and steep, hilly countryside on the right, the route heads south passing Hamei Tiberias (2K), known for its mineral springs and ancient ruins, including some of the largest and most beautiful mosaics from ancient

synagogues in Israel. After running by mostly beaches and fishing areas, the race hits Yardenit and the Jordan River near 10K. Runners reach Deganya Aleph, considered the mother of all Kibbutzim, around 11K before heading along the sea's eastern edge. With the dramatic, green Golan Heights on the right, the race goes by more beaches and camping sites heading down the date palm-lined road to the turnaround (near 23K) in Kibbutz Ein-Gev. From here, you return the way you came, finishing in front of the Moriah Plaza Hotel in downtown Tiberias.

CROWD/RUNNER SUPPORT Like most rural marathons, Tiberias attracts limited spectator support. While most of your inspiration undoubtedly arises from the race's divine location, expect sizeable crowds at the start, along the road as you exit downtown, and at the turnaround. You'll also enjoy the encouragement of fellow runners coming from the opposite direction on the out-and-back course. Aid stations sit every 5K and contain water and sponges. Upon request, race officials place personal drinks along the course.

RACE LOGISTICS Most participants stay in one of the downtown Tiberias hotels, which makes race morning virtually hassle free.

ACTIVITIES Pick up your race number, T-shirt and goody bag on Tuesday, from 2:30 p.m. to 6:00 p.m. and from 7:30 p.m. to 10:00 p.m. at the Radisson Moriah Plaza on Habonimum Street. For your last supper before the race, head to the pasta party at 6:00 p.m. on Tuesday evening. The awards ceremony begins after the race at 2:00 p.m. inside the hotel.

AWARDS Every entrant receives a T-shirt, while finishers receive medals and certificates. The top three males, if under 2:15:59, receive US$15,000, $5,000 and $2,500, respectively. Otherwise, the prize money is reduced by half. The first three women, if under 2:40:29, earn US$2,500, $1,500, and $1,000, respectively. Otherwise, the sums are reduced by half. Bonuses ($5,000 for men and $1,000 for women) are awarded to course record breakers. Top age-group runners earn trophies.

ACCOMMODATIONS The host hotel, the Radisson Moriah Plaza, Habonimum Street (tel. +972/6-679-2233; fax +972/6-679-2320) offers special room rates. Other nearby options include: Four Points Tiberias, 18 Hashomer Street (tel. +972/6-679-1484); Galei Kinneret, 1 Kaplan Street (tel. +972/6-679-2331; fax +972/6-679-0260); and Meyouhas Youth Hostel, corner of Gedud Barak and Hayarden Streets (tel. +972/6-672-1775; fax +972/6-672-0372). If you don't mind staying further away, nice accommodations exist at any one of several Kibbutz that dot the lake's shoreline. Shartours Ltd. (tel. +972/9-862-1343; fax +972/9-862-3082) is the official tour agent, offering three different travel programs for the race.

RELATED RACES A popular 12K race accompanies the marathon. Starting at 9:25 a.m., the out-and-back race follows the first and last 6K of the marathon course.

AREA ATTRACTIONS Biblical sight-seeing dominates most agendas, of course. After exhausting the Sea of Gallilee attractions, head to the nearby cities of Jerusalem, Bethlehem and Nazareth. When ready to relax, stroll past the shops and restaurants along Tiberias' active lakefront promenade.

EGYPTIAN INTERNATIONAL MARATHON

OVERALL: 83.2

COURSE BEAUTY: 9

COURSE DIFFICULTY: 3

APPROPRIATENESS FOR FIRST TIMERS: 7

ORGANIZATION: 8

CROWDS: 2

R A C E   D A T A

Overall Ranking: 77
Quality Ranking: 90
Quickness Ranking: 48
Contact: Egyptian International Marathon
c/o Egytrav
Nile Hilton Business Center
Tahrir Square
Cairo, Egypt
Tel. +20/2-575-5029 or 766-548
Fax +20/2-778-861

Date: Tentatively second Friday in February
Start Time: 7:30 a.m.
Time Course Closes: 1:30 p.m.
Number of Finishers: 115 in 1997
Course: Four loops
Certification: AIMS
Course Records: Male: NA
Female: NA
Elite Athlete Programs: No
Cost: US$50/57
Age groups/Divisions: None
Walkers: No
Requirements: None
Temperature: 68° - 77° (20°C - 25°C)
Aid/Splits: 16 / none

HIGHLIGHTS   Part of the allure of the marathon distance comes from its fabled and lengthy history — that of the Athenian warrior rushing from the Plain of Marathon to Athens to bring news of their tremendous victory over the vastly more numerous Persians. Well, long before that storied run, an ancient civilization flourished across the Mediterranean Sea from Athens. During the latter stages of this great empire (known as the New Kingdom) the city of Thebes amassed vast wealth during its stint as the capital from about 1550 BC to 1070 BC. The pharaohs used this treasure in part to build incredible temples to their gods and tombs for themselves. The heart of this area off the Nile River's West Bank is now called the Necropolis of Thebes near the current city of Luxor. This triangle celebrating ancient death, straddling the edge of the green Nile River valley and the brown desert hills, serves as the course for the youthful Egyptian International

Marathon as runners celebrate life and good health. In this sense, it is perhaps the most historic course in the world. Among the celebrated monuments runners pass during the race are the: Temple of Hatshepsut (1492 BC - 1458 BC), Temple of Ramses III, two Colossi of Memnon, Medinet Habu, Tomb of the Nobles, and Temple of Seti I. Although the marathon itself is quite small, the three combined races attract about 1,500 runners.

COURSE DESCRIPTION The Egyptian International Marathon essentially consists of a four-lap course around the Necropolis of Thebes. The triangular lap starts in the natural amphitheater of the Temple of Hatshepsut. The dramatic cliffs engulfing the graceful temple make for an inspired beginning. As you leave the temple behind, you reach the main road through the temple complex just after 1K. Still in the desert, the course turns right on the main road, ducking into the half-circle road past the Temple of Tuthmosis III (1.5K). The route passes a series of temple ruins, reaching the largest temple in the complex, that of Ramses III, and the Medinet Habu near 3.5K. Runners proceed on a 1.5K "U" into the green Nile River valley, reaching the road to Luxor just after 5K. Near 6K, you pass the twin Colossi of Memnon, the last vestiges of the Temple of Amenophis III. As you approach 7.5K, you turn left at the "new" village of El-Qurna, which never really got settled, about a half mile from the Nile River. Following the El-Fâdilîya Channel from 7.5K to 9.5K, runners turn left at the tiny village of El-Qurna, passing the Temple of Seti I as the course treads between the green valley and the desert's edge. At 10.5K, you must do an abrupt about-face before getting back on the main road through the complex, completing the triangle. Marathoners must complete three more loops before heading up the final 1K to the finish in front of the Temple of Hatshepsut.

CROWD/RUNNER SUPPORT The race attracts small crowds, estimated by race organizers to be in the 2,000 range. The race has aid stations every 2.5K with water and bananas available.

RACE LOGISTICS Race organizers provide air-conditioned buses from the race hotels to the start and back to the hotels after the race.

ACTIVITIES On Thursday morning before the race, runners can warm up during the breakfast run from Luxor Temple to Karnak Temple in Luxor City on the east bank of the Nile. After the short run, there is a breakfast along the Sacred Lake at the Karnak Temple.

AWARDS All runners receive a marathon memento and a race program. Finishers receive a papyrus certificate and medal. The top 3 male and female finishers also earn prizes.

ACCOMMODATIONS Since the race organization is a travel agency, it is best to call or fax them with your lodging needs.

RELATED EVENTS/RACES Those runners who do not wish to run four laps around the temple complex can opt for the larger Luxor Run (2 laps or about 22.3K) or Ramses Run (1 lap or about 12.3K). All three races combined attract about 1,500 runners.

AREA ATTRACTIONS Everyone knows the main attractions of Egypt are Luxor's amazing temples and tombs, and the pyramids and Sphinx around Giza, near Cairo. You may also want to consider a boat trip down the Nile from Aswan to Luxor. If you are interested in Egyptian artifacts, you must visit the Egyptian Museum in Cairo, the world's foremost collection on ancient Egypt.

CAPE TOWN MARATHON

OVERALL: 88.2

COURSE BEAUTY: 9

COURSE DIFFICULTY: 5- (SEE APPENDIX)

APPROPRIATENESS FOR FIRST TIMERS: 9-

ORGANIZATION: 9+

CROWDS: 3-

RACE DATA

Overall Ranking: 43
Quality Ranking: 57
Quickness Ranking: 87
Contact: Old Mutual Cape Town Marathon
Lubellker Sports Management
P.O. Box 2098, Claireinch 7740
South Africa
Tel. & Fax +27/21-683-7214
E-mail: andrew@ctmarathon.co.za
http://mickey.iafrica.com/apisport
Date: Generally fourth Sunday in February
Start Time: 6:00 a.m.
Time Course Closes: 11:00 a.m.
Number of Finishers: 2,800 in 1997
Course: Loop
Certification: AIMS
Course Records: Male: (open) 2:11:46
Female: (open) 2:36:29
Elite Athlete Programs: No
Cost: R80
Age groups/Divisions: <20, 20-34, 35-39, 40-49, 50-59, 60+
Walkers: No
Requirements: 18 years old and pre-registration
Temperature: 70˚ (21˚C)
Aid/Splits: 14 / halfway

HIGHLIGHTS Josia Thugwane's victory in the 1996 Cape Town Marathon launched him to his gold medal performance in the 1996 Atlanta Olympics. While his victory came out of nowhere for some, Thugwane possessed all the raw materials found in a champion. South Africa's young Cape Town Marathon is no different. Offering terrific race organization, an array of race day events, world-class competitors and above all, a wonderful setting, Cape Town stands on the threshold of joining marathoning's heavyweight events. Located near Africa's southern tip and framed by the 3,000-foot cliffs of Table Mountain and the crashing surf of the Atlantic Ocean, Cape Town ranks as one of the most beautiful cities in the world. As the race acquires the seasoning of experience, hopefully the community will spice this event by coming out in force to support it. Then perhaps it can follow in Thugwane's toesteps to the top of the marathon world.

COURSE DESCRIPTION The CTM features a rolling, loop course through the city's suburban and downtown streets including stints through the fashionable Victoria and

Alfred Waterfront and coastal confines of Green Point and Sea Point. Starting at Mutual Park east of downtown in Pinelands, the course runs flat for the first few kilometers before dropping 33 feet from around 3.5K to 4.5K. Rising 50 feet from 4.5K to 6K, the course levels out with a few tricky corners around the green expanses of Rondebosch Common. Running in the shadow of Devil's Peak, the highest point of Table Mountain, runners head mostly downhill on Liesbeeck Parkway. Plateauing near 10K, the race remains mostly flat over the following 13 kilometers through downtown and to the turnaround in Sea Point. At 13K, the large crowd of half marathoners assembling near their start at the Castle of Good Hope (one of the oldest European structures in South Africa and still used as a military base) provides great encouragement as you soon head northwest to the Victoria and Alfred Waterfront, Cape Town's most vibrant area (17K). Watch your footing through

the cobblestones and relic railway track while pondering what post-race waterfront activities you plan to enjoy. Now heading south within feet of the Atlantic Ocean, the course reaches 20K in Green Point, a favorite spot for other local road races, followed by the halfway point in the bustling suburb of Sea Point. After rounding Sea Point's Presidential Hotel at 21.5K, the route backtracks toward downtown, rising on Somerset Street and more abruptly on Buitengracht Street near 27K. Now entering oak-lined Government Street, runners pass the South African Museum, Botanical Gardens (home of the National Gallery), St. George's Cathedral, and the Houses of Parliament. After passing the old City Hall near 30.5K on Darling, you are soon back to the Castle of Good Hope. A short climb and a screaming downhill over the Observatory Bridge take you into the well-manicured grounds of Valkenberg Hospital at 36K. The last several kilometers run level to the finish in Mutual Park.

CROWD/RUNNER SUPPORT Besides the start and finish area, most spectator support comes near the Castle of Good Hope, the V & A Waterfront, and Sea Point. Community support must continue to grow before Cape Town joins the world's big-time marathons. The potential is certainly there and race organizers know it. In 1997, organizers started using the ChampionChip timing system, normally saved for larger events. Several musical groups, including marimba bands, township troupes, and disco groups play along the second half of the course. Aid stations, stocked with water, Coke, and Powerade, sit every 3K.

RACE LOGISTICS You must provide your own transportation to the start. Most hotels and bed and breakfast inns are not within walking distance. Runners choosing the half marathon must catch a free train to the Castle of Good Hope. The race provides day-care for children 2 to 10 years old from 7:00 a.m. to 1:00 p.m. The service must be booked in advanced and costs R20 per child.

ACTIVITIES Pick up your race packet from 9:00 a.m. to 8:00 p.m. on Friday, or 9:00 a.m. to 5:00 p.m. on Saturday at the Sports Expo in the Old Mutual Sports Grounds, Mutual Park. Please note that you must pre-register for the full and half marathons usually at least 10 days prior to race day. You may purchase race T-shirts by adding R20 to your entry fee. At the conclusion of the Sports Expo, a pasta party feeds carbo-seeking runners at the start/finish area. The awards ceremony and random prize drawing start at 11:00 a.m. in Mutual Park.

AWARDS All finishers earn medals. The top three men and women receive R12,000, R5,000, and R4,000, respectively. Top age-group runners receive trophies, extending to tenth place for masters and to fifth place for other age groups.

ACCOMMODATIONS Several lodging options exist in Pinelands. Bed and breakfast inns include: Pine Cottage, 89 Ringwood Drive (tel. +27/21-531-9911); Mr. and Mrs. Slabbert, 5 Central Avenue (tel. +27/21-531-5867; fax +27/21-531-2942); Margaret House, 23 Margaret Avenue (tel. +27/21-531-2623); and Byways Bed and Breakfast, 4 ByWay (tel. +27/21-531-5646). Other accommodations include the Welwyn Lodge, 17 Welwyn Road (tel. +27/21-531-6019). Along the waterfront try the Breakwater Lodge, Portswood Road (tel. +27/21-406-1911; fax +27/21-406-1070); or City Lodge, corner of Dock Road and Alfred Street (tel. +27/21-419-9450; fax +27/21-419-0460).

RELATED EVENTS/RACES A 5K fun run/walk takes place on Saturday evening. On race morning, runners may opt for a half marathon or 10K. The half marathon begins at 7:45 a.m. near the Castle of Good Hope on Strand Street. The 10K starts at 8:00 a.m. alongside the Old Mutual Sports Grounds. In-line skaters are permitted on the half marathon and 5K courses.

AREA ATTRACTIONS While you are likely to spend much of your time admiring its natural beauty, Cape Town offers much more than its good looks. The Waterfront along the Old Harbor bulges with restaurants, bars, music venues and shops. Another popular pastime is a cable car ride up Table Mountain. Besides the dazzling views, there are some excellent walks on the flat summit and over 1,400 species of flowers. You'll find more spectacular flowers and plants at the Kirstenbosch Botanical Gardens, home to 9,000 different species. Chapman's Peak Drive, a fantastic scenic drive along the side of sheer mountain walls, provides a panorama over Chapman's Bay. Head south to find the Cape of Good Hope Nature Reserve filled with trails, beaches, unique flora, baboons, antelopes and birds.

Two Oceans Marathon

OVERALL: 94.3

COURSE BEAUTY: 10-

COURSE DIFFICULTY: 7+ (SEE APPENDIX)

APPROPRIATENESS FOR FIRST TIMERS: NA

ORGANIZATION: 9+

CROWDS: 6

RACE DATA

Overall Ranking:	17
Quality Ranking:	25
Quickness Ranking:	NA
Contact:	Two Oceans Marathon
	PO Box 2276
	Clareinch 7740
	South Africa
	Tel. +27/21-619-407
	Fax +27/21-618-724
	E-mail: twoceans@iafrica.com
	http://www.twooceansmarathon.org.za
Date:	Easter Saturday (April 11, 1998; April 3, 1999; April 22, 2000; April 14, 2001)
Start Time:	6:00 a.m.
Time Course Closes:	12:30 p.m.
Number of Participants:	7,800 in 1997
Course:	Loop
Certification:	AIMS
Course Records:	Male: (open) 3:03:44
	Female: (open) 3:30:36
Elite Athlete Programs:	Yes
Cost:	R150
Age groups/Divisions:	18-19, 20-39, 40-49, 50-59, 60+
Walkers:	No
Requirements:	18 years old & 4:30 marathon after April 1 in the year prior to the race (for non-South African runners)
Temperature:	55° - 73° (13°C - 23°C)
Aid/Splits:	32 / digital clocks at 28K and 42K

HIGHLIGHTS In what started as a 35-mile training run for the world-renown Comrades Marathon, the Two Oceans Marathon (actually 56 kilometers or 34.72 miles) has evolved into a world-class event of its own. Spanning two oceans and two mountains on South Africa's spectacular Cape Peninsula, the race courses through forests and towns and along mountain roads and oceanfront. Chapman's Peak Drive, wedged between clear ocean waters and 1,000-foot cliffs, may be one of the most beautiful stretches of running anywhere, and a bit challenging as well. The race also boasts excellent organization, including the 32 much-needed aid stations along the route. Weather here is very unpredictable and can play a major factor in the race. Note that to be eligible to run in the Two Oceans Marathon, overseas runners must have completed a standard marathon (26.2 miles) in 4:30 or less since April 1 prior to the race you wish to enter.

COURSE DESCRIPTION The Two Oceans Marathon sports a loop course around the Cape Peninsula. Beginning in the dark on Main Road in Newlands, the race rises about 160 feet during the first 4K, and falls about the same during the trip through the Cape Town suburbs of Wynberg and Plumstead. You won't particularly mind running before the sun rises since the scenery here is unremarkable. The course remains largely flat until runners reach 22K at the end of Fish Hoek. At Westlake near 12 to 13K, you may be able to spot Pollsmoor Prison which housed Nelson Mandela for a while during the apartheid regime. As you and the rising sun meet at Muizenberg (16K), you catch your first glimpse of the Indian Ocean. The following 6K stretch through Muizenberg, St. James, Kalk Bay, Clovelly, and Fish Hoek provides an opportunity to enjoy the beautiful view of False Bay bordered by the Peninsula Mountains on one side and the Hottentots Holland on the other. Although flat, runners may encounter a stiff headwind as they trace the False Bay coast.

At the end of town in Fish Hoek (22K), runners make a sharp right turn up a relatively brief climb of about 80 feet. Turning inland across the peninsula, runners face a lonely period from 22K to 25K along Kommetjie Road. After passing through Sun Valley and Louw's Corner, with some gradual ups and downs, runners reach the halfway point (28K) in Noordhoek, just before the deceiving climb up Little Chapman's (31K). Focus on the stunning view across Noordhoek Beach as the Atlantic Ocean greets you rather than concentrating on the climb, because the trek up the real Chapman's Peak (31K to 34K), a 425-foot climb, lies just ahead. This section is among the most challenging and beautiful

of the race. Soak in the view of the mountain above and the sea below as you trudge up the peak. Try to stay patient; each slope appears to be the summit, disappointing you at every turn. Before 34K, the climb is over as you scream down the peak into Hout Bay. The downhill and the severely cambered road hammer your legs as you descend 550 feet over 6K. Runners come opposite the imposing Sentinel guarding Hout Bay near 40K. Check out the batteries built by the British to protect the bay during the Napoleonic Wars. The bronze statue of a leopard lounging on a rock overlooking the bay commemorates a leopard who, legend has it, would sit on this rock for hours on end years ago.

The 650-foot climb to Constantia Nek (46K) begins almost imperceptibly at 40K. Savor the downhill after this tough climb because you still have a couple of nasty surprises ahead, including two hills through the Cecelia Forest between 48K and 50K. From the Kirstenbosch top gate (51K), the course heads straight downhill past Harry's Corner onto Rhodes Drive with the mountains rising on your left. At 53K the route takes a sharp upward turn to the left onto Union Avenue. With Devil's Peak looming alongside, runners enter the Upper Campus of the University of Cape Town. A short jaunt over the rugby fields takes you to the finish line after 56 kilometers of challenge and beauty.

CROWD / RUNNER SUPPORT At times rural and lonely, and at other times boisterous, runners should find a variety of moods along the Two Oceans Marathon course. You encounter generous shows of support from Fish Hoek residents, in Hout Bay, at the summit of Constantia Nek, in parts of the Cecelia Forest, and at the finish. In addition, the aid station volunteers provide excellent assistance, including music and entertainment, particularly atop Chapman's Peak. The 32 aid stations (almost 1 every mile) stock water, sports drink, Coke, and sponge troughs. Massage therapists and first aid are also available at various points along the route.

RACE LOGISTICS You likely will have to find your own way to the start (unless your package tour provides transportation), probably by car. Runners who must drop from the race can catch a ride in one of the rescue buses. The race stores your warm-ups at the tog bag security service. Shower facilities, food vendors, a pasta party, medical treatment, and children's games await you at the finish line.

ACTIVITIES Pick up your race packet or register at the expo in the Indoor Sports Centre at the University of Cape Town. You may request a course tour ahead of time; the tour usually takes place a few days before the race. The pasta party is held on Thursday from 5:00 p.m. in a large tent on the fields alongside the Sports Centre.

AWARDS Each entrant receives a T-shirt, log book, and sponge; finishers receive cloth badges. Runners who finish under 4 hours are awarded the coveted silver medal, while runners under 6 hours receive bronze medals. A blue medal is given to runners completing the course in 6 to 6.5 hours. Gold, silver, and bronze medals are awarded to the top 3 finishers in each division.

ELITE RUNNERS INFORMATION Top ultra marathon runners, sub-2:15 male marathoners, and sub-2:35 female runners could receive round-trip airfare, one-weeks accommodation, expenses, and the chance to win part of the R181,000 in prize money. Send your resume to Chet Sainsbury at the marathon office for consideration. The top 10 men overall receive gold medals. The top 10 men and women also win prize money ranging from R30,000 for first to R500 for tenth. Top veteran and masters runners are also eligible for prize money.

ACCOMMODATIONS The Breakwater Lodge, Waterfront (tel. +27/21-406-1911; fax +27/21-406-1070) and Garden Court Newlands (tel. +27/21-611-105; fax +27/21-641-241) serve as the headquarter hotels for the race. Many runners prefer to stay along the Cape Town waterfront. For other lodging options you can contact the marathon's travel agent, Penthouse Travel Sporting Tours (tel. +27/21-215-670; fax +27/21-252-300), or the Cape Tourist Authority (CAPTOUR), P.O. Box 1403, Cape Town, 8000, South Africa (tel. +27/21-418-5214; fax +27/21-418-5227).

RELATED EVENTS / RACES For runners who may not be up to 35 miles, the race offers a half marathon (13.1 miles) on race morning. The half starts and finishes at the same venues as the marathon and has a 2.5 hour time limit. A series of Fun Runs (2.5K, 5K, and 10K) are held on Good Friday. All Fun Run finishers receive medals.

AREA ATTRACTIONS While you are likely to spend much of your time admiring its natural beauty, Cape Town offers much more than its good looks. The Waterfront along the Old Harbor bulges with restaurants, bars, music venues and shops. Another popular pastime is a cable car ride up Table Mountain. Besides the dazzling views, there are some excellent walks on the flat summit and over 1,400 species of flowers. You'll find more spectacular flowers and plants at the Kirstenbosch Botanical Gardens, home to 9,000 different species. Chapman's Peak Drive, a fantastic scenic drive along the side of sheer mountain walls, provides a panorama over Chapman's Bay. Head south and you'll find the Cape of Good Hope Nature Reserve filled with trails, beaches, unique flora, baboons, antelopes and birds.

SOUTH AFRICA PRESENTS

a Magnificent route around the beautiful
Cape Peninsula
CAPE TOWN - SOUTH AFRICA
Enjoyed by Thousands

CASTLE *Lite*

TWO OCEANS
56 km MARATHON
& HALF MARATHON (21.1km)

11 April 1998 & 3 April 1999

Athletes need to run a qualifying marathon within 4 hours 30 minutes
Enquiries to:
Castle Lite Two Oceans Marathon
P.O. Box 2276
Clareinch 7740
South Africa
Tel 27 21 619407
Fax 27 21 618724
e-mail: twoceans@iafrica.com
web: www.twooceansmarathon.org.za

YOU'VE GOTTA RUN IT TO BELIEVE IT

COMRADES MARATHON

COURSE BEAUTY: 8

COURSE DIFFICULTY: 9 (SEE APPENDIX)

APPROPRIATENESS FOR FIRST TIMERS: NA

ORGANIZATION: 10

CROWDS: 9-

RACE DATA

Overall Ranking:	15
Quality Ranking:	5
Quickness Ranking:	NA
Contact:	Comrades Marathon
	P.O. Box 100621
	Scottsville, 3209
	South Africa
	Tel. +27/331-94-3510
	Fax +27/331-42-7548
	E-mail: comrades@alpha.futurenet.co.za
	http://www.comrades.org.za
Date:	June 16 annually
Start Time:	6:00 a.m.
Time Course Closes:	5:00 p.m.
Number of Participants:	13,000 in 1997
Course:	ASA, IAAF, and AIMS
Certification:	Male: (open) 5:27:42 (up); 5:24:07 (down)
Course Records:	Female: (open) 6:13:23 (up); 5:54:47 (down)
Elite Athlete Programs:	No
Cost:	US$70
Age groups/Divisions:	18-39, 40-49, 50-59, 60+
Walkers:	No
Requirements:	18 years old, pre-registration, and clearance from your athletic federation
Temperature:	37° - 75° (3°C - 24°C)
Aid/Splits:	55 / none

HIGHLIGHTS   The Comrades Marathon, the largest ultramarathon in the world, is a relentlessly hilly 90-kilometer road race between Pietermaritzburg and Durban in KwaZulu/Natal, South Africa. It is also a national treasure, and one of the best organized races in the world. The race debuted in 1921 when a young railroad engineer named Vic Clapham organized a run between his hometown of Pietermaritzburg and the coastal city of Durban to honor South African veterans of WWI. While only 34 stalwarts braved the initial running, the race has grown through apartheid and post-apartheid years to over 13,000 participants in 1997. Though integrated with non-whites and women only since 1975, Comrades has come to represent a unifying force in the country. Perhaps Victor Strugo, a South African nationally syndicated columnist, captures the Comrades spirit when he writes: "The Comrades Marathon is far more than a road-runner's Everest: it's a national institution. For one entire day, the human face of Comrades suffuses a diverse society with a special awareness of harmony, aspiration and unity." Held annually on Youth Day (June 16), a national holiday commemorating the Soweto Uprising, the country's biggest sporting event attracts thousands of spectators and a national television audience glued to the drama. Even South Africa's President Nelson Mandela has participated by presiding over the awards ceremony.

COURSE DESCRIPTION The challenging route follows the Old Main Road connecting Pietermaritzburg and Durban, primarily running through the KwaZulu/Natal countryside, passing chicken farms and several small towns along the way. While saturated with elevation change, the route features five hills that are especially noteworthy. The Big 5 include: Cowie's Hill, Field's Hill, Botha's Hill, Inchanga Hill and Polly Shorts. The lowest point on the route is Durban at sea level and the apex comes at Umlaas Road, 2,700 feet. The start and finish venues for Comrades alternate each year with the direction of the race. The following is a description of the slightly longer down course which features approximately 5,240 feet of uphill and 7,530 feet of downhill.

Beginning at 2,160 feet in front of the Pietermaritzburg City Hall, the race heads slightly downhill for the first kilometer then begins a gradual climb over the next 7K to the top of Polly Shorts (2,472 feet), which is better known for being the toughest hill on the up run. After a nice downhill off of Polly Shorts, runners undulate past the large crowds at Mpushini (12K) and at the race's highest point at Umlaas Road near 20K. With the exception of noisy Camperdown (25K), the next 10K to Cato Ridge run quietly through native bush, dropping 200 feet over the rolling terrain. At Cato Ridge, children three deep line the road screaming their encouragement. Gradually climbing through balmy Harrison Flats, runners enjoy further voracious, youthful support from the disabled children of Et Hembeni School before reaching the top of Inchanga Hill near 43K. Though a rigorous uphill during the up run, Inchanga Hill on the down run treats runners to a fast, 490-foot descent during the 3K to the halfway point in festive Drummond. Don't get too carried away during this stretch, for the next 7K to Botha's Hill Village regain nearly all of the lost elevation. From here, the course drops 1,080 feet over the following 13K, passing the villages of Gillits, Maytime, and Kloof before hitting Field's Hill. Lying 25K from the finish at an elevation of 1,775 feet, Field's Hill affords the competitors a dramatic view of the ocean and Durban. Only 5K later, the route hits Pinetown (1,162 feet) where, according to two-time champion Ann Trason, "The crowd of spectators is so thick and close to you, that you can barely see where you're going." If your quadriceps haven't detached from your femur, the deafening horde and the continuous downhill should hasten your finish. With approximately 14K left, the course joins the freeway for nearly 10K before hitting the city of Durban for the final 4K push to the finish inside the Kingsmead Cricket Stadium. In all, the race loses 1,162 feet over the final 20K. (Note: Unlike most races, kilometer marks along the Comrades course indicate distance from the finish rather than from the start).

CROWD/RUNNER SUPPORT Thousands of South Africans perch along the course. In addition to the huge crowds at the start and finish, expect enthusiastic support at Cato Ridge (31K), Drummond (halfway), Gillits, Maytime and Kloof (between 60K and 65K), and from Pinetown (near 70K) to the finish. Large crowds also congregate at a few freeway access points early on the course: Mpushini (12K), Umlaas Road (20K), and Camperdown (25K). Given the race organizers deftness in moving and supporting more than 13,000 runners over the 56-mile course, Comrades is one of the best-organized running races in the world. Runners come across fifty-five aid stations, containing water, Coke, and Powerade. Many stations also carry cookies, biscuits, oranges, bananas, potatoes and candy. Additionally, 15 physiotherapy stations and 4 diabetic stations disperse along the course.

RACE LOGISTICS Race organizers provide transportation to the start for a R20 fee. You must purchase tickets at registration, the Durban Expo, or at the Comrades House. Buses for the start depart from the Marine Parade Holiday Inn and the front gate of the expo between 3:15 a.m. and 4:15 a.m. The return buses leave the finish line at 5:15 p.m. The race transports your clothing to the finish. Be aware that Comrades maintains an 11 hour time limit with the following cutoffs: halfway (Drummond) – 5.5 hours; 20K to go – 9 hours; and 7K to go – 10.5 hours.

ACTIVITIES Comrades features one of the largest expos in the sport. The two-day event at the Durban Expo Centre, corner of Walnut Road and Ornance Road, occurs June 14th from 8:00 a.m. to 9:00 p.m. and June 15th from 8:00 a.m. to 8:00 p.m. Pick up your race packet at the International Runners Area. International participants can tour the course two days before the race. An awards ceremony starts promptly at 5:05 p.m.

AWARDS Each entrant receives a T-shirt, peak cap, and race program. Finishers receive a medal and cloth badge. The top 10 men and 5 women receive gold medals as well as a portion of the R340,000 in prize money. Trophies are presented to team winners and other unique categories such as: novice, oldest, and last finisher. Silver and bronze medals are presented to all finishers under 7.5 hours and 11 hours, respectively. All finishers qualify for a random drawing for a Nissan car. Read about your accomplishment in the following day's *The Mercury* newspaper which prints the name, time, and place of each finisher.

ACCOMMODATIONS The Durban Hilton, 12-14 Walnut Road (tel. +27/31-336-8100; fax +27/31-336-8200) serves as the official race hotel. A number of hotels offer special rates for Comrades competitors, including: Karos Edward Hotel (tel. +27/31-373-681); and Marine Parade Holiday Inn (tel. +27/31-373-341). In addition, there are a number of caravan/camping parks, youth hostels, motels, holiday flats, beach cottages, and time-share units available. Call the Pietermaritzburg Publicity Association for more information (tel. +27/331-451-348; fax +27/331-943-535). In Durban, call Tourism Durban (tel. +27/31-3044-934; fax +27/31-3046-196). Turners Travel (tel. +27/31-3321-451; fax +27/31-3325-709) is the official travel agency.

AREA ATTRACTIONS Stop at the Pietermaritzburg Publicity House and obtain maps for a self-guided town trail tour exploring the many historic landmarks within the city. Pietermaritzburg also houses many excellent museums and the Comrades Marathon House. In Durban, the primary attraction is the long strand of beach. There are plenty of opportunities to participate in water sports such as: diving, surfing and sailing. If you're looking for a safari, then venture to one of the many nearby game and nature reserves. The reserves are home to a variety of animals including: black and white rhinos, zebras, elephants, hyenas, leopards, cheetahs and giraffes.

MOUNT MERU MARATHON

OVERALL: 88.8

COURSE BEAUTY: 9-

COURSE DIFFICULTY: 4+

APPROPRIATENESS FOR FIRST TIMERS: 7-

ORGANIZATION: 8+

CROWDS: 5+

RACE DATA

Overall Ranking:	37
Quality Ranking:	68
Quickness Ranking:	82
Contact:	Mt. Meru International Marathon
	P.O. Box 855
	Arusha, Tanzania
	Tel. +255/51-2394; Fax +255/57-8226
	E-mail: Hoopoe@form-net.com
	or
	Global Partners for Development
	5145 Burnham Ranch Road
	Santa Rosa, CA 95404-9554 USA
	Tel. (707) 579-5009; Fax (707) 579-1108
Date:	Generally first Sunday in August
Start Time:	8:00 a.m.
Time Course Closes:	NA
Number of Participants:	300 in 1997
Course:	Two separate loops
Certification:	AIMS
Course Records:	Male: (open) 2:13:46
	Female: (open) 2:36:00
Elite Athlete Programs:	No
Cost:	US$20
Age groups/Divisions:	None
Walkers:	Yes
Requirements:	None
Temperature:	68° (20°C)
Aid/Splits:	8 / none

HIGHLIGHTS The safari capital of Tanzania, Arusha rests at the foot of Mt. Meru in the midst of lush green plateaus, coffee plantations, and volcanic peaks. The town is the gateway to some of the country's most famous national parks, including Serengeti and Ngorongoro Crater. Every August during the dry season, Arusha hosts the Mt. Meru International Marathon for those runners with a bold spirit and safari notions. The race completes two loops within the city of Arusha before venturing out at 20K into the neighboring fields of coffee and wheat for a 20K out and back. Once in the countryside, runners can see small volcanic peaks rising from the dry landscape. What many runners remember most are the people and the children, many of whom run the final kilometers with sagging runners, bolstering energy and the heart. Be aware that 90% of the field consists of sub-3:00 runners (most of whom are local). The over three-hour crowd tends to be the overseas entrants. After the race, you have an endless number of options, such as safaris, climbing Mt. Kilimanjaro, cruising Lake Victoria, or heading to the Spice Island, Zanzibar.

COURSE DESCRIPTION The marathon starts at the Clock Tower in central Arusha, which is the exact midpoint of the continent of Africa from north to south, at an elevation of 4,500 feet. Runners make the first loop of the city, a 10K jaunt on decent roads past the major hotels. Although the hills are mostly modest, the section from 8K to 10K toward the Clock Tower is uphill. As the race winds through the city, runners encounter colorful markets, tribal people coming from distant villages, entire families on one bicycle, cars held together with string and wax, a herd of cattle, and maybe even some camels. After passing the Clock Tower, runners complete the second loop, but instead of turning toward the Clock Tower again, the course turns right and heads out of the city. From 18K to 28K, runners head down Arusha-Dodoma Road, the main highway to the national parks of Ngorongoro Crater and Serengeti. Runners find lots of Sunday morning street activity between 18K and 20K (still in town) as they enjoy the gentle downgrade. By 20K, the course passes through brilliant green coffee plantations and blooming flame trees. After passing the municipal airport near 22K, runners roll through rippling wheat fields. Soon the landscape begins to change, however, becoming noticeably drier. This is true Big Sky country (it is also the Maasai people country), as runners can see great distances, and volcanos dominate the hori-

zon. Runners reach the turnaround point at 28K, and they retrace their steps on Arusha-Dodoma Road straight to the Clock Tower (40K). This tends to be the most difficult stretch for runners since spectators have thinned and most of the final 6K into the city is uphill. However, on the return trip runners get to admire the sight of Mount Meru which looms above Arusha. After passing the Clock Tower, the final 1.5K loop back toward the stadium finish on a gentle downgrade. The race gains an estimated total of 650 feet. The city streets are closed for the sub-3:00 marathoners. Slower runners have to stick to the side of the road toward the end of the race.

CROWD/RUNNER SUPPORT A Tanzanian-style brass band provides the beat for race warm-ups in a very entertaining send off. High excitement accompanies the race, especially among the local runners. A good result here could lead to an invitation to a European or U.S. marathon or possibly a spot on the national team. And, of course, the winner's prize money goes a long way in Tanzania. All of the major intersections in Arusha have large crowds, eager to cheer on the runners. After the frontrunners, locals seem to offer their biggest support to the foreigners, shouting words of encouragement and an occasional good-natured ribbing ("run faster, number one runner is long gone!"). Local residents find it quite puzzling why anyone would want to run a marathon when they are not contending for the win. Children in sandals often tag along for miles, chatting and laughing the whole way. The stadium is jammed-packed with spectators to watch the fastest runners finish. The crowds tend to thin out after the four-hour mark. We suggest avoiding the race aid stations, unless your stomach is accustomed to water with a high bacteria content. Two groups of runners from the U.S. (Global Partners) and Japan (World Runners) offer support to all over three-hour runners from start to finish. Drinks, snacks, vaseline, medical aid, and runner pick-up and transportation to the finish are all offered by a number of roving vehicles.

RACE LOGISTICS Many downtown Arusha hotels are within a few minutes walk of the race start. Runners can arrange an inexpensive taxi ride from any other hotel. A taxi stand also sits outside the stadium for rides back to the hotel after the race.

ACTIVITIES Pick up your race packet at the Sheikh Amri Abeid Stadium in Arusha the day before the marathon, or at the press conference held at one of the major hotels in the city. All foreign runners are invited to attend the press conference and introduce themselves. The local elite runners then joke with each other about who will blister whom with their final kick the following day. After the marathon, Global Partners and World Runners hold an unofficial celebratory dinner at the Impala Hotel.

AWARDS All runners receive T-shirts. Special commemorative T-shirts may also be purchased. Finishers receive certificates with their official times. The top ten male and female runners receive trophies and cash prizes. The total purse for the event is about US$13,000, with the male winner receiving $1,600 and the female winner $1,300.

ACCOMMODATIONS The race does not have an official race hotel. Among those convenient to the race start are the four star Novotel Mount Meru Hotel (tel. +255/57-2711 or 2712; fax +255/57-8221 or 8503), about US$135 to $190; New Arusha Hotel (tel. +255/57-8541; fax +255/57-8085), about US$65 to $70; New Safari Hotel (tel. +255/57-3261), about US$25 to $80; Equator Hotel (tel. +255/57-3127 or 8411; fax +255/57-2674 or 4379), about US$45; Hotel Seventy Seven (tel. +255/57-8403 or 8054; fax +255/57-8407), about US$50 to $120; and Impala Hotel (tel. +255/57-7083 or 8448; fax +255/57-8220 or 8680), about US$65 to $154. You can also make tour arrangements through Global Partners for Development in the United States (see contact information above).

RELATED EVENTS/RACES Just before the marathon, runners enjoy the 5K race for boys and the 5K race for girls. The kids warm up by dancing in tune with the brass band, and then bolt down the road at the start. There is also a 10K run/walk for adults.

AREA ATTRACTIONS Arusha is a pleasant small city full of life and loads of good shopping for tourists. The most popular shopping items include ebony and other wood carvings, musical instruments, batiks, weavings, spears, fabrics, handcrafted jewelry and beadwork from the Masai and other local tribal groups, and semi-precious stones, especially tanzanite. Easily the major attraction here is a safari through one of the many area game reserves, including Serengeti and Ngorongoro Crater. Many people like to make the short trip to Mt. Kilimanjaro, at 19,340 feet, Africa's tallest mountain. A short plane ride takes you to Zanzibar of Spice Islands fame, with it's Arabic influence, Stone Town's labyrinth of narrow, winding streets, mosques, palaces, and magnificent Indian Ocean beaches.

ASIA/PACIFIC

MOOREA BLUE MARATHON

OVERALL: 87.7

COURSE BEAUTY: 10

COURSE DIFFICULTY: 3

APPROPRIATENESS FOR FIRST TIMERS: 7

ORGANIZATION: 8+

CROWDS: 2

RACE DATA

Overall Ranking: 48
Quality Ranking: 85
Quickness Ranking: 47
Contact: Moorea Blue Marathon
Tahiti Manava Sports
B.P. 1710 Papeete, Tahiti
Tel. +689/50-57-38
Fax +689/45-16-78
E-mail: tahiti-animation@mail.pf

Date: Generally third Saturday in February
Start Time: 5:15 a.m.
Time Course Closes: No time limit
Number of Finishers: 231 in 1997
Course: Out and partial back
Certification: AIMS
Course Records: Male: (open) 2:21:31
Female: (open) 2:52:32
Elite Athlete Programs: Yes
Cost: US$95/110
Age groups/Divisions: 16-29, 30-39, 40-49, 50-59, 60+
Walkers: Yes
Requirements: 16 years old & register through an official travel agency
Temperature: 75° - 82° (24°C - 28°C)
Aid/Splits: 17 / none

HIGHLIGHTS The exotic Moorea Blue Marathon entices runners with spectacular scenery and relaxed island charm. Held on Moorea, Tahiti's heart-shaped sister island, the race teems with white sand beaches, crystalline lagoons, towering lush volcanic peaks, and the sweet aroma of tiare and frangipuii flowers. While the gorgeous scenery alone should provide more than enough inspiration, further encouragement comes from the many aid stations where Polynesian beauties sway to Tahitian tunes. And remember, it's a smart runner who takes his time at the aid stations and doesn't forget to grab a piece of tropical fruit from the Polynesian canoe. With such compelling attributes, it's difficult to understand why the ten-year-old Moorea Blue Marathon remains a relative shrimp on the international marathon scene. While the warm temperatures and distant location may be partly to blame, neither should be a deterrent. After all, the Moorea Blue Marathon is perfect justification for making a trip to heaven.

COURSE DESCRIPTION   The Moorea Blue Marathon features a mostly flat, out-and-partially-back route around two magnificent bays and through several resort areas. Starting just before sunrise to the beat of the toere (Tahitian drums), the race leaves from PK 20 in Opunohu Bay with flaming torches lighting runner's early steps until the sun appears over 2,694-foot Mt. Rotui (898 meters). Winding around the bay, the marathon passes Archipels Croisieres shortly before 2K and continues to the Moorea Lagoon Hotel at the 6-K mark. From the scuba diving center, the course goes east along the shoreline before hitting the tranquil waters of Cook's Bay near 8K. Runners follow the contours of the deep, narrow bay, passing the impressive yachts resting in Paopao Harbor near 10K. After completely rounding Cook's Bay, the course enters Maharepa, a popular resort area and starting point for the Polymat 5K fun run/walk. Now near the northeastern tip of the island, the course heads south toward the airport and then into Temae (20K) — the eventual finish site. On the out and back from Temae, runners still trace the ocean, passing the Sofitel Ia Ora Hotel, ferry dock, and the towns of Teavaro and Vaiare. With lush Mt. Mouaputa (2,490 feet) to the right, the course approaches the turnaround in Afareaitu. From here, runners pass each other while returning to the finish along the white sand beach surrounding the turquoise lagoon in Temae.

CROWD/RUNNER SUPPORT   With island inhabitants numbering around 11,000 – less than many marathon fields – you won't have huge crowds spurring you along. Though lacking in quantity, the quality of spectator support can be impressive. Beautiful dancers and Tahitian music keep runners entertained while they sip spring water or sports drink and sample exotic fruit at the seventeen aid stations. Since the course is not closed to traffic, supporters can follow much of the race by car, bicycle, or moped.

RACE LOGISTICS   The race provides shuttle service from the hotels to the start in Opunohu Bay. A return service is provided from the finish.

ACTIVITIES   Pick up your race packet Monday through Friday before race weekend at Tahiti Manava Sports (visitors bureau) Fare Manahini Papeete. Thursday night, take in some of the local flavor at the Tiki Theatre Spectacle and Tahitian Buffet. An outrigger canoe picks you up from your hotel and transports you to a Tiki Village. After sampling village life and the local arts of sculpting, carving, and tattooing, feast your mouth and eyes at the traditional Tahitian buffet and dance show. The cost is US$69 for runners and friends. Join other competitors at the pre-race carbo dinner on Friday night at the Moorea Village Hotel. The party goes from 6:30 p.m. to 8:30 p.m. and includes a Polynesian pasta buffet, exotic fresh fruit and great local music. Race participants receive free admission while supporters must pay US$15. Course tours are available the day before the race for US$5. A post-race awards party and Tahitian-style barbecue, complete with Polynesian dancers and a fire eating show, takes place on the beach starting at 5:00 p.m. Saturday. The barbecue is free for athletes and US$30 for others.

AWARDS   All finishers receive a T-shirt, shell medal and certificate. Top men and women vie for US$16,000 in prize money. In addition to money, first place men and women receive Tahitian black pearls and airline tickets to return to Moorea the following year. The top three finishers in each age group receive specially designed shell trophies. Finally, a special trophy goes to the first place man and woman from each country represented.

ELITE RUNNERS INFORMATION   The marathon provides complimentary entry and accommodation to selected athletes based on recent performances and promotional abilities. Contact the marathon office for consideration.

ACCOMMODATIONS   Contact the race for marathon travel packages. Air New Zealand is the official airline and offers special rates for marathon runners.

RELATED EVENTS/RACES   The events menu also includes a half marathon and 5K. The half marathon starts at 5:30 a.m. from Opunohu Bay and traces much of the marathon course. Starting at 6:00 a.m., the Polymat 5K leaves from Maharepa and ends at the

marathon and half-marathon finish in Temae. And if the weekend events have not satisfied your running hunger, head to the neighboring island of Bora Bora for the Mini Run taking place on the Thursday following the marathon.

AREA ATTRACTIONS Sunning, snorkeling, boating, mountain biking, and island hopping lead most agendas.

OKINAWA MARATHON

OVERALL: 84.9

COURSE BEAUTY: 8

COURSE DIFFICULTY: 4

APPROPRIATENESS FOR FIRST TIMERS: 7

ORGANIZATION: 9-

CROWDS: 5+

RACE DATA

Overall Ranking:	63
Quality Ranking:	50
Quickness Ranking:	73
Contact:	Okinawa Marathon
	Okinawa Track & Field Association
	2-1-1 Moromizato, Okinawa City
	Okinawa 904
	Japan
	Tel. +81/98-930-0088
	Fax +81/98-930-0101
Date:	Generally third Sunday in February
Start Time:	9:00 a.m.
Time Course Closes:	3:00 p.m.
Number of Finishers:	11,253 in 1997 (15,000-runner limit)
Course:	Loop
Certification:	AIMS
Course Records:	Male: NA
	Female: NA
Elite Athlete Programs:	No
Cost:	¥3,000
Age groups/Divisions:	None
Walkers:	No
Requirements:	18 years old
Temperature:	62° - 68° (17°C - 20°C)
Aid/Splits:	8 / none

HIGHLIGHTS/COURSE DESCRIPTION Japan's Hawaii, Okinawa has become a winter running retreat for thousands of runners in the Okinawa Marathon. Started in 1993 to showcase Okinawa's central district, the race grew to over 11,000 runners by 1997, and is a favorite with U.S. Marines. Runners assemble at the Okinawa Comprehensive Sports Park Stadium in Awase township. The rolling, loop course essentially runs through the twelve municipalities and townships that comprise central Okinawa. While going along the many city streets, you may think you are in California with all the fast food joints thanks to the presence of the U.S. military bases on Okinawa. In fact, the course cuts through massive Kadema Air Force Base from 26.5K to 29.5K, allowing you to taste a hunk of Americana on Asian soil. The next highlight appears from about 36K to 38K as you pass through Nakajo Joseki (castle) Park. Runners arrive back in the stadium to a usually good crowd of spectators.

CROWD / RUNNER SUPPORT About 5,000 or so locals cheer runners along the course. Aid stations lie every 5K, offering water, brown sugar, bananas, and plums.

RACE LOGISTICS Most hotels lie approximately 20 minutes (3 to 4 kilometers) from the start. Since parking is prohibited at Okinawa Park, runners must use a bus or taxi. The race may also provide some buses from the hotel. Your extra clothes and personal belongings are held at the reception desk in the gym during the marathon.

ACTIVITIES Pick up your race number and T-shirt on Saturday from 1:00 p.m. to 5:00 p.m. at the Okinawa Comprehensive Park Athletic Gym. After the race, stay for the awards ceremony held at the park's main stadium.

AWARDS Every entrant receives a T-shirt, and finishers earn a medal and certificate. Special awards go to the top six male and female finishers, eldest finisher, top male and female foreign competitors, and top team.

ACCOMMODATIONS Okinawa maintains no official race hotel. The closest lodging options include: Laguna Garden Hotel, Kyoto Kanko Hotel, 2-1-51 Goya, Okinawa City (tel. +81/98-933-1125; fax +81/98-933-5528); Diego Hotel, 3-4-2 Chuo, Okinawa City (tel. +81/98-937-1212; fax +81/98-939-5393); and Crown Hotel, 51 Uechi, Okinawa City (tel. +81/98-933-2551; fax +81/98-932-2194). After the marathon, you may want to stay at the west coast beaches. Among the possibilities are: Miwason Minshuku, Moon Beach (tel. +81/98-964-3160); Beachside Hotel, Moon Beach (tel. +81/98-965-4522); and Hotel Moon Beach (tel. +81/98-965-1020).

RELATED EVENTS / RACES Double your chances of winning an award by gathering three friends for the team competition. The team with the best average finish time wins.

AREA ATTRACTIONS Okinawa offers magnificent beaches (including famous Moon Beach) and excellent snorkeling and diving along its west coast. Other island highlights include: Okinawa Prefectural Peace Memorial, war caves, and the lively Heiwa Dori Shopping Arcade.

CHINA COAST MARATHON

OVERALL: 79.8

COURSE BEAUTY: 8+

COURSE DIFFICULTY: 6 (SEE APPENDIX)

APPROPRIATENESS FOR FIRST TIMERS: 5

ORGANIZATION: 8

CROWDS: 1-

RACE DATA

Overall Ranking:	93
Quality Ranking:	99
Quickness Ranking:	92
Contact:	China Coast Marathon
	P.O. Box 28893
	Gloucester Road Post Office
	Hong Kong, China
	Tel. & Fax +852/818-4856
	E-mail: garryl@netvigator.com
	http//www.Hk.super.net/~kff/avohk/ccm98reg.html
Date:	Generally second Sunday in March
Start Time:	7:00 a.m.
Time Course Closes:	1:00 p.m.
Number of Finishers:	220 in 1997
Course:	Double L
Certification:	AIMS
Course Records:	Male: (open) 2:38:40
	Female: (open) 3:14:47
Elite Athlete Programs:	No
Cost:	HK$200/300/400
Age groups/Divisions:	Men: 18-34, 35-39, 40-44, 45-49, 50-54, 55-59, 60+
	Women: 18-34, 35-39, 40-44, 45-49, 50+
Walkers:	No
Requirements:	18 years old
Temperature:	65° - 70° (18°C - 21°C)
Aid/Splits:	8 / none

HIGHLIGHTS   With more painted faces than a Peking Opera, Hong Kong always seems to reveal a fresh new visage. Well known are the dueling British and Chinese cultures, the overwhelming frenzy of the world's highest concentration of humans, and the burgeoning financial district. And then comes the China Coast Marathon. Small. Rural. Rugged. Unexpected. Held 30 miles northeast of downtown around the High Island Reservoir, the marathon follows an L-shaped course with plenty of hills. So many in fact, your voice may sound as high-pitched as the opera divas by the end of it all.

COURSE DESCRIPTION   The China Coast Marathon's challenging course starts and finishes near the entrance to Sai Kung Country Park in Pak Tam Chung, and in between traces a double out-and-back "L" along the High Island Reservoir. Though hilly throughout, one of the route's most egregious hills comes in the first 2K, climbing over 240 feet to the head of the reservoir. When you reach the water, the race turns left along Eastern Reservoir Road for a 2K out and back. Near 4K, the longer part of the "L" ensues along Southern Reservoir Road. This stretch is punctuated by a steep, 130-foot hill at 8K (which you also meet at 15K, 29K, and 36K). Runners follow the reservoir until it ends at the main dam (near 12K). After crossing the dam, the course turns around at the roundabout and retraces its route to the head of the reservoir, reaching it near 19.5K. Now runners embark on a longer, tougher stretch on Eastern Reservoir Road, climbing 240 feet from 21K to the turnaround at 23K. The hill and direct exposure to the sun make this the most difficult portion of the race. Back at the reservoir head (27K), runners complete the final leg to the main dam and back (27K to 40.5K) and descend the 240-foot hill leading to the finish.

CROWD / RUNNER SUPPORT   Due to the relatively remote course, crowd support is practically non-existent. Most encouragement comes from the other runners whom you see several times along the repetitive route. Aid stations lie every 5K.

RACE LOGISTICS   The marathon venue lies 35 minutes (by bus) to the northeast of downtown Hong Kong. Race organizers provide buses to the start, leaving at 5:30 a.m. from Queen's Pier, Central Hong Kong Island, and from Middle Road (behind the YMCA), Tsim Sha Tsui, Kwoloon. The bus fee of HK$50 is payable when submitting your entry. Since limited parking is available at Pak Tam Chung, race organizers strongly encourage using the bus.

ACTIVITIES   A low-key event, China Coast offers no pre-race activities. Race bib numbers are mailed to participants. An awards ceremony gets underway after the marathon.

AWARDS   All finishers receive T-shirts and medals. Runners completing the course under six hours earn a certificate. The top three finishers in each age group win special prizes.

ACCOMMODATIONS   Many inexpensive and convenient rooms can be had within Chung King Mansion at 40 Nathan Road, Tsim Sha Tsui, Kwoloon; or the Imperial Hotel, 30-34 Nathan Road (tel. +852/2-366-2201; fax +852/2-311-2360). If you're in Hong Kong on business or simply prefer nicer digs, try the Holiday Inn Golden Mile, 50 Nathan Road (tel. 800-Holiday; fax +852/2-369-8016).

RELATED EVENTS / RACES   For those runners not ready to sing the Peking Opera, the race holds a half marathon. Starting with the marathon, the race essentially follows the first half of the marathon route.

AREA ATTRACTIONS   Of course, shopping and culinary pursuits rank highest on the list of most visitors, although vibrant Hong Kong is no longer the bargain hunter's paradise. For glorious views of downtown and the water, take a tram to Victoria Peak.

MALANG INTERNATIONAL MARATHON

OVERALL: 76.8

COURSE BEAUTY: 9

COURSE DIFFICULTY: 6+ (SEE APPENDIX)

APPROPRIATENESS FOR FIRST TIMERS: 4

RACE ORGANIZATION: 7+

CROWDS: 3-

RACE DATA

Overall Ranking:	98
Quality Ranking:	100
Quickness Ranking:	93
Contact:	Jongki Sumarhadi
	Malang International Marathon
	Jl. Jemur Andayani 27
	Surabaya 60237
	Indonesia
	Tel. +62/31-843-9827
	Fax +62/31-843-8405
	E-mail: fajarmas@rad.net.id
Date:	Generally last Sunday in March
Start Time:	5:30 a.m.
Time Course Closes:	9:45 a.m.
Number of Finishers:	49 in 1997
Course:	Loop
Certification:	AIMS
Course Records:	Male: (open) 2:24:48
	Female: (open) 2:46:48
Elite Athlete Programs:	No
Cost:	US$10/20
Age groups/Divisions:	None
Walkers:	No
Requirements:	20 years old & times under 3:45 for men and 4:15 for women
Temperature:	75° - 90° (24°C - 32°C)
Aid/Splits:	8 / every 5K by digital clocks

HIGHLIGHTS   In the depths of Java, on the least-touristed, eastern portion of the island, the Malang International Marathon runs along hilly streets and busy regional thoroughfares. The race, teetering on the cusp of the wet and dry seasons, gives runners a lengthy taste of life in East Java. On the menu are wide boulevards lined with airy Dutch colonial buildings, narrow rows crammed with local houses, green forests, rice fields, and endless banana trees with bowing leaves. Two of East Java's most spectacular volcanos, Mount Semeru (Java's highest mountain) and Mount Bromo, lend the area a distinguished air. Distinguished or not, the air here is definitely cooler than in most Javanese cities due to the relatively high elevation of the city (1,475 feet). Be aware that this race is skewed towards faster runners (men under 3:45 and women under 4:15). If you cannot easily meet these times, you should probably consider the much larger 10K.

COURSE DESCRIPTION   This loop course, police monitored but not closed to traffic, begins on Jalan Ijen in front of the Brawijaya Museum. The race heads mostly on a downgrade for the first 5K (except for a 30-foot rise near 2K) through residential parts of the city. Between 5K and 8K the course climbs about 80 feet before flattening, giving you a chance to ready yourself for the first of two tough climbs in the race — 250 feet through the light green rice fields from about 12K to 17K. Near 17K, runners quickly descend 175 feet and then roll through residential areas until 26K. The course now joins the Singosari-Malang highway through the endless East Java villages that line the road (runners must keep to the left of the two-lane highway), falling another 70 feet until 28K. Near 29K, runners begin the second challenging climb up 200 feet over 5K. From 35K to 40K runners scream down 250 feet through residential parts of Malang, leading to a mostly flat last 2K through more neighborhoods, until a final rise into Gajayana Stadium.

CROWD/RUNNER SUPPORT The race attracts a small number of spectators along its course (perhaps 10,000), mostly curious onlookers. Most congregate near the finish area around the stadium. You, however, likely will be the center of people's attention. The race has water stations every 5K. If you need a sports drink, arrange the handoff with your crew at some point along the way. Every 5K is also marked with elapsed time given by clocks.

RACE LOGISTICS Foreign runners have the luxury of complimentary transportation from one of the four race hotels to the start, and from the finish back to the hotels. Note that men must report to the start area by 4:30 a.m. and women by 5:00 a.m.

ACTIVITIES Runners must attend the technical meeting held the evening before the marathon to learn details of the course and other important information. The technical meeting is held at the race headquarters hotel (currently the Graha Cakra). Runners may pick up their race packets at the meeting, or if they prefer, at the marathon office at Jalan Tennis 1-A (near Gajayana Stadium) on Saturday afternoon. The carbo-load party and welcome dinner begins after the technical meeting. Runners accustomed to a pre-race pasta dinner will likely have to settle for rice in Malang. This should pose no difficulty at all, given rice's high carbohydrate content and the wide availability of delicious rice dishes (Indonesia's staple food). In the stadium after the race there is a cultural performance and traditional handicraft exhibition which you can browse and enjoy.

AWARDS Every runner receives a T-shirt, and finishers of the tough course receive certificates. The top 10 male and female runners also earn prize money. The current prize structure is: Rp. 5,000,000 for first, Rp. 3,500,000 for second, Rp. 2,500,000 for third, Rp. 1,500,000 for fourth, Rp. 1,000,000 for fifth, Rp. 500,000 for sixth, Rp. 400,000 for seventh, Rp. 300,000 for eighth, Rp. 200,000 for ninth, and Rp. 100,000 for tenth. In addition, a runner who sets a new course record receives a bonus of Rp. 50 million.

ACCOMMODATIONS The official race hotel is the historic Graha Cakra Hotel (US$60). If you would like to stay at the Graha Cakra, there is no need to contact the hotel directly. Simply make your registration through the race entry form. Other possibilities include the Regent Park Hotel Malang (US$55); Kartika Prince (US$50); and Tugu Park (US$75). The race can give you the latest information on their arrangements with these hotels. There are many other cheaper, simpler, local-style accommodations (called *losmen*) for adventurous runners on a budget.

RELATED RACES Runners not feeling like a marathon should join the large 10K race that goes through Malang's streets. The 10K usually attracts more than 6,000 runners.

AREA ATTRACTIONS One of the most diverse, beautiful and amazing countries on earth, Indonesia is sure to dazzle, overwhelm and frustrate you. Travelers to Indonesia must have Bill Dalton's Indonesia Handbook (Moon Publications), one of the best guidebooks ever written. It will provide you with a lifetime of exploration options. Malang itself is a pleasant small city with numerous interesting temples and stupas. Among the attractions near Malang are sunrise atop eery, beautiful Mount Bromo. East Java is also full of other volcanos including stunning Mt. Semeru, Java's tallest mountain. Further afield is the central Java city of Yogyakarta, near one of the world's great wonders, Borobudur Temple. In addition, Bali is a short flight or long bus and ferry ride away.

KASUMIGAURA MARATHON

OVERALL: 79.9

COURSE BEAUTY: 9-

COURSE DIFFICULTY: 3

APPROPRIATENESS FOR FIRST TIMERS: 7

ORGANIZATION: 9

CROWDS: 2

RACE DATA

Overall Ranking:	91
Quality Ranking:	70
Quickness Ranking:	46
Contact:	Kasumigaura Marathon
	& International Marathon for the Blind
	2-7-36 Shimokozu
	Tsuchiwa-shi, Ibaraki-ken
	Japan
	Tel. +81/29-826-3457
	Fax +81/29-826-3456
Date:	Generally third Sunday in April
Start Time:	10:00 a.m.
Time Course Closes:	4:00 p.m.
Number of Participants:	14,084 in 1997 (all races combined)
Course:	Loop
Certification:	AIMS
Course Records:	Male: NA
	Female: NA
Elite Athlete Programs:	No
Cost:	¥3,000
Age groups/Divisions:	16-29, 30-39, 40-49, 50-59, 60+
Walkers:	No
Requirements:	16 years old
Temperature:	61˚ - 64˚ (16˚C - 18˚C)
Aid/Splits:	7 / every 5K

HIGHLIGHTS The Japanese love elite races. The Nagoya International Women's Marathon, Osaka International Ladies Marathon, Tokyo International Marathon, Lake Biwa Marathon, and Fukuoka International Marathon. A who's who of Japanese marathons, and all races for elite runners only. The Kasumigaura Marathon takes a different approach. Call it the "Inclusive Marathon." In fact, the race doubles as the International Marathon for the Blind, hosting an impressive 170 blind runners in 1997. Over 14,000 runners come to Japan's second-largest lake in Ibaraki-ken Prefecture Kanto, less than two hours from Tokyo. Together they enjoy the marathon, 10K, and 5K races. The mostly rural marathon travels through forest and along the lake's shore, and best of all, can be enjoyed by every runner.

C O U R S E   D E S C R I P T I O N   The Kasumigaura Marathon features a loop course around Lake Kasumigaura and through the surrounding forest. Starting at the Kawaguchi Athletic Park Track & Field Stadium, the route climbs 65 feet to 4K, levels off for 2K, and then rises another 30 feet to 7K. Cutting through the forest, runners descend nearly 90 feet in the following 15K, passing the Dejima Castle near halfway. Hugging the shoreline for the second half of the race, runners return to the stadium for an exciting finish.

C R O W D / R U N N E R   S U P P O R T   Don't expect much crowd support along this remote marathon course. Most of the encouragement comes from the aid station volunteers and your fellow runners. Aid stations start at 10K and come every 5K thereafter. The stations offer sports drink, water, bread, lemons, bananas, chocolate and candy.

R A C E   L O G I S T I C S   Most hotels lie about 6 miles from the start. Runners staying at the host hotel (which is near the train station) can easily take a train to Tsuchiura Station, and walk five minutes to the start. Be sure to take the station's east exit. The late start allows sufficient travel time for runners staying in Tokyo, many of whom also arrive by train.

A C T I V I T I E S   Race organizers typically host an opening ceremony on the eve of the race. Pick up your race packet the night before at the ceremony or near the start on race morning. The awards ceremony takes place in the stadium following the race.

A W A R D S   Each runner receives a T-shirt, and finishers earn medals. The top age-group runners win special prizes.

A C C O M M O D A T I O N S   The Yamazakiya Hotel, a Japanese-style inn, serves as the official race hotel. Contact race organizers for other options near the lake.

R E L A T E D   E V E N T S / R A C E S   If you're not ready to tackle the marathon, organizers stage 5K and 10K races. Starting at 9:50 a.m., the 10K loop course follows the early kilometers of the marathon, while the 5K runs an out-and-back route beginning at 10:20 a.m.

A R E A   A T T R A C T I O N S   People go to Lake Kasumigaura for the natural beauty. Kairakuen, one of Japan's most celebrated landscape gardens, can be found in Mito, six miles to the northeast. And, of course, frenetic Tokyo is an easy train ride away.

FLETCHER CHALLENGE MARATHON

OVERALL: 88.8

COURSE BEAUTY: 9

COURSE DIFFICULTY: 5+ (SEE APPENDIX)

APPROPRIATENESS FOR FIRST TIMERS: 8+

ORGANIZATION: 9+

CROWDS: 4

RACE DATA

Overall Ranking: 37
Quality Ranking: 42
Quickness Ranking: 88
Contact: Fletcher Challenge Marathon
P.O. Box 610
Rotorua, New Zealand
Tel. & Fax: +64/7-348-8448
http://nz.com/rotorua/sport/fletcher/index.htm

Date: Generally first Saturday in May
Start Time: 10:00 a.m.
Time Course Closes: 5:30 p.m.
Number of Finishers: 2,079 in 1997
Course: Loop
Certification: AIMS
Course Records: Male: (open) 2:16:05
Female: (open) 2:37:37
Elite Athlete Programs: No
Cost: NZ$60
Age groups/Divisions: 16-39 (M), 16-34, 35-39 (F), 40-44, 45-49, 50-54,
55-59, 60-64, 65+ (M), 60+ (F)
Walkers: Yes
Requirements: 16 years old
Temperature: 50˚ - 64˚ (10˚C - 18˚C)
Aid/Splits: 16 / digital clocks at 5K, 10K, 20K, halfway, 30K,
& 40K; verbally at 25K & 31-39K

HIGHLIGHTS New Zealand boasts, arguably, the greatest running culture in the world. Virtually every town sports a harrier, track, or marathon club. And whether you know it or not, you probably owe your marathon training program to the famous Kiwi coach Arthur Lydiard, whose LSD (Long Slow Distance) theory enabled even average runners to realize their marathon dreams. With such passion for the sport, it's not surprising that the country hosts countless races throughout the year, the largest and most prestigious being the Fletcher Challenge Marathon. Held in Rotorua, New Zealand's most popular tourist resort, the well-organized race circles beautiful Lake Rotorua through a mixture of city streets and farmland. Before hobbling off and relaxing sore muscles in the area's medicinal thermal pools, be sure to attend the awards ceremony where speedsters split a healthy cash purse and the rest of us hope for a share of the NZ$80,000 in random prizes.

COURSE DESCRIPTION From the Municipal Gardens in Rotorua City, the race traces an undulating, clockwise loop around picturesque Lake Rotorua (which is visible for over half of the race). The first 5K head through downtown streets and suburbs, rising 50 feet to Rainbow & Fairy Springs, a popular visitor attraction featuring native birds, trout pools and farm animals. With the exception of Ngongontana Village (9K), the next 10K pass mostly through farmland, returning to lake level at 15K. The following, relatively flat 3K pass the trimmed golf course, trout pools, and natural spring of Hamurana Springs, providing a brief respite before the race's toughest hill – a 110-footer from 18K to 20K. Once over the top, the course heads downhill to lake level at Ohau Channel (25K), a waterway between Lake Rotorua and Lake Rotoiti. Here, the course rises again, gaining nearly 90 feet before peaking at the 28-K mark. Dropping 95 feet over the next 4K, the course hits the Rotorua Airport at 32K. During the flat to slightly rolling final 10K, the route crosses Holdens Bay Bridge (35K) before proceeding through the small shopping village of Ngapuna, and then the Whakarewarewa Forest in the final stretch to the Municipal Gardens.

CROWD/RUNNER SUPPORT Held annually for thirty-three years, the Fletcher Challenge has become a local institution and a popular spectator event. Large crowds (for the small area) gather at the Municipal Gardens and at many of the small villages around the lake. Sixteen aid stations dot the course, while digital clocks sit at 5K, 10K, 20K, halfway, 30K, and 40K.

RACE LOGISTICS The start and finish lie about 250 meters apart in the Municipal Gardens. Runners must find their own way to and from the Gardens, although several hotels lie within walking distance.

ACTIVITIES Pick up your race number at the three-day sports expo kicking off Friday at 3:00 p.m. at the Sports Drome in Municipal Gardens. You must pre-register for the race, usually at least one month prior to the event. An impressive pasta party (limited to 250) takes place on Friday night from 6:30 p.m. to 9:00 p.m. at the Millennium Hotel, corner of Hinemoa and Eruera Streets. After the marathon, return to the expo site for the well-attended awards ceremony. And Sunday, if you can force yourself out of bed, limp to the post-marathon breakfast (limited to 400) held in the large marquee at the rear of the Sports Drome.

AWARDS   There's no skimping on prizes at this event. Every finisher receives a finisher's T-shirt, certificate and souvenir results book. Runners finishing under 7 hours qualify for a random drawing for NZ$80,000 in prizes, usually including airfare and spending money, trips to the Honolulu Marathon, electronic equipment, furniture, and running shoes and apparel. Top men and women split NZ$25,000, with $5,000 for first, $3,000 for second, $2,000 for third, $1,000 for fourth, and $500 for fifth. Those finishing sixth through twentieth (men) and sixth through tenth (women) earn trophies. Additionally, the top three masters men (over 40 years old) and women (over 35 years old) earn $1,250, $750, and $400, respectively, while the top three in each age group win a special marathon memento. Prizes also go to the fastest male and female first timers. The male and female age-group winners whose times break their age-group records by the greatest margin win a trip to Fletchers' Japanese sister race, the Lake Kawaguchi Marathon. If no age-group record is broken, then the trip goes to the male and female winners whose times are closest to their age-group race record.

ACCOMMODATIONS   The Millennium Rotorua Hotel, corner of Hinemoa and Eruera Streets (tel. +64/7-347-1234; fax +64/7-348-1234), serves as the official race hotel. Other hotels near the start/finish area include the Lake Plaza Rotorua, 6 Eruera Street (tel. +64/7-348-1174); Novatel, 9-11 Tutanekai Street (tel. +64/7-346-3888; fax +64/7-347-1888); and the Rydges Hotel, 272 Fenton Street (tel. +64/7-349-0099; fax +64/7-349-0900). For other accommodations, contact Tourism Rotorua (tel. +64/7- 348-5179; fax +64/7-348-6044).

RELATED EVENTS/RACES   Those not interested in running the marathon may consider the Mayor's Walk. Taking place shortly after the marathon start, the walk travels around some of Rotorua's most interesting and historic sites.

AREA ATTRACTIONS   Whakarewarewa, often called 'Whaka' for short, is Rotorua's largest and best-known thermal zone. It is also a major Maori (early Polynesian settlers) cultural area. Located on Fenton Street about 2 miles from the city center, Whaka contains the Pohutu Geyser, which usually erupts at least once an hour, spurting hot water about 65 feet in the air, and the Maori Arts and Crafts Institute. Marathon runners will probably want to visit the relaxing thermal pools at the Polynesian Spa off Hinemoa Street in the Government Gardens. Just outside of Rotorua lies another active thermal area called Hell's Gate which contains the largest thermal waterfall in the southern hemisphere. Other major attractions include: luge rides, sheep and sheep dog displays, and lake cruises.

THAILAND INTERNATIONAL MARATHON

OVERALL: 86.8

COURSE BEAUTY: 10-

COURSE DIFFICULTY: 7 (SEE APPENDIX)

APPROPRIATENESS FOR FIRST TIMERS: 4

ORGANIZATION: 8+

CROWDS: 2

RACE DATA

Overall Ranking:	55
Quality Ranking:	85
Quickness Ranking:	94
Contact:	Thailand International Marathon
	1099 Prachachuen 35
	Bangsue Bangkok 10800
	Thailand
	Tel. +66/2-585-5700
	Fax +66/2-587-9909
	E-mail: marathon@veerada.com
	http://www.veerada.com
Date:	Generally first Sunday in May
Start Time:	6:00 a.m.
Time Course Closes:	12:00 p.m.
Number of Participants:	2,000+ (combined races)
Course:	Loop
Certification:	NA
Course Records:	Male: (open) 2:27:37
	Female: (open) 3:10:55
Elite Athlete Programs:	Yes
Cost:	US$20/32
Age groups/Divisions:	<20, 20-24, 25-29, 30-34, 35-39, 40-44, 45-49, 50+
Walkers:	No
Requirements:	None
Temperature:	77° - 86° (25°C - 30°C)
Aid/Splits:	15 / none

HIGHLIGHTS You probably think of Bangkok when it comes to Thai marathons. While understandable, Bangkok suffers from excessive traffic, pollution, and noise. A little known alternative takes place at Thailand's most popular resort destination, Phuket Island, 885 kilometers south of Bangkok. While staged on this beautiful resort island, the Thailand International Marathon allows you no time to relax. Extreme temperatures and interior island hills turn your suntanned skin pale. But have no fear. There is plenty of opportunity to get that tan back on Patong Beach later. Now simply enjoy the quiet, tropical air and be glad you're not dodging cars and smog in Bangkok.

COURSE DESCRIPTION Starting at Surakul Stadium, the marathon route heads south on mostly flat Route 4022, passing the island's most sacred temple, Wat Chalong near 8K. Just before the coastal town of Chalong (10.5K), the course turns west, rising nearly 210 feet between

11K and 13K and then descending 240 feet to Kata Beach's Club Med (15K). Runners now go north along the highly developed western shoreline, skirting Karon Beach between 17K and 21K. Near 20K, the 1,500-foot Mt. Khao Krabok comes into view on the right. Veering away from the sea at 21K, the route rises 120 feet before descending into famous Patong Beach at 25K. Mostly flat to 32K, the race climbs sharply into the inner island Kathu District (34K), gaining 280 feet in only 2 kilometers. A well-deserved 350-foot downhill over the final 8K leads to the finish at Surakul Stadium.

CROWD / RUNNER SUPPORT Local residents and some tourists scatter along the course, with many families of runners gathering in Surakul Stadium to cheer on the finishers. Aid stations lie every 2.5K, with sponge stations every 5K.

RACE LOGISTICS If you're staying in Phuket Town, the start lies within walking distance from the hotels. Runners coming from west coast resorts must furnish their own transportation.

ACTIVITIES Pick up your race packet at Surakul Stadium on Thursday through Saturday from 8:00 a.m. to 6:00 p.m. If you register a week prior to the race, your entry fee includes the Saturday evening pre-race dinner held at the Kata Beach Resort. The awards ceremony begins at 10:30 a.m. in the stadium.

AWARDS Every entrant receives a T-shirt, and finishers under 6 hours earn medals and certificates. The top male and female runners earn trophies and compete for about US$40,000 in prize money. The top five local runners and the top three in each age group win trophies.

ACCOMMODATIONS Phuket Island provides a wide range of accommodations, from private bungalows to 5-star luxury hotels. While the Kata Beach Resort (tel. +66/76-330-530) serves as the race hotel, there are a number of large resort hotels along the west coast beaches including: Club Andaman, Patong Beach (tel. +66/76-340-530); Kamala Bay Terrace Resort, 16/12 Moo (tel. +66/76-270-801); Karon Villa Phuket, 36/4 Karon Beach (tel. +66/76-396-139); Diamond Cliff Resort, 284 Prabaramee Road (tel. +66/76-340-501); Phuket Arcadia Hotel & Resort, Karon Beach (tel. +66/76-396-038); Felix Karon Phuket, Karon Beach (tel. +66/76-396-666); and Kata Beach Club Med (tel. +66/76-381-455; fax +66/76-330-461). If you prefer lodging closer to the start try the following Phuket Town hotels: Thavorn Hotel (tel. +66/76-331-333); or P.S. Inn (tel. +66/76-212-216).

RELATED EVENTS / RACES If running a full marathon is 13.1 miles longer than you desire, consider the accompanying half marathon. The race starts 15 minutes after the marathon, running on an out-and-back course along the first 10.5K of the marathon.

AREA ATTRACTIONS Phuket Island, Thailand's largest island and most popular beach resort area, offers tremendous opportunities for water sport enthusiasts and plain sunshine worshippers. On top of the beach and water activities, the island teems with rainforests, waterfalls, pearl farms, and Buddhist temples.

GOLD COAST MARATHON

OVERALL: 92.8

COURSE BEAUTY: 9+

COURSE DIFFICULTY: 2-

APPROPRIATENESS FOR FIRST TIMERS: 9

ORGANIZATION: 10-

CROWDS: 4

RACE DATA

Overall Ranking:	22
Quality Ranking:	28
Quickness Ranking:	6
Contact:	Gold Coast Marathon
	P.O. Box 1986
	Southport BC
	Queensland, 4215
	Australia
	Tel. +61/7-5527-1363
	Fax +61/7-5527-1295
Date:	Generally second Sunday in July
Start Time:	6:30 a.m.
Time Course Closes:	12:30 p.m.
Number of Finishers:	1,810 in 1997
Course:	Near loop
Certification:	NA
Course Records:	Male: (open) 2:10:11
	Female: (open) 2:29:29
Elite Athlete Programs:	Yes
Cost:	NA
Age groups/Divisions:	18-24, 25-29, 30-34, 35-39, 40-44, 45-49, 50-54, 55-59, 60-64, 65-69, 70-74, 75-79, 80+, wheelchair
Walkers:	No
Requirements:	18 years old
Temperature:	50˚ - 64˚ (10˚C - 18˚C)
Aid/Splits:	15 / NA

HIGHLIGHTS Our highest-rated Australian marathon, the Gold Coast Marathon traces a figure-eight route alongside the famous caramel beaches and high-rise hotels of Surfers Paradise. Four separate events with over 10,000 participants between them ensure that every member of the family will reap some exercise in the vacation capital of Australia. The flat, long straightaways and generally superb weather conditions make Gold Coast one of the fastest marathons in the world, and our 6th quickest race. In 1997, South Africa's Gert Thys, running alone for much of the way, went through 32K in world record marathon pace before sputtering near the finish.

COURSE DESCRIPTION The Gold Coast Marathon essentially consists of two loops with long out-and-back sections. With Southport anchoring its middle, the course first heads north for a 25K loop along the beautiful calm waters of Broadwater. This is the playground of the Gold Coast, complete with yachts, powerboats, sailboats, windsurfers, and anglers. Runners

encounter several bridges and a 15-foot hill (which they must "surmount" twice) during this section of the race. After returning to the Southport start, runners head south for the 17K loop (again with a long out and back) along Surfers Paradise. Runners have plenty of time to check out the Pacific waters and the high-rise hotels that line the beaches, until they make their way back to Southport for the finish.

CROWD/RUNNER SUPPORT You find spectators scattered around the Gold Coast, with the largest number near the start/finish area (and 25-K point). Enthusiastic school kids and sports club members man the aid stations located every 2.5K. Sports drink is available at every 5K. Organizers also provide special drink tables every 5K for athletes who wish to supply their own formula.

RACE LOGISTICS A shuttle bus service is available (for a fee) to and from the race from various Gold Coast hotels. The marathon uses the ChampionChip timing system, so make sure you have your Chip strapped on your shoe on race day.

ACTIVITIES Pick up your race packet at the expo held during race weekend at the start/finish site. Note that race registration typically ends in early June. There is a pasta party Friday night.

AWARDS All finishers receive T-shirts and medals; certificates are mailed at a later date. Top male and female runners contend for A$120,000 in prize money. The top three age-group winners earn $200, $150, and $100, respectively. All entrants are eligible for random prizes and can see their name and finish time printed in Monday's newspaper.

ELITE RUNNERS INFORMATION Male runners with sub 2:12 credentials and females with sub 2:32 previous bests may qualify for transportation expenses, accommodations, and appearance money. Contact the marathon office for more details. Prize money goes from A$20,000 for first to $100 for tenth.

ACCOMMODATIONS All accommodation information can be obtained by contacting the marathon's official travel agency, 1-Call Holidays (tel. +61/7-5591-7677; fax +61/7-5591-7761).

RELATED EVENTS/RACES Gold Coast offers three other races in conjunction with the marathon. The accompanying half marathon attracts the largest field, hosting nearly 4,000 runners in 1997. A 10K road race and 10K non-competitive walk round out the race-day events.

AREA ATTRACTIONS The Gold Coast is a unique combination of nature's beauty and man-made attractions. You can run along a perfect white beach, swim in the clear blue ocean, and walk in a breathtaking rainforest. Or, enjoy the international flavor of superb shops and fine cafes and restaurants. The Gold Coast has all that you would expect in a first-class resort area.

MOUNT FUJI CLIMBING RACE

OVERALL: 83.7

COURSE BEAUTY: 9+

COURSE DIFFICULTY: 10

APPROPRIATENESS FOR FIRST TIMERS: 1

ORGANIZATION: 8+

CROWDS: 1-

RACE DATA

Overall Ranking:	70
Quality Ranking:	92
Quickness Ranking:	NA
Contact:	Mount Fuji Climbing Race
	Kaneyama Sports Center
	6200 Kamiyoshida
	Fujiyoshida-shi, Yamasashi-ken 403
	Japan
	Tel. +81/555-24-3633
	Fax +81/555-22-6299
Date:	July 25th annually
Start Time:	7:30 a.m.
Time Course Closes:	12:00 p.m.
Number of Finishers:	1,851 in 1997
Course:	Point to point
Certification:	None
Course Records:	Male: (open) 2:36:23
	Female: (open) 2:51:36
Elite Athlete Programs:	No
Cost:	¥5,000
Age groups/Divisions:	19-44, 45+
Walkers:	No
Requirements:	19 years old
Temperature:	36˚ - 73˚ (2˚C - 23˚C)
Aid/Splits:	3 / none

HIGHLIGHTS As the name suggests, a bunch of crazy runners get together each year to run up 12,389-foot Mt. Fuji, Japan's sacred national symbol. Always held on July 25th, the 21-kilometer trek takes runners along the historic Yoshidaguchi climbing trail. The arduous climb begins in Fujiyoshida City (2,520 feet) before joining the trail near 4K. Dense, lush forest and several historic buildings and shrines adorn the early kilometers before runners break through and struggle over the black, volcanic rock. Celebrating its 52nd anniversary in 1998, the race includes elaborate pre- and post-race ceremonies, such as a Japanese-style lunch. Those quickest up the perfectly sloped cone receive invitations and plane tickets to Mt. Fuji's sister race, the Jungfrau Marathon in Switzerland. Though the Japanese say that to climb Mt. Fuji once is wise, but to climb it twice is foolish, many runners evidently haven't been informed of this proverb because they continue coming back to this well-organized event.

COURSE DESCRIPTION Mt. Fuji's point-to-point course begins in front of Fujiyoshida City Hall (2,520 feet) and finishes 21K later on the summit (12,389 feet). Following city streets for 4K, the race gains 450 feet leading to Fuji Sengen Jinga, a sacred shrine dedicated to Konohanasakuyanhime, the patron of Mt. Fuji. This marks the beginning of the Yoshidaguchi climbing trail. The next 7 kilometers leading to Umagaeshi (11K) head through old forest on generally good trail (at least compared to what lies ahead). Lined with several shrines and monuments, the trail from Umagaeshi to the Fifth Station (15K) becomes steeper and rocky, rising nearly 2,650 feet. Once through the tree line, the route grows even steeper, climbing a brutal 3,800 feet over black, volcanic rock to the Eighth Station (19K). As you're likely doing more walking than running at this point, you're also probably thinking how the mountain that looks so beautiful from afar, can look so unattractive up close. Ascending 1,230 feet in the final 2K, a series of switchbacks deposit you on top of the summit, where you will swear an oath on this sacred mountain never to do that again. But then, you've probably never heard of that Japanese proverb.

CROWD / RUNNER SUPPORT Spectators evidently read proverbs more than runners because they tend to stay off the mountain. The smart ones congregate at the start at Fujiyoshida City Hall. Others take the bus to the Fifth Station checkpoint. From the Fifth Station (15K) to the finish, it's mostly people who happen to be climbing to the summit that day. Three aid stations, carrying water only, assist you along the climb.

RACE LOGISTICS Runners are responsible for their own transportation to City Hall on the morning of the event. Most participants walk or take a taxi to the start. Race organizers provide bus transportation from the finish back to City Hall. Buses depart from the Fifth Station with the last bus leaving at 2:00 p.m. (Note: Runners to the summit must walk back down to the Fifth Station after the race because there are no roads for vehicles above that station!) The race does transport your extra clothing to the Fifth Station, however, so at least you'll be dry while lying on the stretcher. Be aware that the temperature at the summit can be 30°F colder than at the start, so consider taking an extra layer of clothing. Many participants where gloves and knee-pads for protection from the sharp rocks.

ACTIVITIES An opening ceremony takes place at Fujiyoshida City Hall at 7:00 a.m. race morning. The closing ceremony and awards presentation occur at 2:30 p.m. in the inner courtyard at City Hall. (There is no live coverage of the events on television at the local hospital.) Race organizers provide a Japanese-style lunch for participants once they have returned from the mountain. After the awards ceremony, runners are invited to attend the Fujiyoshida City Foundation Festival, an annual city event. Local residents of all ages turn out from 3:00 p.m. to 10:00 p.m. along the city streets. Featuring food, games, music and dance, the festival provides a wonderful opportunity to meet the locals and get a good glimpse of Japanese culture.

AWARDS All finishers receive a certificate and a small medal. The top male and female runners receive airfare and an invitation to run in the Jungfrau Marathon in Switzerland. Additionally, each winner receives an array of trophies including a very elegant one from Japan's Prime Minister. Awards are given for first through tenth place in the men's division and first through sixth place in the women's division.

ACCOMMODATIONS When sending your completed race entry form, you may request that the city make hotel accommodations for you. For ¥6,500, you receive hotel accommodations (shared room) for the night of July 24th as well as two meals. For further information contact Fujikyu Travel, Fujiyoshida Office, 2-4-19 Kamiyoshida, Fujiyoshida-shi 403 Japan (tel. +81/555-22-5551; fax +81/555-23-4309). All accommodations are Japanese-style *ryokan* or *minshuku* (inn).

RELATED EVENTS / RACES On top of the summit race, Mt. Fuji includes a 15K race. Beginning at 9:00 a.m., the 15K follows the summit course gaining 4,845 feet to the finish at Mt. Fuji's Fifth Station. (And you don't have to walk back down.)

AREA ATTRACTIONS Five beautiful lakes and several resorts lie only minutes away from Fujiyoshida in Fuji-Hakone-Izu National Park — the most visited national park in Japan. Once quenched with the area's natural wonders, head to the Fujikyuu Highland Amusement Park, home to the world-class Fujiyama roller coaster, or to the Yamanashi Visitor's Center Museum on the northern edge of Lake Kawaguchi.

SYDNEY MARATHON

OVERALL: 87.6

COURSE BEAUTY: 9+

COURSE DIFFICULTY: 3+

APPROPRIATENESS FOR FIRST TIMERS: 8+

ORGANIZATION: 8+

CROWDS: 3+

RACE DATA

Overall Ranking: 50
Quality Ranking: 75
Quickness Ranking: 56
Contact: John Mallinder
Sydney Marathon
c/o AusFit Events Management Inc.
305 Burwood Road
Hawthorn, Victoria 3122
Australia
Tel. +61/3-9819-6888
Fax +61/3-9819-9477

Date: Generally first Sunday in September
Start Time: 7:00 a.m.
Time Course Closes: 1:00 p.m.
Number of Participants: 1,300 in 1996
Course: Point to point
Certification: AIMS
Course Records: New course in 1998
Elite Athlete Programs: No
Cost: A$80
Age groups/Divisions: <20, 20-24, 25-29, 30-34, 35-39, 40-44, 45-49, 50-54, 55-59, 60-64, 65-69, 70+
Walkers: No
Requirements: 18 years old
Temperature: 54° - 65° (12°C - 18°C)
Aid/Splits: 8 / digital clocks every 5K

HIGHLIGHTS   While you may not have the talent to make the Olympic marathon team, you can still run the marathon course for the 2000 Olympics. Although not yet finalized, the Sydney Marathon traces most of the proposed Olympic route treating runners to a gold medal tour of one of the world's most beautiful cities. Runners pass such landmarks as the Opera House, Sydney Harbour Bridge, the Rocks Precinct, and Mrs. Macquaries Chair. Sponsorship problems forced the cancellation of the 1997 race, but now, the Olympic pressure is on. Hopefully the new organizers use the warming spotlight to turn the Sydney Marathon into one of the world's greats — a place it clearly deserves to be one day. After all, it has the talent to make the Olympic team, all it needs now is the will.

COURSE DESCRIPTION   Due to the construction of the 2000 Olympic Stadium and other areas around the city, the last 22K of the Sydney Marathon course had not been finalized at our press time. The race starts outside North Sydney Oval, the city's rugby complex, and proceeds through North Sidney's business district. Runners then cross the Sydney Harbour Bridge (5K) into Sydney proper and head through the Botanical Gardens. After smelling the flowers, runners pass around Mrs. Macquaries Chair overlooking the Sydney Harbour and its Opera House (10K), the city's most recognizable image. The route goes through the heart of downtown before entering the Rocks district (15K), known for its restaurants and shopping. Next runners hit Darling Harbour (17K), home to the National Maritime Museum and more shopping, and head over the Glebe Island Bridge at 20K. The rest of the course remains under design, but organizers promise that it will follow the proposed Olympic marathon course wherever possible.

CROWD/RUNNER SUPPORT   One area Sydney needs to improve on to achieve Olympic class is crowd support. Currently about 15,000 to 20,000 spectators turn out for the race, with the favorite spots being the Harbour Bridge, the Rocks district, and Mrs. Macquaries Chair. Aid stations lie every 5K, supplying runners with water and sports drink.

RACE LOGISTICS   Runners must drive or take a taxi to the start across the Harbour Bridge, approximately 3 miles from the Rocks district's hotels.

ACTIVITIES   We believe the Sydney organizers prefer light beer, because they sure go light on the race activities. The most exciting pre-race activity is ... the packet pick-up for foreign runners at the race hotel. Do not despair, however. An awards ceremony follows the race.

AWARDS   Marathon finishers receive medals and certificates; a results book is mailed after the race. The top runners vie for prize money, while age-group winners receive trophies. Maybe someday the race will give you a T-shirt.

ACCOMMODATIONS   The ANA Sydney Hotel, 176 Cumberland Street (tel. +61/8-9250-6000; fax +61/8-9250-6250), serves as the official race hotel. Any hotel in the Rocks district is convenient to the start. Some options include: Old Sydney Park Royal, 55 George Street (tel. +61/8-9252-0524; fax +61/8-9251-2093); Harbour Rocks Hotel, 34-52 Harrington Street (tel. +61/8-9251-8944; fax +61/8-9251-8900); and The Stafford, 75 Harrington Street (tel. +61/8-9251-6711; fax +61/8-9251-3458).

RELATED EVENTS/RACES   The Sydney Marathon has a companion 10K race for those inclined to shorter distances.

AREA ATTRACTIONS   Although the marathon doesn't have many activities to keep you busy, pretty Sydney should have plenty to hold your attention. Take in a concert at the Opera House or enjoy free performances on Saturdays and Sundays along its surrounding boardwalks. Hop a jet cat to neighboring Manley and visit Oceanworld. How about some shopping in the Rocks precinct or Darling Harbour area? While in Darling Harbour, check out its Maritime and Powerhouse Museums, and stroll through the Chinese Gardens. Wildlife lovers will enjoy Koala Park and Featherdal Wildlife Park, while beachgoers will relish the excellent Biondi and Manley beaches. When time to eat and relax, head to the revolving restaurant atop 1,000-foot high Sydney Tower and enjoy the stunning harbor views.

BEIJING MARATHON

OVERALL: 83.5

COURSE BEAUTY: 9-

COURSE DIFFICULTY: 1+

APPROPRIATENESS FOR FIRST TIMERS: 1

ORGANIZATION: 9-

CROWDS: 6

RACE DATA

Overall Ranking: 58
Quality Ranking: 43
Quickness Ranking: 3
Contact: Beijing International Marathon
China Athletic Association
9 Tiyuguan Road
Beijing 100763
China
Tel. & Fax +86/10-671-40801

Date: Generally second Saturday in October
Start Time: 8:00 a.m.
Time Course Closes: 11:00 a.m.
Number of Finishers: 300 in 1997
Course: Out and back
Certification: IAAF and AIMS
Course Records: Male: (open) 2:07:35
Female: (open) 2:27:13
Elite Athlete Programs: Yes
Cost: US$60
Age groups/Divisions: None
Walkers: No
Requirements: 18 years old
Temperature: 46˚ - 64˚ (8˚C to 18˚C)
Aid/Splits: 9 / NA

HIGHLIGHTS Geared for swift performances (our third-fastest marathon), the Beijing Marathon boasts one of the fastest median marathon times of any marathon in the world. Held on a lightening-fast course under usually ideal weather conditions in Beijing's "golden season," runners are expected to run fast. Added incentive comes in the form of strictly enforced intermediate and finish time requirements. If you meet the standards (3 hour pace for men and 3:10 pace for women), however, the event offers a nice tour of China's capital city, passing some of its greatest historical landmarks including Tiananmen Square and the Forbidden City. At 3-hour pace though you may not be able to appreciate it very much. (Note: At the time of this writing, organizers are considering changing to a point-to-point course possibly ending at the National Olympic Center. If this occurs, the time restrictions will likely loosen.)

COURSE DESCRIPTION Starting from Worker's Stadium, Beijing's out-and-back course heads south on Dongdaqiao Lu, turning right near 4K onto Beijing's main street. The longest straightaway of the race (8K), the avenue (which changes names every few blocks) takes runners past the embassy and shopping districts before arriving in the cultural heart of the city. The Gate of Heavenly Peace, Tiananmen Square, Museum of Chinese History, Monument to the People's Hero, and Great Hall of the People appear on the left between 7.5K and 10K. On the right, runners glide by the Forbidden City, the largest and best preserved cluster of ancient buildings in China. Continuing flat and straight, the route passes the Cultural Palace of the Nationalities before turning right near 12K, heading in the general direction of the famous Beijing Zoo. A few turns take runners to the turnaround point at the China Theater, and the course backtracks to Beijing's main street (here called Fuxingmennei Dajie). Instead of going back down the main street, however, runners continue straight, turning left on a parallel street, Xuanwumen Xida Jie. The race heads east, skirting the back of Tiananmen Square during another long straightaway. Eventually the street name changes to Chongwenmen Dongdajie before passing the Beijing Railway Station. Following a left turn on Jianguomen Nandajie, runners are back on the main street (here called Jianguomen) until rounding the Beijing Ancient Observatory. Runners now return to Worker's Stadium via the initial few kilometers of the course. Run on a mixture of asphalt and concrete, the course contains only a few overpasses for hills.

CROWD/RUNNER SUPPORT   While huge crowds view the marathon (Beijing is densely populated after all), don't expect raucous cheering. The unfamiliar sight of scantily clad marathon runners tromping through the city's main thoroughfares elicits mostly silent stares instead. This is especially true during the long straightaways on DongChang'an Jie and Xuanwumen Xida Jie. Refreshment stations sit on the right-hand side of the course every 5K, while sponging stations lie approximately halfway between refreshment stations.

RACE LOGISTICS   Runners must provide their own transportation to the start. Race organizers enforce strict intermediate time limits to ensure participants meet either the 3 hour time limit for males or the 3 hour and 10 minute limit for females. You will be escorted from the course if you do not meet the following times: 1:40 at 25K, and 2:20 at 35K for men; and 1:45 at 25K, and 2:30 at 25K for women.

ACTIVITIES   Pick up your race packet at the Chinese Athletic Association. The China Travel Service (CTS) offers a full-service travel package. For details, contact CTS (tel. +86/10-646-12572; fax +86/10-646-12576).

AWARDS   Each finisher within the time limit earns a race T-shirt, certificate, and souvenir badge. The top ten males earn trophies, while the top six females earn medals. Prize money extends ten deep for men, ranging from US$15,000 for first to $200 for tenth; and six deep for women, ranging from $7,000 for first to $500 for sixth.

ACCOMMODATIONS   The Beijing Marathon does not have a host hotel. However, several hotels lie near the start/finish including: Huada Hotel, 8 Xinyuan Naulu (tel. +86/10-500-1166; fax +86/10-500-1615); Ritan Hotel, 1 Ritanlu (tel. +86/10-512-5588); and Hilton Hotel, 1 Dongfang Lu, Dongsanhuan Beila (tel. +86/10-466-2288; fax +86/10-465-3052). If you prefer to stay closer to the downtown area, consider the International Hotel, 9 Jianguomennei Dajie (tel. +86/10-512-6688; fax +86/10-512-9972); or Beijing Toronto Hotel, 3 Jianguomennei Dajie (tel. +86/10-500-2266). For other options, contact the China Travel Service.

RELATED EVENTS/RACES   Runners not confident in making the marathon time limits may consider entering the accompanying half marathon or 10K, both of which start with the marathon.

AREA ATTRACTIONS   Beijing houses some of China's most historic sights, including the Forbidden City, Summer Palace, Tiananmen Square, Temple of Heaven and Lama Temple. Though you'll pass many of these sights during the race, you must return for a closer look. You won't, however, pass the Great Wall during the marathon, but a portion of it can be seen in Badaling, a 50-minute drive from Beijing. A 30-mile drive to the north leads to the Ming Tombs, another popular tourist attraction. And the shopping and food selections in Beijing's Wanfujing and Qianmen areas are supposedly the best in China.

MELBOURNE MARATHON

OVERALL: 83.7

COURSE BEAUTY: 9

COURSE DIFFICULTY: 2

APPROPRIATENESS FOR FIRST TIMERS: 8

ORGANIZATION: 8+

CROWDS: 3+

RACE DATA

Overall Ranking: 70
Quality Ranking: 75
Quickness Ranking: 12
Contact: Melbourne Marathon
AusFit Events Management Inc.
305 Burwood Road
Hawthorn, Victoria 3122
Australia
Tel. +61/3-9819-6888
Fax +61/3-9819-9477

Date: Generally first or second Sunday in October
(October 11, 1998)
Start Time: 8:00 a.m.
Time Course Closes: 2:00 p.m.
Number of Participants: 1,800 in 1997
Course: Loop
Certification: AIMS
Race Records: Male: (open) 2:11:08
Female: (open) 2:33:02
Elite Athlete Programs: No
Cost: A$80
Age groups/Divisions: <20, 20-24, 25-29, 30-34, 35-39, 40-44, 45-49, 50-54,
55-59, 60-64, 65-69, 70-74, 75-79, 80+, wheelchair
Walkers: Yes (6 hour limit)
Requirements: 18 years old
Temperature: 43° - 61° (6°C - 16°C)
Aid/Splits: 9 / digital clocks every 5K

HIGHLIGHTS   The Melbourne Marathon tends to get overshadowed internationally by its sexier brethren, the Gold Coast and Sydney Marathons. Perhaps to compensate, Melbourne revs up runners by starting on the Australian Grand Prix race track. After weaving through the chicanes and hairpins, the marathon takes in many of Melbourne's most pleasant areas, like Port Phillip Bay, downtown, and the Melbourne Cricket Grounds. Runners come in for their final stop on Pit Row, taking in fuel at the post-race refreshment tables.

COURSE DESCRIPTION   The Melbourne Marathon starts in outdoorsy Albert Park, home to Australia's Formula One Grand Prix. Runners make one full lap of the 5K race track at something less than 200 mph before heading down tree-lined St. Kilda Road. After crossing the Yarra River, the course enters downtown, passing Melbourne's Arts Centre, Concert Hall,

Flinders Street Station, and huge new Crown Casino and Entertainment Complex between 11K and 13K. Runners next encounter the Melbourne Cricket Grounds (near 16K), the famous stadium for the 1956 Olympic Games, before running alongside the beautiful Botanical Gardens. The race now embarks on a long stretch through South Melbourne as it reaches for the beach. The long, out-and-back section along the water from Port Melbourne to Elwood is the only exposed part of the course, but given favorable conditions is also one of the most pleasant. Following scenic Port Phillip Bay, the route first heads north to Port Melbourne (26K), and then south to Elwood, passing cosmopolitan St. Kilda (32K). The race returns to Albert Park where runners can finally turn off their engines in Pit Row.

CROWD/RUNNER SUPPORT   Melbourne attracts approximately 15,000 spectators along its course. Popular viewing locations include: Flinders Street Station, Albert Road, Beaconsfield Parade and Birdwood Avenue. Digital clocks and aid stations, containing water and Gatorade, lie every 5K.

RACE LOGISTICS   There are several options to get Albert Park on race morning. The Grand Prix track affords plenty of parking for the 1,800 runners. If you are without wheels, you may consider taking a taxi. If you are on a budget, take one of Melbourne's charming electric trams from downtown.

ACTIVITIES   Melbourne has no pre-race activities. Up to two days before the event, foreign runners may pick up their race packets at the Heritage Hotel, 328 Flinders Street (+61/3-9670-4101). Following the race, enjoy a quick massage before attending the awards presentation at the main stage in Albert Park. Also near the finish, the Lifestyle Expo displays the latest health and sports products, as well as food, refreshments, entertainment, and marathon merchandise.

AWARDS   A medal, certificate and results booklet go to all marathon finishers. The first three male and female runners to see the checkered flag receive trophies and prize money: A$3,000 for first, $2,000 for second, and $1,000 for third. A course record brings A$5,000. Age-division winners take home trophies. The official race results and finisher certificates are mailed eight weeks after the event.

RELATED EVENTS/RACES   Several events accompany the marathon for the less ambitious. In 1997, Melbourne started a Marathon Bike Tour that covers the full marathon course, beginning one hour before the footrace. One hour after the marathon start, the green flag waves for Victoria's largest half marathon and an accompanying 6K. If a relay is more to your liking, gather some friends and enter the six-member marathon relay event.

ACCOMMODATIONS   The Heritage Hotel, 328 Flinders Street (tel. +61/3-9670-4101; fax +61/3-9670-4293), serves as the official race hotel offering special marathon rates. Other nearby choices include: Grand Hyatt Melbourne, 123 Collins Street (tel. +61/3-9657-1234; fax +61/3-9650-3491); Regent of Melbourne, 25 Collins Street (tel. +61/3-9653-0000; fax +61/3-9650-4261); Windsor Hotel, 103 Spring Street (tel. +61/3-9653-0653; fax +61/3-9654-5183); and Banks Hotel, corner of Flinders Street and Spencer Street (tel. +61/3-9629-4111; fax +61/3-9629-4300).

AREA ATTRACTIONS   Take a tour of the city in one of Melbourne's famous trams. Visit the Victorian Arts Center, the National Gallery of Victoria, and the Royal Botanical Gardens. Shoppers delight in the Toorak, South Yarra, and Queen Victoria Market areas, while loafers can relax in Albert Park.

AUCKLAND MARATHON

OVERALL: 81

COURSE BEAUTY: 9-

COURSE DIFFICULTY: 3+

APPROPRIATENESS FOR FIRST TIMERS: 7

ORGANIZATION: 8-

CROWDS: 3+

RACE DATA

Overall Ranking:	85
Quality Ranking:	89
Quickness Ranking:	58
Contact:	BMW Auckland Marathon
	P.O. Box 68615
	Newton, Auckland
	New Zealand
	Tel. +64/9-521-9438
	Fax +64/9-521-9437
Date:	Generally fourth Sunday in October
Start Time:	7:00 a.m.
Time Course Closes:	11:30 a.m. (Finish line open until 1:00 p.m.)
Number of Participants:	500 in 1997
Course:	Double out and back
Certification:	NA
Course Records:	Male: (open) 2:14:03
	Female: (open) 2:39:03
Elite Athlete Programs:	No
Cost:	NZ$63
Age groups/Divisions:	M: 18-39, 40-44, 45-49, 50-54, 55-59, 60+, wheelchair
	W: 18-34, 35-39, 40-44, 45-49, 50-54, 55+, wheelchair
Walkers:	Yes
Requirements:	18 years old
Temperature:	50° - 61° (10°C - 16°C)
Aid/Splits:	16 / every 5K and halfway

HIGHLIGHTS   Known for its fresh air, magnificent scenery, and sailing prowess, New Zealand also boasts a strong running culture. Thus the surprise at the low-profile stature of New Zealand's second marathon, Auckland. Held every October, the Auckland Marathon offers picturesque views of sailboats skimming along the bay and of the extinct volcano rising in Hauraki Gulf. However, the double out-and-back course may prove tedious for some, and the understated race activities may also contribute to the race's small size. Maybe if BMW ponied up a couple of cars for prizes, the race would grow to a stature enjoyed by its spring counterpart, the Fletcher Challenge. Until then, Auckland offers runners a low-key race in a nice setting amongst a great running culture.

COURSE DESCRIPTION   If you believe that familiarity breeds contempt, then you may not like Auckland's course. A double out and back, the route covers the same 10.5K of mostly waterfront scenery the entire race. Although the view is nice, a bit more variety would enhance the race. Starting adjacent to the international ship terminal, the race makes a 2-K loop around downtown before winding for the next 9.5K along the waterfront, one of the most popular training routes for Auckland runners. At 3K, runners get their first unobstructed view across the Hauraki Gulf to Rangitoto, the extinct volcanic island a few kilometers off the coast. The green parks, sandy beaches, and sidewalk cafes of popular Mission Bay lie around 8K. Near St. Helias Bay at 11.5K, runners hit the only significant hill, climbing 130 feet into the Auckland suburbs. Here, you are rewarded with a breathtaking view across the Gulf to the Harbour Bridge and the city. A key-hole loop in the residential area returns runners to the waterfront where they retrace their steps back to downtown. Following the second trip, runners hit the finish line in front of QEII Square on Quay Street.

C R O W D / R U N N E R   S U P P O R T   Due to the out-and-back format, spectators enjoy several opportunities to cheer their favorite runners. Most of the approximately 10,000 spectators gather around the downtown start/finish area and at the 8-K mark in Mission Bay, where supporters line the parks and beaches on one side and relax at the sidewalk cafes on the other. More support comes in St. Helias (11K, 13K, 31K, and 33K). Aid stations containing water, Powerade, Coke, bananas, and sponges extend 50 meters wat 5K intervals.

R A C E   L O G I S T I C S   Runners must provide their own transportation to the start. Many hotels, however, exist within walking distance. The race utilizes the ChampionChip timing system, so you must have a chip to receive an official time and finisher's shirt.

A C T I V I T I E S   Little pomp and circumstance accompany this event. You can typically pick up your race packet Thursday through Saturday from 10:00 a.m. to 7:00 p.m. at the Novotel Auckland Hotel, 8 Customs Street, Auckland City. An awards ceremony and random prize drawing take place at 1:00 p.m. in front of the Central Post Office Building in QEII Square.

A W A R D S   All finishers receive a T-shirt after turning in their ChampionChip. A finisher certificate and results book are mailed within two weeks after the event. The top five men and women receive prize money: NZ$2,000 for first, $1,200 for second, $800 for third, $400 for fourth, and $200 for fifth. Use of a 3-Series BMW for one year is awarded to the first New Zealand man and woman marathoners who break time targets of 2:19 (men) and 2:42 (women). The first three places in five-year age groups receive product awards. Finishers under 6 hours are eligible for over 100 spot prizes and many other random prizes.

A C C O M M O D A T I O N S   The Novotel Auckland Hotel, 8 Customs Street (tel. +64/9-377-8920; fax +64/9-302-0993), serves as the official race hotel and offers special marathon rates. For other options, contact Tourism Auckland (tel. +64/9-307-7999; fax +64/9-358-4684).

R E L A T E D   E V E N T S / R A C E S   A half marathon and corporate marathon relay accompany the marathon. Starting at 8:00 a.m., the half marathon runs one segment of the marathon course. The corporate relay leaves with the marathon at 7:00 a.m. Corporate teams consist of 6 members each running between 5K and 10K.

A R E A   A T T R A C T I O N S   A country for outdoor enthusiasts, New Zealand and Auckland offer plenty of activities. Besides camping, hiking, rafting, and sailing, regular activities include harbor cruising, walking around Rangitoto, and visiting Kelly Tarlton's Underwater World including its Antarctic Encounter.

MT. EVEREST CHALLENGE MARATHON

OVERALL: 82.8

COURSE BEAUTY: 10

COURSE DIFFICULTY: 8

APPROPRIATENESS FOR FIRST TIMERS: 2

ORGANIZATION: 8+

CROWDS: 1-

RACE DATA

Overall Ranking: 79
Quality Ranking: 92
Quickness Ranking: 96
Contact: Mr. C.S. Pandey
Mt. Everest Challenge Marathon
Himalayan Run & Trek Pvt. Ltd.
35-D, Pocket 'A', Group-2, Dilshad Garden
Delhi 110095, India
Tel. +91/11-228-5805
Fax +91/11-222-4811
E-mail: hrtpl@del2.vsnl.net.in
http://www.himalayan.com
Date: Generally late October or early November
(November 12, 1998; October 30, 1999)
Start Time: 7:30 a.m.
Time Course Closes: No time limit
Number of Finishers: 25 in 1997
Course: Point to point
Certification: None
Course Records: Male: (open) 4:07:00
Female: (open) 5:07:00
Elite Athlete Programs: No
Cost: Included in trip package
Age groups/Divisions: None
Walkers: No
Requirements: None
Temperature: 40° - 70° (4°C - 21°C)
Aid/Splits: 13 / given at aid stations approximately every 2.5 miles

HIGHLIGHTS/COURSE DESCRIPTION   One of the relatively new breed of ecological marathons, the Mt. Everest Challenge Marathon tours the Indian Himalayas under the distant gaze of Mount Everest, Mount Lhotse, Mount Makalu, and Mount Kanchenjunga, four of the world's five highest peaks. The feature race in the Himalayan 100-Mile Stage Race, the marathon starts in Sandakphu at 11,815 feet and runs along a dazzling ridge line path until mile 18, all the while staying above 11,000 feet. The course then cuts through lush jungle and remote villages to the finish in Rimbik at 6,350 feet. The one catch to this event is that you must book one of the packages offered by race organizer Himalayan Run & Trek to run the race. Packages include accommodations, meals, ground transportation, aid stations, guides, and porters. You do not have to participate in the entire 100-mile stage race, however.

RACE HISTORY   American Jim Crosswhite founded the stage race in 1991 after growing concerned with the environmental impact of Nepal's increased tourism. He envisioned an event that would promote Himalayan conservation, create a greater awareness of the area's distinctive culture and history, and expand the sport of running in the Indian Himalayas. Of course, offering runners a once-in-a-lifetime running experience was also important. Eventually he wanted to transfer the race rights and organization to an all-Indian company, and starting in 1998, the race will be completely controlled by Crosswhite's long-time assistant C.S. Pandey of Himalayan Run & Trek.

CROWD/RUNNER SUPPORT   Small and intimate in its vastness, the Himalayan 100-Mile Stage Race is beginning to attract a growing interest among area villagers. In fact, many locals now enthusiastically greet participants as they pass through town. Aid stations, fully stocked with water, fruit, sports drink, snacks, and portable toilets, dot the course at approximately 2.5-mile intervals.

RACE LOGISTICS   Race organizers provide jeep/bus transportation during and between event stages. Most events start in a different location than the previous stage finish. Runners interested in doing only the marathon usually arrive early and support runners in the first two stages.

AWARDS   Each participant receives a T-shirt, trophy, certificate, and other gifts.

ACCOMMODATIONS   All accommodations are provided in the various race packages. Mirik Lake Resort serves as the race headquarters and is the arrival and departure site for the runners. During the stage race, accommodations include mountain lodges and huts in Sandakphu and Rimbik.

RELATED EVENTS/RACES   The Mt. Everest Marathon is the third stage and centerpiece of the Himalayan 100-Mile, 5-Day Stage Race. The first stage starts in Maneybanjuang (near Darjeeling, India), and runs 24 miles over trails in Sandakphu National Park to the village of Sandakphu. The toughest stage, it has over 10,000 feet of elevation gain. The second stage heads 10 miles to Molle and back. Stages four and five run on rural roads for 13 miles and 17 miles, respectively.

AREA ATTRACTIONS   Outdoor lovers will be as close to heaven as they ever will be on earth in the Himalayas. After all of that running you may be ready for some spiritual nourishment at the many temples and monasteries in the area.

AMAGASAKI MARATHON

OVERALL: 79.9

COURSE BEAUTY: 8

COURSE DIFFICULTY: 3

APPROPRIATENESS FOR FIRST TIMERS: 7-

ORGANIZATION: 9-

CROWDS: 4

RACE DATA

Overall Ranking: 91
Quality Ranking: 59
Quickness Ranking: 40
Contact: Hajime Yuki
Amagasaki International Marathon
Sankei Building, Shinkan 6F
2-4-9 Umeda, Kita Ku, Osaka 530
Japan
Tel. +81/3-3481-2300
Fax +81/3-3481-2449
E-mail: sanspo@mb.infoweb.or.jp
http://sanspo.com

Date: Generally fourth weekend in November
Start Time: 10:30 a.m.
Time Course Closes: 4:00 p.m.
Number of Finishers: 2,000 in 1997
Course: Point to point
Certification: AIMS
Course Records: Male: (open) 2:23:54
Female: (open) 2:50:06
Elite Athlete Programs: No
Cost: NA
Age groups/Divisions: None
Walkers: No
Requirements: 18 years old
Temperature: 55° - 68° (13°C - 20°C)
Aid/Splits: 8 / digital clocks every 5K

HIGHLIGHTS   Few marathons claim a nobler existence than the Amagasaki International Marathon. The event donates a portion of each entry to Unicef, earmarking a different cause each year. In 1997, the nearly 7,000 participants in the marathon and related events raised thousands of dollars for landmine victims in Cambodia and Amagasaki orphans of the 1995 Kobe Earthquake. The marathon features a point-to-point course through the Amagasaki city center in the early kilometers, and then parallels the placid Muko River the rest of the way. Overseas runners probably will most appreciate its central location in the Osaka-Kobe industrial zone near Kyoto.

COURSE DESCRIPTION   Starting in Amagasaki City Memorial Park Track and Field Stadium, the course runs flat through the city for the first 2.5K. Runners pass Higashinanamatsucho City Hall (2K) and then climb 30 feet to the Hamauracho intersection. After crossing the Meihan Highway near 4K, the race gradually rises 40 feet along the Hankyu Kobe Line train tracks to the Muko River Levee entrance (7.5K). The next 33K run relatively level, back and forth along each side of the Muko River. Leaving the levee at 40.7K, the course descends 30 feet to the finish at the Nishimuko Prefectural Park.

CROWD/RUNNER SUPPORT Most spectators congregate along the downtown streets during the early kilometers. Aid stations refuel runners every 5K.

RACE LOGISTICS Runners must supply their own transportation to the start. The efficient subway system makes it very easy for runners staying near Osaka Station or in nearby Kobe.

ACTIVITIES Don't expect a lot of ceremony attached to this race; no pre-race activities accompany the event. Pick up your number at the stadium on race morning.

AWARDS All finishers receive T-shirts and certificates.

ACCOMMODATIONS The race maintains no official host hotel. There are several hotels in Amagasaki near Osaka Station, 15 minutes from the race start. Contact the race for the latest list. Most foreigners stay in livelier Kobe, not too far from the start. Options here include: Hotel Okura, 2-1 Hatobacho, Chuo-ku (tel. +81/78-333-0111); Shin-Kobe Oriental Hotel, 1-chrome Kitanocho, Chuo-ku (tel. +81/78-291-1121); Oriental Hotel, 25 Kyo-machi, Chuo-ku (tel. +81/78-331-8111); and Kobe International Hotel, 1-6-8 Goko-dori, Fukiai-ku (tel. +81/78-221-8051).

RELATED EVENTS/RACES Nearly 7,000 runners usually compete in the five combined events. Besides the marathon, race day includes a half marathon, 10K, 5K and 3K.

AREA ATTRACTIONS While you may want to spend some time in Kobe strolling, eating, and shopping along fashionable Flower Road, the area's greatest appeal is found 30 minutes to the northeast in Kyoto. Spared from Allied bombing during WWII, Kyoto remains a living museum of Japan's historical and cultural heritage. Besides being renowned for traditional Japanese crafts, the city is home to hundreds of architectural landmarks including: Kyoto Imperial Palace, Nijo-jo Castle and its gardens, Sento Imperial Palace, and Daitokuji Temple. The Municipal Museum of Traditional Industry and the Municipal Museum of Art are also worth a look. And the quiet confines of Japan's largest lake, Lake Biwa, are only minutes from the city.

LAKE KAWAGUCHI MARATHON

OVERALL: 90

COURSE BEAUTY: 10-

COURSE DIFFICULTY: 3

APPROPRIATENESS FOR FIRST TIMERS: 9-

ORGANIZATION: 9

CROWDS: 3-

RACE DATA

Overall Ranking: **32**
Quality Ranking: **66**
Quickness Ranking: **42**
Contact: **Lake Kawaguchi Marathon**
Nikkan Sports Newspaper Planning Department
3-5-10 Tskiji Chuo-Ku
Tokyo 104-55
Japan
Tel. +81/3-3547-0900
Fax +81/3-5550-8912

Date: **Generally last Sunday in November**
Start Time: **8:30 a.m.**
Time Course Closes: **1:30 p.m.**
Number of Participants: **14,000 in 1997**
Course: **Double loop**
Certification: **NA**
Course Records: **Male: (open) NA**
Female: (open) NA
Elite Athlete Programs: **No**
Cost: **¥4,000**
Age groups/Divisions: **Men: 18-34, 35-44, 45-54, 55-64, 65+**
Women: 18-34, 35-44, 45-54, 55+
Walkers: **No**
Requirements: **18 years old**
Temperature: **50° - 68° (10°C - 20°C)**
Aid/Splits: **8 / digital clocks every 10K**

HIGHLIGHTS Perhaps the Lake Kawaguchi Marathon would better be called In the Shadow of Mount Fuji Marathon. Non-Japanese runners would have a much better sense of what this race is all about with that perhaps overly long name. Japanese runners may not need the clarification because 14,000 of them show up to the Five Fuji Lakes region in Fuji-Hakone-Iza National Park in late November. With the race's new unofficial name, you don't need us to tell you that the course offers spectacular views of Mount Fuji. And its official name gives you the correct impression that you spend much of the race running around Lake Kawaguchi, one in a string of five major lakes near Japan's sacred symbol. These factors, combined with its convenient location less than two hours from Tokyo, makes it one of Japan's best marathons for overseas runners, confusing name notwithstanding.

COURSE DESCRIPTION Starting in front of the Fuji Lake Hotel on Lake Kawaguchi's southeastern shore, the race heads south toward the perfectly symmetrical cone of Mount Fuji. After U-turning near 2.5K, runners return to the lake slightly after 5K. Bordered by woods on the right, the course now traces the winding outline of the lake for two, 17K counterclockwise loops. Although the course is scenic and rural, runners pass a few landmarks, including the Fujikyuu Highland Amusement Park at 21K and again at 38K, and a handful of hotels and ryokan. Be aware that the course may not be entirely closed to traffic, although the roads are well maintained.

CROWD/RUNNER SUPPORT Most of the crowds on this pastoral route come in front of the hotels and the amusement park. Runners' entourages provide encouragement near the start/finish area which runners pass twice during the race. Aid stations lie approximately every 5K.

RACE LOGISTICS To get to Lake Kawaguchi from Tokyo, you have to take two trains: first a limited express train on the JR Chuo Hansen Line from Tokyo's Shinjuku Station to Otsuki (1 hour), and then a Fujikyu Line train from Otsuki to Lake Kawaguchi (50 minutes). Once in the area, you still need to find your own way to the start, unless you are lucky enough to have a room at the Fuji Lake Hotel.

ACTIVITIES Pick up your race number the night before the race at the Runners Cultural Fellowship Party, where you can meet lots of Japanese runners.

AWARDS Every finisher receives a T-shirt and medal. Top overall runners and age groupers receive special gifts.

ACCOMMODATIONS The Fuji Lake Hotel, 1 Funatsu, Kawaguchiko (tel. +81/555-72-2209), serves as the host hotel. Other nearby hotels include: Fuji-View Hotel, 511 Katsuyam-mura (tel. +81/555-83-2211); and Hotel Kogetsukan, 4014, Funatsu, Kawaguchiko (tel. +81/555-72-1180). Budget conscious runners may consider the Kawaguchiko Youth Hostel (tel. +81/555-72-1413); or a "people's" lodge like Fuji Kawaguchiko Kokumin Shakusha, Kawaguchiko-machi (tel. +81/555-72-7611).

AREA ATTRACTIONS Do you really need us to tell you? Okay, did we mention Mount Fuji? For even better views of Mount Fuji and Lake Kawaguchi, take the ropeway station gondola to the top of Mount Tenjozan. If the kids are around, take them to Fujikyuu Highland Amusement Park, and let them ride its scary roller coaster. The Five Fuji Lakes area is a year-round vacation spot offering fishing, hunting, camping, hiking, lake cruises, and hot-spring spas, not necessarily in that order.

NAHA MARATHON

OVERALL: 92.4

COURSE BEAUTY: 9-

COURSE DIFFICULTY: 4 (SEE APPENDIX)

APPROPRIATENESS FOR FIRST TIMERS: 9

ORGANIZATION: 9+

CROWDS: 9-

RACE DATA

Overall Ranking: **24**
Quality Ranking: **18**
Quickness Ranking: **66**
Contact: **Naha Marathon Association**
Okinawa Times Building
2-2-2 Kumoji
Naha City, Okinawa
Japan
Tel. +81/98-862-9902
Fax +81/98-869-2109

Date: **Generally first Sunday in December**
Start Time: **9:00 a.m.**
Time Course Closes: **3:00 p.m.**
Number of Finishers: **19,934 in 1996**
Course: **Loop**
Certification: **NA**
Course Records: **Male: (open) 2:23:54**
Female: (open) 2:47:15
Elite Athlete Programs: **No**
Cost: **¥3,000**
Age groups/Divisions: **None**
Walkers: **No**
Requirements: **16 years old**
Temperature: **68˚ - 73˚ (20˚C - 23˚C)**
Aid/Splits: **15 / every 5K**

HIGHLIGHTS Dubbed the Festival of Sun, Sea and Runners, the Naha Marathon started in 1985 to commemorate the 25th anniversary of the sister city bond between Naha and Honolulu. Perhaps not coincidentally, the race is held near the anniversary date of the Pearl Harbor bombing and runs past many of southern Okinawa's WWII memorials. Naha and Honolulu share many similarities. Both located in tropical climates, they also rank as their respective country's largest marathons. (And they both have a lot of Japanese runners.) The Naha Marathon is our top-rated Japanese race, and the 24th-ranked marathon overall.

COURSE DESCRIPTION The Naha Marathon makes a rolling, clockwise loop around southern Okinawa, taking in many heartrending monuments to those who died here during WWII. Starting in Onoyama Track & Field Stadium, the race heads past the shops, restaurants, and fast food establishments on lively Kokusai Dori (International Street). Continuing flat, runners enter the southern Naha countryside after 6K. Running through hibiscus and bougainvillea covered hills, past farmhouses and family tombs, you climb nearly 245 feet from 6K to the halfway point in Okinawa Peace Memorial Park. Here, the course veers right, losing 130 feet while cutting across the island's southern tip, hitting Nashiro Beach near 28K. Near 25K, runners pass Okinawa Old Battlefield Quasi National Park and its Himeyurinoto ("cave of the virgins") Monument honoring the 200 young women who died in the crossfire during the closing days of the war. Although the course runs mostly level to 38K, the sea breezes may cool you off and slow you down at the same time. Fields of chrysanthemums lead you to Itoman (32K) and Onaga (35K). It was here in Onaga at the Old Japanese Underground Headquarters that General Ota and his 4,000 men committed *seppuku* (ritual suicide). Continuing north, the course rises 60 feet between 38K and 39K before skirting Naha International Airport. A welcome 60-foot downhill in the final kilometer returns runners for the dramatic stadium finish.

CROWD / RUNNER SUPPORT   Naha attracts nearly 200,000 spectators, most on International Street, and near 8K, 11K, 17K, halfway, 32K and 38K. Added inspiration comes from the many entertainers playing drums and various Japanese stringed instruments. Runners come across aid stations every 2.5K after 6K, with water being the usual refreshment. Several unofficial aid stations with assorted foods pop up along the way.

RACE LOGISTICS   Most runners take the bus or taxis to the start, about 10K from the major hotels. As with many Japanese races, intermediate time limits are enforced. Runners must remove themselves from the race if they lag behind the following times: halfway at 3 hours; 32.5K by 4.5 hours; and the finish within 6 hours.

ACTIVITIES   Pick up your race packet on Saturday between 10:00 a.m. and 4:00 p.m. during the opening ceremonies at Onoyama Track and Field Stadium. In 1998, race organizers plan to hold a race expo for the first time at Onoyama Park. An awards ceremony follows the race at 3:30 p.m.

AWARDS   Every runner receives a T-shirt, and finishers receive certificates and medals. The top ten male and female competitors earn special prizes, while the 11th through 20th finishers receive certificates of merit.

ACCOMMODATIONS   There is no official host hotel for the Naha Marathon. Some of the hotels closest to the start include: Naha Tokyu (tel. +81/98-868-2151); Palace on the Hill Okinawa (tel. +81/98-864-1111); and Pacific Hotel Okinawa (tel. +81/98-868-5162).

AREA ATTRACTIONS   Perhaps the most westernized Japanese city, Naha fascinates in many ways. Mixed in with neon signs and fast food establishments are many temples and shrines including: Gokoku Otera, the main temple of the Shingon sect; Naminoue Jingu, one of the eight famous shrines of Okinawa which overlook the ocean; and Sojen-ji Ishimon, the remains of the Sojen-ji Temple which held the spirits of the Ryukyu kings. Many war memorials, such as Peace Memorial Hall and Okinawa Peace Museum, lie south of Naha. Shoppers feel right at home on Kokusai Dori, while beachgoers have plenty of options minutes from downtown. If you tire of fast-paced Naha, hop to one of the quiet neighboring islands of Iriomote, Kumejima, or Taketomi.

LATIN AMERICA/CARIBBEAN

BERMUDA INTERNATIONAL MARATHON

OVERALL: 87.0

COURSE BEAUTY: 9+

COURSE DIFFICULTY: 5 (SEE APPENDIX)

APPROPRIATENESS FOR FIRST TIMERS: 8+

ORGANIZATION: 8+

CROWDS: 1

RACE DATA

Overall Ranking: 51
Quality Ranking: 75
Quickness Ranking: 56
Contact: Bermuda International Marathon
P.O. Box DV 397
Devonshire DV BX
Bermuda
Tel. (441) 236-6086

Date: Generally third Sunday in January
Start Time: 9:00 a.m. (7:00 a.m. for early starters)
Time Course Closes: 3:00 p.m.
Number of Finishers: 527 in 1997
Course: Double loop
Certification: USATF
Course Records: Male: (open) 2:15:20
Female: (open) 2:42:47
Elite Athlete Programs: Yes
Cost: US$25/40
Age groups/Divisions: 16-19, 20-29, 30-39, 40-49, 50-59, 60-69, 70+
Walkers: Yes
Requirements: 16 years old
Temperature: 65° (18°C)
Aid/Splits: 10 / mile 1 and halfway

HIGHLIGHTS Mark Twain once said, "Sometimes a dose of Bermuda is just what the doctor ordered." Although not toasty warm in January, Bermuda remains a place to relax and enjoy the pink sand beaches, lush subtropical flora, and decidedly English flavor before or after tackling the marathon or one of the triangle of other races. You can wear your shorts runner-short or Bermuda-long while soaking in the beautiful course around the narrow island. The thinness of Bermuda makes the race especially crowd-friendly for those on bicycles or mopeds. Your support crew can easily catch you at several points along the two-loop course. Without a doubt, the Bermuda International Marathon is your best off-shore bet for southern Atlantic or Caribbean running.

COURSE DESCRIPTION The Bermuda International Marathon's double-loop course features all that is Bermuda: subtropical flora, meticulously manicured parks and gardens, nature reserves, scenic coastline, and, of course, a smattering of traditional pastel-colored cottages with whitewashed roofs. Held mostly on narrow, coral and flower-lined roads, the race departs Hamilton from Barr's Bay Park, passing Front Street's popular shops and restaurants. After going by the Bermuda Exploration Institute, the route heads south, rising 65 feet from mile 1 to mile 1.5 on Trimingham Road. Runners turn left onto South Road which parallels (but does not border) the southern coast of Bermuda for the next 4 miles. The race skirts the beautifully land-scaped areas of the Botanical Gardens and Palm Gardens before climbing McGalls Hill, the tough-est hill on the course, rising nearly 130 feet between miles 3.5 and 4. A gradual downhill leads to your first view of the Atlantic Ocean near the Spittal Pond Nature Reserve, the island's largest wildlife sanctuary. At mile 6, the course goes northwest along the shore of Harrington Sound on the way to scenic Flatts Village (mile 7). Now on the island's northern edge, miles 7 to 11 gently roll, running within a discuss toss of the ocean passing more parks and the Government House on the return to Hamilton. The last two miles run along Pitts Bay Road, featuring many old Bermuda homes, and then Front Street to complete the loop. Following one more lap, you finish opposite the No. 6 Passenger Terminal.

CROWD/RUNNER SUPPORT A few thousand spectators usually turn out to encourage the runners. The local paper publishes the runners' names and bib numbers so spectators often surprise visitors by calling out their name. Favorite viewing spots are along Front Street in Hamilton and in Flatts Village. Two factors make Bermuda an extremely spectator-friend-ly race: the double-loop course, and the narrow island. The marathon is fairly runner friendly as well with aid stations every 2.5 miles.

RACE LOGISTICS The start line is within easy walking distance of hotels and guesthouses. Taxis, ferry service and rented mopeds are other means of traveling to the start. The race provides an early (7:00 a.m.) start for walkers and runners who anticipate finishing in over 5 hours.

ACTIVITIES Pick up your race number from 4:00 p.m. to 7:00 p.m. on Thursday or Friday at No. 6 Passenger Terminal. A colorful British military ceremony called the Regimental Musical Display follows the mile races on Friday night. Your last chance for registration and num-ber pick-up takes place on Saturday from 10:00 a.m. to 1:00 p.m. at the National Sports Centre on Montpelier Road in Devonshire. After the race, you should have plenty of time to nap before head-ing to the awards ceremony starting at 7:00 p.m. at Pier 6 on Front Street.

AWARDS   All entrants receive T-shirts, and finishers receive medals and certificates. Prize money goes to the top three male and female runners: $2,500, $1,500, and $800, respectively. A $10,000 bonus is awarded for a new course record. Age category winners receive $200.

ELITE RUNNERS INFORMATION   The race provides travel expenses and accommodations to elite runners based on recent performances. Contact the race for more details.

ACCOMMODATIONS   Bermuda offers a wide variety of lodging options, ranging from the big, luxurious resorts to small guesthouses. The following choices lie closest to the start and finish area in Hamilton: The Princess (large resort), 76 Pitts Bay Road (800-223-1818); Rosedon (small hotel), Pitts Bay Road (800-742-5008); Waterloo House (small hotel), Pitts Bay Road (800-468-4100); and The Oxford House (guesthouse), Woodbourne Avenue (800-548-7758). Other lodging opportunities exist throughout the island, including many properties with private beaches. Call the Bermuda Department of Tourism (800-223-6106) for other accommodations.

RELATED EVENTS/RACES   The weekend's running events blast off Friday night with the Bank of Butterfield Mile races featuring local celebrities, children, area residents and world-class competitors. Saturday brings the Bank of Butterfield Bermuda International 10K and Charity Walk starting at 10 a.m. at the National Sports Centre in Devonshire Parish. The loop course offers runners and walkers a condensed version of the scenic marathon route. Held in tandem with Sunday's marathon, the half marathon completes one loop of the marathon course.

AREA ATTRACTIONS   Ordinarily, heading to the beach would be one of your first moves after arriving in Bermuda. However, keep in mind that it's winter time in Bermuda and, unlike its Caribbean counterparts and even the Bahamas, average air and water temperatures range from the cool low 60s to the mid 70s. Strolling the beaches then may take precedence over sunning and swimming. Offering pale pink sand, Elbow Beach in Paget Parish and Warwick Long Bay Beach in Warwick Parish may provide the best settings. Since island law prevents you from driving a car, consider renting a bicycle to tour the 21-mile length of the island. Walking around historic St. George's Town and the City of Hamilton, Bermuda's government seat and major shopping area, should fit into your schedule. For a spectacular view of the Atlantic Ocean, climb the 185 steps of the Gibbs Hill Lighthouse, the oldest cast-iron lighthouse in the world. The Old Royal Naval Dockyard in Sandy Parish is the number one tourist attraction on the island, with its Bermuda Maritime Museum, Neptune Theatre, Crafts Market, and Bermuda Arts Center. Also worth your time is a tour of the Crystal Caves in Hamilton Parish.

CARIB CEMENT INTERNATIONAL MARATHON

OVERALL: 76.8

COURSE BEAUTY: 7+

COURSE DIFFICULTY: 4

APPROPRIATENESS FOR FIRST TIMERS: 6+

ORGANIZATION: 8+

CROWDS: 1-

RACE DATA

Overall Ranking:	98
Quality Ranking:	88
Quickness Ranking:	79
Contact:	Carib Cement Jamaica Marathon
	Caribbean Cement Company Limited
	P.O. Box 448
	Kingston, Jamaica
	Tel. (876) 928-7530/928-6231
	Fax (876) 928-6096
	E-mail: marathon@caribcement.com
	http://www.caribcement.com/marathon
Date:	Generally third Sunday in February
Start Time:	6:00 a.m.
Time Course Closes:	12:00 p.m.
Number of Participants:	176 in 1997
Course:	Out and partial back
Certification:	JAAA & AIMS
Course Records:	Male: (open) 2:23:05
	Female: (open) 2:46:25
Elite Athlete Programs:	Yes (contact the race)
Cost:	US$30/40
Age groups/Divisions:	≤19, 20-29, 30-39, 40-49, 50-59, 60-69, 70+
Walkers:	No
Requirements:	None
Temperature:	75° - 86° (24°C - 30°C)
Aid/Splits:	23 / every mile after mile 3

HIGHLIGHTS While most Caribbean marathons were created with tourism in mind, the Carib Cement Jamaica Marathon's goal is to develop Jamaican distance runners to complement the country's well-known sprinters. This explains why the marathon is less aesthetic than most other Caribbean races. Held mostly in the tawdry capital Kingston, the marathon takes runners through Port Royal, once called the "wickedest city on earth" thanks to the exploits of notorious buccaneers like Henry Morgan. The race also goes through some more recently notorious spots. If you are one of the many elites chasing the race's fairly generous prize money, you won't care much about the less-than-nice sections of the course. But all of the slow pokes out there may wish they were on a moped in a few areas. Fast guys also favor this race because it is regularly featured on ESPN, and everyone likes a little air time, even runners who can't jump. While the marathon course may not be storybook, everyone benefits from the 23 aid stations and the generally solid organization. Of course, the marathon is only one morning (unless you're having a very bad day), and Jamaica offers plenty of distractions for hibernating runners.

COURSE DESCRIPTION   With the mile-high Blue Mountains to the east, Jamaica's flat, out-and-partially-back course starts at the National Stadium in north Kingston. After a brief stint through area side streets, including a jaunt past the statue of Jamaica's music legend Bob Marley, the race runs south on Mountain View Avenue through a mostly industrial area located east of downtown. At mile 2, runners turn left onto Windward Road passing the Rockfort Mineral Spa and Caribbean Cement Company Sports Complex, the eventual finish site, before rounding the eastern edge of Kingston Harbour. Now heading west toward Port Royal, the race takes competitors along the narrow Palisadoes Sand Spit for the next 10 miles. This strip of sand helps protect the harbor from the sea. The course passes popular Gun Boat Beach (mile 12), followed by the cast iron Plumb Point Lighthouse and Norman Manly Airport. Runners enter Port Royal near the 14-mile point, circle St. Peters Church, and then return to the CCC Sports Complex with the Blue Mountains in the distance.

CROWD/RUNNER SUPPORT   The race has yet to capture the attention and interest of most Kingstonians, so spectator support is minimal. You're more likely to experience an occasional snicker than heavy applause. Race organizers counter the hot and humid conditions with aid stations every mile after mile 3 (sports drink is available every other mile). Both water and sports drink come in handy sachets rather than cups. Sponges are also available at 6 points along the course.

RACE LOGISTICS   American Airlines usually offers marathon participants 50% off their normal airfare to Jamaica. The race provides ground transportation from the airport to area hotels, and also shuttles to the race start beginning at 4:30 a.m. Race organizers transport your belongings to the finish.

ACTIVITIES   Pick up your race packet at the Caribbean Cement Company Sales Office in Rockfort, Kingston starting two days before the race. A bus tour of the course is available the day before the race, leaving from the Jamaican Pegasus Hotel at 10:00 a.m. Beginning at 7:00 p.m. on Saturday evening, a pasta party (US$10) takes place at the Jamaican Pegasus. After the race, stick around for the awards ceremony beginning at 1:00 p.m. in the finish area.

AWARDS   Every finisher receives a T-shirt and medal. A US$30,000 total prize purse is generously distributed throughout the various age categories. Prize money for open division men and women extends from $3,000 for first to $100 for eighth. A $400 bonus goes to a course-record setter. The top three men and women in all other age groups receive $500, $300, and $200, respectively.

ACCOMMODATIONS   The Jamaican Pegasus Hotel, 81 Knutsford (tel. 800-225-5853; fax 876-929-4855) serves as the official race hotel. A number of hotels offer special marathon rates including: Wyndham, 77 Knutsford (tel. 800-822-1400); and Morgan's Harbour, Port Royal (tel. 876-924-8464; fax 876-924-8562/8146).

AREA ATTRACTIONS   Let's face it. You come to Jamaica for the beach and water. There are other diversions, however, when you tire of lounging. Centered around William Grant Park in the heart of downtown, The Parade is an active shopping and dining area with reggae and Jamaican folk music echoing in the background. The Bob Marley Museum is perhaps the largest tourist attraction in the area. Also popular is a trip into the Blue Mountains or a visit to one of the resort areas outside of Kingston.

SANTIAGO INTERNATIONAL MARATHON

OVERALL: 78.3

COURSE BEAUTY: 8+

COURSE DIFFICULTY: 2+

APPROPRIATENESS FOR FIRST TIMERS: 6

ORGANIZATION: 7

CROWDS: 3-

RACE DATA

Overall Ranking:	96
Quality Ranking:	102
Quickness Ranking:	25
Contact:	Rodrigo Salas Moncado
	Marathon International de Santiago
	3008 Bilboa
	Providencia, Santiago
	Chile
	Tel. +56/2-339-7075
	Fax +56/2-339-7076
	E-mail: olimpo@entelchile.net
Date:	Generally second Sunday in April
Start Time:	8:30 a.m.
Time Course Closes:	2:30 p.m.
Number of Finishers:	455 in 1997
Course:	Loop
Certification:	AIMS
Course Records:	Male: (open) 2:14:40
	Female: (open) 2:35:34
Elite Athlete Programs:	Yes (contact the race)
Cost:	US$50
Age groups/Divisions:	Male: 18-19, 20-39, 40-49, 50-54, 55-59, 60-64, 65+
	Female: 18-19, 20-34, 35-39, 40-44, 45-49, 50+
Walkers:	No
Requirements:	18 years old
Temperature:	46° - 64° (8°C - 18°C)
Aid/Splits:	13 / none

HIGHLIGHTS Chile's largest and most prestigious running event, the Santiago International Marathon debuted in 1990, just months after the demise of dictator General Augusto Pinochet's turbulent rule. The marathon takes in the broad, statue-clad Avenue de Bernardo O'Higgins in downtown Santiago, the fashionable shopping area of Providencia, and the wealthy residential areas of Las Condes and Nunoa. Spacious parks, plazas, and gardens mark the course, while the imposing, snowcapped Andes form an inspiring backdrop. As with many Latin American races, traffic control remains a common problem here. Perhaps in a plea to improve this situation, organizers dedicated the 1997 race to the Chilean Police (who celebrated their 70th birthday on race weekend). We'll have to wait and see if this little bit of flattery does anything to beef up future course patrol.

COURSE DESCRIPTION The Santiago International Marathon features a mostly flat loop through some of the most popular streets and avenues of Santiago and the neighboring municipalities of Providencia, Vitacura, Las Condes, Nunoa, and Macul. Starting in front of the presidential viewing stand at O'Higgins Park, the course leaves the green behind by crossing Ercilla Square. Near 1.5K, the route turns on Avenue of the Liberator Bernardo O'Higgins (also called Alameda), Santiago's version of the Champs-Elysees. While on the sweeping avenue, runners pass several statues of former presidents, soldiers, and poets. Two significant landmarks also stamp this street – the Palacio de La Moneda (3.5K), the former residence of many Chilean presidents, and the San Francisco Church (5K), one of the city's oldest buildings and home to the Colonial Museum of Art. After crossing Baquedano Square, the race enters Providencia (7K), Vitacura (11K), and Las Condes (17K), the three of which are fast becoming Santiago's most important financial and commercial areas. Towering 2,850-feet high, San Cristobal Hill emerges on your left between 8K and 9K. Views of the Andes usually appear on the left (depending on smog conditions) when cutting through the tree-lined streets in the increasingly stylish residential district of Nunoa between 22K and 29K. In the final 13K, runners navigate the southern district of Macul, before returning to O'Higgins Park for the finish.

CROWD / RUNNER SUPPORT Unfortunately, the marathon has yet to capture the interest of Santiago and its nearby communities. Though the race follows many central boulevards and avenues, only an estimated 5,000 spectators turn out. Traffic control has been a chronic problem as many motorists consider the race an unneeded nuisance. Aid stations, located every 3K, supply beverages and fruit.

RACE LOGISTICS Most hotels lie three kilometers from the start, which runners must traverse on their own. Most visiting runners walk or take the easily accessible Metro.

ACTIVITIES Pick up your race number and goody bag during the brief expo on Saturday from 4:30 p.m. to 6:30 p.m. at the Holiday Inn Crowne Plaza. Following the expo, stick around for the spaghetti feed (free for race entrants).

AWARDS Each runner who crosses the finish line receives a T-shirt and certificate. Finishers under 6 hours earn medals. Top men and women compete for 7,000,000 pesos in prize money, with the following breakdown: 500,000-first; 350,000-second; 300,000-third; 250,000-fourth; and 100,000-fifth. Time bonuses are also offered for men under 2:15:30 and women under 2:35:30. Bonuses range from 100,000 to 1,000,000 pesos. Masters men and women winners each receive one airline ticket to the Buenos Aires Marathon (from Chile). Age-group winners receive medals and prize money.

ACCOMMODATIONS The Holiday Inn Crowne Plaza, Alameda 136 (tel. +56/2-638-1042; fax +56/2-633-6015) serves as the host hotel. Other choices nearby include: Galerias, San Antonio 65 (tel. +56/2-638-4011; fax +56/2-633-0821); Hotel El Libertador, Alameda 853 (tel. +56/2-639-4212; fax +56/2-633-7128); and Hotel Panamericano, Teatinos 320 (tel. +56/2-672-3060).

RELATED EVENTS / RACES Those not ready for the full distance may choose the accompanying 13K, which runs concurrently with the marathon.

AREA ATTRACTIONS Any trip to Santiago should include a visit to Cerro San Cristobal. Just as the Christ on Corcovado stands guard over Rio de Janeiro, a 110-foot statue of the Virgin Mary graces the top of 1,200-foot San Cristobal Hill over Santiago. Spacious Parque Metropolitano houses several restaurants, snack bars, and coffee shops at the base of the hill. A convenient walk from the park takes you to the popular Providencia shopping district. Cerro Santa Lucia, another elevated park filled with gardens, footpaths and fountains, offers visitors splendid views of the snowcapped Andes and downtown Santiago. Day trips to the coastal resorts of Valparaiso and Vina del Mar are also popular.

SAO PAULO MARATHON

OVERALL: 79.0

COURSE BEAUTY: 8-

COURSE DIFFICULTY: 3

APPROPRIATENESS FOR FIRST TIMERS: 8-

ORGANIZATION: 9-

CROWDS: 4

RACE DATA

Overall Ranking: 95
Quality Ranking: 59
Quickness Ranking: 40
Contact: Ricardo Gomes
Sao Paulo Marathon
R. Oscar Freire 379/18
Sao Paulo-SP, 01426-001
Brazil
Tel. +55/11-253-8866
Fax +55/11-253-8635
E-mail: rgomes@ibm.net

Date: Generally first Sunday in June (April 5, 1998)
Start Time: 9:00 a.m.
Time Course Closes: 3:00 p.m.
Number of Finishers: 4,610 in 1997
Course: Point to point
Certification: AIMS
Course Records: Male: (open) 2:17:07
Female: (open) 2:42:13
Elite Athlete Programs: Yes
Cost: US$20
Age groups/Divisions: NA
Walkers: Yes
Requirements: None
Temperature: 66° - 72° (19°C - 22°C)
Aid/Splits: 13 / none

HIGHLIGHTS Perhaps no other marathon in the world influences its brethren more than the New York City Marathon. A model for the symbiotic relationship between a community and a race, New York has inspired the birth of many marathons around the world. Brazil's Sao Paulo Marathon is one such event. Only four years old, the race stands as the country's largest and most prestigious marathon. Like New York, the Sao Paulo Marathon travels through a host of communities, finishing next to the city's largest and most beautiful park. And while New York has its signature bridges, Sao Paulo is characterized by three traffic-free tunnels toward the end of the course. Despite the similarities, Sao Paulo has a ways to go before joining the world's marathon elites, especially in improving crowd support. Normally held in early June, the 1998 marathon takes place in April due to the Soccer World Cup (Brazilians are much more passionate about their soccer than their running).

COURSE DESCRIPTION The Sao Paulo Marathon's point-to-point course begins in front of historic Pacaembu Stadium in the fashionable Pacaembu residential district. After traveling through several neighborhoods for the initial kilometers, the course rises into downtown on Elevado Costa e Silva. Leaving the business district near 6.5K, runners climb for 3K on Sumare Avenue leading to the Perdizes neighborhood. Near 12K, the route descends along Henrique Schumann Avenue through residential Pinheiros. Becoming mostly commercial along Teodoro Sampaio Street, the route turns right on Pedroso de Morais Avenue (near 13.5K), the longest straightaway of the race. At 16K, runners pass Praca Panamericana (Pan American Plaza) while coursing past the beautiful homes in Alto de Pinheiros. After going by Villa Lobos Park near 18K, the route soon crosses the Pinheiros River and enters Sao Paulo University near halfway. Normally bustling with the activity of 60,000 students, the campus is eerily quiet on race morning, closed to all but the runners. The next 9K through the campus pass beautiful trees and well-designed buildings, but also include several challenging grades. Between 30K and 35K, runners cross and recross the Pinheiros River before gliding by the Joquei Club (horse race track). The tunnels begin at 36K. First in line is the 1.2K Janio Quadors Tunnel under the Pinheiros River. Now on Presidente Juscelino Kubitschek Avenue, the Tribunal da Justica Tunnel lasts .8K. Only seconds later, runners reach the 1.4K Ayrton Senna Tunnel, named for the late Brazilian Formula 1 racer. Breaking out of the tunnel, runners see the monument to Senna, make a quick left turn, and finish in front of the Commons State Building alongside lovely Ibirapuera Park. The route is completely closed to vehicle traffic.

CROWD/RUNNER SUPPORT Although Sao Paulo ranks as the most populous city in South America, its marathon draws only modest enthusiasm from residents. Areas of noticeable support include: Avenida Sumare, Dr. Arnaldo Bridge, Parque Villa Lobos, and Praca Panamericana. The aid stations, placed at 3K intervals, provide water, sports drink and sponges.

RACE LOGISTICS Pacaembu Stadium is a two kilometer (1.2 miles) walk from many area hotels. If you'd rather avoid the walk to the start, take the subway or a bus instead. While you have to run, race organizers transport your extra gear to the finish. Be aware that the tunnels along the course stay 3 to 4 degrees cooler than the outside air, which may be a blessing in hot weather but can also be a shock for some runners.

ACTIVITIES Pick up your number the day before the race at the Ibirapuera Park Marquis. Race organizers plan to have a pasta party the night before the marathon. A lively post-race party awaits runners in the finish area.

AWARDS All marathoners receive T-shirts at the packet pick-up, and finishers receive medals and certificates. Finishers also qualify for a drawing to win one of many prizes. The top five male and female runners compete for a share of the US$110,000 prize purse, while the fastest Brazilians win a new car. The best age-group runners receive special prizes.

ELITE RUNNERS INFORMATION Race organizers offer a combination of transportation, hotel and food expenses, and appearance money. Contact the race for more details.

ACCOMMODATIONS The race does not have an official host hotel. However, there are several hotels within two kilometers of the start. Among them are the: Hilton Hotel, Avenue Ipiranga 165 (tel. +55/11-256-0033; fax +55/11-257-3137); Brasilton, R. Martins Fontes 330 (tel. +55/11-258-5811; fax +55/11-258-5812); and Grand Hotel Ca d'Oro, R. Augusta 129 (tel. +55/11-256-8011; fax +55/11-231-8011). For less expensive lodging, try: Plaza Maraba, Avenue Ipiranga 757 (tel. +55/11-220-7811); or Terminus, Avenue Ipiranga 741 (tel. +55/11-222-2266).

AREA ATTRACTIONS Sao Paulo offers all of the features you expect in a large city: fine shopping, dining, museums, cinemas, gardens, and lively nightlife. The most popular tourist attraction is the Butanta Snake Farm and Museum which contains over 70,000 snakes, spiders, scorpions, and lizards. Spacious Ibirapuera Park houses a planetarium and several museums, including: Museu de Arte Contemporaneo, Arte Moderna, Aeronautica, and Folklore. For coastal excursions, head southeast for one-and-one-half hours to the exceptional beaches and resorts of Santos and Guaruja.

LIBERTADOR MARATHON

OVERALL: 80.4

COURSE BEAUTY: 9-

COURSE DIFFICULTY: 4+

APPROPRIATENESS FOR FIRST TIMERS: 6

ORGANIZATION: 7+

CROWDS: 3-

RACE DATA

Overall Ranking:	89
Quality Ranking:	100
Quickness Ranking:	85
Contact:	Marathon Libertador Caracas
	Globalbest Travel Services
	Avenida Sucre Los Dos Caminos
	Conjunto Centro Parque Boyaca
	18th Floor, Office #182
	Caracas 1071, Venezuela
	Tel. +58/2-285-6704 / 286-0131
	Fax +58/2-283-6170
	E-mail: travel@cantv.net
Date:	Generally third Sunday in July
Start Time:	7:30 a.m.
Time Course Closes:	12:30 p.m.
Number of Participants:	885 in 1997
Course:	Loop
Certification:	NA
Course Records:	Male: (open) 2:19:25
	Female: (open) 2:52:46
Elite Athlete Programs:	No
Cost:	US$60
Age groups/Divisions:	18-39, 40-44, 45-49, 50+ (M), 50-54, 55-59, 60+ (F)
Walkers:	No
Requirements:	18 years old
Temperature:	66° - 75° (19°C - 24°C)
Aid/Splits:	12 / none

HIGHLIGHTS/COURSE DESCRIPTION Though South America trails most other continents in the number (and quality) of marathons, the neophyte Sao Paulo and Libertador Marathons have generated a spark of interest in many foreign runners. With its northern location, Caracas may become a favorite among the growing number of North Americans intent on running a marathon in each continent. With only three races under its belt, Libertador has already doubled its field, with a respectable 885 runners participating in 1997. The race's name stems from the organizers' wish to honor Simon Bolivar, the father of Venezuela's independence. The rolling loop course runs through Caracas, a beautiful city in the foothills of Monte Avila National Park. Runners assemble amongst the statues and gardens of Los Proceres, a national monument for Venezuela's Independence Heroes. Barreling south, runners pass the soccer and baseball stadiums used for the 1983 Pan American Games, before touring downtown Caracas. After a stint through a military area, runners return to Los Proceres for the finish.

CROWD / RUNNER SUPPORT   Approximately 20,000 spectators encourage the runners, with most applauding at Los Proceres and downtown. After 5K, aid stations come every 3K or so, with sports drink available after 21K. Like many South American marathons, Caracas suffers from poor traffic management. Be careful, especially when running through downtown.

RACE LOGISTICS   Most foreign runners stay downtown and take a 15-minute taxi ride to the start.

ACTIVITIES   The race organizers haven't gotten around to hosting a bunch of activities, like a pasta party or race expo. You'll have to settle for the awards ceremony, but you'll probably skip it anyway.

AWARDS   All runners receive T-shirts, and finishers earn medals. Top male and female overall and age-group performers receive special prizes.

ACCOMMODATIONS   There is no official race hotel. However, several hotels lie within a 15-minute drive of the start. Since the race organization is a travel agency, let them offer suggestions for your lodging while in Caracas.

AREA ATTRACTIONS   On race weekend, Caracas' already festive atmosphere cranks up a gear with several celebrations of the city's anniversary and the birthday of its liberator Simon Bolivar. When partied out, relax on the long white-sand beaches of Islas Los Roques, a beautiful Caribbean atoll, or take a hike through quiet Monte Avila National Park. Another worthwhile excursion is to the touristy mountain town of Colonial Tovar. Settled in 1843 by German immigrants, the town abounds with quaint shops and restaurants, and is still populated by blond-haired, blue-eyed, inhabitants. If you have more time, head to Angel Falls – the world's highest waterfall at 3,204 feet – in Parque Nacional Canaima, several hours southeast of Caracas.

PANAMA ULTRAMARATHON

OVERALL: 75.3

COURSE BEAUTY: 9

COURSE DIFFICULTY: 8-

APPROPRIATENESS FOR FIRST TIMERS: 1

ORGANIZATION: 8+

CROWDS: 1-

RACE DATA

Overall Ranking:	101
Quality Ranking:	92
Quickness Ranking:	NA
Contact:	Arturo Bouche
	Ultramarathon de Panama
	815-0306 Zona 15
	Panama City, Republic of Panama
	Tel & Fax +507/236-2876
	http://www.gnw.net/ultramaraton
	or: Jonathan DeHart
	139 Harrison Avenue
	Glenside, PA 19038 USA
	Tel. (215) 887-5825
Date:	Generally first Saturday in September (scheduled for July 31, 1999)
Start Time:	10:00 p.m. (yes, p.m.)
Time Course Closes:	Within reason
Number of Participants:	33 in 1997
Course:	Point to point
Certification:	USATF and PAF
Course Records:	Male: (open) 5:53:47
	Female: (open) 7:20:32
Elite Athlete Programs:	No
Cost:	US$80
Age groups/Divisions:	NA
Walkers:	No
Requirements:	None, but recent marathon or 50-mile ultra finish recommended
Temperature:	75° - 90° (24°C - 32°C)
Aid/Splits:	A support crew is provided for $75 charge / none

HIGHLIGHTS What other race offers this bragging right to its finishers, "I ran from the Atlantic Ocean to the Pacific Ocean in one night!"? This distinction can be yours after finishing the Panama Ultramarathon. Starting at 10:00 p.m., the challenging 50.4-mile adventure runs through the night along the Trans-Isthmus Highway, roughly paralleling the Panama Canal. With the headlights of support vehicles illuminating the way, the small field cuts through a primary-growth tropical rainforest during one memorable section. The jungle fauna, tropical birds, and exotic, though harmless, mammals create a welcome distraction from the harsh hills and heat. At the finish, runners witness a phenomenon unique in the Western Hemisphere to Panama: the sun rising over the Pacific, starting a new day at the end of your long night.

RACE HISTORY The origin of the race can be traced back to 1940 when friends dared a young corporal in the U.S. Army Air Corps to run across Panama from ocean to ocean. At the time, there was no road through the country, but Corporal Fay Steele completed the trek in his $1.50 Ked sneakers. Forty-three years later the first official race took place, and twenty of the twenty-three starters finished the course. In 1990, Mr. Steele, at age 74, completed the race for the fifth time in 10:09:43. His personal record of 8:47:28 (which he set at age 70) remains the course record for the 70 and over age group.

COURSE DESCRIPTION The Panama Ultramarathon features a point-to-point route from Colon on the Atlantic Ocean to Fort Amador on the Pacific Ocean. For the first 30 miles, the course undulates through hills covered with tropical fauna and small farms. Using the right lane, runners share the road with local people walking on foot and light highway traffic. From the Chagre River Bridge (mile 27) to Forest Road, runners encounter a 6-mile gradual incline. A right turn onto Forest Road takes you over the Continental Divide through a dripping rainforest, where the course reaches its highest point of 500 feet. This is where you can really enjoy the fauna, exotic birds, and jungle mammals. The most challenging hill on the course comes one mile after the turn onto Forest Road. Following the 6 miles in the rainforest, runners continue along Gaillard Highway for 11 miles, closely paralleling the Panama Canal, including a section along the lock at Pedro Miguel. A steep, 1-mile downhill on Paraiso Hill deposits you near mile 42. The final 8.5 miles head generally downhill, but include a few steep and gradual uphill sections. From Fort Clayton (49.5 miles), you can look across the Pacific entrance to the Panama Canal and see the Bridge of the Americas lying 4.5 miles away, all the while watching the sun rise over the Pacific. The "S" shape of the Isthmus places the Pacific entrance to the canal further east than the Atlantic entrance. If the distance alone is not challenging enough, the formidable hills coupled with the heat and humidity make this race a very difficult adventure.

CROWD/RUNNER SUPPORT You may be crazy enough to run across Panama in the middle of the night, but don't expect many spectators to join you. Besides a few curious bystanders during the first mile in Colon, a handful of cantina partiers, and a few animals in

the jungle, most noise and support comes from your race-supplied crew. Of course, a small contingent of runners' family and friends are on hand for the finish. Fluids, food and lighting are provided by your support vehicle. A Red Cross ambulance and doctors patrol the course.

RACE LOGISTICS Each participant, or group of runners who have decided to stick together, must have a support vehicle. For $75, the race provides a vehicle, driver, and an explorer scout trained in first aid. This vehicle or one you obtain can transport you to the start of the race.

ACTIVITIES Pick up your race number and meet your fellow adventurers at the pre-race dinner held at a local sports bar. Contact the race for details.

AWARDS Each hearty finisher receives a T-shirt, while the top three men and women earn modest prize money.

ACCOMMODATIONS The Executive Hotel, Cl. A de la Guardia y C152 (tel. +507/269-3333; fax +507/269-1944), serves as the race hotel for the 1998 and 1999 events. Plenty of other hotels lie near the finish in Panama City's business district. These include: El Panama, Apdo 6-999 Zona 6 (tel. +507/223-1660; fax +507/220-5017); Hotel Costa del Sol (tel. +507/223-7111; fax +507/223-6636); Suites Ambassador, Cl. D El Cangrejo (tel. +507/263-7274; fax +507/264-7872); and Hotel Central (tel. +507/262-8044).

AREA ATTRACTIONS Several indoor and outdoor shopping areas lie near the hotels, including El Dorado, La Alhambra, Plaza Paitilla, and Tocumen. Old Panama City and Colonial Panama City contain many interesting sites. Colon lies near the ruins of Portobelo with its impressive Spanish forts. Not far from Colon are attractive beaches at Isla Grande and Isla Mamey. Contadora Island, a beach resort on the Pacific coast, is only 15 minutes by air from Panama City. The Pan-American Highway provides access to other beautiful Pacific beaches, including Coronado, Gorgona, Punta Chame, Rio Mar, San Carlos, and Santa Clara. The dense jungles of Darlene Province, home of the Choco Indians, are an hour flight from Panama City. And, of course, the Panama Canal and its impressive locks are within a short drive.

BARBADOS MARATHON

OVERALL: 79.8

COURSE BEAUTY: 9

COURSE DIFFICULTY: 4

APPROPRIATENESS FOR FIRST TIMERS: 7

ORGANIZATION: 8

CROWDS: 1-

RACE DATA

Overall Ranking: 93
Quality Ranking: 98
Quickness Ranking: 72
Contact: Barbados Marathon
The Barbados Tourism Authority
P.O. Box 242
Harbour Road
Bridgetown, Barbados
Tel. (246) 427-2623
Fax (246) 426-4080

Date: Generally first Sunday in December
Start Time: 5:30 a.m.
Time Course Closes: 11:00 a.m.
Number of Participants: 150 in 1997
Course: Point to point
Certification: AIMS
Course Records: Male: NA
Female: NA
Elite Athlete Programs: Yes
Cost: US$20
Age groups/Divisions: ≤29, 30-39, 40-49, 50-59, 60+
Walkers: No
Requirements: None
Temperature: 72° - 81° (22°C - 27°C)
Aid/Splits: 8 / none

HIGHLIGHTS   The most easterly of the Caribbean Islands, Barbados mixes British institution with African-style hospitality. Offering runners a welcomed interlude from the wintry climes of the north, the Barbados Marathon features a point-to-point course run almost entirely within meters of the island's scenic southern and western coasts. Even some of the locals drop their cricket mallots to take part in the marathon, 10K, 20K walk, or triathlon that comprise Run Barbados weekend.

COURSE DESCRIPTION   The Barbados Marathon features a point-to-point course generally staying within 300 feet of the Caribbean Sea. Starting at Grantley Adams International Airport on Barbados' southeastern tip, the race goes west through the fishing town Oistins near 5K on the way to the palm tree-lined beaches and lively strip of hotels, nightclubs, and restaurants of St. Lawrence Gap (11.5K). Normally bustling with activity, this area is relatively quiet when trundling through around 6:30 in the morning. Still skirting the shoreline, the race enters

Bridgetown, the busy capital city, near 18K. Leaving north from Bridgetown, the second half of the race traces the western coast on Highway 1. Elegant private homes and luxury resorts, lying amid leafy mahogany trees and pink and white beaches, dominate this portion of the course. Runners pass Holetown (near 34K), the center of the Gold Coast resort area, en route to the finish at the Almond Beach Village just outside the port city of Speightstown.

CROWD/RUNNER SUPPORT Approximately 20,000 spectators cheer on the runners with most gathering in Oistins, Bridgetown, Holetown, and the finish. Aid stations lie every 3 miles which, considering the toasty Barbados temperatures, may be a bit infrequent for some runners.

RACE LOGISTICS Race organizers provide bus transportation to the start. Buses pick up runners outside their hotels along the main highway.

ACTIVITIES Pick up your race packet during race week at the Caribbee Hotel, located just outside of Bridgetown in Hastings, Christ Church.

AWARDS The first 100 finishers receive medals and running vests. The top male and female runners receive a one-week, all-expenses paid trip for two to the following year's race. Age-group winners receive plaques.

ACCOMMODATIONS The Caribbee Hotel in Hastings (tel. 246-436-6232), serves as the official race hotel. Hotels fill the southern and western shores of Barbados. Hotels north of Bridgetown are predominately self-contained resorts. In addition to the Almond Beach Village, Hwy 1 (tel. 800-425-6663; fax 246-422-1581), other options near the finish include: Sandridge, Roadview (tel. 246-422-2361; fax 246-422-1965); and Cobbles Cove Hotel, Hwy 1 (tel. 800-890-6060; fax 246-422-1460). Many less expensive hotels sit closer to the start in Christ Church Parish. Among them are: Oasis, Worthing (tel. 246-435-7930; fax 246-435-8232); and the Sandy Island Resort, Worthing (tel. 246-435-8000; fax 246-435-8053).

RELATED EVENTS/RACES Barbados offers an event to suit just about anybody. Marathon weekend starts Saturday with a 20K walk beginning on Harbor Road in St. Michael and ending at the marathon finish. At 4:00 p.m. the same day, the popular 10K runs through the streets of Bridgetown. Finally, while the tail end of the marathoners stream into the finish area, a children's triathlon (ages 7-17) blasts off from Heywoods Beach at 9:00 a.m.

AREA ATTRACTIONS Barbados' year-round hot and sunny weather makes basking in the sun a first priority for most visitors. The calm, clear waters of the West Coast make for excellent snorkeling, scuba diving, and swimming. Great shopping and dining exists along Bridgetown's Broad Street and in the St. Lawrence Gap area. Five minutes north of Bridgetown lies the Mount Gay Rum Visitor's Center where you can learn the story behind the world's oldest rum and the rum-making process. In St. Thomas Parish, visit Harrison's Cave where a one-hour tram tour leads you through this pale-gold limestone cavern complete with a 40-foot waterfall.

Appendix

MARATHON RANKINGS
AND COURSE PROFILES

WORLD'S TOP 100+ DESTINATION MARATHONS

Name of Marathon	Crowd	Course Scenery	Race Organization	Overall Rating
1. Stockholm	8	10-	10-	100.0
2. Berlin	10	8+	10	99.7
2. London	10	8+	10	99.7
4. New York City	10+	8	10	99.3
5. Big Sur	5-	10+	10	98.8
6. Hamburg	9-	9+	10	98.7
7. Venice	8	9+	9+	98.5
8. Twin Cities	9-	10	10	98.4
9. Chicago	9-	8+	10	98.1
10. Boston	10+	8	10	97.8
11. Medoc	8	9+	9+	97.6
11. Rome City	9+	10	9-	97.6
13. Madrid	9+	8	9 +	95.7
13. Marine Corps	5-	10-	10-	95.7
15. Comrades	9-	8	10	95.4
16. Paris	5-	10-	9+	94.8
17. Two Oceans	6	10-	9+	94.3
18. Lausanne	5-	10-	9+	94.2
19. Dublin	7-	9-	9+	93.9
20. Jungfrau	4	10+	9	93.7
21. St. George	4	9	10-	93.0
22. Honolulu	6	9	9+	92.8
22. Gold Coast	4	9+	10-	92.8
24. Noha	9-	9-	9+	92.4
25. Florence	5-	10-	9-	92.1
26. Vancouver	6	9-	9+	91.4
27. Frankfurt	9-	8+	10-	91.0
27. Los Angeles	10	6+	9+	91.0
29. Catalunya-Barcelona	6	8+	9	90.7
30. San Francisco	5+	10-	8+	90.3
31. Prague	4	9+	9-	90.1
32. Lake Kawaguchi	3-	10-	9	90.0
32. Maui	2	10-	9	90.0
34. Lisbon Half	6	9	9	89.9
35. Helsinki	5-	9+	9+	89.7
36. Route du Vin Half	4	10-	9	88.9
37. Fletcher Challenge	4	9	9+	88.8
37. Mount Meru	5+	9-	8+	88.8
39. Rotterdam	8	7+	10	88.6
39. Royal Victoria	4	9	9-	88.6
41. Seville	5-	9-	9	88.5
41. Vermont City	5-	9	9	88.5
43. Cape Town	3-	9	9+	88.2
43. Columbus	7+	8+	10-	88.2
45. Pittsburgh	8	8-	10-	88.0
45. Rock "N" Roll	4	9+	9	88.0
47. Antwerp	5+	9-	9	87.9
48. Napa Valley	2	9+	9	87.7
48. Moorea Blue	2	10	8+	87.7
50. Sydney	3+	9+	8+	87.6
51. Portland	6	8	10	87.0
51. Oslo	5-	9	9	87.0
51. Bermuda	3+	9+	8+	87.0
54. Budapest	4	9+	9-	86.9

Name of Marathon	Crowd	Course Scenery	Race Organization	Overall Rating
55. Thailand International	2	10-	8+	86.8
56. Echternach	4	9	9	86.7
57. Grandma's	4	9-	10-	86.6
58. Beijing	6	9-	9-	86.5
59. Vienna City	5-	8+	9	86.1
60. Loire Valley	1+	9+	9-	85.9
61. Houston	9-	6+	10	85.8
62. Walt Disney World	4	9-	9	85.7
63. Okinawa	5+	8	9-	84.9
64. Kiawah Island	2	9+	9	84.7
65. Copenhagen	3+	9-	8+	84.6
66. Turin	5-	8	9+	84.1
66. Reykjavik	4	9	9-	84.1
68. Chambord	1-	9	9-	84.0
69. National Capital	4	9	9-	83.8
70. Mount Fuji	1-	9+	8+	83.7
70. Melbourne	3+	9	8+	83.7
70. Catalina Island	1+	10-	9-	83.7
73. Humboldt Redwoods	1-	10	8+	83.5
73. Avenue of the Giants	1-	10	8+	83.5
75. Canadian International	5-	7+	9	83.4
75. Cleveland	5+	8-	9+	83.4
77. Egyptian International	2	9	8	83.2
78. Midnight Sun	3-	9-	9-	83.1
79. Mount Everest Challenge	1-	10	8+	82.8
80. Malta Challenge	4	9	8	82.3
81. Vigarano	5-	8-	9+	82.0
82. Istanbul-Eurasia	3-	8+	8-	81.9
82. Calgary	3-	8	9	81.9
84. Pikes Peak	1-	9	9-	81.6
85. Auckland	3+	9-	8-	81.0
86. Italian	5-	7+	9+	80.7
86. Valencia	5-	7+	9+	80.7
86. Siberian International	7+	8	8+	80.7
89. Libertador (Caracas)	3-	9-	7+	80.4
90. Belgrade	4	8-	9	80.0
91. Amagasaki	4	8	9-	79.9
91. Kasumigaura	2	9-	9	79.9
93. Barbados	1+	9	8	79.8
93. China Coast	1-	8+	8	79.8
95. Sao Paulo	3-	8-	9-	79.0
96. Santiago	3-	8+	7	78.3
97. Montreal	4	8-	8	77.8
98. Malang International	3-	9	7+	76.8
98. Carib Cement	1+	8-	8+	76.8
100. Tiberias	2	8	8	75.4
101. Panama Ultra	1-	9	8+	75.3
102. Athens	2	8	6	74.9
102. Bucharest	2	8-	8+	74.9
104. Vardinoyiannios	1+	9-	7+	73.8

THE PR CHASE
WORLD'S TOP 30 FASTEST MARATHONS

Name of Marathon	Crowd	Race Organization	Difficulty	Overall Rating
1. Chicago	9-	10	1+	100.0
2. Rotterdam	8	10	1+	99.7
3. Beijing	6	9-	1+	97.3
4. Berlin	10	10	2-	96.7
4. London	10	10	2-	96.7
6. Gold Coast	4	10-	2-	93.5
7. Antwerp	5+	9	2-	93.4
7. Italian	5-	9+	2-	93.4
7. Vigarano	5-	9+	2-	93.4
10. Frankfurt	9-	10-	2	92.8
11. Houston	9-	10	2+	90.2

Name of Marathon	Crowd	Race Organization	Difficulty	Overall Rating
12. Melbourne	3+	8+	2	88.8
13. Bucharest	2	8+	2	88.2
14. Chambord	1-	9-	2	87.9
15. Cleveland	5+	9+	2+	87.8
16. Turin	5-	9+	2+	87.5
17. Rock "N" Roll	4	9	2+	86.9
18. Prague	4	9-	2+	86.6
19. Twin Cities	9-	10	3-	86.2
20. Copenhagen	3+	8+	2+	85.8
21. Columbus	7+	10-	3-	85.2
21. Loire Valley	1+	9-	2+	85.2

Name of Marathon	Crowd	Race Organization	Difficulty	Overall Rating
23. Humboldt Redwoods	1-	8+	2+	84.6
23. Avenue of the Giants	1-	8+	2+	84.6
25. Santiago	3-	7	2+	84.3
26. Vardinoyiannios	1+	7+	2+	83.9
27. Grandma's	4	10-	3-	83.6
27. Valencia	5-	9+	3-	83.6
29. Canadian International	5-	9	3-	83.4
30. Echternach	4	9	3-	82.9
30. Walt Disney World	4	9	3-	82.9

MARATHON RANKINGS

The Raving Beauties

Most Scenic Marathons

1. Jungfrau
2. Big Sur
3. Rome City
4. Moorea Blue
5. Twin Cities
6. Mount Everest Challenge
7. Humboldt Redwoods
8. Avenue of the Giants
9. Paris
10. Maui
11. Stockholm
12. Florence
13. Catalina Island
14. San Francisco
15. Lausanne
16. Two Oceans
17. Thailand International
18. Marine Corps
19. Lake Kawaguchi
20. Route du Vin Half
21. Gold Coast
22. Medoc
23. Budapest
24. Prague
25. Loire Valley
26. Hamburg
27. Rock "N" Roll
28. Venice
29. Sydney
30. Bermuda

I'm Going to ...

Top Destination Marathons by Region

North America

1. New York City (4)
2. Big Sur (5)
3. Twin Cities (8)
4. Chicago (9)
5. Boston (10)
6. Marine Corps (13)
7. St. George (21)
8. Honolulu (22)
9. Vancouver (26)
10. Los Angeles (27)
11. San Francisco (30)
12. Maui (32)
13. Royal Victoria (39)
14. Vermont City (41)
15. Columbus (43)

Europe

1. Stockholm (1)
2. Berlin (2)
2. London (2)
4. Hamburg (6)
5. Venice (7)
6. Medoc (11)
6. Rome City (11)
8. Madrid (13)
9. Paris (16)
10. Lausanne (18)
11. Dublin (19)
12. Jungfrau (20)
13. Florence (25)
14. Frankfurt (27)
15. Catalunya-Barcelona (29)
16. Prague (31)
17. Lisbon Half (34)
18. Helsinki City (35)
19. Route du Vin Half (36)
20. Rotterdam (39)

Africa/Middle East

1. Comrades (15)
2. Two Oceans (17)
3. Mount Meru (37)
4. Cape Town (43)
5. Egyptian International (77)
6. Tiberias (100)

Asia/Pacific

1. Gold Coast (22)
2. Naha (24)
3. Lake Kawaguchi (32)
4. Fletcher Challenge (37)
5. Moorea Blue (48)
6. Sydney (50)
7. Thailand International (55)
8. Beijing (58)
9. Okinawa (63)
10. Mount Fuji Climbing Race (70)

Latin America/Caribbean

1. Bermuda (51)
2. Libertador (Caracas) (89)
3. Barbados (93)
4. Sao Paulo (95)
5. Santiago (96)
6. Carib Cement (98)
7. Panama Ultra (101)

MARATHON RANKINGS

Looking for a Fast Time?

Fastest Marathons by Region

North America

1. Chicago (1)
2. Houston (11)
3. Cleveland (15)
4. Rock "N" Roll (17)
5. Twin Cities (19)
6. Columbus (21)
7. Humboldt Redwoods (23)
7. Avenue of the Giants (23)
9. Grandma's (27)
10. Canadian International (29)
11. Walt Disney World (30)
12. Pittsburgh (32)
13. Napa Valley (35)
13. Kiawah Island (35)
15. Calgary (42)

Europe

1. Rotterdam (2)
2. Berlin (4)
2. London (4)
4. Antwerp (7)
4. Italian (7)
4. Vigarano (7)
7. Frankfurt (10)
8. Bucharest (13)
9. Chambord (14)
10. Turin (16)
11. Prague (18)
12. Copenhagen (20)
13. Loire Valley (21)
14. Vardinoyiannios (26)
15. Valencia (28)
16. Echternach (30)
17. Budapest (32)
18. Reykjavik (32)
19. Siberian International (37)
20. Hamburg (38)

Africa/Middle East

1. Egyptian International (48)
1. Tiberias (48)

Asia/Pacific

1. Beijing (3)
2. Gold Coast (6)
3. Melbourne (12)
4. Amagasaki (40)
5. Lake Kawaguchi (42)
6. Kasumigaura (46)
7. Moorea Blue (47)
8. Sydney (56)
9. Auckland (58)
10. Naha (66)

Latin America/Caribbean

1. Santiago (25)
2. Sao Paulo (40)
3. Bermuda (56)
4. Barbados (72)

What Was I Thinking?

Most Difficult Marathons

1. Mount Fuji Climbing Race
2. Pikes Peak
3. Jungfrau
4. Mount Everest Challenge
5. Catalina Island
6. Thailand International
7. Malang
8. China Coast
9. Big Sur
10. Malta Challenge

The Well-Oiled Machines

Best Organized Marathons

1. London
2. Chicago
3. Portland
4. Berlin
5. Comrades
6. Boston
7. New York City
8. Hamburg
9. Rotterdam
10. Twin Cities
11. Houston
12. Big Sur
13. Stockholm
14. Columbus
15. Frankfurt
16. St. George
17. Grandma's
18. Marine Corps
19. Pittsburgh
20. Medoc
21. Venice
22. Two Oceans
23. Honolulu
24. Madrid
25. Los Angeles

Screamin' Meemies

Marathons With Best Crowd Support

1. New York City
2. Boston
3. London
4. Los Angeles
5. Berlin
6. Rome City
7. Madrid
8. Hamburg
9. Chicago
10. Comrades
11. Frankfurt
12. Naha
13. Houston
14. Twin Cities

M A R A T H O N   R A N K I N G S

Virgin Voyages
Top Marathons For First Timers

1. London
2. Berlin
3. Chicago
4. New York City
5. Hamburg
6. Marine Corps
7. Twin Cities
8. Frankfurt
9. Rotterdam
10. Portland
11. Dublin
12. Paris
13. Rome City
14. Venice
15. Columbus
16. Medoc
17. Stockholm
18. Rock "N" Roll
19. Los Angeles
20. Madrid
21. Houston
22. Pittsburgh
23. Vancouver
24. Walt Disney World
25. Grandma's
26. Naha
27. Helsinki City
28. Florence
29. Cape Town
30. Gold Coast

The Road Less Traveled With Plenty of Leg Room
Best Small Marathons (under 500 runners)

1. Mount Meru
2. Moorea Blue
3. Budapest
4. Beijing
5. Reykjavik
6. Humboldt Redwoods
7. Avenue of the Giants
8. Egyptian International
9. Midnight Sun
10. Mount Everest Challenge

Cream Rises
Highest Quality Events

1. Boston
1. New York City
3. Berlin
3. London
5. Comrades
5. Chicago
5. Hamburg
5. Houston
5. Twin Cities
10. Rotterdam
11. Frankfurt
12. Los Angeles
13. Stockholm
13. Pittsburgh
15. Madrid
16. Columbus
17. Portland
18. Naha
19. Venice
19. Medoc
21. Big Sur
22. Rome
23. Dublin
24. Marine Corps
25. Honolulu
25. Two Oceans
25. Vancouver
28. Gold Coast
28. Grandma's
28. St. George

COURSE PROFILES

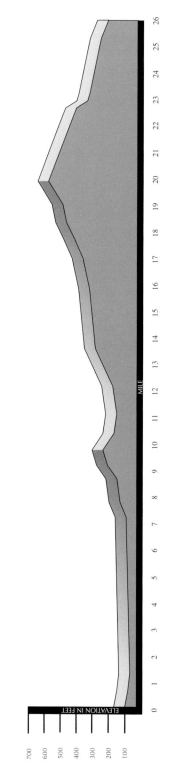

ATHENS MARATHON

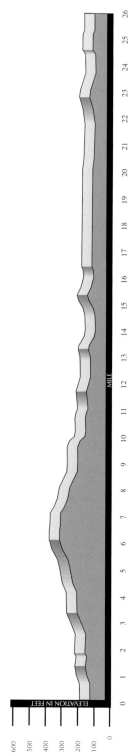

AVENUE OF THE GIANTS MARATHON

Course Profiles

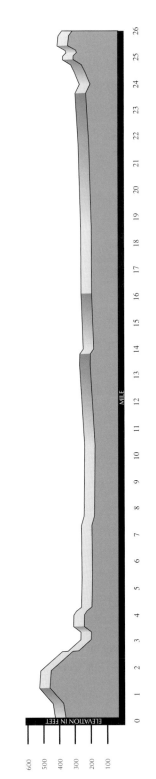

Belgrade Stark Marathon

Berlin Marathon

Course Profiles

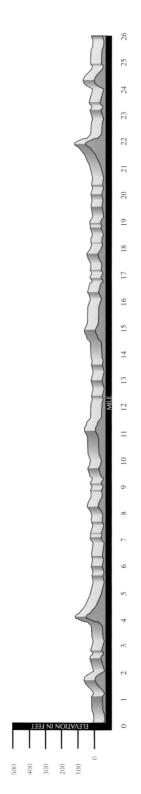

Bermuda Marathon

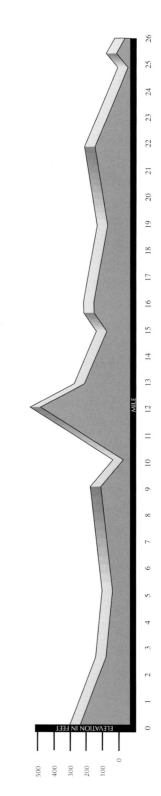

Big Sur International Marathon

COURSE PROFILES

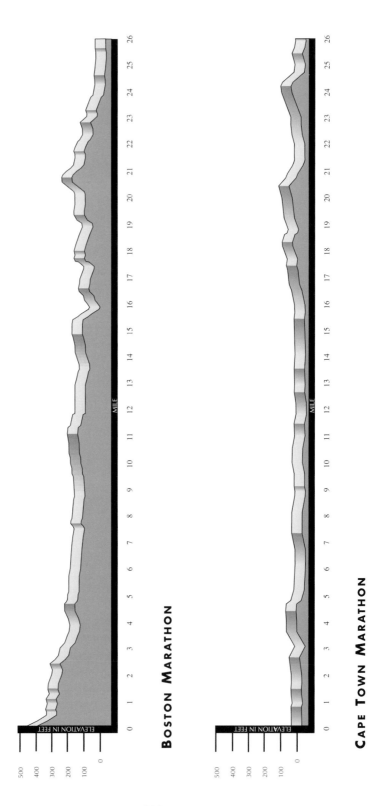

BOSTON MARATHON

CAPE TOWN MARATHON

Course Profiles

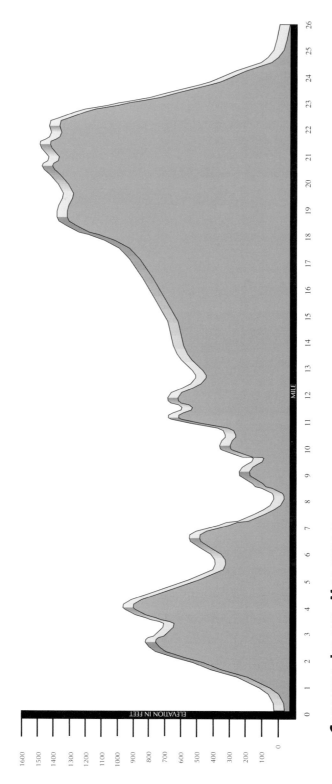

ELEVATION IN FEET

CATALINA ISLAND MARATHON

319

Course Profiles

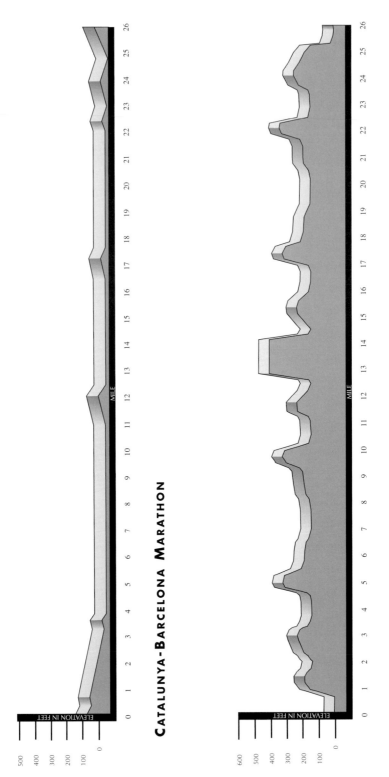

Catalunya-Barcelona Marathon

China Coast Marathon

COURSE PROFILES

COLUMBUS MARATHON

COMRADES MARATHON
(NOTE: DOWN COURSE AT 500-FOOT INCREMENTS)

COURSE PROFILES

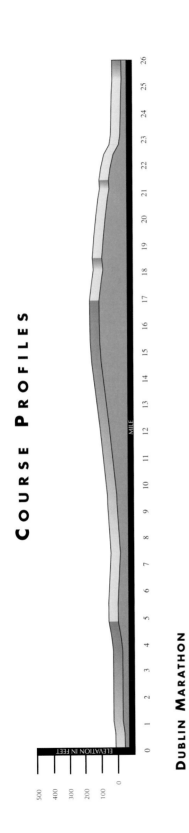

DUBLIN MARATHON

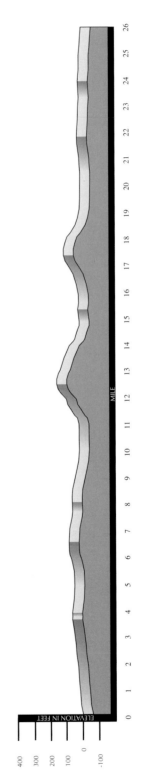

FLETCHER CHALLENGE MARATHON

COURSE PROFILES

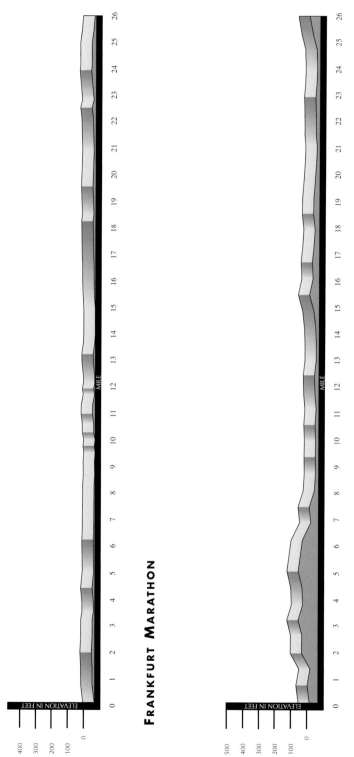

FRANKFURT MARATHON

HAMBURG MARATHON

COURSE PROFILES

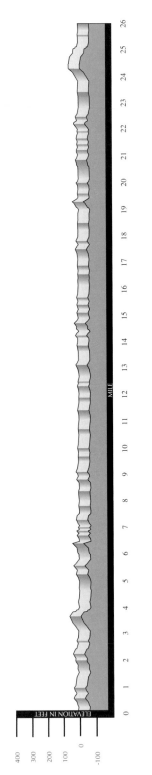

HELSINKI CITY MARATHON

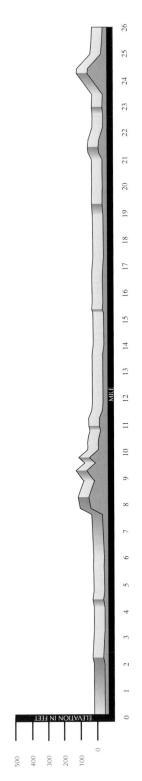

HONOLULU MARATHON

COURSE PROFILES

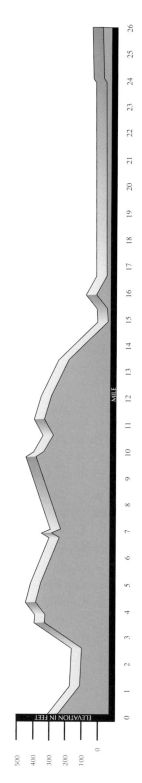

HUMBOLDT REDWOODS MARATHON

ISTANBUL EURASIA MARATHON

COURSE PROFILES

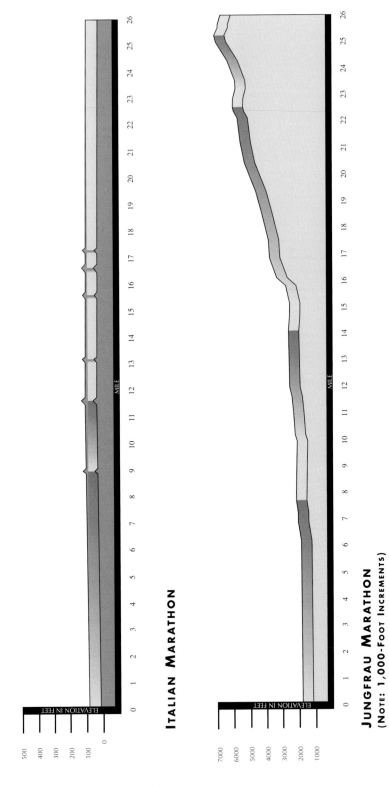

ITALIAN MARATHON

ELEVATION IN FEET

500 · 400 · 300 · 200 · 100 · 0

MILE

0 1 2 3 4 5 6 7 8 9 10 11 12 13 14 15 16 17 18 19 20 21 22 23 24 25 26

JUNGFRAU MARATHON
(NOTE: 1,000-FOOT INCREMENTS)

ELEVATION IN FEET

7000 · 6000 · 5000 · 4000 · 3000 · 2000 · 1000

MILE

0 1 2 3 4 5 6 7 8 9 10 11 12 13 14 15 16 17 18 19 20 21 22 23 24 25 26

COURSE PROFILES

LONDON MARATHON

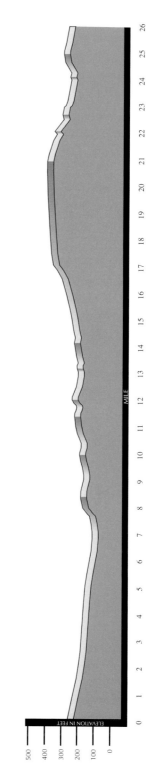

LOS ANGELES MARATHON

COURSE PROFILES

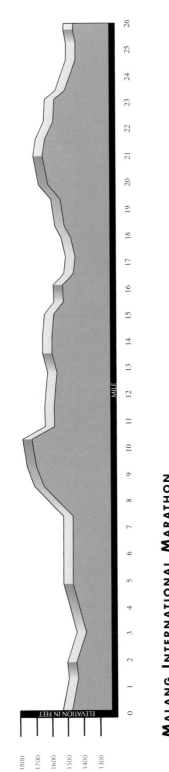

MALANG INTERNATIONAL MARATHON

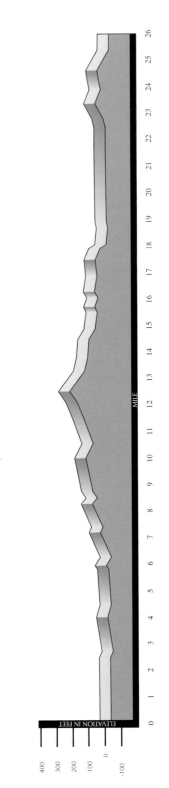

NAHA MARATHON

COURSE PROFILES

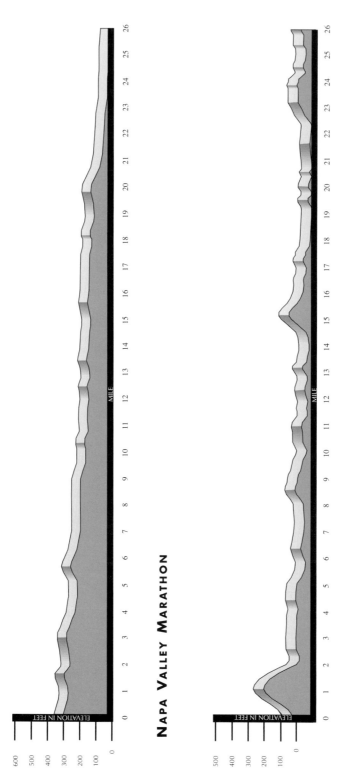

NAPA VALLEY MARATHON

NEW YORK CITY MARATHON

COURSE PROFILES

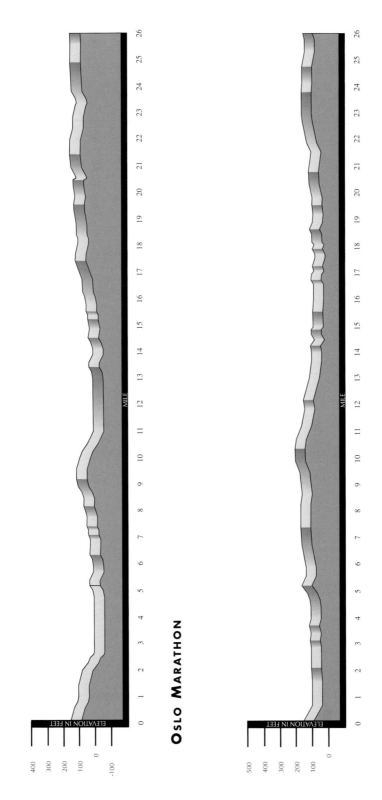

OSLO MARATHON

PARIS INTERNATIONAL MARATHON

Course Profiles

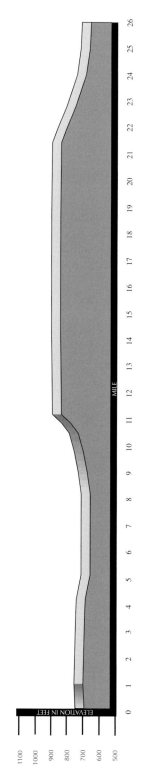

PITTSBURGH MARATHON

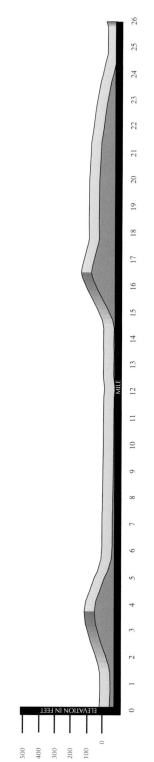

PORTLAND MARATHON

Course Profiles

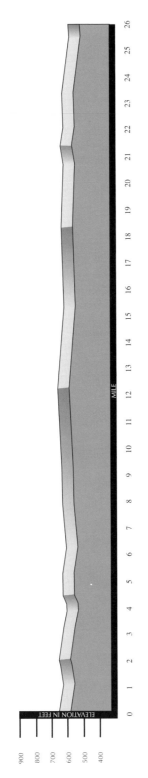

Prague International Marathon

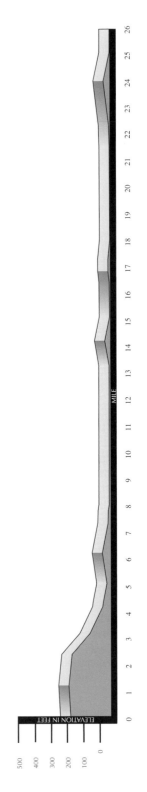

Rock "n" Roll Marathon

COURSE PROFILES

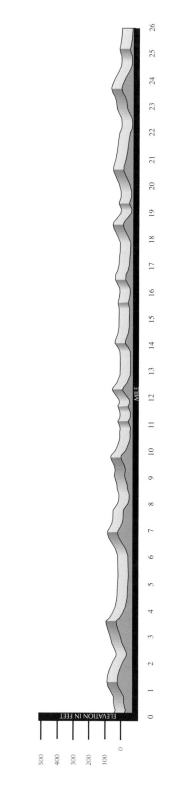

ROTTERDAM MARATHON

ROYAL VICTORIA MARATHON

Course Profiles

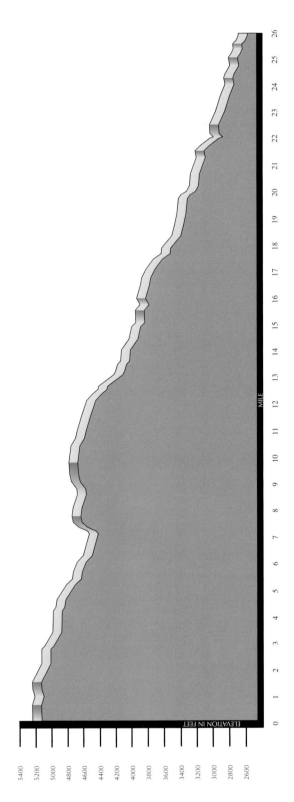

St. George Marathon
(Note: 200-Foot Increments)

ELEVATION IN FEET

MILE

COURSE PROFILES

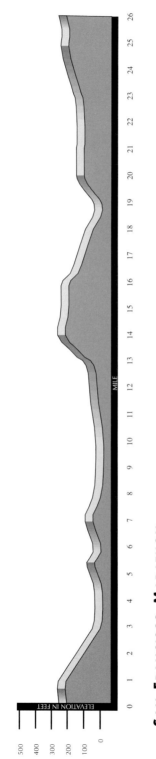

SAN FRANCISCO MARATHON

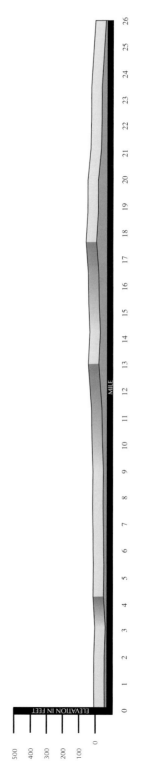

SEVILLE MARATHON

COURSE PROFILES

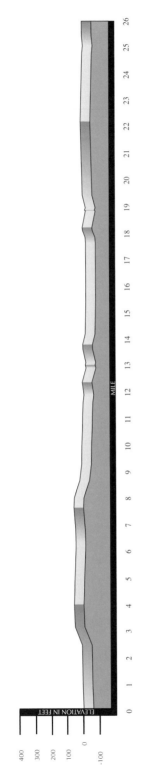

SIBERIAN INTERNATIONAL MARATHON

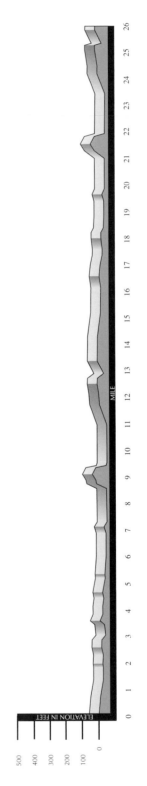

STOCKHOLM MARATHON

Course Profiles

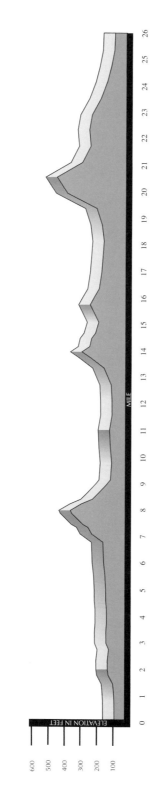

ELEVATION IN FEET

MILE

THAILAND INTERNATIONAL MARATHON

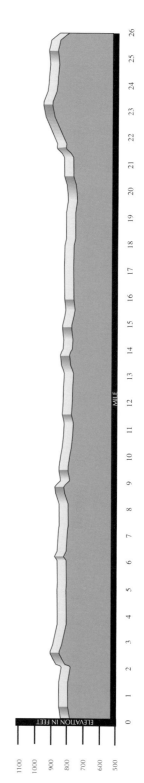

ELEVATION IN FEET

MILE

TWIN CITIES MARATHON

COURSE PROFILES

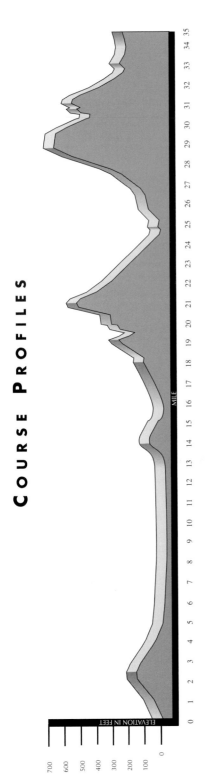

TWO OCEANS MARATHON

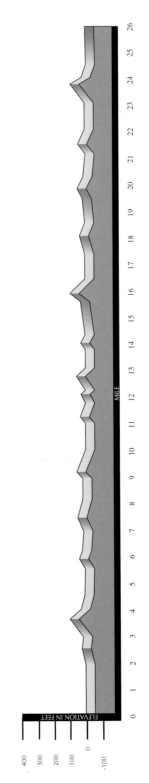

VANCOUVER INTERNATIONAL MARATHON

338

COURSE PROFILES

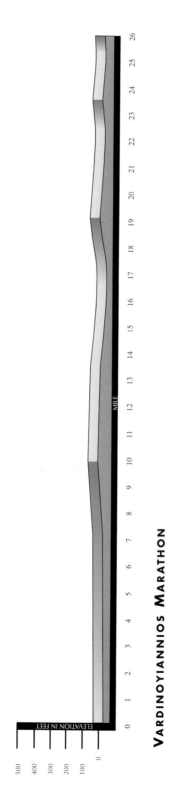

VARDINOYIANNIOS MARATHON

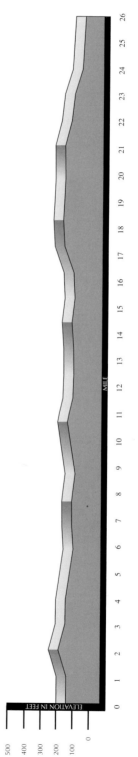

VERMONT CITY MARATHON

COURSE PROFILES

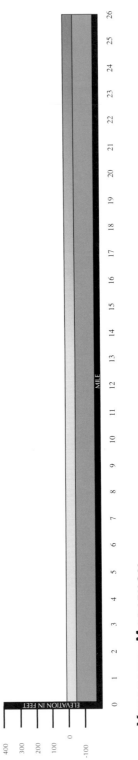

VIGARANO MARATHON

ELEVATION IN FEET

400
300
200
100
0
-100

MILE

0 1 2 3 4 5 6 7 8 9 10 11 12 13 14 15 16 17 18 19 20 21 22 23 24 25 26

INDEX

BY COUNTRY

Germany
Berlin Marathon, 194
Frankfurt Marathon, 214
Hamburg Marathon, 146

Great Britain
London Marathon, 156

Greece
Athens Marathon, 210
Vardinoyiannios Marathon, 222

Hungary
Budapest Marathon, 199

Iceland
Reykjavik Marathon, 185

India
Mt. Everest Challenge Marathon, 281

Indonesia
Malang Marathon, 258

Ireland
Dublin Marathon, 219

Israel
Tiberias Marathon, 231

Italy
Florence Marathon, 226
Italian Marathon, 206
Rome City Marathon, 137
Turin Marathon, 163
Venice Marathon, 216
Vigarano Marathon, 127

Japan
Amagasaki Marathon, 283
Kasumigaura Marathon, 260
Lake Kawaguchi Marathon, 285
Mt. Fuji Climbing Race, 270
Naha Marathon, 287
Okinawa Marathon, 254

Luxembourg
Echternach Marathon, 212
Route du Vin Half Marathon, 197

Malta
Malta Challenge Marathon, 224

Netherlands
Rotterdam Marathon, 149

New Zealand
Auckland Marathon, 279
Fletcher Challenge Marathon, 262

Norway
Midnight Sun Marathon, 179
Oslo Marathon, 192

Panama
Panama Ultramarathon, 302

Portugal
Lisbon Half Marathon, 134

Romania
Bucharest Marathon, 202

Russia
Siberian Marathon, 183

South Africa
Cape Town Marathon, 235
Comrades Marathon, 242
Two Oceans Marathon, 238

Spain
Catalunya-Barcelona Marathon, 131
Madrid Marathon, 160
Seville Marathon, 125
Valencia Marathon, 123

Sweden
Stockholm Marathon, 172

Switzerland
Jungfrau Marathon, 187
Lausanne Marathon, 208

Tahiti
Moorea Blue Marathon, 251

Thailand
Thailand Marathon, 265

Tanzania
Mt. Meru Marathon, 245

Turkey
Istanbul-Eurasia Marathon, 204

United States
Avenue of the Giants Marathon, 47
Big Sur Marathon, 41
Boston Marathon, 38
Catalina Island Marathon, 26
Chicago Marathon, 99
Cleveland Marathon, 49
Columbus Marathon, 112
Grandma's Marathon, 65
Honolulu Marathon, 115
Houston Marathon, 20
Humboldt Redwoods Marathon, 103
Kiawah Island Marathon, 118
Los Angeles Marathon, 34
Marine Corps Marathon, 105
Maui Marathon, 29
Napa Valley Marathon, 23
New York City Marathon, 108
Pikes Peak Marathon, 75
Pittsburgh Marathon, 52
Portland Marathon, 80
Rock 'N' Roll Marathon, 68
San Francisco Marathon, 72
St. George Marathon, 85
Twin Cities Marathon, 89
Vermont City Marathon, 62
Walt Disney Marathon, 17

Venezuela
Libertador Marathon, 300

Yugoslavia
Belgrade Marathon, 151

PHOTOGRAPHER CREDITS

Cover, Tim Matthews/AllSport • **15,** courtesy BSIM • **19,** courtesy Walt Disney World Marathon • **21,** courtesy Houston Marathon • **25,** Ken Lee • **27,** Lois Schwartz • **31,** Media Systems Maui, Hawaii • **36,** Tina Schmidt/AllSport • **40,** Victah Sailer • **43,** courtesy BSIM • **44,** Dave Stock/courtesy BSIM • **56,** courtesy VIM • **61,** courtesy National Capital Marathon • **63,** courtesy Vermont City Marathon • **67,** John Kelly • **73,** Ken Lee • **81,** courtesy Portland Marathon • **87,** Tim DeFrisco • **88,** Tim DeFrisco • **91,** John Kelly • **100,** Victah Sailer • **107,** Ken Lee • **109,** Jack Gescheidt • **113,** Victah Sailer • **116,** Ken Lee • **119,** Photo-Graphics • **121,** courtesy Jungfrau Marathon • **129,** courtesy Vigarano Marathon • **133,** courtesy Catalunya-Barcelona Marathon • **135,** courtesy Lisbon Half Marathon • **142,** AllSport • **143,** Agence Shot • **147,** courtesy Hamburg Marathon • **152,** Ken Lee • **157,** Simon Bruty/AllSport • **159,** Mark Shearman • **161,** Jose Gonzalez Fotografos/courtesy Madrid Marathon • **166,** courtesy Copenhagen Marathon • **169,** Dennis Craythorn • **173,** courtesy Stockholm Marathon • **180,** courtesy Midnight Sun Marathon • **182,** courtesy Helsinki City Marathon • **186,** courtesy Reykjavik Marathon • **188-189,** courtesy Jungfrau Marathon • **195,** Victah Sailer • **200,** courtesy Budapest Marathon • **217 & 218,** courtesy Venice Marathon • **220,** courtesy Dublin Marathon • **227,** courtesy Florence Marathon • **229, 236, & 243,** Tertius Pickard/Touchline • **232,** courtesy Tiberias International Marathon • **239,** Thomas Turck/Touchline • **246,** courtesy Global Partners for Development • **249,** courtesy Gold Coast Marathon • **253,** Mark Shearman • **255,** courtesy Okinawa Marathon • **263,** courtesy Fletcher Challenge Marathon • **268 & 269,** courtesy Gold Coast Marathon • **271,** courtesy Mount Fuji Climbing Race • **282,** courtesy Jim Crosswhite • **284,** courtesy Amagasaki Marathon • **289 & 292,** Bermuda Tourist Authority • **303,** Jonathan DeHart • **306,** Victah Sailer • **Appendix,** courtesy Jungfrau Marathon • **Author portrait,** Rudy Meyers / MVP Photography • **Back cover,** Ken Lee

MAUI MARATHON SWEEPSTAKES

NO PURCHASE REQUIRED FOR ENTRY

LIMIT ONE ENTRY PER PERSON

Maui Marathon and the Valley Isle Road Runners Association congratulate you on your purchase of **THE ULTIMATE GUIDE TO INTERNATIONAL MARATHONS.** The International Guide is a valuable tool in selecting marathons best suited to your interests. In order to encourage participation in the exciting sport of marathon running, Maui Marathon and the Valley Isle Road Runners Association are pleased to provide one lucky winner, subject to the terms and rules indicated below, a trip for two to the 1999 Maui Marathon. The trip will consist of the following:

• Complimentary entry for one person and one accompanying person into the 1999 Maui Marathon and all race-related activities, including the pre-race dinner;

• Complimentary, single-room accommodations for one person and one accompanying person at the Headquarters Hotel, the Maui Marriott, for four days and three nights;

• Complimentary rental of one compact car for 4 days during the 1999 Maui Marathon; and

• Complimentary round trip economy airfare for two persons traveling together from any city in the continental United States served by a major airline with service to Honolulu. The Maui Marathon reserves the right to approve the travel route and airline.

No purchase is necessary in order to enter this sweepstakes. Rules and terms are listed below.

How To Enter:

Send the following information on a 3" x 5" postcard to the address indicated below:

Your name, address, phone number, age on December 15, 1998, country of citizenship, signature, where you heard about The International Guide, and, if you purchased The International Guide, the place of purchase.

Maui Marathon International Sweepstakes
c/o Marathon Publishers, Inc.
P.O. Box 19027
Sacramento, CA 95819

Rules & Terms:

Please print or type your entry. Entries must be postmarked by November 15, 1998 to be eligible for the drawing. All entries postmarked after November 15, 1998 will not be entered into the drawing and will be discarded.

The Winner will be randomly chosen in a drawing conducted by the officials of Marathon Publishers on or before December 15, 1998. Only the winner will be notified of the results. By entering the Maui Marathon Sweepstakes, the winner agrees to allow his or her likeness to be used by the Maui Marathon, and/or the Valley Isle Road Runners Association for any promotional purposes.

Winner agrees to hold Maui Marathon, Valley Isle Road Runners Association, Marathon Publishers, Inc. and any of their owners, officers, agents or employees harmless for any injury or damages that result from any portion of the trip or events discussed herein. Winner agrees that if the Maui Marathon is canceled as the result of an Act of God or other unforeseen occurrence, the entire trip will be canceled, and Winner shall not be entitled to any compensation whatsoever.

All travel arrangements must be coordinated with and approved by the Maui Marathon and/or the Valley Isle Road Runners Association. You must be at least 18 years of age on or before December 15,1998 to enter the 1999 Maui Marathon Sweepstakes. All entrants must be U.S. citizens or U.S. legal residents. This sweepstakes promotion is void where prohibited by law.

METRIC PACE CHART

MIN./MILE	MIN./KM	MARATHON	MIN./MILE	MIN./KM	MARATHON
5:00	3:06	2:11:06	10:00	6:13	4:22:07
5:10	3:13	2:15:28	10:10	6:19	4:26:29
5:20	3:19	2:19:50	10:20	6:25	4:30:51
5:30	3:25	2:24:12	10:30	6:31	4:35:13
5:40	3:31	2:28:34	10:40	6:37	4:39:35
5:50	3:37	2:32:56	10:50	6:44	4:43:57
6:00	3:44	2:37:19	11:00	6:50	4:48:19
6:10	3:50	2:41:41	11:10	6:56	4:52:41
6:20	3:56	2:46:03	11:20	7:02	4:57:03
6:30	4:02	2:50:25	11:30	7:09	5:01:25
6:40	4:08	2:54:47	11:40	7:15	5:05:47
6:50	4:15	2:59:09	11:50	7:21	5:10:09
7:00	4:21	3:03:31	12:00	7:27	5:14:31
7:10	4:27	3:07:53	12:10	7:33	5:18:53
7:20	4:33	3:12:15	12:20	7:40	5:23:15
7:30	4:39	3:16:37	12:30	7:46	5:27:37
7:40	4:45	3:20:59	12:40	7:52	5:31:59
7:50	4:52	3:25:21	12:50	7:58	5:36:21
8:00	4:58	3:29:43	13:00	8:04	5:40:43
8:10	5:04	3:34:05	13:10	8:11	5:45:05
8:20	5:11	3:38:27	13:20	8:17	5:49:27
8:30	5:17	3:42:49	13:30	8:23	5:53:49
8:40	5:23	3:47:11	13:40	8:29	5:58:11
8:50	5:29	3:51:33	13:50	8:35	6:02:33
9:00	5:35	3:55:55	14:00	8:42	6:06:55
9:10	5:41	4:00:17	14:10	8:48	6:11:17
9:20	5:48	4:04:39	14:20	8:54	6:15:39
9:30	5:54	4:09:01	14:30	9:00	6:20:01
9:40	6:00	4:13:23	14:40	9:06	6:24:23
9:50	6:06	4:17:45	14:50	9:13	6:28:45
			15:00	9:20	6:33:07

NOTES

NOTES

NOTES

ABOUT THE AUTHORS

Dennis Craythorn writes and runs in Sacramento, California. His work has appeared in *Runner's World*, *The American River Literary Review*, and many other publications. He has spent over two years traveling in North America, Europe, and Asia, including several months for this book. Mr. Craythorn obtained his MSFS from Georgetown University and BA from the University of California — Davis.

Rich Hanna is a veteran of more than 35 marathons and ultramarathons. He is a two-time U.S. National 100K champion and has represented the United States in several international competitions. With a personal best 2:17 marathon, Mr. Hanna qualified to run in the 1996 U.S. Olympic Marathon Trials. Mr. Hanna contributes his extensive marathon experience as a personal running trainer and coach of the Sacramento Chapter of the Leukemia Society's Team in Training program in his spare time. Mr. Hanna received his BA from the University of California — Davis.

Both authors wrote the bestselling **ULTIMATE GUIDE TO MARATHONS**.